Sustainable Marketing Planning

There are two major parallel challenges facing managers and leaders: first, how to adapt to global changes in markets, competition and supply, and second, how to grow a business while observing recognisably sustainable practices. Companies must now align their values with customers who increasingly seek people-friendly and planet-friendly products and services. Using sustainable marketing techniques to create value ultimately leads to improved customer satisfaction, better professional relationships and increased effectiveness.

With marketing planning absent from the current textbook offering, this book provides practical insights, tools and frameworks to help readers produce tactically and strategically appropriate marketing plans. Showing how to embed sustainability in these strategies and reflecting on the historical and current criticisms aimed at marketing, students will be shown how to implement changes while being encouraged to reflect on why they are needed. Full of tools and frameworks to improve comprehension, including chapter-by-chapter learning outcomes, summaries, exercises, applied activities and mini case studies, it bridges the gap between theory and practice effectively and accessibly. Finally, PowerPoint lecture slides and Multiple Choice Questions sections are provided for each chapter as electronic resources.

Presenting contemporary themes and challenges at the cutting edge of business research and practice, this book should be core reading for advanced undergraduate and postgraduate students of sustainable marketing, marketing planning and marketing strategy, as well as professionals seeking to improve the competitive advantage of their organisations.

Neil Richardson is the course director for postgraduate marketing programmes for Leeds Business School, UK. He has extensive experience as an academic and practitioner, including working with world-class companies in sales, marketing and customer services. He has published several books and academic articles on sustainable marketing.

Sustainable Marketing Planning

Neil Richardson

LONDON AND NEW YORK

First published 2020
by Routledge
2 Park Square, Milton Park, Abingdon, Oxon OX14 4RN

and by Routledge
52 Vanderbilt Avenue, New York, NY 10017

Routledge is an imprint of the Taylor & Francis Group, an Informa business

British Library Cataloguing-in-Publication Data
A catalogue record for this book is available from the British Library

Library of Congress Cataloging-in-Publication Data
Names: Richardson, Neil, 1963 January 25– author.
Title: Sustainable marketing planning / Neil Richardson.
Description: New York : Routledge, 2019. | Includes bibliographical references
    and index.
Identifiers: LCCN 2019025793 (print) | LCCN 2019025794 (ebook) |
    ISBN 9780367025205 (hardback) | ISBN 9780367025212 (paperback) |
    ISBN 9780429399114 (ebook)
Subjects: LCSH: Green marketing. | Consumption (Economics)—Environmental
    aspects. | Social responsibility of business.
Classification: LCC HF5413 .R53 2019 (print) | LCC HF5413 (ebook) | DDC
    658.8/02—dc23
LC record available at https://lccn.loc.gov/2019025793
LC ebook record available at https://lccn.loc.gov/2019025794

ISBN: 978-0-367-02520-5 (hbk)
ISBN: 978-0-367-02521-2 (pbk)
ISBN: 978-0-429-39911-4 (ebk)

Typeset in Sabon
by Apex CoVantage, LLC

Visit the eResources: www.routledge.com/9780367025212

Contents

Figures

Introduction

First, I would like to take this opportunity to thank you for buying this book. Having bought it, you're now one of my customers, which means a lot to me. As you progress through the chapters, you'll recognise the theme of marketers creating value for customers. My sincere hope is that you will take value from this book during your studies and later in your professional career.

Marketing draws on many of the great discourses, namely philosophy, sociology, economics and psychology. Indeed, many marketers see it as a form of applied psychology that shapes how managers make decisions and then implement changes (based on these decisions). Hence, this text will be a practical resource to those studying marketing decision-making and implementation. It supports undergraduate, postgraduate and professional marketing students. The fundamental principles are covered in order to provide a thorough underpinning for strategy, planning and metrics-related modules. Furthermore, the text features teaching tools to improve comprehension: each chapter has learning outcomes, key findings, applied activities and practical examples. It critiques the theory and brings the real world into the classroom.

Throughout my career, I've worked for (and with) organisations such as charities, SMEs and genuinely world-class companies. I've witnessed management decision-making that has at times been inspired but also ill-informed. Marketing managers face two parallel challenges: first, how to adapt to changes (in fragmenting markets, hyper-competition, oversupply or globalisation), and second, how to grow a business while practising recognisably sustainable practices. Companies must align their values with their customers, who increasingly seek products and services that create customer value while remaining people- and planet-friendly.

Organisational drivers rarely change (e.g. attracting/retaining customers, developing customer relationships and growing satisfaction); however, the sustainability challenges are introducing previously unseen complexities into everyday business. Marketing is changing almost daily – for example, media ethics (think Leveson), emergent consumer concerns (banking, fair trade) and ever-evolving business needs. Using sustainable marketing (SM) techniques to create value ultimately leads to improved customer satisfaction, better professional relationships and increased effectiveness. This text is unique in that it extensively covers marketing planning and addresses key sustainability challenges simultaneously.

All business students must be interested in the issues of corporate failure, recovery and turnaround techniques. No doubt, there are many factors that contribute to failure, and each scenario is unique. I'll discuss these factors throughout the text; however, I have no doubt that *the largest threat to a company's future is likely to be ineffective marketing.*

Poor marketing; nothing more, nothing less. Many (ill-informed) people think marketing is superficial, ephemeral or at worst deceptive. So I'll consider the role of critical marketers, the persistent marketing myths and why scepticism exists.

Some say the digital age has increased the power of consumers' making purchasing decisions. Hence, firms must adopt a more customer-centric approach. Digitalisation has benefited both consumers (who have more choice) and companies (who have improved market access and reduced costs). The networking nature of social media makes it easier for marketers to collaborate with communities and achieve reputational endorsement. That said, networks are often the source of many societal and green problems for companies. Think of the child-labour scandals that arise and the reputational damage they inflict. Potential buyers will seek to take value from certain brands above others in the same product category. To achieve this, companies strive to build brand awareness and equity. However, such brands are increasingly viewed through the prism of sustainability. The two issues are now inextricably linked.

When teaching Chartered Institute of Marketing (CIM) students over the last 15 years, I've been asked a diversity of questions. I've incorporated the answers to these questions into this book and offered honest, sometimes critical answers. These students (both client-side students and agency-side students) represent the whole spectrum of companies involved in marketing. Many marketing texts focus on larger, specifically manufacturing, organisations. They promote theories or tools that don't apply (meaningfully) to many enterprises today. Hence, this text is for students interested in all organisations: virtual, large or small, new or old, profitable, ecological or charitable.

Planning is absent from many current sustainable texts; hence, this book provides a bottom-up approach with the latest thoughts on tactical and strategic SM. It reflects on the role of sustainability in the contexts of contemporary themes, including entrepreneurialism, internal marketing, international marketing, small firms and digital marketing (among others).

Finally, employers increasingly want graduates to be better marketing practitioners rather than simply "academics". Most texts fail to address this discrepancy; hence, this book bridges this gap by adopting a "pracademic" approach. Students will be given insights into how to implement changes while being encouraged to reflect on why they are needed.

Best wishes,
Neil

1 Why Sustainable Marketing?

Abstract

Whilst the notion of the sustainable consumer is relatively recent, the debates about consumption, consumer behaviour and consumerism are ancient (see Fig 1.1). Hence this Chapter will first consider the historical view of consumption and then it will define the elusive sustainable consumer. It draws on the work of Professor Tim Jackson who in 2005 produced a detailed review of consumer decision making from a sustainability perspective. It is comprehensive and should be compulsory reading for marketers. Stakeholder theory is used to identify create sustainable segments shaped by the TBL. The notion of sustainable consumption is developed and considering how purchasing decisions are increasingly influenced by sustainability. Marketers who identify the key influences affecting decision-making, will establish a deeper understanding of customers' behaviour and will be better placed to create value for (and support) the customer. Furthermore, sustainable marketing cannot ignore the criticisms aimed at marketing. Hence critical marketing is discussed and the persistent myths associated with marketing. Marketing research is at the heart of most marketing decisions. To remain competitive, innovative and attractive to the customer, marketers must constantly develop their products, services and even organisations. Marketing Research is central to providing the data and information to do this successfully. Finally this chapter considers the role of systems and their influence on adopting sustainable practices.

Learning outcomes

At the end of this chapter, students will be able to do the following:

- Discuss the historical influences on sustainable marketing (SM);
- Examine the role of internal marketing;
- Assess the nature of sustainable entrepreneurship;
- Evaluate the application of sustainable brands;
- Analyse how sustainability informs global marketing;
- Discuss techniques to manage digital marketing;
- Explain alternative marketing approaches for SMEs, charities and not-for-profit organisations.

When considering the challenges facing companies, a key question is, why would clients buy your products or services rather than those of a competitor? Finding good answers to such thoughts is crucial. One answer is that when buying goods, consumers increasingly want to buy from companies that are motivated by more than "business as usual" or the traditional bottom line. Another answer is that consumption is social in that when "buying", consumers take on attitudes, beliefs, opinions and values of others. These attitudes are increasingly shaped by information shared digitally, often generated by people "outside" of the companies. Hence, those companies unaware of changes in society run the risk of alienating customers. This is the case with sustainability, which despite being missing from many marketing texts is increasingly important to key stakeholders.

Marketing – a definition

Singularly the most important word for marketers is "customer", and marketing is about understanding customers (past, present and future), being able to anticipate their requirements and ultimately satisfying their needs. All of the work organisations undertake (not just the marketing department) should therefore be created and implemented to delight customers. This should be reflected in any definition.

The definition by the Chartered Institute of Marketing (hereafter CIM) is cited widely. It describes marketing as "the management process responsible for identifying, anticipating and satisfying customer requirements profitably" (CIM, 2019). This definition is useful in understanding the key facets of marketing. That said, there are issues with the definition.

First, marketing is seen as a management process. Since marketing covers strategic elements, it can be fully embedded into the culture of an organisation only if it has "buy-in" from top management. However, all employees can influence the customers (or prospective customers) who have contacted an organisation and, say, been cut off or have been spoken to in an unprofessional manner or not given solutions to problems. The customer may have become frustrated by poorly trained or demotivated staff. Not all staff members are involved in sales and marketing; many are in accounts, logistics or tech support, and yet customers do not distinguish between the different roles if they are dissatisfied. They see the company holistically. Hence, marketing is everybody's responsibility, because everyone plays a part in creating the customer experience.

As the CIM definition suggests, marketing is an ongoing process. It is neither linear nor a one-off. As customers change, businesses must adapt and evolve to transition with the times. Because marketers must try to anticipate customers' future wants, needs and values, organisations must be focused on the future. Because it can take years to develop new products (or services), marketers must be aware of changing customer perceptions. Increasingly, social media are being used as a research tool to identify insights into how users (and influencers) see their needs changing in the future.

The American Marketing Association defines marketing as "the activity, set of institutions, and processes for creating, communicating, delivering, and exchanging offerings that have value for customers, clients, partners, and society at large" (AMA, 2019). This complements the CIM definition by introducing value and the role of society.

The traditional view is that customers buy products and services from organisations in exchange for money. This simple exchange view is somewhat outdated. The reality is that organisations cannot "give" customers value (a mistake repeated in many marketing texts). Some argue that the exchange brings the organisation and the customer together, and here they co-create value. Others argue that customers provide money so that they can seek value from companies. Marketers must focus on creating circumstances where customers can seek and co-create or simply take value. These two options (co-creation and value seeking) reduce the risk for organisations because they promote a customer-centric approach. Since value seeking and value taking involve bringing (at least) two parties together, relationships are formed, and many marketers today try to capitalise on that initial relationship by finding out as much as they can about the customer and their needs.

The one constant is change. Customer needs are constantly changing, and technology is enabling quicker, easier decision-making. Consider the role of cost-comparison websites such as gocompare.com and moneysupermarket.com that not only compete with each other but also with organisations that "represent" the customer. For many organisations, the marketplace is a difficult, dynamic, dangerous and highly competitive place. When the market or environment changes, marketers must change and adapt; otherwise, they risk being left behind. Those that do not adapt may incur customer dissatisfaction and suffer attrition: lose their customers to the competition. If the customer has a positive experience, they will be more likely to tell their family and friends, and if they have a bad experience, chances are that they will tell even more people about it.

Since the advent of Web 2.0, the use of user-generated content (UGC) on websites, blogs and social media sites has increased immeasurably. Some sites have failed to react to changes (e.g. Vine), while others are being challenged by newcomers. Facebook is still a colossus in social networking; however, it is questionable whether it will be so in, say, 10 years' time. After all, how many people still use Friends Reunited?

To be more successful, organisations must be externally focused, not just internally focused upon production techniques, products and processes. Many organisations suffer from such navel gazing and develop tunnel vision for their business activities. This is often referred to as marketing myopia: a short-sightedness that can often result in the loss of customers and business failure. Some argue that the current business environment is so turbulent that all marketers are to a degree blind to the future.

> *Example* Toys "R" Us. This retail giant's core customers' needs were changing, and new competition entered the high street. Changes occurred in the wider external environment; for example, young children were increasingly being given smartphones and tablets as presents. These were available extensively online and from a much wider range of suppliers. The UK government had changed the rates charged and introduced new taxes, such as the Apprenticeship Levy. Toys "R" Us, like many retailers, seemed to pay high rent values to landlords. On top of this, their cashflow was inherently seasonal. Consequently, they were vulnerable despite having had after a sustained period of success. As individuals, we can become complacent when we are not challenged. Unsurprisingly, organisations run by humans can react in a similar way.

Companies who have survived similar scenarios (think Marks and Spencers in the 1990s) were able to make changes, which permeated their management culture and went through a process of recovery, where the focus of their philosophy incorporated identifying, anticipating and delighting the customer. They addressed social issues related to supply chains and later led the way in adopting sustainable policies under their Plan A programme, where they aimed for a carbon-neutral delivery method of goods.

That said, most organisations have limited resources: financial, staff, equipment and so on. Therefore, they must seek to satisfy their customers efficiently (with as little wastage as possible) and profitably. However, now more than ever, business activities should also be undertaken and managed in an environmentally friendly and socially responsible manner.

1.1 Sustainable marketing and its influences

While the terminology and the context of sustainable consumption are relatively recent, the debates about consumer behaviour and consumerism are much older and

Aristotle	Pleonexia (the insatiable desire for more)
Thorsten Veblen	Conspicuous consumption
Pierre Bourdieu	Analysis of social distinction
Jean Baudrillard	Semiotic analysis
Fred Hirsch	Positional goods
Mary Douglas	Symbolic interactionism
Abraham Maslow and Erich Fromm	Humanistic psychology
Edward Wilson and Richard Dawkins	Biological analogies
John Kenneth Galbraith	Sociopolitical critique of the affluent society
Juliet Schor	Downshifting
Duane Elgin	Voluntary simplicity

Figure 1.1 Different approaches to consumption and consumer value approaches

Source: adapted from Jackson (2005, pp. 20–21)

run much deeper (Jackson, 2005). Many commentators have reflected on how consumers have demonstrated different values (Figure 1.1).

This list of commentators is not exhaustive; however, it partly explains why there is a long-standing tradition of ethical and socially responsible companies in most parts of the world, dating back many generations (Barkemeyer et al., 2009) without registering the same degree of impact in many marketing texts.

Sustainability – a historical perspective

Adam Smith recognised the idea of voluntary exchanges: transactions between producers and consumers where both parties benefited (Smith, 1776). Smith suggested abandoning the assumption of the zero-sum game (i.e. a fixed amount of wealth) and talked about wealth creation, especially through labour and voluntary exchange (Donaldson, 2008). Donaldson describes Adam Smith as

> "a young moral philosopher (who) suggested that we throw out the assumption of the zero-sum game (i.e. assuming that there was a fixed amount of wealth) and begin to talk about how wealth is created, especially through labour and voluntary exchange".
>
> (2008, p. 173)

Smith's text, while undoubtedly important, is not a blueprint for business. Organisations were obviously not high on his agenda given that he devoted only two paragraphs to corporations. He insisted that the only organisations with a real future would be in canal building and banking (ibid). Furthermore, his discussion of the (economic only) value of slaves is repugnant to all right-minded people in the 21st century. Adam Smith may well have been a "moral" philosopher of his time, but societal values and attitudes to slavery have rightly changed. This resonates with those who argue that value is always temporal (Heinonen, 2006).

Smith's idea of the pursuit of growth could be argued to be the genesis of the Dominant Social Paradigm (DSP), ultimately leading to the neo-liberal agenda (Jackson, 2005) and globalisation based on the assumption that the march of progress is not only inevitable but also ideal, something to be striven towards (Jones et al., 2009).

Economists expressed alarm during the Industrial Revolution over the lack of social wealth (Tilley and Young, 2009). In the 19th century, Hobbes noted the pervasive anxiety of a society characterised by unlimited materialist value perspectives. Victor Hugo suggested that the two main problems faced by 19th century society were the production of wealth and its distribution (Jackson, 2005). Gerald Alonzo Smith's (1996) review of the historic perspective of the purpose of wealth suggested many 19th-century economists questioned the proposition that economic growth was an end rather than a means. He cited John Ruskin (1819–1900) as stating "Something was wrong with an economy that produced so much quantity with so little quality, yet brutalised so many people in doing it". Smith also cited Sismondi (1834), who opined that "The too much of everything is the evil of the day". This sentiment resonates with the oversupply and fragmentation evident in today's society.

The 19th-century economist Thomas Malthus was concerned with the production of food and suggested that supply would be outstripped by population growth, developing the idea that nature is not simply a never-ending resource. Marx (and many others) decried the fetishism of commodities that characterised capitalism. On the cusp of the 20th century, Thorsten Veblen coined the phrase "conspicuous consumption" (Veblen, 1898), which still resonates today.

From the time of Adam Smith through to the present day, organisations have been allowed (or even encouraged) to develop in line with capitalist, neo-liberal traditions. Developments since the adoption of the neo-liberal agenda (such as globalisation and deregulation) mean "some corporations have gradually come to replace the most powerful institution in the traditional concept of citizenship, namely government" (Garriga and Mele, 2004, p. 57). With Facebook, Amazon, Alphabet Inc, Microsoft etc., this is arguably more relevant today than ever before. It is, however, too simplistic to say that globalisation has generated only negative impacts. It can be argued that material well-being has increased dramatically for many people as a result of globalisation (Rosling, 2010).

Clear divides were evident in the mid 20th century. Bowen's seminal 1952 text *Social Responsibilities of the Businessman* was responsible for bringing the issue to the wider community. Davis (1960, cited in Agle et al., 1999) attacked the assumption of the classical economic theory of perfect competition that precludes the involvement of the firm in society besides the creation of wealth. Davis warned that whoever does not use their social power responsibly will lose it. Agle et al. (1999) refer to this as Davis's Iron Law.

There has been a shift from shareholder interests reigning supreme to a scenario where different stakeholders compete to influence the business agenda. In this scenario, shareholder interests are simply one of many. Businesses have to meet increasing public expectations and to address legal obligations around environmental and sustainability issues (Jones et al., 2009). The need to make profit can coincide or conflict with a company's stated ethical aims and objectives.

Sustainability should be viewed in terms of commitment within the wider context of stakeholder relationships. Improving relationship management requires understanding stakeholders who may have interpersonal (consumers) or person-to-firm (company) perspectives (Wong and Sohal, 2002; Sparks and Wagner, 2003). Stakeholders with competing and differing needs, rights and obligations have to be managed to minimise conflict. Whether stakeholders can be managed is a moot point. Hence, it is necessary to reflect on the nature of stakeholders.

Stakeholder theory

Freeman provided a language and framework for examining how companies relate to stakeholders. It established legitimacy for parties (other than shareholders) whose interests can shape a manager's actions (Margolis and Walsh, 2003). He defined "stakeholders" as groups or individuals who can influence (or be influenced by) the achievement of the organisation's objective (Freeman, 1984). The effect can be beneficial or harmful. This was developed to include those whose rights may be violated or should be respected by the business (Solomon et al., 2006) or who claim ownership in organisational activities (Mendes et al., 2009).

Figure 1.2 is useful because it maps the stakeholders according to their connectedness to the organisation. Those directly employed have the highest degree of connection (and control by management), because they usually have contractual obligations. Shareholders have no contractual obligations, because they can always sell their shares. Large institutional investors have higher power and access, whereas small shareholders have little real power. There are exceptions, of course, one being John Lewis, the renowned retailer who uses a cooperative business model. Their staff members also own shares in the business and take part in regular profit shares. So for John Lewis, the shareholders would be in the centre.

The following are some of the reasons for involving stakeholders:

- Needing to understand the complexity of the cultural system;
- Ensuring management systems identify potential conflicts inherent to objectives;
- Resolving areas of conflict and counterbalancing existing patterns of interaction.
                          (adapted from Mendes et al., 2009)

Agle et al. (1999, p. 521) refer to "a stakeholder class system – in which shareholders, employees, and customers were privileged, and government and communities were less so". *Primary* stakeholders are those without whom the company cannot

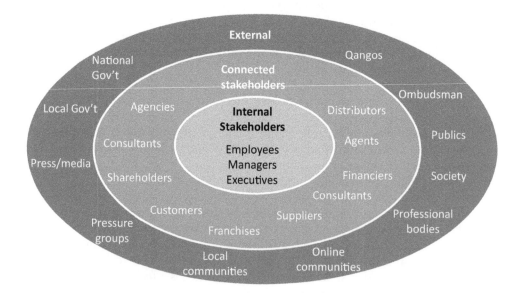

Figure 1.2 Stakeholder connectedness

survive, whereas *secondary* stakeholders represent those who influence or affect (or are influenced or affected by) the company but are not essential for survival. Hence, a power-based ranking system can be established that ranges from having only interest (low-power) to having an effect (medium power) to assuming ownership (high power). However, stakeholders may have interest only in a single project rather than, say, a company's corporate objectives.

Acknowledging this (power and interest) has, to a degree, encouraged businesses to re-evaluate their activities. Indeed, Freeman argued that

> "maximizing profits is more like creating value for stakeholders than others might read in *Capitalism and Freedom* (Friedman, 1962). Does that mean that I believe that "maximizing profits" is the goal or purpose of the corporation? Absolutely not. . . . It is an outcome of a well-managed company, and that stakeholder theory is an idea about what it means to be well managed . . . (and) . . . is not about markets and how they work. . . . It's not a theory of the firm. Rather it is a very simple idea about how people create value for each other".
>
> Freeman (2008, pp. 164–166)

Freeman insists that better stakeholder theory focuses us on how "companies and entrepreneurs are out there creating value, making our lives better, and changing the world" (ibid). The notion of personal and organisational values is central to marketers.

Strong stakeholder theory versus weak stakeholder theory

Strong stakeholder theory suggests that all stakeholders, irrespective of power and/or interest, are dealt with equally. Figure 1.3 summarises the key issues regarding strong stakeholder theory versus weak stakeholder theory.

View	Attribute	Comment
Strong	Each stakeholder has a legitimate claim to management attention. Management must balance stakeholder demands.	Managers who account to everyone actually account to no one. With no criteria for performance, managers cannot be evaluated in any principled way. Managers decide on the balance between stakeholders. It confuses a stakeholder's interest in a firm with a person's citizenship of a state.
Weak	Satisfying stakeholders is a good thing, but only because it enables the business to satisfy its primary purpose: the long-term growth in owner wealth.	People have interests, but this does not give them rights. Stakeholder attributes are variable rather than steady states. Stakeholder priorities can change for any group or stakeholder–manager relationship.

Figure 1.3 Strong stakeholder theory versus weak stakeholder theory

Source: adapted from Jensen (2008) and Agle et al. (1999)

A critique of strong stakeholder theory is that it assumes

> "managers would do the right thing so as to benefit society as a whole. That position is naive . . . (because they) . . . would have no way to know how to best benefit society. . . . Furthermore, there would be widespread disagreement on how and what to do".

(Jensen, 2008, p. 168)

Marketers must be aware of the degree of urgency, interest and/or power that stakeholders possess. As discussed in Chapter 1.1, the notion of power alludes to the degree to which managers prioritise competing stakeholder claims. Such *salience* is often attributed to shareholders, customers, government and communities. Institutional shareholders can be dominant stakeholders and therefore salient to a degree; however, it is heightened shareholder urgency that concerns senior management. Figure 1.4 clearly illustrates a range of stakeholders with different combinations of attributes (i.e. power, legitimacy and urgency) resulting in of different saliences (Mitchell et al., 1997).

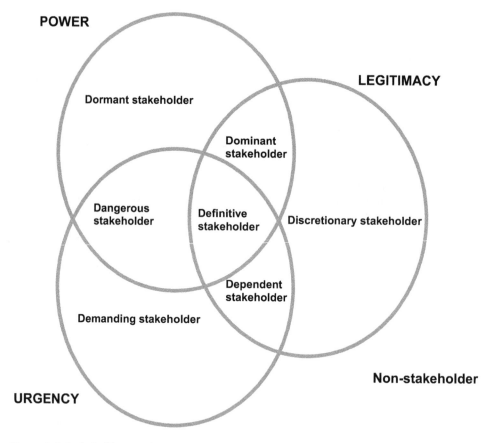

Figure 1.4 Stakeholder typology: one, two or three attributes

The idea of the *non-stakeholder* is replaced in marketing by a *public*, which represents a stakeholder who may be interested in the organisation but is not directly involved or "connected". Naturally, today's public could easily become tomorrow's engaged stakeholder.

This raises the challenging issue of bargaining power and communication (Figure 1.5).

Some companies will have inclusive cultures, whereas others will be authoritarian. Progressive marketers are, however, recognising that not only consumers are more discerning but they also have more choice than ever before. Marketers must be transparent in their communications and should consult with networks of suppliers and stakeholder communities. As previously discussed, many companies with marketing myopia have failed. Communication is the problem to the answer.

Stakeholders will have different attributes due to combinations of power, legitimacy and urgency. These must inform any stakeholder communications. Consider the following questions:

- Which publics are important, and is the degree of importance changing?
- How strong are company-stakeholder relationships?
- What is the impact of corporate actions on these publics?
- What is the impact of these publics on corporate actions?
- How do the interests of the relevant publics differ?
- Which groups pose a threat and which an opportunity?

Friedman versus Freeman

In 1970 Friedman challenged those firms that contemplated making investments in social objectives and public interests other than economic ones. His article is seminal and often cited by libertarians who insist that enterprises should have no objectives

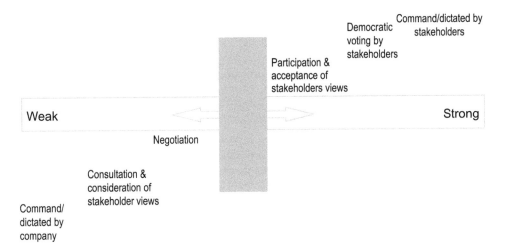

Figure 1.5 Stakeholder bargaining strength

Source: adapted from Megicks, Donnelly and Harrison (2009)

other than those with an economic focus, namely the bottom line. He insisted that property rights, the invisible hand of the market, and the government are entrusted to solve society's problems, whereas corporate managers are to play no direct role in ensuring the social welfare of society (Friedman, 1970).

For centuries, "family-run businesses with social value such as Cadbury, Lever and Rowntree had shown that businesses could be run in ways that were profitable and that benefited others, particularly employees and the local community" (Emery, 2012, p. 11). These enterprises complemented the traditional bottom line with other values. Indeed, they thrived while refuting the bottom-line-only focus in favour of mutual benefit. However, Friedman challenged the idea of mutual benefit, arguing that the only responsibility of business towards society is the maximisation of profits to shareholders. Often paraphrased as "the business of business is business", this is arguably one of the most-cited quotes in organisational management theory literature. It should not, however, be taken at face value, however, because he qualified this point by stressing that business should work within the legal framework and the ethical custom of the country (ibid).

Friedman was not alone in voicing this view. Jensen (2008) argued that two hundred years' worth of work in economics and finance indicate that social welfare is maximised when all firms in an economy maximise total firm value. Jensen conceded that companies must attend to multiple constituencies in order to succeed, but ultimately (he argued), firms must be guided by wealth creation only (Margolis and Walsh, 2003). Jensen concluded that long-term market value is the one objective that best advances social welfare. Those subscribing to this view believe that if shareholder wealth is maximised, social welfare will be maximised as well (ibid). Certainly, as "long as society wants high investment returns, job security and higher wages, and lower prices, CEOs are bound to respect these norms" (Agle et al., 1999, p. 522). So it can be argued that Friedman was merely reflecting a view from society. Friedman "did not deny the existence of social problems; he simply claimed that it is the state's role to address them" (Margolis and Walsh, 2003, p. 272).

In other words, no money should be taken as "rent" from the shareholders. Notably, Jensen (2008, p. 167) suggests that there is nothing special "about stockholders in the firm . . . it is time we take it as given that maximising the value of a firm's equity will not produce maximum value of the firm as a whole. And it will certainly not produce maximum value for society".

Regarding the conflict between taking account of relevant stakeholders and attending to long-run interests, Jensen (2008, p. 170) goes on:

> "When I look at the maladaptive behavior in corporations (and goodness knows there's lots of it), what shocks me is how much of it is purposeless. . . . . The behavior doesn't accomplish what the people who are taking those actions nominally want to accomplish, which let us assume is power and wealth."

This illustrates the fundamental problem with Friedman's position that business is a part of society and not apart from society. While in no way belittling the role of organisations in modern society, it is important that they not be demonised. *Business* has rights as well as obligations and has competing needs to meet and address. These rights, obligations and needs change over time and between contexts (Jones et al., 2009).

Another flaw in the arguments posited by Friedman and his supporters is the role of (and anticipated reaction from) society and stakeholders. Clearly, they expect stakeholders (and society) to be passive, which is simply not the case. Margolis and Walsh (2003, pp. 289–290) allude to street protests against the World Trade Organization, the International Monetary Fund and the World Bank. Ranganathan (1998) listed 47 initiatives where investors have "pressured" firms to be more responsive to social problems.

Wood (2008, p. 160) insists "we know too much about the institutional role of business in society to be persuaded by arguments about the glories of unfettered free markets with actors solely in pursuit of maximizing their economic self-interest". Clarkson (1988) argued it has been demonstrated that the pursuit of this single measure was self-defeating. Hence, stakeholder theory is worthy of consideration even if it runs contrary to maximising shareholder returns.

Most economic models focused on the firm and/or its markets rather than coming from a societal (or even customer-centric) position. However, studies have consistently found that with or without a stakeholder focus, corporate performance is very much the same. This suggests stakeholder-focused management does no harm to shareholder interests while also benefiting a larger constituency (Agle and Mitchell, 2008).

Scholars have rightly been criticised for paying too little attention to the relationship between the firm and society, focusing too much on internal organisational processes, to the neglect of any analysis of the societal effects of the firm (Walsh et al., 2003). Businesses that ignore this relationship are remiss in that ethics, social responsibility and sustainability in business have moved from the margins to the mainstream, and it can no longer be argued that the business of business is purely business (Emery, 2012).

Corporate Social Responsibility (CSR)

If ethics has any meaning whatsoever and is to be meaningful,

> "it will be because we need to justify our lives to ourselves and to others, as Sartre and other thinkers have shown us. . . . (And if) . . . business is on one side and ethics is on the other, then we'll have a gap that may come to be known as corporate social responsibility (CSR)".
>
> (Freeman, 2008, p. 164)

CSR is complex: it draws on economics, politics, social integration and ethics (Garriga and Mele, 2004). It is an eclectic field with loose boundaries, multiple memberships and different training/perspectives, and it is broad rather than focused and interdisciplinary (Carroll, 1994). Many companies address ethical and societal concerns by adopting CSR policies, which may benefit both the company and their stakeholders.

Many studies have found positive correlations between improved profitability after adopting progressive CSR measures, such as employee relations, product innovation/ safety, environmental stewardship and community relations. Carroll (1979, 1991) and Wood (1991) are widely cited as having played key roles in CSR and have contributed to building definitions of the different levels at which organisations respond to social responsibilities (Figure 1.6).

Discretionary level	Organisation goes beyond stakeholder views of everyday expected duty and what is just and fair, often involving philanthropy, and is an exemplary corporate citizen.
Ethical level	Organisation views its responsibility to satisfy society's expectations to go beyond basic legal requirements and do what is just and fair, and their practices reflects this. It is focused on business ethics in a wide stakeholder context.
Legal level	Organisation obeys all the laws and rules applied by the state (e.g. taxes, regulations, etc.). It is concerned with the law and legal rights, duties, rules and obligations.
Economic level	Organisation produces products and services that society wants, and it sells them at a profit. Its base starting points are the economy and economic performance, which are seen as pivotal.

Figure 1.6 Carroll's pyramid portraying levels of organisational CSR

Source: adapted from Carroll (1979, 1991) and Wood (1991), as cited in Jones et al. (2009, p. 302)

Jones et al. (2009), however, point out a number of issues with Carroll's pyramid:

- The levels are not mutually exclusive;
- It is a *staged* hierarchy where movement is supposedly based on fixed criteria, but that is not necessarily the case;
- The dynamism that characterises the social, economic and business world is only partially captured;
- It is a theoretical abstract removed from the complex realities of the world it seeks to explain.

Customers can be the forgotten stakeholders (Belz and Peattie, 2009) since organisations are not necessarily consistent in their approach in that their focus on CSR may change with time. Where companies seek (unfair) competitive advantage by abusing the reporting of their CSR practices, the reactions online are often swift and hostile. Social media sites often form the platforms for well-organised pressure groups to coordinate their communications efforts in order to influence corporate behaviour. Marketers must monitor such sites and respond by clearly articulating their company's position. They can create a digital Marcomms campaign (discussed in more detail in Chapter 2.1), highlighting positives from sustainability audits as well as identifying how changes will be implemented. Many examples exist of companies that have benefited from positive Word of Mouth (WoM) by improving their CSR and in turn becoming increasingly sustainable.

Patterns emerge from the adoption of CSR across different organisations. Highly motivated companies may adopt idealistic stances or even one of enlightened self-interest, whereas stakeholders on whom they rely may only adopt CSR practices when coerced (Haberberg et al., 2010). This potentially poses a risk for some companies; for example, Nike's poor Public Relations (PR) due to allegations of child labour generated negative publicity that spread rapidly via social media. Trust in supply networks is discussed in more detail in Chapter 2.2.

Wicked problems

Wicked problems are multifaceted and highly complex societal problems, such as poverty, obesity and environmental degradation (Kennedy and Parsons, 2012). Gerard Hastings argues that the truly wicked problems now faced demand more than nudges and off the shelf solutions. They require everyone to take responsibility and engage in finding intelligent solutions. Wicked problems include impersonal interactions that require institutional guidance and (normative) frameworks. These, in turn, present a vehicle for solving social problems. What, how and how much is exchanged is decided by society and perpetuated through institutions (Kennedy, 2015).

Sustainability-related solutions should be led by a government; however, Tadajewski and Hamilton (2014) argue that government action is not necessarily as effective as it should be. This has to be seen in the context of post-credit crunch "austerity" programmes, where many national governments (often at the behest of bodies such as the European Union) are cutting social budgets in response. National governments are increasingly washing their hands of problems and devolving social causes to the third sector. Third-sector enterprises practice Social Marketing, which is "inherently political, especially when undertaken by public sector organizations" (Kennedy, 2015, p. 5). Belz and Peattie (2009) insist that many social problems remain stubbornly intractable. Local governments – along with communities, institutions, and individuals – may need to be part of long-term plans to create such society-wide change (Kennedy and Parsons, 2012).

Social Marketing

Kotler and Levy proposed extending marketing technologies to non-business arenas in their seminal 1969 article "Broadening the Marketing Concept". They advocated Social Marketing as an approach for social ideas and causes, which can be applied to places (cities, regions, nations) or people (Kotler and Levy, 1969). Kotler later defined it as "the design, implementation, and control of programmes seeking to increase the acceptability of a social idea, cause or practice among a target group" (Kotler and Armstrong, 2006, p. 239). This suggests a range of approaches and different solutions to different problems, which is not ideal from a sustainability perspective, where global solutions are needed. Also, it can be inferred (from the definition) that what matters is the supply-side selling of products and services through programmes.

Social Marketing is often used to influence consumer behavioural change; however, many people do not have the information or the processing capability in certain situations to make logical choices (Kennedy, 2015). When auxiliary products (e.g. educational programmes) support change, people must be told how to obtain them and what actions constitute a purchase (ibid, p. 5). Hence, Kotler's "inward-out" orientation may contribute to cognitive dissonance because it lacks specifics about social responsibility, ethics and community or environmental sustainability.

A further challenge is that Social Marketing can be undertaken by commercial, non-profit and government organisations (Kotler and Lee, 2005), not all of whom will necessarily be au fait with "commercial marketing". The International Social Marketing Association (ISMA) develop this by suggesting it

"seeks to develop and integrate marketing concepts with other approaches to influence behaviours that benefit individuals and communities for the greater social good. Social Marketing practice is guided by ethical principles. It seeks to integrate research, best practice, theory, audience and partnership insight, to inform the delivery of competition sensitive and segmented social change programmes that are effective, efficient, equitable and sustainable".

This refinement provides better balance between the upstream supply and downstream demand side. It resonates with the notion that actors in a marketing system can be individuals, groups, businesses or networks (Kennedy, 2015) and offers clear overlap with sustainable consumption (see Jackson, 2005). Ultimately, upstream organisations cannot force those downstream or midstream to (for example) be happy, satisfied or green. All they can hope to achieve is to create the circumstances where value-seeking customers and influencers can "take value" from the company (Vargo and Lusch, 2004).

Apropos the aforementioned governmental involvement in Social Marketing, Kennedy and Parsons (2012) advocate questioning whose values are being implemented and hope that in democratically elected and governed societies, democratic values are the ones implemented. It is difficult to challenge this logic; however, in times of reduced "purse" (i.e. government spending), national and local governments may not share the same values. Kennedy (2015) alludes to the use of Social Marketing by those who shape the social context, seeking societal-level rather than individual-level change. It can be argued, however, that the implementation of such policies will be more effective if both societal- and individual-level change is sought. Social Marketing has traditionally focused on sociocultural change when more emphasis is needed on creating sustainable value. Although Social Marketing was a key stepping stone, it has not addressed growing ecological concerns in the way sustainability does.

Defining sustainability

The best way to define and measure sustainability is contested. Terms such as "ethical", "organic", "eco", "green" and "fair trade" are used interchangeably, though clearly, they are not interchangeable. In companies, terms such "CSR" and "sustainability" are vague enough to gloss over differences among definitions, stakeholder interests and involvement while being powerful enough to draw the commitment of many different actors, including consumers, other companies and (inter)national organisations.

Unsurprisingly, many terms are used to represent new concepts, such as sustainability. Even well-established terms, such as the "environment", are used in myriad ways in different texts and in some cases by the same author. Consumers often connect with broader environmental issues. Their environmental interaction is important, often emotional and often influences their purchasing decisions.

The 1987 Brundtland Commission definition is widely cited. They define sustainability as

"development that meets the needs of the present without compromising the ability of future generations to meet their own needs".

(1987)

In the late 1990s, the issue was brought to wider audiences when Elkington coined the phrase "Triple Bottom Line" (TBL) in the *Harvard Business Review*. Since TBL was coined, the sustainable business development concept has grown, often being referred to as people-planet-profit. This may still be new to many practitioners (and academics); however, elements therein have been practised for centuries. In TBL, the traditional economic focus (i.e. the company's bottom line) is complemented by adding new foci, namely societal and ecological responsibilities.

It has been argued that Friedman's libertarian position leads to acting in a non-sustainable way. Commentators increasingly think pursuing short-term profits over all other considerations contributed to the 2008 economic meltdown. Companies need to be able to position (or reposition) themselves within their markets in order to make effective decisions. All marketers must ask the following two questions:

1 How do you rate your company in terms of sustainability?
2 How do your customers rate your company in terms of sustainability?

If research shows that there is a mismatch in perceptions (i.e. a perceptual gap), then the organisation must implement changes. To do otherwise may create a disadvantage that competitors could exploit.

Sustainability and business

Many companies have extolled their green credentials via blogs, vlogs and social media. However, simply insisting they are green is no longer sufficient. Such claims will be challenged, and those who have engaged in greenwashing (i.e. sought to gain from false or exaggerated environmental claims) will suffer reputational damage and collateral damage to their brand. Marketers must respond to the social media narrative *and* demonstrate that they operate in increasingly sustainable ways.

Elkington argued that the standard business-as-usual approach was changing as a result of seven "revolutions" that were changing businesses' behaviours and leading to a more-sustainable future. These "revolutions" are portrayed in Figure 1.7.

Clearly, the "revolutions" do not stand apart; rather, they can energise or constrain each other. Nor are they chronologically linear or constant across different cultures. The complex nature of the revolutions is exacerbated by the (mis)use of the word "sustainability" itself.

That said, to depict consumption simplistically as "bad" is naïve and potentially damaging. According to Mary Douglas (1976 as cited in Jackson, 2005), "An individual's main objective in consumption is to help create the social world and to find a credible place in it." In other words, consumption can be viewed as an attempt to improve individual and collective well-being by providing the goods and services necessary to meet people's desires. Needs and desires are central considerations for marketers.

In practice, it is not always clear where corporate governance and sustainability "ownership" reside: should it be hosted by marketing (representing the customer), HR (representing the staff), production (reducing green impacts), quality control (ethical supply policies), purchasing (if greening the supply chain) or all of the above? This is partly due to different approaches regarding what should be sustained, where and

Markets	Increased competition in more demanding, volatile markets, making businesses more susceptible to the effects of economic crises.
Values	Worldwide shift in human/societal values, making businesses susceptible to values-based crises when society finds them wanting.
Transparency	Increased transparency resulting from more open access to information, more authority of stakeholders to demand information and the adoption of scrutiny and reporting systems.
Life cycle technology	Acceptability and appraisal of products at point of sale loses significance, and the focus rests on the whole of the supply chain from acquisition of raw materials, manufacture, transport and storage through to disposal or recycling after consumption.
Partnerships	Business partnerships will become more varied as campaigning groups enter relationships with business organisations once regarded as enemies.
Time	Sustainability issues lengthen time considerations, making planning for sustainable business a matter of years, decades or even generations.
Corporate governance	Evolving corporate governance to include the representation of all relevant stakeholders, not just shareholders, keeping the corporate board focused on all aspects of the sustainable agenda.

Figure 1.7 Elkington's seven revolutions to a sustainable future

Source: adapted from Elkington (2004)

when. Furthermore, companies may face disadvantages when pursuing "costly" sustainable actions; consequently, costs may not be borne by competitors (Pacheco et al., 2010). A way to address ownership issues is to arrange for cross-functional, interdepartmental teams to contribute to (and coordinate) sustainability-related matters.

Some organisations recognise sustainability's importance, as evidenced by elements of their mission statements. This has been seen in the use of purpose statements, where organisations clearly state their different objectives and related stakeholders. Such statements help with maintaining sustainability responsibility among stakeholders: the company, the consumer, the community, the regulator or the government. Consumers and others "downstream" can develop different types of involvement in activities, objects, ideas or even social issues. Higher involvement results from stakeholders being committed to a cause or by being affected by one, such as the local community might be affected. Creating sustainable value may be subject to time constraints or may be impossible given certain resource allocations. Furthermore, while some are able to implement sustainable practices immediately, others may need to accrue the resources to initiate changes (Pacheco et al., 2010).

Some sustainable ventures do not seek to grow their enterprises, being content to remain in their niche. Hockerts and Wüstenhagen (2010) argue that those who are active in a high-end social niche but who have no intention to broaden their impact on a wider market are "social bricoleurs" who often come from the voluntary sector and who may be opposed to consumerism and growth because they worry about abandoning their ideals. This is harsh as new entrants will simply see the opportunity and strive to grow their company while the sustainable first-mover continues or declines.

There are those who describe sustainability as a megatrend (Prothero and McDonagh, 2015) because megatrends are larger in magnitude, longer in duration and deeper in its effects than normal trends, fads or fashions (Mittelstaedt et al., 2014). If it were a megatrend, the issues raised by businesses' adopting and implementing sustainability would be relevant. Consumers increasingly consider problems to be beyond the capacity of government alone to solve, as was demonstrated after the 2016 Brexit referendum. The public expects companies to be problem-solvers. However, inertia or fear of change is often cited as a reason for businesses to be conservative or risk averse. Companies need clear definitions and sustainable marketing tools or frameworks.

Sustainable Marketing

Van Dam and Apeldoorn (1996) coined the phrase "Sustainable Marketing" (hereafter SM) in 1996, when they discussed the inadequacy of green and/or ecological marketing. SM is the process of creating, communicating and delivering value to customers in such a way that both natural and human capital are preserved or enhanced throughout (Martin and Schouten, 2012). Richardson (2015) developed the following definition:

> "Sustainable Marketing (SM) is principled and predicated on the foci of the triple bottom line. SM decisions should be ethically and ecologically sound and companies should divert profits into people and planet foci to enable implementation. Sustainable business practices must be informed by continuous dialogues with all stakeholders. Ultimately, this is the only way to resolve the tensions between customer (and stakeholder) demands, long-term interests, companies' requirements, society's long-run interests and the need for environmental balance".
>
> (Author's PhD thesis)

This definition should act as a springboard for companies. SM needs to be sold on the basis of future gains using communications platforms for external stakeholders and internal marketing techniques to overcome resistance to change (see Chapter 4.2). It should inform mission/vision/purpose statements, marketing objectives and strategies. SM largely uses the same frameworks and tools as conventional marketing. However, marketers will have to adapt the information used to make decisions *and* the criteria used to measure performance. Sustainability audits may be required.

SM involves cascading information regarding the best sustainable practices to producers, stakeholders and consumers alike. It must promote environmental stewardship based on minimising the depletion of non-renewable resources while promoting environmental regeneration. SM is an evolution of being marketing oriented (see Chapter 1.3). Hence, it is inherently long term, and marketers will have to sacrifice short-term profit by incorporating environmental and social costs into pricing decisions.

There is an ongoing debate regarding whether the advent of Web 2.0 (featuring consumer-generated tools such as blogs, price-comparison websites, etc.) has changed how marketing fundamentals are applied. Undoubtedly, the power of consumers has grown in their making purchasing decisions, and companies must adopt a more customer-centric approach if they wish to *sell, not tell*. Companies of all sizes can now reach millions of new customers on a global scale that until recently was available only to major corporations. It is the most exciting time there has ever been for starting and growing smaller companies. Marketers can tap into this as long as they recognise changing consumer behaviours.

Some use the term "sustainability-driven marketing" to reflect the values of marketers who more strongly associate the meaning of it with the process of sustainability as opposed to the process of sustaining anything (Tilley and Young, 2009). This raises the same problems as the increasingly outdated notion of a value proposition (see Chapter 1.4). Value (whether sustainable or other) cannot be "given" to consumers. They can co-create or take it, but companies cannot simply give it. Hence, the all-encompassing concept of SM is preferred, and now, more than ever before, SM encourages marketers to align their values with the increasingly ethical and/or green behaviour of consumers. Marketers must find out not only what consumers think but also what they value, which in turn will provide insights into the networks and communities of users, prospects, friends, colleagues and even families.

1.2 Sustainability . . . the new organisational orientation

Marketing is a social science. In short, this means matters are rarely clear-cut. Answers to questions are often conditional and shaped by the context. In some ways, context is everything, because answers taken out of context may be damaging. There are many ways to create, grow and sustain a business, depending on the type of market, available resources (both hard and soft), leadership skills, entrepreneurialism and serendipity (or sheer luck). Economists categorise markets into three types, as shown in Figure 1.8.

Incipient markets pose a problem for companies that aim to provide solutions on the basis of customer dialogue. Customer dialogue is usually needed for successful launches. Two exceptions (where the drivers were internal rather than external from the market) are the Sony Walkman in 1979 and the iPhone in 2007. Both were radical and examples of technological competence being matched with a vision and understanding of the application of that specific technology.

Globalisation is a key influence on markets. The BRIC countries (Brazil, Russia, India and China) have been complemented with Mexico, Indonesia and Turkey to form the E7. Markets will continue to open in the E7, which brings opportunities for Western companies. Companies will have to avoid overly relying on the E7 economies, which can lead to complacency.

> *Example* In 2018 Jaguar Land Rover (JLR) announced 4500 redundancies in their UK workforce. Brexit played some role since it had lowered the value of sterling; diesel engines suffered reputational damage from the Volkswagen (VW) emission cheat debacle; and some local authorities were actively considering introducing pollution charges in cities, akin to the congestion charge in London. But above everything else, the Chinese economy slowed down, and China's burgeoning middle class bought JLR products in much smaller numbers.

Chinese investors have acquired hundreds of European companies over the past decade. Many of them were German or British companies, including those in the automotive sector: Rover (UK); MG (UK); and Volvo (Sweden). This saw cars previously manufactured in Europe being made in China. It is possible that the country of origin (CoO) effect may have had an influence, as Chinese consumers may have preferred to

Market type	Traditional role	Customer-centric implications
Existing markets	Customers are satisfied with existing products or services. Competition is largely based on price and promotional spend. Innovation/additional benefits seem to be absent	Customers or consumers benefit from progressively lower prices for given categories of products or services. This in turn requires companies to pay close attention to costs and marketing spend to maintain profitability, suggesting a cost leadership approach often found in production orientation.
Latent markets	Needs are defined but not yet met – e.g. much improved battery technology to support the introduction of genuinely non-polluting vehicles or cures for Alzheimer's disease or type 2 diabetes.	Investment is needed in technology: new diagnostic tools and therapies. These require using high tech, which lends itself to production and product orientations.
Incipient markets	Customers do not yet recognise their need or problems that need solving; however, the appearance of a new solution triggers their problem recognition.	Research with customers will not show support for genuinely innovative products and services.

Figure 1.8 The role and nature of markets

Source: adapted from Richardson et al. (2015, pp. 28–29)

buy products made locally. The competitive landscape is dynamic and presents challenges. Companies have to be prepared; otherwise, they may face a loss in market share or profitability or even face organisational failure.

The forces stimulating the development and growth of E7 markets will see native companies reciprocate – that is, seek to become established in developed countries. The nature, or orientation, of the companies will largely shape their approach to selling domestically and internationally. Hence, it is wise to consider the different business orientations (Figure 1.9), each of which has strengths and weaknesses.

Production orientation is the oldest form; Henry Ford has been attributed with introducing new manufacturing techniques since he launched the Model T Ford in 1908. The old adage of "you can have any colour you want as long as it's black" is often attributed to Henry Ford. This is clearly far from a customer-centric attitude, and yet Ford sold 15 million Model T Fords while revolutionising car manufacturing. Ford did not invent the automobile, and his were not necessarily the best vehicles available; however, they were affordable and led to the democratisation of independent transport in the United States. It was a similar story with the Honda C90. Launched in 1958, over 27 million units have been sold, and a new iteration (known as the Honda Super Cub) is still being sold.

If there is a market, why should anyone introduce radical, costly changes? Production-oriented companies focus on production techniques, reducing costs, marginal gains and efficiency issues. It typically involves high-volume, low-margin business with low R&D or innovation. It has an inwards-looking focus, which is problematic

Orientation	Nature	Driver	Motivation to change	Marketing Activities	Marketing Oriented
Production	High volume, low margin, little risk, minimal R&D and innovation. Imitates first movers.	Internal (in-out; top-down).	Take share by cost leadership. Towards end of extended product life cycle (PLC). Often target late majority and laggards. Little NPD. Low risk. Products often cash cows.	Yes	No
Product	Add to existing ideas. Market follower of new products. Some tailoring of product offer. Medium volume, occasional high margins.	Internal (in-out; top-down)	Improve existing product or adapt/develop rivals' offering. Target early majority, niche or new overseas markets. Risks trademark and intellectual property infringements.	Yes	No
Sales	High focus on above-the-line advertising. Seeks high brand awareness and recall. Not necessarily the first, the best or the cheapest. Can take large market share.	Internal (in-out; top-down)	Take share from competitors by having higher awareness. Single transactions. Heavy reliance on promotion – some use of mass media, others through sales teams. Strong branding. Can miss changing customer patterns.	Yes	No
Marketing	Sell what customers want. Seek to innovate with products and services. Customer-centric – i.e. customer at heart of all business decisions.	External (out-in; bottom-up)	Seek to identify customer needs that are not satisfied by rivals, and provide solutions. Look to develop customer relationships. Heavy reliance on market research. Promote loyalty schemes. Seek to sell benefits and create value for customers to take.	Yes	Yes
Market	Sell what customers want. Gather insights internally (from other departments) and externally (from customers, suppliers, competitors, etc.). Often end up market leaders. Seek to innovate with products and services.	Internal + external (out-in; in-in; bottom-up)	Adopt all aspects (and accepts benefits) of a marketing orientation. Complement customer-centric approach with full understanding of markets (i.e. competitors, suppliers, pressure groups, trade bodies, etc.) and focus on developing inter-functional relationships. Use internal marketing techniques.	Yes	Yes

Figure 1.9 Attributes of pre-sustainability organisational orientations

Source: author

if the market, competition and customers change. Some changes may be imposed by governments, such as. banning the sales of traditional light bulbs. Organisations following this inwards-looking approach may not know how or when to change. They may struggle in fast-paced marketplaces. Blackberry smartphones were "technologically superior" products, but the company struggled to react to changes in a post-iPhone world.

Product orientation involves focusing mainly on developing existing product features or offering improvements on competitor's products. The Apple iPad is a brilliant concept, but many of its components have existed for decades (displays, solid state storage, touch screens, etc.). It was not the first tablet to market; however, it was the first to have substantial customer take-up. Apple is a unique company, some might argue the exception to the rule, as most product-oriented organisations adopt an inward focus at their peril. They will be successful initially, but when newer, more innovative and competitive products enter the market, they will usually suffer. Apple is still a technological force today.

Sales orientation features a focus on selling the products (or services) with little regard to the market. This approach relies on above-the-line communications (see Chapter 2 and sales techniques. This approach became popular in the 1950s, when customers were offered a greater choice of products and services. Historically, hard-sell techniques were often used in this approach to help persuade the customer to buy one particular product or service rather than the competition's product. Today, hard selling is considered unethical, though not necessarily illegal. Recent scandals in the United Kingdom highlighted aggressive selling techniques in banking and other financial services, energy, cosmetic surgery and, perhaps most reprehensibly, pensions products and services to the elderly.

A more enlightened example of a sales-oriented company is Dell. Consumers who take subscriptions to, say, the *Times* would see Dell's massive investment in advertising. Most days sees half or full-page advertisements, not to mention TV, radio, and other media. A straw poll of classes over the past few years has never failed to produce a cluster of students who have bought Dell machines. Dell did not invent the PC, and they may not be the cheapest unit on the market, but you have to go a long way to find a company that advertises its products more effectively than Dell.

These orientations are transactional. The focus is on closing the deal rather than building a relationship. Furthermore, there is no sense that feedback from the customer, let alone any longer-term relationship beyond these individual transactions, is expected or desired.

Marketing-oriented companies recognise that the customers are their most important "assets". Irrespective of whether a company is product or service based, or indeed a charity, it must place the customer at the heart of all the decision-making and planning (not just the marketing) decisions. Where customer needs drive all the business decisions a marketing philosophy has been truly adopted and implemented. This can only be achieved by entering into regular, honest dialogue with customers. Every time a marketer receives customer feedback, their organisation has grown stronger. Furthermore, all employees must be customer-centric and not merely those who interact with the customers. This is generally known as the marketing concept. Organisations who adopt the marketing concept are said to be marketing oriented.

A market orientation signals the importance placed on an organisation's approach to its customers and (unlike a marketing orientation) its competitors and microenvironment. All staff are responsible for supporting the market orientation. Customers are key information sources but so are suppliers, distributors, intermediaries, representative bodies and trade associations. Both formal and informal methods must be used when adopting a market orientation. Thus, the conduct of formal marketing research (see Chapter 1.6) is essential. The dialogue should be ongoing and undertaken with their wider networks. The intelligence gathered by sales staff is particularly important; however, there may be internal politics when extracting information from the market. Internal Marketing (see Chapter 4.2) should be used to encourage non-customer-facing functions (R&D, production or QA) to contribute. Their insights are valuable; however, there are no quick or free options in developing a market orientation.

Market orientation – a definition

Market orientation involves understanding current and future customers' needs to develop offerings where customers can seek and take more distinctive value than that which the competition is offering; market-oriented companies undertake ongoing research to improve relationships with (internal and external) customers and key stakeholders.

Meaningful "buy-in" from senior management will reduce the risk of interdepartmental competition and politics. Information must not remain in functional "silos", and best practice must be shared. It has to be embedded through formal contractual means and through reward systems (with input from the HR function) that recognise the importance of this activity. All employees must embrace market orientation. It is naïve to assume that the adoption of a market orientation will guarantee success. As discussed, many successful companies do not follow this approach and are unlikely to do so in future. They have taken market share and often thrived on using different orientations.

Benefits of adopting a market orientation

There is a positive correlation between adopting a market orientation and organisational success. The following are some of the benefits of adopting a market orientation:

- Increased market share, revenues and profitability;
- Improved customer satisfaction, retention and loyalty;
- Lower customer attrition and more new customers;
- Improved staff morale and motivation and lower churn;
- Improved WoM, reputation and competitive advantage.

Satisfied customers tend not only to return to purchase for themselves once again but also to recommend their purchase to their friends, families and colleagues. Conversely, if they have a poor experience, they tend to tell even more people about it. This applies now more than ever with the advent of new technologies. Web 2.0 has seen an explosion in the use of user-review websites (see www.imdb.com), blogs, social media sites and cost-comparison websites such as Kelkoo or moneysupermarket.com.

Marketers must avoid becoming overly internally focused on analysing and crunching sales and market share figures, staffing issues or buying in new capital equipment. Companies certainly need excellent production techniques, products and sales initiatives, but the need for customer awareness and understanding factors in the wider environment is paramount. Wherever and whenever markets or environments change, marketers must change and adapt; otherwise, they risk being left behind.

A market orientation can be embraced and implemented in any size or type of organisation. Indeed, it is arguably more important that small firms monitor the market forces that can affect the customer.

1.3 Critical marketing

Marketing has been practiced for millennia; however, as a theoretical domain, it has been considered only since the early 20th century. Many commentators have reflected on how consumers have demonstrated different values. Adam Smith, David Ricardo and Karl Marx elaborated on value in exchange. Marx also differentiated between value in exchange and value in use (Boztepe, 2007).

The argument is, in essence, whether profit should be exclusively used to improve Return on Investment (ROI) or also invested into a Return on Objectives (RoO) designed to satisfy stakeholders other than shareholders. ROI is the performance measure used to evaluate the economic efficiency of an investment, whereas RoO aims to gauge an investment's efficiency according to achieving other corporate and/or functional objectives.

In the absence of adequate regulation, free markets can run out of control. Consumerism has been described as the "shame of marketing" for the simple reason that if sellers abided by the marketing concept, then the interests of buyers would be given equal attention to those of sellers and so would avoid conflicts of interest that bring many marketing practices into disrepute (Baker, 2009). Consider the matter of household waste. Defra offered the following figures for household waste in England in 2016–2017:

- 23.6 million tonnes of waste produced.
- 10.3 million tonnes of waste recycled.
- 43.7% overall waste recycling rate for England.
- 411 kg average amount of waste produced per person per annum.

Clearly, the consumer cannot be responsible for the total amount of waste produced and recycled. This falls on the manufacturers, government (local and national) and recycling organisations. Most of the plastic food containers that householders wash out after use and put in the recycling bin cannot actually be recycled by local government authorities. The Local Government Association (LGA) observed that two-thirds are sent to landfill, while a third is recycled (BBC, 2018b). Around 525,000 tonnes of plastic pots, tubs and trays are used by households annually in the United Kingdom; however, only 169,000 tonnes of this waste are recyclable, largely due to the use of polymers, some of which are of poor quality (ibid).

The LGA report comes after a study from the National Audit Office that suggests half the packaging reported as recycled is sent abroad to be processed (BBC, 2018). Hence, the carbon footprint of the waste materials is increased, and concerns are raised about the working conditions of those tasked with recycling. Examples of child labour working in poor conditions are common.

Example Microwave meals are often supplied in black plastic, as it is more aesthetically appealing. It also conveys a sense of "luxury" and suggests a premium product. However, materials can be recycled only once they have been sorted. Some manual sorting takes place; however, as recycling volumes increases, optical scanners provide an effective solution. However, black is the only colour that cannot be easily scanned by recycling machines; changing the colour would significantly increase the recycling rate (BBC, 2018). Margarine and ice cream tubs often contain the polymer polypropylene, which is difficult to recycle. An alternative approach would be to make them from the same plastic as water bottles, which is easily recycled. Yoghurt pots are often made from a mixture of polypropylene and polystyrene. An alternative is to use polyethylene terephthalate, which is also used in plastic bottles and can be easily recycled (ibid).

The LGA, which represents councils in England and Wales, says the government should consider a ban on low-grade plastics. In 2018 the LGA was arguing that the UK government should make plastics manufacturers pay for the costs of collecting and disposing of unrecyclable plastics. The Recycling Association identified nearly 350 different collection systems in the United Kingdom and cited widespread confusion and a lack of awareness among consumers. Hence, it is incumbent on marketers to improve awareness and the adoption of such schemes. The annual cost of dealing with UK household packaging is circa £1 billion. UK manufacturers cover up to £20 million of the cost, unlike some of their European counterparts, who have to cover the whole cost. The UK's GDP is £1.6 trillion, so £1 billion is a relatively small amount; however, as always, someone will have to pick up the cost. More often than not, it is the consumer, because companies will want to maintain profits and dividends for shareholders. A better alternative may be to incentivise marketers to adopt easily recyclable materials and designs. This carrot-and-stick argument has been around as long as companies have existed.

However, the manufacturers, the authorities and the consumer can all share responsibility for the waste per person. 411 kg per UK citizen per annum is staggering. Clearly, this is but a single snapshot, and what is needed is research into the barriers of consumer recycling.

Marketers are put under pressure to be global and local, centralised and decentralised, large and small, planned yet flexible and to serve different markets, with standardised and customised products, at premium and penetration prices, through restricted and extensive distribution networks and supported by national yet targeted promotional campaigns (Brown, 1995). With these demands, it is no surprise that, as previously discussed, companies fail. The cause is often due to inappropriate marketing.

The term "inappropriate" here covers not only poorly implemented marketing but also that which is neither legal nor ethical. With so many high-profile cases in recent years, marketers should not be shocked to hear that there is much cynicism towards marketing. A basic premise of this book is that by acting sustainably, marketers will be more likely to build trust. Too often, marketing has focused on what is needed to be done *to* customers, whereas modern, progressive marketers should be asking themselves (and their colleagues) what can they do *for* their customers. This mindset will improve relationships with consumers and other stakeholders.

Arguably, anything that is sold is marketed. Hence, those involved in, say, prostitution or ticket touting could be argued to be marketers. The counter to this argument is to be ethical in everything. If there are doubts about the ethical or environmental

		Legality		
		High	*Low*	*Zero*
Ethicality	High	A	B	C
	Low	D	E	F
	Zero	G	H	I

Figure 1.10 Absolute marketing: ethics and legality matrix

Source: original diagram

impact of a company's actions (Figure 1.10), they should think carefully before proceeding.

Figure 1.10 covers the full spectrum of marketing activities. Thankfully, it is harder than ever before to keep illegal and/or unethical practices secret. Most marketers are ethical and comply with the law.

Corporate Social Irresponsibility (CSI)

"Corporate social irresponsibility" (CSI) is a term better suited to describing the workings of the "old" shareholder business models, whereas corporate social responsibility (CSR) is more applicable to the workings of the nascent stakeholder business model. CSI extends Carroll's work on definitional constructs by re-examining some of the theoretical frameworks that underpin, inform and guide CSR (Figure 1.11).

Jones et al. (2009) describe their model as a conduit of corporate governance that enables action and assists planning. The model facilitates a potentially better-managed, more productive, socially responsible and profitable business (ibid). The use of a continuum seems appropriate because organisational decisions are rarely as clear-cut as many business texts suggest. It can be inferred from Figure 1.11 that some organisations may be positioned towards CSR on some issues but closer to CSI on others. Companies with clear, coherent CSR strategies should gravitate towards one end. The CSI–CSR continuum provides a useful tool for organisational positioning and benchmarking. It does, however, suffer from the drawback of not informing managers of how they should implement changes. Furthermore, the continuum includes ecological concerns within the "social" concept of CSR, which some may deem incongruous. Although CSR predates the SM movement, including ecological matters, Emery, 2012 suggests that it fails to provide a complete answer to the issues raised by the sustainability agenda.

Organisation and management theory scholars are still criticised for paying too little attention to the relationships between firms and society. They have focused excessively on internal organisational processes and firms adapting to their proximate environment, much to the neglect of any analysis on the effects of the firm on society (Walsh et al., 2003). Many marketing texts draw from the experiences of large American companies. They are often behind the curve on key areas, such as sustainability, customer centricity and digital marketing. Professor Stephen Brown (an influential critical marketer) argued that the traditional, linear, step-by-step marketing model of analysis, planning, implementation and control no longer seems applicable,

	CSI	CSR
Pollution & Environment	Environmental degradation & pollution are inevitable & little can/should be done	Environmental degradation & pollution are avoidable & should not be tolerated. Raising awareness/commitment to action is vital
	Employees are resource to be exploited	Employees are to be valued
	Minimal community consultation or involvement is necessary	Community consultation should maximise engagement
	Compliance: failure/reluctant/basic CSR legislation compliance	Compliance with policies & practical actions beyond minimum legal requirements
	Ethical issues if relevant are on the periphery of operations	Ethical issues are central to the organisation
Diversity & Equal Opportunities	Social exclusion is an inevitable by-product of markets	Socially inclusive – helps to correct market inefficiencies
New Technologies	New technologies should be developed/introduced to market	New tech should be developed & introduced to the market if safe
Corporate Governance	Governance of companies is best left to shareholders/management	Corporate governance involves a wide range of stakeholders
Customers & Suppliers	Stakeholder Attitude – treat suppliers/customers unfairly	Work fairly with suppliers and customers
	Pragmatic approach to CSR issues	Principled & pragmatic approach to CSR issues
Human Resources / Community involvement	Sustainability defined as business survival	Sustainability defined as business, environmental & community survival/mutual growth
Ethical Standards / Profit	Profit is the sole purpose of business & should be achieved at any cost	Profit should be achieved but not at any cost

Figure. 1.11 The CSR versus CSR dichotomous model and potential outcomes

Source: adapted from Jones et al. (2009, pp. 301–304)

appropriate or even pertinent to what is actually happening on the ground (Brown, 1995). This is interesting as a critique; however, extensive interaction with practitioners has shown that they want some form of structure to implement planning. Implementation is everything.

The company's relationship to "the problem" also influences how it ought to respond to a societal ill (Margolis and Walsh, 2003). Consider the following three perspectives:

1   A problem created (or contributed to) by the firm will impose a stronger duty to act than one not of the firm's making;
2   The relevance of the firm's capabilities and resources to the societal ill shape the strength of an imperative to respond;
3   The response required may vary with a company's proximity to the community in which the need arises.

Freeman (2008) insists that better stakeholder theory focuses us on the many ways that companies are "out there creating value, making our lives better, and changing the world". G. E. Moore (as cited in Freeman, 2008, p. 164) posited the open question argument: for any decision that a manager or other organisation member makes, can the following questions be answered?

1   If this decision is made, for whom is value created and destroyed; who is harmed; and who benefits?
2   Whose rights were respected or violated?
3   What kind of person will I be if I make this decision in this particular way?

Businesses can and do fail by not answering these questions. These questions clearly link values with sustainability and SM. Values that may be addressed include the monetary outlay to buy a related product but also include time, energy and social/psychological costs of obtaining or not obtaining a product or behaving in a certain way (Kennedy, 2015).

The PR industry has long been associated with CSI by producing propaganda, often during times of conflict or unrest. PR has been used by dictators when the messages were based on a twisted form of idealism rather than reality. Criticism is often aimed at businesses and organisations who do not practise what they preach or who spin the story to include a heavily biased opinion in favour of the message sender (see Chapter 2.1). PR practitioners (often referred to as spin doctors) representing political parties are frequently criticised for their part in manipulating (or being economical with) the truth. Sometimes their role has been more insidious, as was demonstrated in the Bell Pottinger debacle in South Africa. Lured by fees of £100,000 a month, the PR firm ran a secret campaign to stir up racial tension on behalf of its billionaire clients. Bell Pottinger was accused of inciting racial tension and operating fake Twitter accounts to mount racially driven campaigns (Guardian, 2017). Francis Ingham, director general of the Public Relations Consultants Association (PRCA), said in an interview,

> "In my years of running the P.R.C.A., I have never seen anything worse, never seen anything equal to it. . . . The work was on a completely new scale of awfulness. Bell Pottinger may have set back race relations in South Africa by as much as 10 years".

By the end of 2018, all 250 employees were laid off, and Bell Pottinger was wound up (*NY Times*, 2018). It is a salutary lesson for all involved in marketing, PR and journalism.

> *Example* Philip Morris International (PMI) makes six of the world's 15 bestselling brands of cigarettes and is the world's biggest tobacco firm. In 2018 PMI staged "a disgraceful PR stunt" by offering to help NHS staff quit smoking to help mark the service's 70th birthday (*Guardian*, 2018). PMI prompted anger among doctors, MPs and health campaigners by making its offer to all NHS bodies in England. Steve Brine, the public health minister, branded the proposal "entirely inappropriate" and said "Our aim to make our NHS – and our next generation – smoke-free must be completely separate from the commercial and vested interests of the tobacco industry" (ibid). Under the World Health Organisation's Framework Convention on Tobacco Control (see WHO, 2019), governments that are signatories (including Britain) must ensure that tobacco manufacturers play no role in public health. The guidance states that "Parties should not accept, support or endorse partnerships and nonbinding or non-enforceable agreements as well as any voluntary arrangement with the tobacco industry or any entity or person working to further its interest"
>
> (ibid).

> Mark MacGregor, PMI's director of corporate affairs in the United Kingdom and Ireland, said the following in a letter: "To support the 70th anniversary of the NHS, we are keen to work with you to help the 73,000 NHS employees who currently smoke, to quit cigarettes. This would be a collaborative campaign: you would provide cessation advice for quitting nicotine altogether, and for smokers who do not quit we can help them switch to smoke-free alternatives".
>
> (*Guardian*, 2018)

> The Royal College of Physicians (RCP), which represents hospital doctors, estimated that NHS staff who smoke take 56% more days off sick than colleagues who do not, costing the NHS £101 million a year and a further £6 million in treatment costs. Professor Jane Dacre, the president of the RCP, added that "We are deeply suspicious of the motives of Philip Morris International in their opportunistic attempt to become involved in smoking cessation in hospitals".
>
> (ibid)

In the United Kingdom, there are laws to protect against libel and slander. Cases are increasingly being brought for online comments. The law applies whether online or in hard copy. Cases of libel action being brought against PR practitioners are rare, but high-profile practitioners have found themselves facing high-court rulings for promoting stories that were falsified. Similarly, newspapers are treated with the same legal action for reporting stories, often promoted by PR practitioners, that are defamatory and may cause anxiety for those misrepresented.

Identity

The issue of identity needs to be given serious consideration as brands increasingly use social media, featuring groups, communities and tribes who share common interests, ideals and values. Organisations seeking to market themselves online face fundamental challenges regarding the issue of identity. Who are the users? Are users and customers the same thing? Can Twitter users be treated in the same way as those on Facebook or LinkedIn? Marketers will struggle to identify prospects, users and/or buyers. Segmentation will become increasingly harder as users of Facebook, Twitter, Instagram and Pinterest (among others) disaggregate (i.e. put their best face forward). An individual's identity may well vary across different social platforms. Wang (2014) refers to this as the elastic self. Furthermore, the nature of online social behaviour is influenced by perceived anonymity. Have no doubt that the identities of users of social media are multifaceted, fluid and often deceptive.

Online communications, social media profiles and interactions form identities online, which can change rapidly. It is increasingly important for marketers to manage their company's reputations online. A number of approaches can be used:

- Socialise campaigns – users use multiple social networks for different reasons: Facebook for personal use, Twitter for conversations and LinkedIn for business;
- Develop a personality – people have personalities and visit networks to socialise. Do not sell on social networks;
- Location – mobile devices have access to improved network connectivity, and multitaskers can no longer be assumed to be at a fixed point. Consider whether they can be reached by geofenced campaigns;
- Timing – multitaskers tend to go online in the evening. Hence, communicating with them between 6.00 p.m. and 9.00 p.m. can be effective;
- Communicate to convert – multitaskers are heavily influenced by WoM. Monitor and listen to the conversations;
- Reputation – be aware of how companies are represented and discussed online, and strive to manage this discussion effectively;
- Monitoring – monitor the macroenvironment continuously (see Chapter 3.3).

Despite the complexity of so many approaches a company's reputation is still worth preserving, since the customer's "spending" is shaped by the thoughts, feelings and actions of those around them. Consumers adopt attitudes, beliefs, opinions and values of their family, friends, communities, colleagues, reference groups, opinion leaders and so on. So, with social media, new forms of identity are being shaped by networks and communities.

However, some seeking to market to users, customers and prospects on social networks are impeded by the ethically dubious practices of identity theft and fake profiles. Identity, profile or personality theft is present on all social networks. Facebook (2014) reported that up to 1.2% of Facebook profiles were fake. With billions of users worldwide, this suggests that there are many millions of fake Facebook accounts. If someone wished to portray themselves as more socially successful, they could simply "buy" Twitter followers – for as little as $10 per 1,000 or 30,000 YouTube views for $150 (*Wired*, 2013). In an era where online popularity is paramount, there will always be a supply for such demand.

Example   Conservative Party strategists bought friends, or likes, for David Cameron's Facebook profile in March of 2014 (*Guardian*, 2014). Whether or not this is deemed to be unethical, it was certainly an opportunity for public ridicule and poor PR, which given Cameron's background was ironic to say the least.

Such practices are in the minority since most consumers are ethical and increasingly discerning about such practices. Social networks have to offer extensive privacy settings for users to help protect their identity, even if at times these lack clarity or simplicity. The onset of the General Data Protection Regulations (GDPR) was directly attributable to such sharp practices by digital marketers.

The negative side of loyalty

Marketers dedicate a great deal of resources to building relationships with customers (see Chapter 4.1) by seeking increased satisfaction and loyalty. There may, however, be a negative aspect to loyalty. Some consumers' relationships with banks, insurance companies or energy providers are less than totally satisfying. The consumer often feels "locked in" as the effort needed to switch suppliers tends to make customers stay with the existing provider. This tendency results from inertia, risk aversion and even apathy. It would be instructive to know how many service providers factor in consumers' perceptions of feeling "locked in" in their discussions with customers. In the United Kingdom, legislation permits easy and quick switching between banking and energy providers. It remains to be seen to what extent these desirable developments affect customer behaviour and loyalty.

Myths perpetuated by (or about) marketers

Marketing practitioners, unlike some business functions (e.g. HR, PR, accounts, production, etc.), must challenge the orthodoxy. No marketer will be appointed if their pitch involves doing the same as the incumbent. Being a continuity candidate will not land the job. No marketing agency will win deals if they offer the same as their predecessor. Marketers have to be agents of change. However, in seeking such change, they are often accused of the following:

- Creating false desires and fostering materialism;
- Producing too few social goods;
- Creating cultural pollution and bombarding people with advertisements;
- Having too much political power;
- Driving prices higher by adding to the cost of the product or service;
- Deceiving consumers about pricing, promotion and packaging;
- Lacking a customer focus and concentrating on closing the deal;
- Selling poor-quality products;
- Designing products with built-in obsolescence to accelerate their replacement.

This list is not exhaustive, and marketers must reflect on why other stakeholders hold such views. These views have accumulated over a considerable period of time. As consumers become more discerning, marketers need to recognise and react to scepticism. Worryingly, some of the more cynical perceptions are often held by fellow professionals who should really know better. Partially, this may be due to marketing myths:

1 Marketing is just advertising

Marketing is not just about advertising and promotional work. People perceive it as such because promotional work (i.e. advertising, PR or sales promotions) is often the most visible part of a marketing team's effort to the outside world. Communications are increasingly being used progressively to engage in dialogue with consumers and stakeholders.

2 A satisfied customer is a loyal customer

Satisfied, loyal customers are more likely to provide good WoM, improve reputations and increase customer acquisition (i.e. more new customers). Managers often confuse satisfaction with loyalty. In some cases, loyalty is simply down to customer apathy as the perceived benefits of changing supplier does not outweigh the hassle of moving. This is often the case with retail banking and utilities such as gas suppliers who arguably overly rely on systems. This raises the question whether being good at systems, such as Customer Relationship Management (CRM), has replaced identifying customers thoughts, feelings and concerns.

3 A strong brand is invincible

Strong brands are far from invincible, as has been proven time and time again.

> *Example*   Microsoft are undoubtedly one of the world's strongest brands, and yet they are under attack from all sides. On one front is the advance of open source software (e.g. Linux, Mozilla, Google Chrome) and shareware. Another is the technological changes such as cloud computing (e.g. word processing) or the challenges presented by the 5G generation of mobiles: the Google phone based on Android.
>
> They have recognised this threat and had the financial strength to diversify into hardware. The Xbox range cost billions of dollars to develop; however, they saw it as a future hub for home communications. In 2014 they acquired Nokia's mobile phone division for $8 billion. Within a matter of months, they announced that 18,000 jobs were to be cut, many of which were in Scandinavia, much to the concern of those who built the Nokia brand.

4 A big name brand can sustain a higher price

Critical marketers are often scathing about some of the most widely used tools, such as the marketing mix (see Brownlie and Saren, 1992). Pricing is a contentious issue and presents many challenges for marketers (see Chapter 2.4).

Dell has high levels of brand awareness and recognition; however, they offer a value-for-money proposition. McDonalds is one of the world's most easily recognised brands, and yet their prices are by no means excessive. Ultimately, what matters is whether the customer sees value in the goods or services. Remember that it is not about being the cheapest, as many iPhone owners *think* their phone is the best value for money available.

5 The customer is always right

The customer is not always right, but they are always the customer. Undoubtedly, the most important "assets" for organisations are their customers, and organisations must place them at the heart of all the decision-making and planning (not just the

marketing) decisions. Customer insights and engagement must drive all business decisions, which can be achieved only by entering into regular, honest dialogue with customers. Every time marketers receive customer feedback, their organisation has grown
stronger.

> *Example*   Microsoft launched Office versions for the iPad in 2014, four years
> after Apple effectively created a new tablet market. This was clearly a result of
> muddled thinking on Microsoft's part. It lacked customer centricity. As soon as
> the iPad was launched, Microsoft should have launched Office. That said, Apple
> themselves have been equally obstinate (to the detriment of customers): to this
> day, the original iPad cannot have its iOS updated beyond 5.1.1 even if the item is
> fully functional. This prevents access to key sites such as LinkedIn. So customers
> who bought an iPad on day one of its release (at £699 in the United Kingdom)
> would have a different level of support from those who bought a MacBook on the
> same day for a similar price. This form of built-in obsolescence (see Chapter 2.3)
> may explain why Apple lost their first-mover advantage in tablets.

6 Members of distribution channels do not influence marketing

Distribution channels are often key to organisational success. At best, poor distribution can irritate customers. At worst, it can lead to organisational failure. Technology
has made it easier than ever for companies to distribute their own goods and services.
This is what Chris Andersen calls the "long tail": everything is available online some-
where. Marketers must not confuse being online with being popular or profitable.
There are thousands of apps on the Apple App Store or Google Play that have never
been downloaded even though the "distributor" is highly visible with brand recognition of the highest level.

7 Advertising always affects sales

Advertising *should* always affect sales; however, some advertising campaigns have
actually driven customers away. Good advertising can have a long-term effect,
although most of it leads to a short-term sales boost. Not all advertising is good.
Mobile advertising is gaining ground, since it has the unique ability to be seen by
the smartphone user. This and other technological changes are causing havoc in the
advertising industry. Customers have evolved into multitaskers who access different
social media sites on a range of platforms (online, mobile, tablet, TV, etc.), which creates challenges for those wishing to target them with marketing communications (see
Chapter 2.1). When coupled with the aforementioned disaggregation, advertising is
harder than ever before to be assured of a RoMI (return on marketing investment).

8 Marketing is used only by large organisations

Governments recognise that Small to Medium-sized Enterprises (SMEs) are a key driving force for economic growth and development. However, the characteristics of SMEs
are essentially different in nature from those of larger companies (see Chapter 4).
Despite this, traditional approaches to marketing have largely been based on or developed from experiences in larger companies. The size of an organisation has affects its

ability to communicate with different stakeholders. If anything, a "market" orientation is more important for SMEs than it is for larger companies. Small businesses do not have the low cost base or substantial financial resources of large companies. But where they often have the advantage is in their ability to move much closer to the customer, to form a strong alliance with them and to make them feel valued. SMEs have the ability to be flexible and move quickly with changing customer needs and market dynamics. Finally, many SME owners are entrepreneurs whose values are not limited to financial profit or economic wealth creation but instead reflect personal and wider value systems, including sustainability.

9 Business causes the problems rather than solves them

One of the myths regarding business is that it's part of the problem, not the solution, and that issues such as sustainability should be the concern of politicians and governments rather than "business". Upon reflection, however, this approach is contradictory, because "business" needs to be at the forefront of the sustainability debate as trade largely takes place between companies, not governments. In 2012 global merchandise trade was estimated to be $18 trillion. Hence, "business" has enormous potential to promote sustainable trade patterns. Also "business", rather than government, has the knowledge and skills to trade sustainably and help to shape global sustainability guidelines and practices. If the Cooperative can thrive for 160 years, then other businesses can.

10 Companies should focus only on making profit

The raison d'être of Elkington's TBL was to complement the existing focus of profit with the new foci of people and planet. Moving from a single focus to multiple foci creates challenges for academics and practitioners alike. Is business purely about being profitable? "Profit" is considered (by many) to be the way to secure long-term survival. On the other hands, reinvesting profit into people and/or planet may be another way to secure long-term survival. Can, say, a city hedge fund or a charity that is worthy but losing money be sustainable? Certainly, there's little value in a company committing to sustainability if, in doing so, it loses out to non-sustainable competitors and ultimately fails.

1.4 Corporate values versus customer-centric values

Company failures may happen suddenly or may have been years in the making. *Any* business can fail. Indeed, the average lifespan of a company listed in the Standard & Poor's (S&P 500) index of leading US companies has decreased from 67 years in the 1920s to just 15 years in the 21st century. Soon, more than three-quarters of the S&P 500 will be companies that are relatively new.

It is generally accepted that the larger the organisation, the more difficult it is to change direction. Lou Gerstner, the CEO who transformed IBM from a failing computer manufacturer into a profitable service and knowledge provider, entitled his memoirs *Who Says Elephants Can't Dance?* The size and structure of larger companies add layers of complexity when change is required. Inertia results from a combination of complacent executives, the abundance of procedures/processes inherent in large organisations and dominant corporate values.

Corporate values

One of the critical factors that determines failure or success is whether those leading large organisations can react to changes in the business environments (i.e. the internal environment, microenvironment and macroenvironment). Some companies seem to be vulnerable after a long period of continued success (think Woolworths, HMV, Toys "R" Us, etc.). This may result from internal inertia, risk aversion or the aforementioned marketing myopia. As discussed previously, leaders have to do two things well: they must make decisions, and then they must implement changes based on those decisions.

> *Example*   In 1997–1998 Marks & Spencer (M&S) reported profits in excess of £1 billion and was set to challenge Walmart as the world's most profitable retailer. However, soon after, profits dropped substantially as a result of various short-term issues (e.g. the acquisition of Littlewoods stores and international expansion). Institutional investors had unrealistic expectations, so even in decent years (when M&S made say £500 million profit), the shares would be marked down. Some problems were long term, though. M&S suffered brand issues in that it was perceived that their quality had deteriorated; they had lost touch with their customer base; and they were struggling to attract a newer, younger demographic.

Spending between November and January (sometimes referred to as the Christmas season) generates approximately 40% of retailers' takings. The British Retail Consortium (see BRC.org.uk) described the Christmas 2018 "season" as the worst in a decade. However, Tesco and Morrisons were the best performing "big" retailers with the Christmas year-on-year (YoY) growth of 2.2% and 3.6% respectively. This compared with Aldi (10%) and Lidl (8%), who admittedly have a smaller base. The discount retailers have growth strategies based on expansion via opening new stores. They will continue to take market share for the foreseeable future.

Clearly, there is no room for complacency in marketing. Hiding behind the status quo and being unwilling to accept the need for continuous change will ultimately lead to failure. That said, it must be the right change. Change for its own sake is rarely a recipe for long-term success.

> *Example*   Tesco, a genuinely world-class retailer, did not respond adequately to consumer changes after the 2007 credit crunch. Before 2007 £1 in every £7 spent by UK consumers was spent with Tesco. Discount retailers were nothing new; however, consumers from higher socioeconomic segments changed their attitudes, perceptions and behaviours by shopping in Aldi & Lidl. They do so to this day. The big four supermarkets have accepted that in the long term, profit margins will be markedly lower than in previous years. Tesco's foray into the US market with the Fresh & Easy brand proved a costly failure. However, they have launched their new sub-brand (Jack's) to take the discount retailers head on.

For a number of key sectors (banking, insurance, transport, energy, etc.), government regulations will continue to be key factors. Companies must recognise this and develop appropriate strategies. When sectors misbehave, they are given the opportunity to self-regulate; however, governments are increasingly legislating (if companies do not regulate) against misbehaviour. Some deregulation is likely to be reversed; for example, there is increasing support in the United Kingdom for nationalised railways. This support was underpinned when LNER was resurrected in 2018 to replace the failed attempts of the private sector. Currently, many financial service providers are addressing the impacts of continuing re-regulation as a consequence of the crisis in developed markets in 2008. They also have to manage changes introduced by GDPR.

Changes in technology – particularly digital technologies – have hugely affected such companies as Blackberry, who ultimately were given little option other than to change their business model. Blackberry no longer sees itself as a smartphone provider; rather, they see their technology as providing solutions to problems in the growing Internet of Things (IoT). Some companies cannot react in time to changes; e.g. video rental company Blockbuster did not recognise or respond quickly enough to demise of VHS and rise of streaming. Some companies may be able to buy themselves time to change.

> *Example*   In 2018 HMV was in administration for the second time in six years. Such turbulence is the norm in the music industry. Graham Jones, in his excellent text *The Last Shop Standing*, cites over 2000 record shops closing since the advent of the compact disc (**Jones, 2014**). Also, music sales have shrunk as established music companies struggle to adapt to the distribution of digital content online and as a new generation of consumers do not appear to respect traditional intellectual property. DVD sales are in decline as streaming gathers momentum. Whether HMV can survive these changes in the long term will be of interest to music fans. The remaining 250 independent music shops are showing signs of health. They suffered at the hands of the large corporate providers; however, having diversified (into selling "gig" tickets and vinyl), they are now in a position to better serve customers.

Unless organisations and their leaders continue to look outside of their companies, they will run the danger of reinforcing attractive but dangerous assumptions. In marketing terms, companies must recognise and engage effectively with all stakeholder groups. Large organisations must be wary of the groupthink phenomenon, where directors and employees accept organisational values and norms set by senior management. Managers often refuse to challenge leaders because they think they can benefit from silence (i.e. they suspect that career opportunities won't be available to those who "rock the boat"). Alternatively, they may fear sanctions if they do not agree with autocratic leaders. Weak leaders seek inputs only from those with "halos" and refuse to interact with those with "horns". This may be acceptable in certain areas; however, in marketing, the orthodoxy must be challenged.

> *Example*   The global credit crunch followed the collapse of a number of American institutions one of which was AIG. Their CEO (Mr Greenberg) had set annual targets of 15% revenue growth, 15% profit growth and 15% return on equity. Apparently, he would suffer no contradictions and refused to entertain discussions or revision of these objectives. He had, in short, become disconnected from the realities of the marketplace. Company culture is clearly a key issue here. If staff members are not encouraged or permitted to present challenging information (and analysis), problems can and will arise. Recent examples of cultural issues in organisations include Bell Pottinger, Ted Baker and WPP (one of the world's

leading marketing agencies). Margolis (2008) argues that engaged and empowered employees represent an important and largely untapped resource. He points out that if we assume that the 80:20 rule (the so-called Pareto principle) applies, 80% of the effort and contribution typically given by employees comes from just 20% of the workforce. Think about what an organisation could achieve if it could tap into just a quarter of the potential of the remaining 80%.

Margolis also recognises the importance of 360-degree reviews. He quotes Hank Paulson, former CEO of Goldman Sachs, as saying, "One of the things that we have done for years is 360 reviews. It's amazing when you go to a leader and say, 'There are 30 people who reviewed you, and 30 of them trust you. But all 30 say you don't listen well'. It makes an impact." In sustainable marketing organisations, 360-degree reviews should really be expanded to 540-degree equivalents in order to include customers and key stakeholders in the microenvironment (see Chapter 3). This suggests that a meaningful two-way conversation with customers and stakeholders remains essential if a company is to survive and prosper, which central to being market oriented. Effective and continuing marketing research (see Chapter 1.6) supported by relevant information systems is critical to success. For companies to prosper, they must make sense of the abundance of raw data. They must identify customers' values.

Key commentators such as Kotler and Porter have argued that companies should put most of their resources into value-building investments and activities, because marketers

> "may raise sales in the short run but add less value than would actual improvements in the product's quality, features or convenience. Enlightened marketing calls for building long-run consumer loyalty and relationships, by continually improving the value that consumers receive. . . . By creating value for customers, the company can capture value from consumers in return".
>
> (Kotler et al., 2009, pp. 97–98)

Enlightened marketing calls for building long-term consumer loyalty and relationships, by continually improving the value that consumers receive from the firm's market offerings. By creating value for customers, the company can capture value from consumers in return, or "co-create" value.

The Value Proposition (VP)

Value is not a permanent state; rather, it can be created or destroyed. Wagner (2013) posited two linked but separate questions about value:

- Does the business have a value proposition that is genuinely distinctive from that of its competitors?
- Can it communicate that value proposition in (a) clear, concise and compelling fashion?

Much of the research in marketing is based on models featuring the creation of "value" by manufacturers of goods. In these models (e.g. Porter's Value Chain

Analysis), manufacturers "give" value to customers through what is referred to as a value proposition, or VP. The term "Value Proposition" is becoming increasingly contentious (Richardson et al., 2015). It justifies why a consumer should purchase a particular product or service – through "giving" more value to the customer and/or better solving a problem than other competing offerings. The VP approach is problematic because the instruments and processes may be unable to adequately capture the customers' values and priorities. As discussed in Chapter 1.3, the VP may even undermine "locked-in" customers, promoting in their place values and social constructs that reflect the priorities of the company (Blowfield, 2004).

Stakeholders face disadvantages when pursuing "costly" sustainable actions, and consequently, costs may not be borne by competitors (Pacheco et al., 2010). Neither the methods nor the sought changes of SM are value-free. Marketers often address (and try to encourage and change) the norms and values of a target group (Kennedy, 2015).

Jensen (2008, p. 171) protests: "value issues go unaddressed. These important issues are not getting nearly enough attention from those of us in business and in economics, as well as in the rest of the social sciences". Hence, it is appropriate to reflect on the nature of value seeking and values held by consumers.

Consumer values

Social institutions are made up of beliefs, practices, codes, values and behaviours (Kennedy, 2015). Values such as altruism may derive from an individual's life orientation, which Spedale and Watson (2014) define as the meanings attached at a particular stage of their life to their personal and social circumstances. This can unfold over a lifetime, being shaped by personal history, present circumstances and a host of broad and/or specific cultural and discursive factors. Values and costs that may be addressed include the monetary outlay to buy a related product as well as the time, energy and social/psychological costs of obtaining or not obtaining a product or undertaking a given behaviour (Kennedy, 2015).

Meaning is clearly derived from or influenced by values. Consumer preferences are not formed on the basis of the products or services themselves but on the attributes that those products possess and the values of those attributes for individual consumers (Jackson, 2005). Marketers should recognise that consumers have value in themselves and that values depend on social contexts, among other things. This chimes with strong stakeholder theory.

Not only do consumers have value in themselves, but different value orientations also coexist in the same individual and may all influence behaviour (ibid). Values also exist in groups, organisations, subcultures, networks, communities and societies. It goes without saying that these "values" vary from group to group and have enormous power for both good and bad.

The notion of value creation is central to current marketing thinking, and marketers should tailor their strategies towards a new approach, one that focuses on their relationship, interaction and cooperation with consumers. Vargo and Lusch (2004) reached a similar conclusion, recognising consumers as co-creators of value rather than as "targets". The emergence of consumers as co-creators or seekers of value has stimulated much interest in marketing circles.

Co-creating value

Clearly, key issues need to be addressed. First, not all stakeholders are equal, with customers being the primary stakeholder for any marketer; second, value can be meaningfully added only in how customers perceive the organisation, rather than, say, between departments, within databases, in the supply chain and elsewhere in the microenvironment.

Co-creating value counters the idea of giving or proposing value, by suggesting that value is mutually created. The notion is not new: indeed, Freeman (2008) suggests that just as we have been watching the stars for a long time, we've also been creating value and trading with each other since long before corporations. This is a challenge for marketers because decisions may be linked and supported by common values. Alternatively, they may be unconnected and affected by the external (situational) environment (see Chapter 4.2).

As discussed, consumers have values that they attach to sustainability criteria in their decision-making (see Chapter 1.5). These values can be functional, emotional, cognitive, social and/or conditional. Hence, we have to conclude that decision-making is far from simple.

The notion of value propositions or proposed value simply being "given" has been challenged by those who argue for the co-creation of value or enabling value seeking (Figure 1.12).

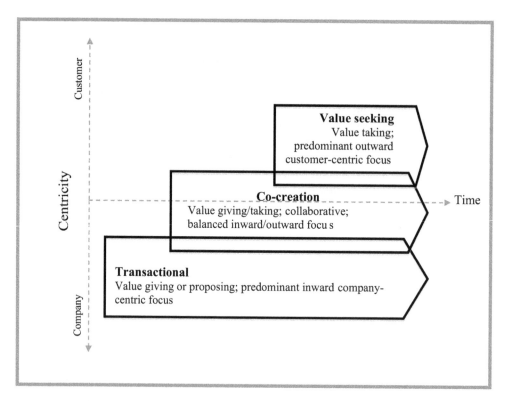

Figure 1.12 Chronology of changes in value

Source: adapted from Richardson (2015, p. 60)

Figure 1.12 shows the chronology of how value has changed. While transactional companies exist (think the low involvement nature of withdrawing money from an ATM), the move towards more services being offered (see Chapter 2.5) has led to companies increasingly seeing "value" from the customer's perspective. Some want to co-create value, whereas others believe that the best they can do is to create the circumstances in which customers will seek to take value from their company. Co-creating value and enabling value seeking are inherently more centred on the customer than the traditional notion of a VP.

1.5 The sustainable consumer and buyer behaviour

Many brands fail because they lack awareness among prospective customers. This may be because they lack what Michael Baker calls a JND (Just Noticeable Difference), which enables them to be recognised in a crowded marketplace. Occasionally, brands have a USP (Unique Selling Point), which can be used to help them stand out. These are few and far between. At times, a powerful price advantage may itself attract attention. Companies with little or no differentiation or price advantage will struggle.

Clearly, understanding how customers make purchasing decisions is critical to the development of an effective marketing Mix (see Chapter 2). The factors within the Mix influence each other. While Marketing Communications (or Marcomms) are key for raising brand awareness, the impact will be diluted or lost if the Distribution (or Place) function has failed to make the subject matter available for inspection and evaluation (Baker, 2009).

The likelihood that someone will respond positively to something new is strongly influenced by five characteristics, identified in Rogers's RACCOT test:

- Relative advantage – the degree to which an innovation is perceived as better;
- Compatibility – whether the product "fits" and solves the customer's problem;
- Complexity – the extent of learning needed for the product;
- Observability – the visible effectiveness of the new product;
- Trialability – the extent to which a product can be tried before purchasing it.

By applying the RACCOT test to customers' wants, marketers should be able to identify those who are most likely to be receptive and build this into their segmentation strategy (see Chapter 3).

Needs and wants are the building blocks of buyer behaviour. A need refers to the gap between a consumer's actual state and their ideal or required state. When the gap is sufficiently large, the consumer becomes motivated to satisfy the need. Needs can be physical or have psychological functions; for example, hunger and thirst are physical, whereas status is psychological. Needs can lead to wants for products and services. Wants are culturally and socially influenced. Needs may produce different wants for different consumers. Needs theorists argue that "true" human needs are finite, few and universal (Maslow, 1954). Part of progressing towards a more-sustainable economy requires a greater understanding of what constitutes a "want" as compared to a "need" while understanding that "humans have a complex set of wants and needs that can interact and even conflict" (Belz and Peattie, 2009, p. 74).

Consumers do not buy products; they buy benefits. A product or service should provide the consumer with a benefit that satisfies a need or want:

- They can see products as solving several problems and thus providing multiple benefits;
- They are attracted to the products that offer the largest assortment of benefits.

Hence, marketers must undertake research to better understand consumers' needs, wants and desires and their corresponding benefits. Sustainability-motivated consumers are often willing to pay more for the blend of benefits. And sustainability marketers must communicate the benefits of the people, planet and profit approach.

Norms

The term "norm" refers to a standard of conduct or rule of behaviour. Norms can be cultural, social or personal and reflect what is normally (or should be) done. They exist in social settings to the extent that an individual's behaviour may lead to the approval or disapproval of others or even punishment by others when seen not to be acting appropriately. Norms bring uniformity of behaviour, since their introduction encourages conformity. Sanctioning behaviour may be essential for a norm.

Margolis and Walsh (2003) argue that "normative" refers to the underlying justification that gives moral weight. Moral weight implies a degree of risk; for example, food and drink choices are based on cultural norms (Mitchell and Harris, 2005) of, say, health concerns or conscience consumption.

Personal norms invoke feelings of strong moral obligation that people experienced when engaging in pro-social behaviour and may determine pro-social behaviours. What appears to interfere with personal norms in the success of pro-environmental behaviours is the existence of external social or institutional constraints (Jackson, 2005).

Social norms reflect the behavioural expectations of the moral rules and guidelines of one's tribe. Jackson argues that the existence of social norms can be a powerful force, both in inhibiting and in encouraging pro-environmental behaviour. Social norms operate in two distinct ways: they provide behavioural examples that may be helpful in selecting appropriate behaviour, or they relate to the social outcomes associated with the performance of a given behaviour (ibid).

Examples of "sustainable" norms include codes of conduct, behaviour contracts, partnership agreements and third-party certification programmes (e.g. Forest Alliance, Fairtrade, Soil Association). Such evidence of sustainable norms is attractive to the ever-increasing number of consumers who are concerned about sustainability and buy food products that are identified as fair trade or other ethically produced goods (Ethical Consumer, 2018).

Harnessing social norms will be important for pro-sustainability behaviour (Belz and Peattie, 2009). However, some consumers are not willing actors in the consumption process, capable of exercising rational or irrational choice in the satisfaction of their own needs and desires. They find themselves "locked into" unsustainable patterns of consumption, either by social norms or the constraints of the institutional context. It can be argued that modern consumer society is being locked into a "social pathology" driven to consume by a mixture of greed, social norms and the persuasive power of unscrupulous producers (Jackson, 2005). This implies that consumers are passive, which is clearly not always the case. It does, however, explain some antipathy towards marketing and underpins the argument for the co-creation of value.

The elusive sustainable consumer

Customers are the marketer's most important stakeholders, and consumer behaviour is the largest area of research in marketing. This is reflected in the wide variety of models identified in the seminal work of Jackson (2005). Every time a consumer makes a decision, it has the potential to contribute to a more or less sustainable pattern of consumption. Because marketing is about aligning brands with customer perceptions, it makes sense for the definition of a sustainable consumer to align with that of sustainable marketing:

> "sustainable consumers' values enable decision-making that complies with the tenets of the triple bottom line. Their decisions are guided by sustainable practices, socially and ecologically. In seeking value that chimes with the TBL approach, they recognise that the short-term sacrifice of paying more may be the only way to balance their wants and long-term interests with companies' requirements, society's long-term interests and the need for environmental balance".

The challenge lies in the nature of consumers. They are often not rational; indeed, at times they are downright contradictory. To assess how interested stakeholders may be, consider the power they wield, how legitimate their claims are and how soon companies need to react to those claims. Figure 1.13 illustrates how power, legitimacy and urgency create segments when fused with the three elements of TBL: people, planet and profit.

Each of these segments may need a different communications approach. Marketers can use digital marketing tools to support any proposed changes aimed at resolving stakeholder conflicts (including sustainability matters) by doing the following:

- Building bases for understanding by sharing information;
- Creating plans for the implementation of sustainable marketing;
- Investing resources and ensuring that people are aware of the financial commitment;
- Demonstrating managerial commitment;
- Encouraging participation and contributions throughout the company;
- Sustaining internal marketing programmes, creating healthy responses to sustainability ideas.

Tensions are caused by consumers having a range of competing values. Such tensions are clearly a barrier to behavioural change. Emery (2012, p. 114) develops this, suggesting that

> "As citizens the public want to avert the socioeconomic and environmental crises by behaving more sustainably but as consumers the public want to drive cars, take flights and buy products which they quickly get tired of only to replace them with more".

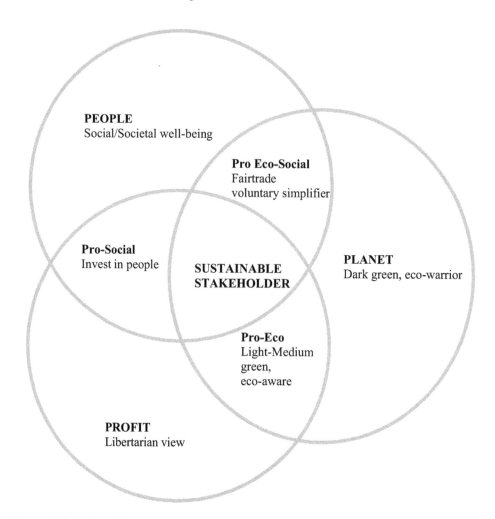

Figure 1.13 Stakeholder positions assuming trade-off model of sustainability

Source: adapted from Mitchell et al. (1997), Jackson (2005) and Richardson (2015)

Ultimately, to meet the needs, wants and expectations of customers, marketers need to map how and where value is created – either with the customers or in the co-creation of a service (see Figure 1.12).

It is particularly useful to know how customers behave when they buy products or services and what influences their behaviours. Through understanding their values and behaviours, marketers can provide them with information and the resources to ease their decision-making. Traditionally, marketers refer to two markets: Business-to-Consumer (B2C) and Business-to-Business (B2B).

The consumer (B2C) Decision-Making Process (DMP)

The B2C market is where the consumer (end user) buys the offering for their own consumption, for the use of their family and/or friends and not for profit-making purposes. Consumers generally move through a psychological process when purchasing products. This is often referred to as the consumer buying process or the Decision-Making Process (DMP). The consumer DMP contains a number of simple steps and is affected by many factors (Figure 1.14).

In Figure 1.14, the solid lines represent the flow of influences on the DMP, whereas the dashed lines illustrate how decisions feed forward – that is, influence future purchases.

In "problem recognition", the word "problem" seems to be problematic for many students. A problem is simply a need or want that needs to be satisfied. Most consumers start the buying process when they realise that they have a problem – for example, their washing machine has broken, they want new clothes or their car needs to be serviced.

Information search is the DMP stage most impacted by communications as the consumer searches for information on brands that will provide a solution. This search could involve looking at a diverse assortment of sources, including websites, magazines, newspapers, social media and retail outlets. Different consumers come with different degrees of complexity in their decision-making, owing to their use of information. Information seeking is present to some degree for all consumers. The challenge for marketers seeking to increase sustainability adoption is to employ a variety of information sources as part of their integrated marketing communications (see Chapter 2.1).

A consumer's "power" during service consumption depends on individual factors (that reside in the consumer) and social or interpersonal factors. Consumer knowledge was cited as a cause of high power, where retail patrons were better informed than those involved in other services. Traditionally, marketing campaigns encouraged customers to buy products and/or services – that is, they sought to close the deal. Marketers too often simply listed features of the product. Before Web 2.0, this may have been enough to satisfy customers, but these days, customers are seeking information about benefits.

Those strongly committed to causes compatible with sustainability (with green, charitable or ethical motives) will be more critical and (willing to) undertake more research in the information search and evaluation stages of the DMP (see Figure 1.14). Research suggests that they are more cynical regarding claims made and buy into the notion of greenwashing. They also tend to be sceptical of claims made regarding CSR policies. Hence, they go to greater lengths to evaluate whether companies practise what they preach.

The different nature of consumer products will be discussed in Chapter 2. Marketers know that most people spend little time searching for information and evaluating the alternatives before making their purchase decision for Fast Moving Consumer Goods (FMCG), such as a loaf of bread. For more sophisticated purchasing scenarios, say buying tickets for a family attending a festival, consumers deal with complex choices by eliminating options. They will, say, select key aspects (e.g. price, location, lineup, facilities, how green the option is, etc.) by which to assess their options, eliminating those that may cause confusion. Acting this way allows consumers to make important but complex decisions in an informed, intelligent way that reduces risk.

These mental shortcuts, known as heuristics, reduce the amount of effort needed to act and in effect make the process simpler. It is well known that consumers often make choices on the basis of simple signals like price. The irony of this will not be lost on marketers, who recognise that pricing represents one of the most complex

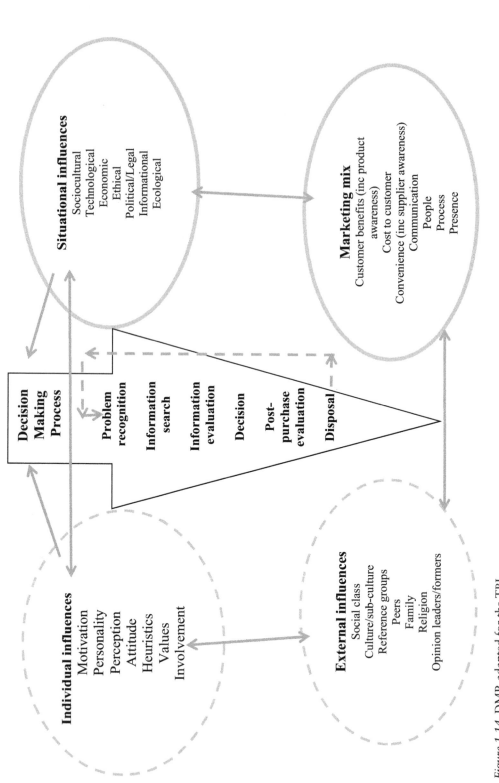

Figure 1.14 DMP, adapted for the TBL.
Source: adapted from Blackwell et al. (2001)

issues in the domain. Consumers also deal in general perceptions rather than comparing every detail, so emotional issues such as ethics or green goods could easily shape decision-making (Mitchell and Harris, 2005). The role of heuristics may help marketers understand how criteria interact and support or create barriers when the consumer is forming priorities.

Consumers may wish to evaluate something on a trial basis before committing to a purchase. This should be encouraged, as it is better than the consumer buying items that are immediately disregarded or sent to landfill. Where such trials are not possible, consumers may seek the opinion of others who have bought, used or reviewed the object in question. At this point, the marketer has ceded control, if they ever had it in the first place.

Finally, consumers trust other consumers and "independent" third parties, both of whom can generate WoM, which is arguably the most powerful and most trusted form of communication available to consumers. A range of means to evaluate alternatives exist, such as the JD Power survey (see www.jdpower.com/), which uses consumer feedback for three-year-old cars and covers several key issues, such as reliability, economy and service quality.

Having considered the options, consumers make their purchasing decision. Some may question their own decision before, during and after the purchase. This cognitive dissonance is more likely to manifest when the item bought has a higher level of risk (socially and financially). These doubts are natural, and marketers should allay the customer's fears. It can be as easy as congratulating the customer on the wisdom of their choice. This is why most consumer durables are accompanied by literature that supports their choice, reaffirms the benefits of the product and highlights the security that the guarantee brings.

By understanding how consumers make purchasing decisions, marketers can create the correct materials, environments and additional activities to support them. Furthermore, the advent of digital marketing has shifted the emphasis to helping consumers to make decisions before the purchasing decision itself.

Once consumers have worn their new item of clothing, they form opinions about the product during the post-purchase decision review. If, say, the perception is that it is poorly made, they may choose to avoid the brand in future. Their car may still be going strong and remaining reliable several years later. This could lead to their purchasing the same product/brand once again. They increasingly create consumer-generated media (CGM), which includes comments, posts, brand complaints, reviews, testimonials, social media posts and simply sharing experiences within brand communities (see Chapter 4.4).

Example Digital technologies have changed the way consumers can exert post-purchase influence. Consider the role of blogs, websites and social media. Trip Advisor (see www.tripadvisor.co.uk/) is now widely cited in the hotel sector. Customers leave a star rating and often much more insightful qualitative feedback, some of which can be hard hitting.

"Marketing rarely considered the post-use behaviour of consumers beyond the opportunity for a repeat purchase" (Belz and Peattie, 2009, p. 76). Traditionally, DMP models ignore the increasingly important aspect of disposal – that is, the fate of goods after their useful life. This is remiss. However, those designing goods are increasingly thinking of disposal. Historically, cars were designed to last as long as possible for the amount spent. Today, cars are designed to last *and* have 90% of their parts recyclable on disposal.

There is often a learning process as consumers move through the DMP. What is learned informs the process next time, and this extends to options after use, including reusing, recycling, upcycling or redistribution. Consumers always move through the DMP, but they move through at different speeds, depending on the items they are buying. Marketers should migrate from being engaged in trying to sell what they think consumers want. Rather, marketers must find out what information consumers need so that customers can make better decisions. Those who are too focused on trying to merely close the deal could be in trouble.

Individual internal human influences

The irrationality of consumers is what often undermines those who expect rational behaviour. A key component of sustainable consumption is to encourage environmental citizenship, which involves asking consumers to reflect on the attitudes that inform their behaviour (Young et al., 2010) and may lead to behavioural change that outlasts more short-term financial incentives. Figure 1.14 illustrates the key internal characteristics that influence the B2C DMP. These factors are not prioritised and may influence one another.

While there are numerous internal influences in the DMP, one that is clearly linked to the price of goods is motivation. What is needed is a clearer understanding of consumers' "motivations and the barriers they face to making sustainable choices" (Belz and Peattie, 2009, p. 82). Those who are highly motivated will arguably pay any price. Generally, people are motivated to know and understand what is going on, to learn, discover and explore. They prefer acquiring information at their own pace and answering their own questions and are motivated to participate and play a role in what is going on around them. However, they hate being disoriented, confused and/or feeling incompetent or helpless (Jackson, 2005). Consumers often have multiple motivations.

The most-cited motivational models are Maslow's hierarchy of needs and Herzberg's dual factor theory. Maslow's hierarchy (Figure 1.15) implies that consumers need to satisfy needs in a rising scale from physiological needs to safety, belonging, esteem and finally self-actualisation. It is a simplistic tool, but it serves a number of useful purposes for marketers. It reminds marketers that consumers may have a substantial concern that they wish to address first. If the marketer is trying to communicate other issues (deemed less important by the consumer), these will effectively be "noise" (see Figure 2.1) and will have little resonance. So the lesson is to deal with the big issue first. Then the position on the hierarchy depends on context. Someone who is established in a community may feel safe and have a sense of belonging. They may be looking to improve their achievement and esteem. Should they move to a different community, they will adopt a new position lower in the hierarchy and start to climb the stages again.

Care must be taken when applying such models across international boundaries. Western societies have well-defined health and safety regulations, so a worker should feel physically safe in the work environment. Law and order generally apply, so consumers *should* feel safe in society at large. Wealthier consumers have greater disposable

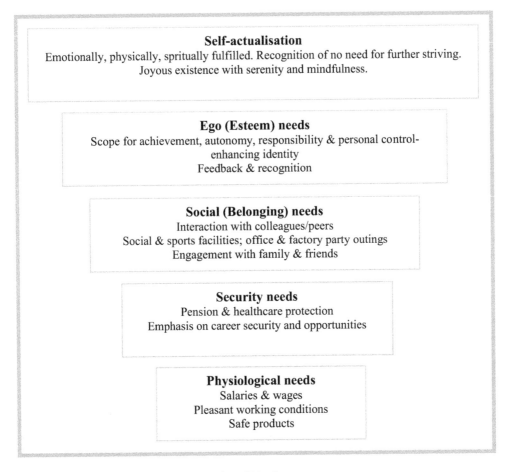

Self-actualisation
Emotionally, physically, spritually fulfilled. Recognition of no need for further striving.
Joyous existence with serenity and mindfulness.

Ego (Esteem) needs
Scope for achievement, autonomy, responsibility & personal control-enhancing identity
Feedback & recognition

Social (Belonging) needs
Interaction with colleagues/peers
Social & sports facilities; office & factory party outings
Engagement with family & friends

Security needs
Pension & healthcare protection
Emphasis on career security and opportunities

Physiological needs
Salaries & wages
Pleasant working conditions
Safe products

Figure 1.15 Abraham Maslow's Hierarchy of Needs
Source: adapted from Maslow (1943)

income to lavish on activities that may help them strive towards self-actualisation. These conditions may not be the case in Less-developed Countries (LDCs). Marketers targeting LDCs may struggle with brands in the self-actualisation category. That said, even in LDCs, there are segments of people who will have disposable income, and care must be taken to avoid simplistic stereotypes. Finally, self-actualisation is largely an abstract concept, particularly in Western materialistic societies. Maslow himself said that only 1% of 1% would self-actualise. Apparently, there is always a new gadget to buy for Western consumers. This may be changing; however, there is a long way to go.

Herzberg's Theory (Figure 1.16) suggests a distinction should be made between factors causing satisfaction (i.e. motivators) and those that could lead to dissatisfaction (i.e. hygiene factors). Hygiene factors cover those things that people take for granted (e.g. health and safety in the workplace, equitable treatment of suppliers or sensible disposal of waste materials). People do get a sense of satisfaction from these factors;

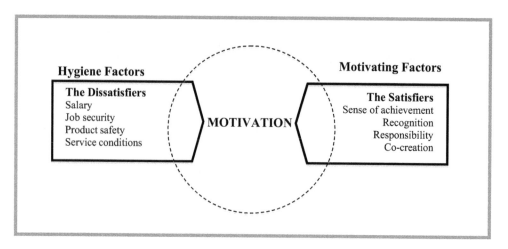

Figure 1.16 Frederick Herzberg's dual factory theory of motivation

Source: adapted from Herzberg et al. (1959)

however, it is short-term. This is akin to the lower levels of Maslow's hierarchy. Motivators can have a longer-term impact and derive from achievement, recognition, responsibility and/or personal growth. The values associated with sustainability can be motivators or hygiene factors depending on the circumstances. Consumers assume councils will recycle the items placed in a green bin. This is taken for granted and is a hygiene factor. Those who support, say, protecting and replenishing threatened marine life will be motivated to support the establishment of Marine Conservation Zones.

A key finding is that the removal of a dis-satisfier would not necessarily produce satisfaction. Marketers should avoiding dis-satisfiers and actively promote of major purchasing satisfiers.

The degree of involvement is another factor. Three types of involvement exist namely situational, enduring and response involvements. Consumers can develop many different types of involvement with activities, objects, ideas or even social issues. Certainly, consumers experience involvement when objects or events "connect" to important goals or centrally held values e.g. being environmentally friendly (Mitchell and Harris, 2005). This "connectedness" with the broader environment features intense emotional commitments that in turn increasingly influence their consumption. Research into consumer behaviour cites different modes of involvement, namely:

- Interest in a product or service
- Pleasure in the form of emotional appeal
- The extent to which the product represents the consumer
- The likelihood of it going wrong and the degree of risk

Other human factors

Consumers are influenced by external factors e.g. family life cycle, disposable income, education (among others). Many products and services are particularly sensitive to cultural differences. The role of the family has deep meaning and belief for many cultures. Many purchasing decisions often involve more than one member of the family. Families build up portfolios of purchase (or non-purchase) decisions, which may be underpinned by their values. Furthermore, consumers are influenced by friends, colleagues, peers and people they respect for social or technical reasons.

Allied to these factors is the question of lifestyle, whether this is what consumers have achieved at a moment in time or would like to achieve. Consumers are influenced by emotional considerations and by how they perceive their place in their families and with their friends and colleagues.

Consumer purchasing scenarios

The following are the different types of decisions or problems that consumers need to solve:

Routine problem-solving can usually be solved quickly with little expense and risk for the customer. FMCG items such as bread, vegetables and fruit fall into this category, because there is often little thought that goes into purchasing them. Therefore, the customer will go through the DMP quickly and few marketing-related support activities are required.

Limited problem-solving involves problems that are not as quickly solved as routine problems, because the product may be expected to last longer and have a higher value. Products such as washing machines may fall into this situation. The customer will spend longer moving through the search and evaluation steps. Customers may have less experience in purchasing these products. By nature, these products tend to involve a longer customer commitment – for example, a new washing machine should last several years.

Extended problem-solving involves purchases that require considerable thought before purchase. Customers will take some time moving through the DMP, primarily because the purchase represents a high risk for them; this could be financial risk, social risk (what will people think), performance risk and indeed ego risk. These "problems" tend to feature long-term commitment and will be around for some time, so customers will want to take the time to arrive at the right decision.

A substantial purchase, for many families, is a car. Even with the assistance of price-comparison websites, most prospective customers prefer to test-drive a car before they buy it.

Kia recognised that customers were concerned about the reliability of their cars. This concern could easily contribute to cognitive dissonance. Hence, they chose to adopt (and promote) a seven-year warranty for their cars. Consider the purchase of a 4 × 4 vehicle (sometimes known as an SUV). In reality, how many are bought by those who need them (e.g., people living in/working in rural and remote areas and/or where winter weather makes them a necessity), and how many are purchased by those who see them as a status symbol? The reality here is that (for many) owning a vehicle of this kind sends a message of conspicuous consumption. It is a want rather than a need. It suggests that the driver *could* (but most probably will never) go "off the beaten track", to get away from the normal combination of work and domestic life.

The planet and the consumer DMP

Green consumers consider environmental factors when shopping (a weekly activity) but engage more frequently in (non-purchasing) activities such as switching off lights and recycling paper (daily activities). It is arguable whether sustainable (i.e. societal and green) values have anything other than a weak influence on the DMP of many consumers. Analysing why these values may have a weaker influence on the DMP is key to understanding and changing consumer behaviour towards sustainable consumption. Weaker green influences may result from the following:

- Brand strength;
- Culture;
- Demographic characteristics;
- Finance;
- Habit;
- Lack of information;
- Lifestyles;
- Personalities;
- Trade-offs between different ethical factors.

(Young et al., 2010)

Pro-environmental behaviour arises from individuals' specific value orientations (Jackson, 2005). Environmental problems stem in part at least from societal values, attitudes and beliefs. Jackson identified three main societal value orientations:

- self-enhancement (i.e. self-regarding);
- self-transcendent (i.e. other regarding, which is pro-social or altruistic);
- biospheric (i.e. valuing the *environment*, as distinct from other people).

Biospheric or pro-environmental behaviour involves both purchasing behaviour and non-purchasing behaviour. Green consumers' contexts and values frame the purchase according to the motivation to pursue green criteria. It is influenced by the consumer's knowledge of the relevant issues and by how previous purchase experience influenced the consumer. Primary and secondary green criteria are formed by researching the ethics of a product (and its manufacturer), talking to friends and family or browsing online (Young et al., 2010). Barriers and key factors to facilitate buying green products and factors that could improve adoption are shown in Figure 1.17.

Marketers have increasingly sought to identify and communicate with green and ethical consumers, but with mixed results. There is a real need to understand more about consumers and whether they purchase sustainable goods, services and experiences instead of alternatives.

> *Example*   In the case of music festivals, consumers are clearly purchasing an "experience". That said, food and drink provisions are major contributors to the profitability of music festivals. The notion of consumers' values shaping their purchases resonates with the music festival sector. Increasingly, consumers buy food products that are identified as fair trade or locally produced. Demand for such goods and services is growing, and interest is growing in how such issues can build and enhance brands. This has led to more festivals providing local goods and services.

Barriers to buying green products	Key factors that will help green purchases
Lack of time to research details – e.g. a company's CSR programme	The consumer's green value is strong
The price of a (green) product	They have purchasing experience
	They can afford and is prepared for the financial costs
The lack of available information on the environmental and social performance of products	They have plenty of time for research and decision-making and to trust certain information sources, labels or organisations, providing a shortcut to choosing a greener product
The cognitive effort in researching, decision-making and searching for the products	They have good knowledge of the relevant environmental issues
Prioritising non-green criteria	Green products are reasonably available, and the customer feels guilt for having other (non-green) priorities, not prioritising green criteria, not being able to purchase the greenest product

Figure 1.17 Contrasting consumer barriers and facilitating factors

Source: adapted from Young et al. (2010, pp. 27–29)

Consumers do not always differentiate between sustainability issues, though. Clearly, some consumers regard being ecologically sound as an ethical or even moral matter. For many (though not all), the environment is rated as the most important ethical driver during purchasing decisions, followed by human rights and then animal rights/welfare issues. This conflation of issues presents challenges in marketing communications.

Organisational buying behaviour . . . the B2B market

For some organisations, the customer is often another organisation. Dyson sells its vacuum cleaners through retailers such as Argos. These retailers are Dyson's customers. Dyson are operating initially in the B2B market, whereas Argos and others are in the B2C market. The B2B DMP for a television manufacturer is shown in Figure 1.18. Clearly, it differs from the consumer model. This is because of a number of differences in the factors relating to buyer behaviour: organisational buyers

- are fewer in number;
- are skilled in the art of buying and negotiating;
- have qualifications from professional bodies such as the Chartered Institute of Purchasing and Supply (see www.cips.org);
- buy in large quantities often over a long time;
- often seek single source supply deals.

Influences on business buyers

B2B buyers will be aware of macro factors such as economic uncertainty, legislation, currency fluctuations and other PEST factors covered in Chapter 3. They will also be aware of internal and microenvironmental factors such as the organisation's

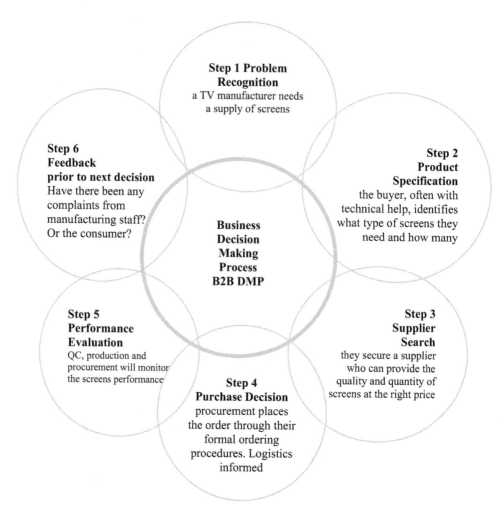

Figure 1.18 B2B DMP applied to a TV manufacturer

Source: original diagram

objectives, policies, procedures and systems. However, on a day-to-day basis B2B buyers are influenced most by a combination of hard (economic) and soft (non-economic) factors.

When referring to hard, quantifiable economic factors the emphasis is on a small "e". This is not PEST as it is internal to the company. Buyers will always be influenced by price, lead times, quantities, shipment sizes, failure rates, warranty length, payment terms or penalties. These involve "hard" figures that can be negotiated and are highly visible.

The non-economic, soft, interpersonal factors derive from the human nature of B2B buyers. Factors such as age, sex, expertise, relationships, prestige, reputation, career stage, ambition and attitude to risk (among others) can all affect the buying process.

Business people make decisions every day. Some are minor, but others may have far-reaching consequences. All decisions are made with an element of fear, uncertainty or doubt (aka FUD). If there is no FUD, then there is no decision to be made; rather, only an administrative action is required. Because most managers and leaders make decisions in uncertainty, they would be prudent to reduce risk and create more certainty when making decisions. Decision-making is rarely binary – that is, choosing between option A and option B. There are often varying answers to questions. Marketing research can help provide the information to help make the most appropriate decision within a given set of circumstances or parameters.

1.6 Sustainable marketing research

Business history is littered with examples of ill-prepared communication campaigns for product launches or repositioning efforts failing due to a lack of research. Carrying out good-quality research is undoubtedly the best way to prepare for any marcomms strategies that marketers intend to undertake because it provides the information needed to make the most appropriate decisions. Chris Fill, one of the leading writers on marcomms, is often cited as suggesting consumers are in an era of information overload, being exposed to 3000–4000 marketing messages every day. In truth, the figure could be much higher.

Cognitive processing . . . or chunking

Of the aforementioned 3000–4000 messages, only seven can be processed at any one time. This is the limit of cognitive processing also referred to as chunking. Some of the other 3993 messages may be processed subconsciously; however, the realm of the subconscious is for other textbooks. Consumers are able to simultaneously process only between five and nine "chunks" of information (with an average of seven). The actual number varies depending on a range of factors, including age and occupation.

The amount of data that can be processed can be increased through training. London Black Cab drivers traditionally had to pass "The Knowledge" before their licence was granted. This formidable test featured learning all of the key roads in London and alternative ways of travelling from A to B (aka spatial navigation). It took years to learn and subsequent research found that the drivers had stimulated their hippocampus (the part of the brain related to memory). Clearly, it is not reasonable to expect consumers to be subjected to such rigorous mental training.

Traditionally, younger people exhibit better chunking skills than their elders. Recent studies have found that younger generations now have less capacity for chunking compared to people in their 40s and 50s. It is suggested that those generations who have grown up with mobile phones have less need for natural recall, and consequently, their hippocampi may be underworked. Hence, the way marketers communicate may have to change to reflect these developments.

Information overload may be alleviated by using powerful search engines (e.g. Google) or alternatives such as Wikipedia. If search engines cannot find the right keyword, they are just as likely to access misleading information. Marketers should emphasise accessing relevant information and being able to relate it to problem-solving in order to enhance customer understanding. Hence, it is critical to be able to distinguish between what knowledge is important and the kind of information that is merely useful (Baker, 2009). This can be done only by carrying out marketing research.

Areas of marketing research

Three common areas of marketing research involve products, distribution and (arguably the most important) markets.

Product research focuses on the features or desirability of the product. This is often used in the process of New Product Development (NPD), where the core focus centres on understanding the actual product(s) (see Chapter 2.3). Alternatively, it can also be used if marketers encounter problems with their products.

During the development of a marketing strategy, the decision regarding how to distribute the product is key. Marketers must undertake distribution research to better understand where the products ought to be sold and (more importantly) how convenient is it for customers to purchase the goods. Sustainable marketers should be undertaking 540-degree feedback as a matter of routine. This feedback can provide useful intelligence on developments in distribution networks.

Market research is usually undertaken on the market's size, type, condition, or value. This research is particularly useful when seeking to grow in existing markets or when entering new markets (see Ansoff's model in Chapter 3). Marketers often struggle when they seek out credible information about the competition. The following are some of the sources of competitor intelligence:

- The Internet/social media;
- Marketing materials, such as exhibitions;
- PR and press articles;
- Annual reports and accounts;
- Customers, including feedback from sales staff;
- New recruits.

Some of this information may arrive through different functions in the organisation; for example, HR may gather information from the recruitment process and new recruits. Procurement may identify useful competitor information from suppliers. Remember that to be market oriented, companies must develop inter-functional relationships.

Market research and the sales department

The sales department is always a source of knowledge regarding competitors and market developments generally. One of the great tasks for marketers is working seamlessly with their sales teams. Marketers *must* be able to identify their most important and most valuable customers. In B2B selling, one of the most satisfying results is when a small account develops into a key account. The challenge is recognising this nascent account. Furthermore, key accounts can wither and should not be assumed to last forever. That said, the sales team should be able to identify the most valuable customers now and in the future. Their input should inform the organisation's strategic direction and tactics.

Ultimately, research needs to satisfy academics and practitioners alike. Academics should find the contributions to knowledge, whereas practitioners should be able to use outputs to improve their implementation. Research in business schools should always have *impact* and seek to inform implementation.

Academic research

Research needs to make a contribution to the existing pool of knowledge. Many students will undertake research in the form of a dissertation, which involves findings and discussions that can then be challenged. Masters students should have an appreciation of higher research concepts, such as ontology and epistemology.

Higher concepts

Langdridge (2007) suggests that ontology, as the philosophical study of being (existence), concerns the nature of reality, which is determined by people rather than by objects and external factors (Easterby-Smith et al., 2012). Objectivism and subjectivism are two parts of ontology. Collins (2010) suggests that objectivism represents the position that social entities exist in reality *external* to social actors concerned with their existence. Subjectivism holds that social phenomena are *created* from the perception and consequent actions of those social actors concerned with their existence.

A study is ontologically subjectivist when social phenomena are created through the perceptions of affected actors. Hence, research should seek to understand their subjective reality and seek an improved understanding of their perceptions. The phrase "improved understanding" is apt in that it is impossible to fully understand how others perceive phenomena and trends. A critique of subjectivist research is that it simply captures or retells individual, subjective accounts involving "indulgent navel gazing", as a naïve form of subjectivism that reproduces everyday cultural understandings without subjecting them to critical analysis (ibid).

Defined narrowly, epistemology is the study of knowledge and justified belief. More broadly, it is about creating and disseminating knowledge in particular contexts. Clearly, there are different ways of inquiring into the nature of physical and social worlds (Easterby-Smith et al., 2012). Epistemology concerns what constitutes acceptable knowledge in a field of study and is concerned with the following questions:

- What are the sources of a belief?
- What is its structure?
- What are its limits?
- How is it justified?
- What makes justified beliefs actually *justified*?
- Is justification internal or external?

(adapted from Collins, 2010, p. 36)

These questions provide a useful epistemological starting point for those undertaking such research.

Subjectivism is often associated with social constructionism, which views reality as being socially constructed. Constructionism recognises the existence of reciprocal and interdependent relationships between objects in the world and social consciousness. It accepts multiple interpretations of objects, none of which is objectively "true" or "valid", and emphasises the cultural and institutional origins of meaning (Collins, 2010).

Collins insists that for social constructionists, the world is "waiting to be discovered" and is "loaded with meaning". Social constructionism and positivism share the broadly empiricist understanding that knowledge arises as a direct result of experiences of the world, but for constructionists, things mean nothing until the meaning-making subject interprets them and until the world and things in it "give something essential of themselves to the conscious subject so that what we come to learn or understand is not simply another subjective account of a phenomenon" (ibid, pp. 38–39). In other words, social constructionists offer accounts that essentially reflect significant qualities of both their culture and of the phenomenon. They aim to offer insights with broad social relevance. The practical reality is that research rarely falls into only one philosophical domain.

The research process

Marketers (whether practitioners or students) are usually more successful when they follow a logical research process (Figure 1.19).

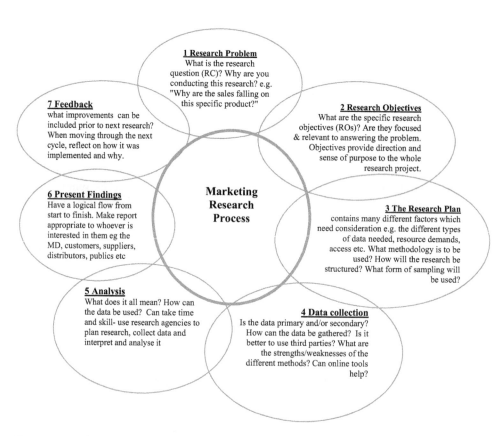

Figure 1.19 The Systematic Marketing Research Process

The research question (RQ)

This is key in that it provides the rationale for (and focus to) the research project. To define the RQ, researchers must reflect on why they are conducting this research and why it is relevant at this juncture. The RQ must be relevant today, specific and preferably unambiguous. It is better to avoid the use of "and" in RQs, because it often suggests two different problems. If the RQ is too broad, the research may not generate specific insights; however, if it is too narrow, it may not consider all germane issues. Once researchers have identified the RQ, they need to set and test research objectives.

Research objectives (ROs)

ROs are used to unpack the RQ and provide direction and a purpose for the whole project. They must not be confused with outputs; rather, they should identify the areas of theory necessary to generate questions for the respondents. All ROs have to be tested to have the minimum needed. A study with three ROs that are tested is preferable to one with four ROs where only three are tested. Most research texts advocate for the use of SMART objectives (see Chapter 3.4). This suggests a positivist approach where everything can be measured. Clearly, the key element of the SMART mnemonic (or memory device) is *specificity*. ROs must be specific, singular (i.e. no use of "and"), focused and relevant to answering part of the RQ. When aspects of the RO can be measured, the objective can approach being SMART.

> *Example* To identify if brand awareness has increased among the West Yorkshire business community by more than 3% year-on-year.

The research plan

The research plan contains many different factors, such as the research structure, different types of data needed, resource demands, access and so on. Management "buy-in" is a factor for practitioner research. Few CEOs would be willing to reorganise an entire business on the basis of an effort undertaken by the consumer research department in isolation. For research to have the greatest impact, business executives must be directly involved from the beginning and take ownership of the research (BCG, 2008).

Methodology refers to the design needed to research a topic and is informed by the researcher's epistemological position. To be clear "methodology" refers to the research design, whereas "method" refers to the tools used to capture the data. No methodology is "better" than any other. The following are the three most common methodologies that students use:

1 Survey;
2 Case study;
3 Observation.

Other methodologies exist (e.g. ethnography), but they are often longitudinal (long term) or involve complex research processes (e.g. experimentation). Survey is used when the research problem needs to be representative or subject to statistical analysis. Few students undertake representative research. The survey methodology enables decisions to be made that can be applied to a larger population

It largely uses questionnaires to gather quantitative, numerical information. The following are some of the pragmatic reasons for conducting surveys with respondents:

- There are often many more respondents than other types of stakeholders – such as surveying customers of a store compared to the staff therein.
- They use more in-depth methods, which may be problematic due to factors such as the duration (i.e. potentially up to an hour), location and available respondent time. A detailed questionnaire can be undertaken in considerably less time per respondent. Respondents should be advised in advance regarding the length of time needed to complete the questionnaire.

Case study is a research design that enables researchers to receive rich, empirical descriptions of particular instances of phenomena (Yin, 1994). It is useful when seeking insights into how, say, an organisation, a network, community or a sector behaves. This largely uses focus groups and/or interviews but occasionally smaller-scale questionnaires with open questions. Case studies often use "qual" data to provide description and test or generate theory. The data can be drawn from multiple sources and improves understanding the dynamics present within settings (Eisenhardt, 1989). A caveat is that the wealth of information provided must be balanced against the small sample size common in "qual" research.

To generate meaningful insights from case studies, the context has to be clearly understood. Contexts include situations and locations and enable researchers to factor in wider social or historical considerations. The relevant social contexts may be a group, organisation, institution, culture, society, time frame (within which action takes place), spatial context and/or the network of social relationships (Dey, 1993).

Observation can be used to collect data to gauge the reaction of customers to new products or services. Usually, there is no direct contact with the respondent. Many psychologists observe behaviour to study the difference in children's behaviour by watching them from behind a glass mirror. They may introduce a new toy to the child to see if their behaviour changes.

> *Example*   Mystery shopping originally compared the shopping baskets (i.e. pricing) of retailers (essentially "quant"); however, it has evolved into observational research generating insights into more complex factors such as staff attitude (essentially "qual"). To ensure it is undertaken in an ethical manner. The Market Research Society (see MRS.org.uk) has excellent guidelines. Indeed, mystery shopping techniques are used by the National Health Service to monitor service standards according to visitors and outpatients.

The research structure is dictated by the research problem and subsequent research objectives. Structurally, research can be qualitative, quantitative or a combination of both (known as a mixed approach).

Quantitative (hereafter "quant") research refers to collecting numerical data, which generates statistics to be analysed. It is usually gathered when seeking answers that either represent a larger population or enable statistical analysis, from which insights can be drawn.

> *Example* When psephologists at Ipsos Mori carry out research to predict UK general elections, they often use quantitative data that seeks to represent the whole voting population. They typically poll a sample of 1500–2000 prospective voters and generate results that are accurate to (+/-)3%. Sometimes 3% may not be accurate enough, so a much larger sample is needed. Alternatively, researchers can undertake a meta-analysis that combines the results from similar (though not necessarily identical) studies.

Phone surveys are now the most common form of political poll, and subsequently, more research is being carried out via mobile phones. Throughout the 2016 Brexit campaign, there were differences between phone and online polls with the former scoring higher results for Remain. Professor John Curtice (of Strathclyde University) provided a stunningly accurate forecast by sampling over 20,000 voters who were leaving the polling stations. To reduce bias, rather than simply asking how people had voted, he replicated the voting action by asking them to record their answers secretly in an exit poll. This addressed the "shyness" resulting from social desirability, which is increasingly an issue when researching sensitive subjects. Marketers could learn much from Curtice's approach.

Qualitative (hereafter "qual") research refers to collecting "soft" data, based on people's attitudes, opinions, feelings and perceptions. How consumers feel is often a greater force than how they think logically. New emergent theory is always fertile ground for "qual" research. It is often used to ascertain consumers' feelings regarding new products or services.

> *Example* Twitter allows real-time research; for example, one wine merchant organised wine tasting at multiple locations and asked the "tasters" to tweet their responses to each wine. The merchant then analysed the results, which were detailed and provided useful feedback.

"Qual" is often used for methodologies other than the survey, including participant (and non-participant) observation, unstructured interviewing and group interviews. It usually questions how actors perceive their situations and explains their motives (Dey, 1993). Interviews can efficiently gather rich data, especially when the phenomenon of interest is highly episodic and infrequent (Eisenhardt and Graebner, 2007). The speed of data collection is a major advantage of interviews.

With "qual" research, the length, detail, content and relevance of the data are not determined by the researcher but instead recorded "as spoken" or "as it happens" (Dey, 1993). Outputs are often recorded using audio and/or video formats, which allows the interviewer to concentrate on the respondents' perceptions.

Topic guide

To interpret data in social research, it may be more important to use meaningful categories than to obtain precise measures (Dey, 1993) and then look for similarities or differences. To create a degree of structure, researchers may use Dey's meaningful categories approach to create a topic guide. Categories can be suggested by the research problem or by existing literature (Eisenhardt, 1989). This can influence the implementation and may provide a starting point for thematic analysis. A common mistake happens when students take a list of questions into an interview. This often results in short, shallow interviews that fail to generate unexpected insights. A topic guide can be as simple as including the following:

- Community;
- Servicescape;
- Broader environment;
- CSR;
- Networks;
- Sustainability;
- Marketing;
- Communications.

The topic guide provides the areas to be investigated. If the researcher is properly prepared, they will be able to draw on their literature review and conduct the interviews with a degree of fluidity and thus may generate interesting, unexpected insights.

"Mixed methods" is the general term used when both "qual" and "quant" research are combined. When a pattern from one data source is corroborated by the evidence from another, the finding is stronger and better grounded (Eisenhardt, 1989). Researchers compare and contrast findings from both "quant" and "qual" research. Using different data collection techniques in one study enables triangulation, which ensures that the data achieves its objectives and provides stronger substantiation of constructs and hypotheses (ibid). Using mixed methods to triangulate data in a meaningful way necessitates carefully designing "quant" questions, which must be mapped (Figure 1.20) against the "qual" topic guide.

Those who adopt a mixed approach must do so for *positive* reasons and not simply because they cannot decide.

Primary data versus secondary data

Researchers often collect secondary data before collecting primary data, because the former already exists. Sources can be internal – such as company reports – or external – such as government publications or directories. Online sources enable secondary research to a greater extent than ever before, although its scale is problematic given recent estimates of 65 billion pages on the Web. External sources, such as government publications, newspapers, magazines or directories, are also useful.

Secondary data come with disadvantages: they are not specific to the marketer's research question and are neither up to date nor particularly accurate. They can, however, support the researcher in their search for the optimum direction. Secondary data are cost-effective, are relatively quick to collect and often do not need a skilled researcher to collect or use them. Existing problems can be revisited in light of changes in the business environments (i.e. internal, Micro or Macro – see Chapter 3).

Primary data are specific, relevant, timely and (assuming appropriate collection and analysis) accurate. Researchers often collect secondary data before primary data because the former is cost-effective (it already exists) and it is relatively quick to

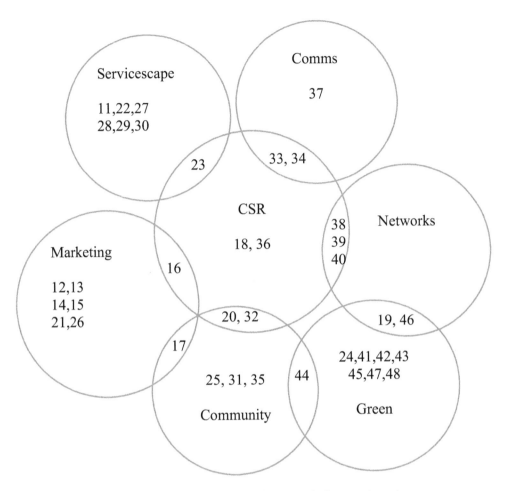

Figure 1.20 Triangulating the eight topic guide themes with the questionnaire

collect. It can come from internal sources such as company reports or previous market research reports.

Before ROs are tested, the population, sample and sampling method must be determined. The concept of a population is crucial: it defines the set of entities from which the sample is drawn and helps define the limits for generalising the findings (Eisenhardt, 1989). Research will be more credible if it can be contrasted with similar, existing studies and the sampling techniques therein. Most students use non-random sampling methods. Undertaking random sampling is not easy; however, it is essential for empirical studies. Common sampling modes used by students include theoretical, probability and snowball sampling. These can be used to choose cases that may replicate or extend emergent theory. A key approach to generating useful insights from research is using numerous and highly knowledgeable informants who view the phenomena from diverse perspectives. These respondents can include organisational actors from the internal environment, microenvironment and sometimes macroenvironment. They can be from different internal hierarchical levels, functional areas and groups or from other relevant organisations and publics.

Data collection

There are different *methods* or tools used to collect primary data. When choosing the data collection method, the first consideration is whether "quant" or "qual" data are needed. The choice (or perhaps the use of both) is governed by the RQ and ROs. The collection of primary data may require the researcher to have certain skills, depending on the method.

Questionnaires

"Quant" research often uses questionnaires to collect data from a large number of people. Key issues to consider are the time, money and resources needed to question the larger population. Ideally, researchers should question a representative sample of the target audience. If the sample is not representative, the number of responses must be big enough to carry out useful statistical analysis. The more people questioned in the target audience, the greater the degree of accuracy; however, resources will always limit the sample size.

A good questionnaire should be neither too long nor too short. It should pose questions to collect the required responses to help answer the RQ/ROs. Generally, the type of data collected from a questionnaire is "quant"; however, they do provide the opportunity to also ask open-ended questions to collect "qual" data, such as "What is your opinion on banning smoking in public places?" Care is needed because qualitative data is analysed in a different way. All questions should be analysed and the results presented to the "reader".

Questionnaires can be administered in a number of ways:

- Face to face with either self or respondent completed;
- Via telephone (mobile or landline);
- Via the post;
- Via email;
- Online – that is, pop-up questionnaires.

Each of these presents challenges with regard to the questionnaire design. The respondents may not understand the question. Alternatively, they may find some questions leading or even too similar. In some cases, respondents are left to their own devices to complete the questions, whereas other researchers will make themselves available to address any queries that arise. Bias can arise from both approaches. The response rate needs to be high, and this will be shaped by to the amount of time allocated to the process and the presence of the researcher. Hence, it is prudent to consider the issues germane to the mode of administering the questionnaire (Figure 1.21).

Many studies use an interviewer-supervised self-completion method, where respondents are left to complete the interview themselves but with the researcher in attendance to answer any queries. Interviewers may notice that the respondents have misinterpreted a question. Great care needs to be taken to only *clarify* questions if prompted; hence, some questions may be left blank, and answers must not be amended. This is

	Interviewer-administered questionnaires	*Self-completed questionnaires*
Advantages	Flexible	Flexible
	Inexpensive to set up	Wide reaching
Disadvantages	Requires data entry	Requires high-quality production
	Limited routing	Respondent can "read through"
		No spontaneous measures
		Limited rotations

Figure 1.21 Comparison of interviewer-administered and self-completed questionnaires

Source: adapted from Brace (2004, p. 41)

preferable to leading the respondent, which is a form of respondent bias that may be deemed acceptable, as ultimately it is better to respect respondents' views. Furthermore, it allows a fuller picture of their perceptions (including misconceptions).

When researchers seek answers to open questions, they need to allow the respondents to use short phrases if they cannot provide single words. Remember that closed questions will usually generate simple yes/no answers.

Common examples of ordinal variables in social research include how various options are perceived and ranking preferences. Ordinal variables provide more meaning since responses are ranked within a pecking order (Dey, 1993). Jackson (2005) advocates respondents' evaluating purchasing characteristics on point scales such as Likert scales. However, with repeated questions, such as rating scales, respondents can fall into a pattern or habit. In such cases, their responses may differ from their attitudes. Hence, some questions should be designed to elicit a response that encourages respondents to relocate their answers on the questionnaire. This necessitates care when analysing the results. For example, a "control" question could be

"Ticket prices should be lowered by being less environmentally friendly".

Alternatively, if it was not a control question, it may have been

"Ticket prices should be raised to include environmentally friendly practices".

This may have been easier to understand and generated positive correlations. Care must be taken when interpreting the results of control questions.

Questionnaire validity

The question must be clearly understood by the respondent. Similarly, the response must be understood by the researcher as intended. This necessitates reflecting on the validity of the questions. Validity is the extent to which scores generated measure the characteristic or variable they are intended to measure for a specific population (Figure 1.22).

Traditionally, researchers seek to provide one or more of three types of evidence, namely content-related validity, criterion-related validity and construct-related validity (Onwuegbuzie et al., 2007). Alternatives include face validity (a form of content

Mode	*Description*	*Comment*
Face validity	The extent to which the questionnaire provides adequate coverage of the investigative questions	Judgement is through careful definitions of the research via the literature review and prior discussion with others – e.g. subjected to experts. Deemed relatively weak, since it is the most subjective mode of testing validity
Internal or measurement validity	The ability of questionnaires to measure what they are meant to measure – i.e. whether it represents the reality of what is being measured	Researchers use their own judgement and/or look for relevant evidence to support answers found in the questionnaire
Content validity	Whether the questions and resulting scores are representative of all the possible questions that could be asked about the content or skills – i.e. the extent to which the items on a questionnaire represent the content being measured	Best performed by experts who evaluate whether the questionnaire content accurately assesses all of the fundamental aspects
Criterion-related or predictive validity	Concerned with the ability to measure (questions) to make accurate predictions Whether scores from a questionnaire are a good predictor of some outcome (or criterion) or are related to an independent external/ criterion variable believed to directly measure the underlying attribute or behaviour	In this assessment, responses to survey items are compared to a "gold standard"
Construct validity	Refers to the extent to which measurement questions actually measure the presence of those constructs they are intended to measure	Often used with as attitude scales Should be evaluated if specific criteria cannot be identified that adequately define the construct being measured Determines the significance, meaning, purpose and use of scores from a questionnaire – i.e. whether it can be interpreted as a meaningful measure of some characteristic or quality

Figure 1.22 Comparison of questionnaire validity modes

Source: adapted from Creswell (2014); Saunders et al. (2012) and Onwuegbuzie et al. (2007)

validity) and internal (or measurement) validity. Internal or measurement validity refers to the ability of a questionnaire to measure the phenomenon.

Most student research features non-random samples that are often too small to be representative. Hence, they are too small for predictive validity and more often than not will comply with content validity.

Some surveys are administered longitudinally – that is, over a long period of time. These are used to identify trends. An example is the UK Chambers of Commerce seek quarterly responses from businesses in their economic outlook. The questionnaire and target audience are always the same. This way, researchers can develop tools for contrasting results or "gold standards".

Pilot questionnaires

A poorly written questionnaire will provide poor or even incorrect data. Hence, a pilot survey is often administered to respondents similar to those to be studied. Pilot questionnaires can identify difficulties with phrasing, length and question sequences. "Problematic" questions can be tailored or removed. Removing such questions enhances the integrity of the survey and improves the efficiency of data analysis. Changes (between the pilot and the final questionnaire) should be captured in the methodology section of any thesis. Both versions should be in the appendices because seeing the research tool helps others to understand the research.

Sources of questionnaire bias

Questionnaires should avoid providing detailed lists of possible answers as pre-codes for respondents. Such lists can distort perceptions because they can effectively "prompt" the respondents. They cannot accurately record behaviour, though, and the alternative of allowing for all possible responses is too complicated to process and analyse.

Likert scales can be problematic as one respondent's 5 may not be the same as another's. The gap between say a 4 and a 5 may differ among respondents, who also may be reluctant to mark at the extreme ends. Issues arise with how researchers interpret findings even when using tools such as SPSS. For example, when is an aggregated response deemed to be "high" or "good"? With 1.0 being a minimum and 6.0 a maximum, only 5 ranges exist. Often, marks over the halfway point are deemed positive, so a 4.5 (mildly agree) is biased towards being more positive since it's closer to the 5 (agree). Similarly, a 4.4 is deemed purely "mildly agree".

Long, complex questions and technical jargon (e.g. ISO 20121 or BS8901) are best avoided if not commonly used by the respondents. The detailed nature of the questionnaire will influence the response rates, as respondents will suffer fatigue. Always be honest and provide information on the time needed to complete the questions. Data generated from partially completed surveys can still be used; however, the closer to full compliance the better. If respondents will typically complete the questionnaire in ten to 12 minutes, quote the higher figure. Under-promise and over-deliver. If they finish in ten minutes, they will be happier and more likely to help you find other respondents if using, say, snowball sampling.

Problems with green questionnaires

Different respondents may have different reasons for partaking in research. Their willingness to *meaningfully* answer questions may suffer if the questions relate to issues low down in their priorities. Questions seeking insights into how green the respondents consider themselves (to be) are useful when seeking to segment a market. Self-rating is likely to be an issue, though; for example, one consumer may consistently act in a "dark green" (say recycles extensively) fashion but may regard it as a "norm" rather than something extraordinary. Someone else may simply make a tokenistic effort that overstates the importance of such acts. There could also be social desirability bias, since people may want to be seen to be green.

Furthermore, respondents may limit their response to the context (i.e. being at a festival) or may answer more generally. Environmental research is often undertaken in the field. Outdoors research may be subject to the capricious nature of the weather, and researchers may have limited time for research, such as before an event starts.

Complete accuracy is almost impossible when using consumer questionnaires to measure attitudes and behaviours. Research tends to collect data on consumers' behavioural intentions rather than actual behaviour. For research into sustainability to be meaningful, it must have an impact – that is, lead to changes in behaviour. When researching sustainable behaviour, many marketers undertake attitudinal research. Marketers must understand that attitudes and behaviour do not always match.

Focus groups

Focus groups are a method for collecting "qual" data, usually involving six to 12 respondents from the target audience. They provide excellent insights when developing new products or services (see Chapter 2.3). A typical use of a focus group would be to introduce a prototype and ascertain their thoughts and feelings regarding its design, size, colour, weight, name and so on. The mediator must be skilled at managing groups. Some people will over-contribute, whereas others will under-contribute. Focus groups raise problems when the issue is sensitive. Care must be taken when selecting the respondents.

Interviews

Students often use semi-structured in-depth interviews to collect "qual" data. The key difference is that each interview has only one respondent. Therefore, the interviewer can probe for in-depth answers, feelings, opinions and so on. Interviews are a useful way to collect sensitive data. Traditionally, interviews have been regarded as costly; however, the results often justify the investment. That said, smartphones (with video and audio capture facilities) are increasingly used to interview people in remote locations. A future development will be the use of Voice over Internet Protocol (VoIP) interviews (e.g. using Facetime or Skype), and videoconferencing will enable groups of people to be interviewed simultaneously.

Analysis

"Qual" data must be analysed to identify themes and trends. Simply offering a few respondent quotes is not usually enough, because quotes alone do not necessarily identify trends. "Qual" analysis involves describing phenomena, classifying them, and seeing how concepts interconnect. However, description has a

> "low status in social science. Descriptive studies can be contrasted unfavourably with more analytic and theoretically oriented research, as though description is a "low level" activity hardly worth attention. This is somewhat ironic, since

description permeates scientific theory and without it theories could have neither meaning and nor application".

(Dey, 1993, pp. 31–32)

Good "qual" research generates insights into themes and trends. In the United States and the United Kingdom, the majority of consumer research is "qual" in nature. The analysis can be undertaken manually or by using computer-aided techniques (such as nVivo, Freemind and Wordle) to better identify themes and provide textual analysis.

Some academics advocate joint collection, coding and analysis of data (Glaser and Strauss, 1967). Data classification enables regularities, variations and singularities to be examined. A caveat is that classification is a conceptual process in that research-ers "don't just break the data up into bits, we also assign these bits to categories or classes which bring these bits together again, if in a novel way" (Dey, 1993, p. 46). Hence, coding involves inevitable subjective decisions. Categorisation involves funnel-ling the data into relevant categories for analysis. The data loses its original shape, but researchers gain by organising it in ways that are more useful for analysis (Dey, 1993).

"Quant" data is easier to analyse since it is suited to statistical analysis, spread-sheets or simple graphs. Packages such as Microsoft Excel and SPSS exist to facilitate analysing large amounts of data. Descriptive statistics is often used as a means of summarising numerical data, to make them more easily interpretable. When using Likert scales to analyse attitudes, descriptive statistical analysis can produce range, mean, mode, median and standard deviation figures. These are the building blocks of "quant" and can provide insights.

More experienced researchers will want to undertake advanced statistical analysis. This starts with identifying correlations that link the data generated by different parts of the questionnaire. Linking data provides a powerful tool for empirically identify-ing relationships between different parts of the data (Dey, 1993). Comparing the data from one question (or variable) with those of another (variable) creates a bivariate analysis. Bivariate analysis is undertaken (across the range of questions in a question-naire) to ascertain whether correlations existed (either positively or negatively) and the strength of the correlation.

The most common correlation coefficients are Pearson's indexes of linear correla-tion, which range from 1.00, for perfect positive linear correlation; to zero, for no lin-ear correlation; to -1.00, for perfect negative linear correlation (Coleman and Pulford, 2006). Either researchers can seek correlations to predict significant relationships, support theories or hypotheses, or they can see which relationships arise based purely on their strength. Neither approach is better than the other.

Most student research is limited in its resources (finances and time). Where a large number of correlations are generated, the researcher will have to make a subjective decision about which will be considered. They may choose to consider only positive correlations of ≥ 0.65 or negative correlations of ≤ -0.35. These decisions should be pragmatic and can be guided by the practices of previous research. Some correlations of lesser strength may still generate interesting insights.

In relation to the significance to be applied to the correlation coefficient, within SPSS, two-tailed significance is the default. Coefficients significant at the 0.01 level are iden-tified with a double asterisk. The two-tailed significance of this correlation is 0.000, which does not mean exactly zero; rather, it is less than 0.001 ($p < 0.001$) (ibid).

Care needs to be taken when using bivariate analysis on the control questions.

Presenting findings

Once the analysis is complete, the findings must be presented to the audience: line management, directors, customers and so on. Good knowledge gained from well-designed research can only strengthen a company's position: in this way, others outside of the intended audience may find the results and conclusions interesting. Marketers must put effort into making the report stand out. A common mistake is to make the report easy for the author instead of the reader.

Students in business schools must use the report format with headings and a numbering system. Businesspeople do not write essays; rather, they produce structured reports. Have a structure with a logical flow from start to finish. The introduction must provide a rationale – that is, establish why the research is of interest to the reader (not the author) and detail what is involved. After the findings are discussed, provide a clear conclusion that summarises the main points and offers recommendations when appropriate. A common error occurs when students discuss new issues in the conclusion section.

A common approach to help the reader is to include an executive summary or an abstract; however, few students understand the difference. An abstract answers the following questions:

- Why is the research of interest to the reader?
- What is involved in the research?

An executive summary complements the above steps with answers to the following questions:

- What are the key findings/conclusions?
- What is recommended?

Abstracts or executive summaries should be single spaced on a single page, and references are optional. The abstract should be approximately 150 words, compared to the longer executive summary's approximate 300 words.

"Qual" research is highly descriptive and focuses on revealing how theory operates in particular contexts: to help the reader by providing visual summaries using tables, matrices, word clouds and associative (semantic) diagrams. Graphic representations make it easier for the reader to understand complex phenomena. Tables and other visual aids can summarise the descriptions of social settings, featuring related case evidence. Summarising the case evidence complements the selective story descriptions of the text and further emphasises the rigour and depth of the theory (Eisenhardt and Graebner, 2007).

A common technique is to provide a discussion matrix, which summarises the respondents' outputs and provides improved analysis. In "qual" research, not all topics are necessarily discussed by all respondents. This is common in interpretive studies. Some matrices merely identify the areas discussed, while others allocate respondents' word counts to show areas that generated more discussions across the sample. It is still useful to see which areas generated the most discussion; however, care should be taken when interpreting importance on the basis of a word count. The matrix can also provide structure for the thematic analysis, providing the platform for the first pass at coding the data. It enables themes among the respondents' views by topic and sub-themes embedded in the narratives to be identified. Some findings can be located on more than one topic, and the number (of sub-topics) does not necessarily correlate with impact. Furthermore, the matrix does not forecast how categories or themes will interact with or influence each other.

Word clouds are a powerful tool for capturing or conveying meaning. However, they do not provide links or correlations; nor do they offer reasons and meanings without further interpretation. They can suffer from the dominance of a particular theme and may need to be refined to identify other issues. Marketers often use semantic (or associative) networks as a means of identifying links between different themes, topics or insights. They are useful because they help to build a narrative of what influences consumers.

Mobile research

Value can be added to a company's knowledge and decision-making by using the mobile platform during research. Marketers can use it for several purposes:

- To provide valuable information from colleagues;
- To listen to advocates, consumers, bloggers, influencers and so on;
- To find out what people are saying about the company, brands, campaigns or competitors;
- To test out new concepts/ideas;
- To help shape strategies.

Mobile marketing research allows marketers to connect with consumers on a large scale. Marketers are increasingly looking at social media sites as places to advertise to targeted audiences.

> *Example* Facebook and Nielsen tested an online research tool that measures the effectiveness of advertisements. The tool, Nielsen BrandLift, placed opt-in polls on Facebook users' homepages that gauged their attitudes to advertisements on the site and measured their purchasing intent. The frequency of polls was controlled to prevent users being asked to participate too often. Nielsen said that no personally identifiable information would be collected. The surveys were placed in positions where users saw sponsored messages. Facebook's chief operating officer, Sheryl Sandberg, said that "The combination of our unique ability to quickly and effectively poll a sample of our more than 300 million users and Nielsen's expertise in data analysis will give marketers access to powerful data they can use to understand and improve current and future campaigns" and that Facebook "wants to be the first place marketers turn to when they want to engage consumers".
>
> Now tools are offered by both organisations with Nielsen's Total Brand Effect with Lift and Facebook's cross-platform brand Lift, both offering advertisers the ability to evaluate the impact of their campaigns across Facebook and TV.

Such tools can produce substantial amounts of data. Raw data is not the same as information, though: marketers must turn raw data into useful information. The information should provide insights that improve the marketers' understanding or knowledge. This knowledge should lead to improved wisdom or, if preferred, decision-making. Remember this adage: knowledge is knowing that a tomato is a fruit, whereas wisdom is knowing that one should not put tomatoes in a fruit salad.

Analysing the data can take time and skill, so many marketers use specialist research agencies to plan their research, collect the data and interpret and analyse those data.

Marketing agencies

The approach to marketing research can be academic, practitioner oriented or a combination of both (i.e. applied research). Marketers must understand the focus of their research, the information required and the problem being solved. Even if marketers have the resource to employ a marketing research agency, they must understand the research process as they will be ultimately responsible and will have to respond to the data once it is presented. Large research agencies, such as Mintel and Nielson, also publish research reports that can be bought or commissioned. However, they can be costly.

Barriers to effective research

Each methodology, method and analysis technique has strengths and weaknesses. Researchers need to acknowledge these and recognise bias, which is the bane of good research. All research is biased, though, including pure, scientific empirical research. When planning research, consider the sensitivities of the researcher *and* the respondent. Hence, some questions would probably be better asked in a non-face-to-face way, such as by phone or online.

> *Example*   The following comes from a Market Research Society (MRS) research bulletin: "Today, a lesson in the importance of questionnaire wording. According to a CBS/New York Times poll, 70% of Americans support *gay men and lesbians* serving in the military. But when it comes to *homosexuals*, it's a different matter – only 59% are in favour of them serving".

Surveys encounter two types of errors: sampling errors and non-sampling errors. Apropos non-sampling errors, interviews often provoke

> "a 'knee-jerk' reaction that the data are biased in which impression management and retrospective sense making are deemed the prime culprits. . . . Is the theory just retrospective sense making by image-conscious informants"?
>
> (Eisenhardt and Graebner, 2007, p. 28)

When using snowball sampling, exercise caution if the first point of contact acts like a gatekeeper. This could be problematic since they may restrict access unless they can see personal or commercial benefits. Furthermore, bias may result from subsequent respondents (knowing the gatekeeper and) not wishing to be overly critical. Obsequiousness towards power, pressures to conform, fears of embarrassment or conflicts of interest can distort behaviour and disguise individual motivations (Dey, 1993). On a more positive note, deception and denial can also derive from more generous qualities, such as politeness and civility (ibid). While laudable, this still represents a source of potential bias that could skew the analysis.

The issue of how researchers interpret meaning is relevant. Researchers will be able to understand what is happening only if they see the bigger picture – that is, understand the social structures that influence or create the phenomenon under consideration. Researchers can record only those factors that interviewees are conscious of and not the influences residing in the subconscious. Respondents perceive and define situations, including their own intentions, according to their understanding "of their own motivations, and of the contexts in which they act, . . . and we have to allow for the usual mix of ignorance and self-deception, delusions and lies" (Dey, 1993, p. 37).

1.7 Systems and customer centricity

To a degree, the Malthusian idea of a never-ending population explosion has been countered, and those interested should seek out the works of Hans Rosling. The earth's population is still growing, but it will level out, and the issue is how will we all live together. In 2019 scientists produced a diet that could feed a global population of ten billion while using current levels of technology. This would entail wholesale changes of eating patterns, with much less red meat being consumed. Still it is useful to see positive solutions being offered.

A simple means of illustrating how problems of increasing consumption (resulting from population growth) continue to this day is the Five Planets Theory.

The five planets theory

This is used to measure countries' respective levels of consumption. If all countries consumed resources in the same way as the United States, 4.0 planets would be needed. For the United Kingdom, 2.7 planets would be needed, whereas for India, only 0.4 planets would be needed. Two points, first the UK figure has come down from 3.0 planets. So post-industrial societies can change their impact for the better. Second, Rosling (2010) predicts the planet's population plateauing at nine to ten billion by 2050 (assuming average family sizes continue to reduce in developing countries). Clearly, if all countries had India's impact, the earth's population would be able to coexist with current levels of resources. Realistically, though, this won't happen as the current economic systems are not "geared up" to make the necessary changes.

Economic systems

Traditionally, many of the social and environmental costs of doing business were not met by companies or reflected in the prices that their customers were charged. They were treated as "externalities", or as bills for others to pick up and pay. In theory, these "others" were meant to be governments using the taxes that they had raised on consumers and producers, but in practice, it has often meant passing those costs down to future generations (cfsd, 2019).

There are three kinds of industrial economies: linear, circular and performance. A linear economy uses natural resources: raw materials to create products in a way that hopefully creates value for the customers. The linear "take, make, dispose" economic model relies on large quantities of cheap, easily accessible materials and energy

Key Authors	Topic
Lifset and Graedel (2001)	Industrial Ecology
McDonough and Braungart (2003)	Cradle to Cradle Design
Benyus (2003)	Biomimicry
Stahel (2006)	The Performance Economy
Hawken et al. (2008)	Natural Capitalism
Pauli (2010)	Blue Economy

Figure 1.23 Influences on the circular economy

Source: adapted from MacArthur (2015)

(MacArthur, 2019). Once the decision-making process has been completed, ownership and responsibility transfer to the consumer. At the end of the product's useful life, the consumer decides if the product should be disposed, reused, recycled, repurposed or remanufactured. This assumes that they are aware of their choices or, indeed, are motivated to do so. In a linear economy, consumers are assumed to be continuously seeking the next best thing in what is often a saturated, fragmented, overly supplied market where goods are disposable. Linear economies involve overcoming scarcity while wasting resources.

The concept of the circular economy has been around since the early 1970s.

A circular economy seeks to avoid sending goods to landfills or for incineration. Rather, it seeks to turn goods at the end of their serviceable life into resources for others, closing loops in industrial ecosystems and minimising waste. It is

> "restorative and regenerative by design and aims to keep products, components, and materials at their highest utility and value at all times, distinguishing between technical and biological cycle".
>
> (MacArthur, 2019)

The remanufacturing, repair or repurposing of products creates skilled jobs and is better for the environment. New jobs will be created, and systems are needed at each step. Consumers will need access to collection points to return products to the manufacturers. Communications will have to be tailored to ensure consumers are aware of the processes involved. Initially, incentives may need to be offered; however, in time, new behaviours will become the norm, and thus, sustainable practices will proliferate. A study of seven European nations found that a shift to a circular economy would reduce each nation's greenhouse gas emissions (GHGs) by up to 70% and grow its workforce by about 4% (see go.nature.com/biecsc).

Circular economy business models either promote reuse and extended product life cycles through repair, remanufacture, upgrades and retrofits or repurpose pre-owned items into new offerings featuring recycled materials. The reprocessing of goods and materials saves energy while reducing resource consumption and waste. A milk bottle that is used 20–30 times has a lower carbon footprint than that of a single-use plastic bottle. Dairies report common recycling figures of 40–50 reuses per bottle. Cleaning a glass bottle and using it again is faster and cheaper than recycling the glass or making a new bottle from minerals. In a circular economy, the objective is to maximise value at each point in a product's life.

A performance economy features renting, leasing and sharing goods rather than selling them. The supplier retains ownership of the product and is responsible for its upkeep. Taxis are facing competition from car clubs in major cities, and the users are not faced with issues such as depreciation, maintenance or servicing. The performance economy features buying products with service-based solutions and is inherently inclined towards reducing waste.

Organisational systems

When discussing audits with practitioners, it is rarely long before the political nature of companies is discussed. Some managers protect their departments jealously, possibly lacking a vision of the bigger picture. Hence, these departments or functions (e.g. HR, accounts, logistics, marketing, etc.) often have their own systems, which do not necessarily work in harmony. This may result from companies being too "inwards" focused or having "systems" that do not create value for the customer. Such companies are often process or systems driven when they should be customer driven.

Companies are made up of different systems that interact with each other and their respective environments. Mintzberg argues that organisational success will be dictated by the "overlaps" between systems: How well does the Human Resource Management (HRM) system recruit, motivate and reward marketing staff? Are the recruits customer-centric? How well do the systems interact with the environment in which business activity takes place?

Systems have natural and human-built boundaries, such as departmental structures. Organisational systems are technical, informational and social. These systems can be closed systems, open systems or hybrid (semi-open) systems.

Open systems connect and interact with the organisation's environments. Hence, they are influenced by the company's environments (see Chapter 3.2). These influences can energise the organisation, or they can act as constraints. Open systems such as wikis tend to be stable but continuously changing due to the user-generated nature of the content. There are issues regarding the reliability of the data contained therein since contributors may not be experts or may have vested interests.

Closed systems (e.g. process control in a factory) are isolated from the company's environments – that is, the system is independent, with no influence exerted either way. In practice, few systems are entirely closed. Many are semi-open, meaning some stakeholders in the business environments can access the system's information or even input data. Hence, there is a degree of influence, depending on the stakeholders and the nature of the system.

> *Example* Universities have Virtual Learning Environments (VLEs) where the students have password access. The university staff can usually upload lectures, whereas the students can file assessments online. The students are connected to and interact with its environment.

Senior management often access a Management Information System (MIS) where others input data, whereas production may use a Distributed Process Control (DPC) system. Different sectors use different systems. For example, for retailers, service tills (EPOS) and Radio Frequency ID (RFID) tags are visible elements of process systems, whereas booking systems for festivals, hotels or concert venues represent "back-office" elements. Interestingly, there are few contemporary discussions in the literature about information systems.

Undoubtedly, operational aspects and systems are important, but not at the expense of focusing on the customer. They will all link to databases within CRM systems, particularly with the increasing acceptance of Big Data.

The Marketing Information System (MkIS)

A key system for marketers is the MkIS.

Figure 1.24 shows how a typical MkIS behaves in the marketing function (designated by the dashed line); however, in Micro environments, it extends beyond the company to the stakeholders. Internally, the MkIS overlaps with the systems in other functions (e.g. HRM, procurement, production, etc.). This is reflected in tools that evaluate the internal environment such as value chain analysis (see Chapter 3). As previously discussed, to be market oriented, companies must develop their inter-functional communications and cooperation. Useful insights from non-marketers must be fed via the MkIS to the marketers making key decisions.

Hollensen (2011) identifies how an MkIS works:

- It develops closer customer relationships.
- It avoids the increasing cost of making the wrong decisions.
- It understands and factors in increasing market complexity (and dynamism and turbulence).
- It combats increased levels of aggression on the part of competitors.

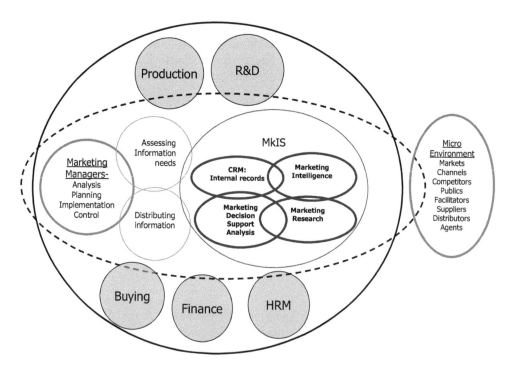

Figure 1.24 Another comparison of interviewer-administered and self-completed questionnaires

Source: Richardson, James and Kelley (2015)

In building and operating such systems, ensure to do the following:

- Process raw data to provide useful and useable information.
- Agree on what information is needed and to whom it may be communicated.
- Effectively disseminate information.
- Use the information system to drive strategy and planning.
- *Continuously* gather information.
- Incorporate feedback loops so that the implementation of the marketing plan informs the data (and quality) of the information system.

CRM

The term "Customer Relationship Management" (CRM) is misleading, because marketers should seek Customer Satisfaction Management (CSM) rather than simply hosting their customers' data in their internal records. CRM was developed in the mid 1990s in the context of Information Technology (IT) systems. The idea was for companies to use databases to maintain and develop customer knowledge and understanding. Improved understanding should lead to better relationships with customers, prospects and even suppliers.

CRM provides the necessary means to monitor levels of activity. It is regarded by some as the solution to many marketing problems, whereas others see it as the cause. Simply put, having an enormous database of contacts will not guarantee success if the customers cannot, or will not, take value from the brand. CRM should act as the platform to serve and nurture customers over their lifetime rather than in a single transaction. This makes good business sense, as existing customers are, on average, five to ten times more profitable.

Chaffey (2014) argues that e-CRM is packed with fundamental common-sense principles; however, surprisingly, many companies do not adhere to them. Progressive marketers who promote customer centricity are not surprised that some companies misuse their data. Users of sites such as Facebook generate enormous amounts of data, and marketers need to manage the data to produce information effectively and efficiently in order to make knowledgeable decisions. Hence, CRM programmes undoubtedly have something to offer, but they are no substitute for genuine customer insight.

CSM is a different approach that lends itself well to digital marketing. As customers change, their desires, needs, and information requirements also change. If companies do not respond to changes, they will start to dissatisfy customers and suffer attrition to the competition. Hence, all databases have to be massaged to ensure the information extracted from the data is good enough to support decision-making, knowledge management and, ideally, adopting a market orientation. Furthermore, as previously discussed, all data must be managed in accordance with the GDPR.

Top ten findings

1 Customer centricity should inform all business decisions, objectives strategies and categories. Stakeholders increasingly influence whether organisational objectives are achieved.

2 The traditional orientations are being complemented by the market orientation in which all staff are responsible for supporting the marketing concept. Organisations

should be both inwardly and externally focused to truly understand changing customer needs and trends. SM is an evolution of the market orientation.

3 Buying is always guided by consumers' thoughts, feelings and actions. Consumers take on the attitudes, beliefs, opinions and values of others. Hence, companies who are not aware of changes in society run the risk of alienating customers.

4 All companies need to be aware of their sustainability position in order to make appropriate strategic and operational decisions. Progressive managers should remove barriers to adopting sustainability.

5 Critical marketers recognise the flaws inherent in marketing and how myths exist relating to marketing and its negative perception.

6 Providing customers with what they require by anticipating their needs and satisfying them will entice them to come back time and time again. Companies are increasingly seeing "value" from the customer's perspective.

7 Poor corporate governance has led to many corporate failures, often owing to the inability of non-executive directors (NEDs) to monitor and control the actions and decisions of executives.

8 Marketers must understand how customers (B2B, B2C) behave, to ensure that they are supported throughout the DMP and that they have the requisite information to help them make confident and correct decisions. Consumers have complex influences and spend more time searching for information before and after a sale. Organisational buyers are influenced by personal, organisational and environmental factors.

9 Marketing research should underpin marketing decisions. Systematic research provides contemporary, accurate information to help marketers support (and develop relationships with) customers. Many organisations fail to effectively conduct customer research.

10 Effective systems allow marketers to measure and monitor CSM. CSM is a different philosophical approach that lends itself well to SM in the digital age. After GDPR, it is not enough to simply amass a huge database. Marketing systems must inform decision-making and knowledge management and support internal implications, such as training needs, restructuring and so on.

Ten activities

1 Identify companies or particular sectors that show characteristics of each individual orientation. Is it easy to do this? What evidence can support the findings?

2 Identify ten key sources that should be included in a MkIS for companies in B2C markets and B2B markets. How do the lists differ?

3 Review organisations that are successful while still adopting sustainability. Reflect on the Cooperative's world-class CSR platform (it is transparent and independently audited). Review the policies of companies in the FTSE4Good and Dow Jones Sustainability Indices (DJSI).

4 Useful insights that can inform sustainability adoption are sustainable value (see www.sustainablevalue.com) and the International Social Marketing Association (ISMA) site (see www.i-socialmarketing.org).

5 The Chartered Institute of Purchasing and Supply (aka CIPS) is a well-respected organisation for B2B "buyers". Visit their website (see www.cips.org/) to tap into current issues.

6 Download the MRS Code of Conduct (from www.mrs.org.uk). It gives invaluable insights into how to conduct research and provides guidance for conducting research in an ethical fashion.

7 Visit www.gartner.com/marketing/digital/and register as a user. This will provide access to useful webinars, blog posts and free resources regarding digital marketing and research.

8 Use Google's Customer Barometer (see www.consumerbarometer.com) to generate insight into how customers use both online and offline information sources in their DMP.

9 Visit Google's Zero Moment of Truth (ZMOT) site (see https://thinkwithgoogle). It provides interesting case studies and support materials. Does this differ from the B2C DMP? If so, how?

10 The IT Toolbox site (see https://it.toolbox.com/tags/crm) provides interesting insights into CRM and issues arising from poorly designed systems.

References

Agle, B.R., Mitchell, R.K. and Sonnenfeld, J.A. (1999). Who matters to CEOs? An investigation of stakeholder attributes and salience corporate performance and CEO values. *Academy of Management Journal*, 42(5), pp. 507–525.

Agle, B.R. and Mitchell, R.K. (2008). Introduction: Recent research and new questions from Academy of Management 2007 Symposium. https://pdfs.semanticscholar.org/34da/1e558e7d 68aea9d51b6d305ea1ae63176942.pdf [accessed 18-09-19].

AMA (2019). Available at: www.ama.org/AboutAMA/Pages/Definition-of-Marketing.aspx [Accessed 15 Jan. 2019].

Baker, M. (2009). Aided recall and marketing mnemonics. Guest lecture presented by Professor Michael Baker to Leeds Business School. November 2009.

Barkemeyer, R., Figge, F., Holt, D. and Hahn, T. (2009). What the papers say: Trends in sustainability – A comparative analysis of 115 leading national newspapers worldwide. *Journal of Corporate Citizenship*, Spring 2009(33), pp. 69–86.

BBC (2018). Ola to challenge Uber in UK ride-hailing market. Online article. www.bbc.co.uk/news/business-45095091 [accessed 18-09-19].

BBC (2018a). Plastic food pots and trays are often unrecyclable, say councils. Available at: www.bbc.co.uk/news/science-environment-45058971 [Accessed 21 Sept. 2019]

BBC (2018b). Recycled packaging "may end up in landfill", warns watchdog. Online article. Author: Roger Harrabin. Published 23 July 2018. Available at: www.bbc.co.uk/news/business-44905576. [Accessed 19 Feb. 2019].

BCG (2008). Available at: www.bcg.com/documents/file15287.pdf.

Belz, F.-M. and Peattie, K. (2009). *Sustainability marketing – A global perspective*. Chichester: Wiley & sons.

Benyus, J. (2003). *Biomimicry*. New York: HarperCollins.

Blackwell, R.D., Miniard, P.W. and Engel, J.F. (2001). *Consumer behaviour*. London: Harcourt College Publishers.

Blowfield, M. (2004). Implementation deficits of ethical trade systems: Lessons from the Indonesian cocoa and timber industries. *Journal of Corporate Citizenship*, 13, pp. 77–90.

Blowfield, M. (2005). Corporate social responsibility: Reinventing the meaning of development? *International Affairs*, 81(3), pp. 515–524.

Boztepe, S. (2007). User value: Competing theories and models. *International Journal of Design*, 1(2), pp. 55–63.

Brace, I. (2004). *Questionnaire Design- How to plan, structure and write survey material for effective market research*. London: Kogan Page.

Brown, S. (1995). *Postmodern marketing.* London: Routledge.

Brownlie, D. and Saren, M. (1992). The four Ps of the marketing concept: prescriptive, polemical, permanent and problematical. *European Journal of Marketing,* 26(4), pp. 34–47.

Bruntdland, G.H. (1987). "Our common future" world commission on environment and development's. Available at: www.un-documents.net/our-common-future.pdf [Accessed 9 Feb. 2018].

Carroll, A.B. (1979). A three-dimensional conceptual model of corporate performance. *Academy of Management Review,* 4(4), pp. 497–505.

Carroll, A.B. (1991). The pyramid of corporate social responsibility: Toward the moral management of organisational stakeholders. *Business Horizons,* 34(4) July–August, pp. 39–48.

Carroll, A.B. (1994). Social issues in management research: Experts' views, analysis and commentary. *Academy of Management Journal,* 27, pp. 42–56.

cfsd (2019). *Pricing & distribution.* Available at: www.cfsd.org.uk/smart-know-net/links/pricing.htm [Accessed 6 Feb. 2019].

Chaffey, D. (2014). *Digital business and E-commerce management.* 6th ed. Harlow: Pearson Education Limited.

CIM (2019). Chartered Institute of Marketing. Available at: www.cim.co.uk/Home.aspx [accessed 15 Jan. 2019].

Clarkson, M.B.E. (1988). Corporate social performance in Canada 1976–86. In: L.E. Preston, ed., *Research in corporate social performance and policy,* vol. 10. Greenwich: JAI Press, pp. 241–265.

Clarkson, M.B.E. (1995). A stakeholder framework for analyzing and evaluating corporate social performance. *Academy of Management Review,* 20(1), pp. 92–117.

Coleman, A. and Pulford, B. (2006). *SPSS for Windows.* 3rd ed. Oxford: Blackwell Publishing.

Collins, H. (2010). *Creative Research: The theory and practice of research for the creative industries.* Lausanne: AVA Publishing.

Creswell, J.W. (2014). *Educational research: Planning, conducting and evaluating quantitative and qualitative research.* 4th ed. Boston: Pearson International.

Davis, K. (1960). Can business afford to ignore corporate social responsibilities? *California Management Review,* 2(3) (Spring), pp. 70–76.

Dey, I. (1993). *Qualitative data analysis- a user-friendly guide for social scientists.* Routledge: London.

Donaldson, T. (2008). Two stories. Article from Academy of Management 2007 Symposium printed in Agle, B.R., Donaldson, T., Freeman, R.E., Jensen, M.C., Mitchell, R.K. and Wood, D.J. (2008). Dialogue: Toward superior stakeholder theory. *Business Ethics Quarterly,* 18(2), pp. 153–190.

Easterby-Smith, M., Thorpe, R. and Jackson, P. (2012). *Management research.* 4th ed. London: Sage.

Eisenhardt, K.M. (1989). Building theories from case study research. *The Academy of Management Review,* 14(4) (oct. 1989), pp. 532–550.

Eisenhardt, K.M. and Graebner, M.E. (2007). Theory building from cases: Opportunities and challenges. *The Academy of Management Journal,* 50(1), pp. 25–32.

Elkington, J. (2004). *Enter the Triple Bottom Line* as cited in Henriques, A. and Richardson, J., eds. (2004). *The triple bottom line: Does it all add up?* London: Earthscan. Available at: www.johnelkington.com/TBL-elkington-chapter.pdf [Accessed 24 July 13].

Emery, B. (2012). *Sustainable marketing.* Harlow: Pearson Education.

Ethical Consumer (2018). Ethical consumer markets report. Available at: www.ethicalconsumer.org/research-hub/uk-ethical-consumer-markets-report. [Accessed 9 Feb. 2019].

Freeman, R.E. (1984). *Strategic management: A stakeholder approach.* Boston: Pitman.

Freeman, R.E. (2008). "Ending the so-called "Friedman-Freeman" debate" article from Academy of Management 2007 Symposium, printed in Agle, BR, Donaldson, T, Freeman, RE, Jensen, MC.

Friedman, M. (1962). *Capitalism and freedom*. Chicago: University of Chicago Press.

Friedman, M. (1970). The social responsibility of business is to increase its profits. *New York Times Magazine*, 13th September 1970.

Facebook (2014). newsroom.fb.com, 2014 Facebook Newsroom (2014) [Online]. Available at: http://newsroom.fb.com/company-info/.

FTSE4Good. Available at: www.ftse.com/Indices/FTSE4Good_Index_Series/index.jsp [Accessed 20 Feb. 2018].

Garriga, E. and Mele, D. (2004). Corporate social responsibility theories: Mapping the territory *Journal of Business Ethics*, 53, pp. 51–71.

Glaser, B. and Strauss, A.L. (1967). *The discovery of grounded theory: Strategies of qualitative research*. London: Wiedenfeld and Nicholson.

Guardian (2014). David Cameron mocked for paying for Facebook friends, *The Guardian* [Online]. Available at: www.theguardian.com/media/2014/mar/10/davidcameron-facebook-friends-twitter-selfie

Guardian (2017). The deal that undid Bell Pottinger: inside story of the South Africa scandal. Available at: www.theguardian.com/media/2017/sep/05/bell-pottingersouth-africa-pr-firm. *The Guardian*. [Accessed 27 Jan. 2019].

Guardian (2018). World's biggest tobacco firm under fire over "disgraceful" PR stunt. Available at: www.theguardian.com/business/2018/jul/19/worlds-biggest-tobacco-firm-under-fire-over-disgraceful-pr-stunt. *The Guardian*. [Accessed 9 Feb. 2019].

Haberberg, A., Gander, J., Rieple, A., Martin-Castilla, J-I and Helm, C. (2010). Institutionalizing idealism: The adoption of CSR practices. *Journal of Global Responsibility*, 1(2), pp. 366–381.

Hawken, P., Lovins, A. and Lovins, L.H. (2008). *Natural capitalism: Creating the next industrial revolution*. New York: BackBay.

Heinonen, K. (2006). Temporal and spatial e-service value. *International Journal of Service Industry Management*, 17(4), pp. 380–400.

Herzberg, F., Mausner, B. and Snyderman, B.B. (1959). *The motivation to work*. New Brunswick, NJ: Transaction Publishers.

Hockerts, K. and Wüstenhagen, R. (2010). Greening Goliaths versus emerging Davids – Theorizing about the role of incumbents and new entrants in sustainable entrepreneurship. *Journal of Business Venturing*, 25(5), pp. 481–492.

Hollensen, S. (2011). *Global Marketing: A decision oriented approach*. 5th ed. Harlow: FT/Prentice Hall, pp. 197–198.

Jackson, T. (2005). Motivating sustainable consumption- a review of evidence on consumer behaviour and behavioural change; a report to the Sustainable Development Research Network January 2005. Funded by the Economic and Social Research Council's Sustainable Technologies Programme (STP).

Jensen (2008). Non-rational behavior, value conflicts, stakeholder theory, and firm behavior article from Academy of Management 2007 Symposium printed in Agle, B.R., Donaldson, T., Freeman, R.E., Jensen, M.C., Mitchell, R.K., and Wood, D.J. (2008). Dialogue: Toward superior stakeholder theory. *Business Ethics Quarterly*, 18(2), pp. 153–190.

Jones, G. (2014). *Last shop standing- What ever happened to record shops?* 6th ed. London: Proper Music Publishing.

Jones, B., Bowd, R. and Tench, R. (2009). Corporate irresponsibility and corporate social responsibility: competing realities. *Social Responsibility Journal*, 5(3), pp. 300–310.

Kennedy, A.-M. (2015). Macro-social marketing. *Journal of Macromarketing*, pp. 1–12.

Kennedy, A.-M. and Parsons, A. (2012). Macro-social marketing and social engineering: A systems approach. *Journal of Social Marketing*, 2(1), pp. 37–51.

Kotler, P. and Levy, S.J. (1969). Broadening the marketing concept. *California Management Review*, (Winter) XII(2).

Kotler, P. and Armstrong, G. (2006). *Marketing – an introduction*. 8th ed. Harlow: Prentice Hall.

Kotler, P. and Lee, N. (2005). *Corporate social responsibility*. Doing the most good for your company and your cause. New York: Wiley.

Kotler, P., Wong, V., Saunders, J. and Armstrong, G. (2009). *Principles of marketing*. 5th European ed. Harlow: Prentice Hall.

Langdridge, D. (2007). *Phenomenological psychology – theory, research and method*. Pearson: Harlow.

Lifset, R. and Graedel, T.E. (2001). Industrial ecology: Goals and definitions. In: R.U. Ayres and L. Ayres, eds., *Handbook for industrial ecology*. Brookfield: Edward Elgar.

MacArthur, E. (2015). *Towards a circular economy: Business Rationale for an accelerated transition*. Published by the Ellen MacArthur Foundation. November 2015.

MacArthur (2019). Ellen MacArthur Foundation website. Available at: www.ellenmacArthurfoundation.org [Accessed 21 Sept. 2019].

Margolis, J.D. (2008). Why companies fail. *Employment Relations Today*, 35(1). http://dx.doi.org/10.1002/ert.20183 [Accessed Jul. 2014].

Margolis, J.D. and Walsh, J.P. (2003). Misery loves companies: Rethinking social initiatives by business. *Administrative Science Quarterly*, 48, pp. 268–305.

Martin, D. and Schouten, J. (2012). *Sustainable marketing*. Harlow: Pearson Education.

Maslow, A. (1954). *Motivation and personality*. New York: Harper & Row.

McDonough, W. and Braungart, M. (2003). Toward a sustaining architecture for the 21st century: The promise of cradle to cradle design, Industry and Environment. April–September 2003. pp. 13–16. www.c2c-centre.com/sites/default/files/McDonough%20-%20Towards%20a%20sustaining%20architecture%20for%20the%2021st%20century-%20the%20promise%20of%20cradle-to-cradle%20design_0.pdf [accessed 18-09-19]

Mendes, J., Guerreiro, M. and Valle, P. (2009). Sustainable planning for community venues. Chapter 15. In: R. Razaq and J. Musgrave, eds. *Event management and sustainability*. Oxon: CABI.

Mitchell, R.K., Agle, B.R. and Wood, D.J. (1997). Toward a theory of stakeholder identification and salience- defining the principle of who and what really counts. *Academy of Management Review*, 22(4), pp. 853–866.

Mitchell, V.W. and Harris, G. (2005). The importance of consumers' perceived risk in retail strategy. *European Journal of Marketing*, 39(7/8), pp. 821–837.

Mittelstaedt, J.D., Shultz, C.J., Kilbourne, W.E. and Peterson, M. (2014). *Sustainability as megatrend: Two schools of macromarketing thought*. Journal of Macromarketing, 34(3), pp. 253–264.

NYTimes (2018). How Bell Pottinger, P.R. firm for despots and rogues, met its end in South Africa. Available at: www.nytimes.com/2018/02/04/business/bell-pottinger-guptas-zuma-south-africa.html. [Accessed 27 Jan. 2019].

Onwuegbuzie, A.J., Witcher, A.E., Collins, K.M.T., Filer, J.D., Wiedmaier, C.D. and Moore, C.W. (2007). Students' perceptions of characteristics of effective college teachers: A validity study of a teaching evaluation form using a mixed-methods analysis. *American Educational Research Journal*, 44(1, March), pp. 113–160.

Pacheco, D.F., Dean, T.J. and Payne, D.S. (2010). Escaping the green prison: Entrepreneurship and the creation of opportunities for sustainable development. *Journal of Business Venturing*, 25(5), pp. 464–480.

Pauli, G. (2010). *Blue economy: 10 years, 100 innovations, 100 million jobs*. New York: Paradigm Publications.

Prothero, A. and McDonagh, P. (2015). Introduction to the special issue: Sustainability as megatrend II. *Journal of Macromarketing*, 35(1), pp. 7–10.

Ranganathan, J. (1998). Sustainability rulers: Measuring corporate environmental and social performance, World Resources Institute. Available at: http://www,wri,org/meb/sei/state,html.

Richardson, N., James, J. and Kelley, N. (2015). *Customer-centric marketing: Supporting sustainability in the digital age*. London: Kogan Page.

Richardson, N.A. (2015). The adoption of sustainable marketing practices within the UK music festivals sector. PhD thesis. Available at: http://etheses.whiterose.ac.uk/13578/1/The%20 adoption%20of%20sustainable%20marketing%20practices%20within%20the%20 UK%20music%20festivals%20sector.pdf.

Rosling, H. (2010). Hans Rosling: Global population growth, box by box. TED talks. Published 9 Jul. 2010. Available at: www.youtube.com/watch?v=fTznEIZRkLg. [Accessed 9 Feb. 2019].

Saunders, M., Lewis, P. and Thornhill, A. (2012). *Research methods for business students*. Harlow: Pearson Education Ltd.

Smith, A. (1776). The wealth of nations.

Smith, A.S. (1996). The purpose of wealth: A historical perspective. In: H.E. Daly and K.N. Townsend, eds., *Valuing the earth: Economics, ecology, ethics*. London: MIT Press, pp. 183–209.

Solomon, M., Bamosy, G., Askegaard, S. and Hogg, M.K. (2006). *Consumer behaviour: A European perspective*. 3rd ed. Harlow: Pearson.

Sparks, L. and Wagner, B.A. (2003). Retail Exchanges: A research agenda. *Supply Chain Management: An International Journal*, 8(3), pp. 201–208.

Spedale, S. and Watson, T.J. (2014). The emergence of entrepreneurial action: At the crossroads between institutional logics and individual life-orientation. *International Small Business Journal*, 32(7), pp. 759–776.

Stahel, W.R. (2006). *The performance economy*. London: Palgrave Macmillan.

Tadajewski, M. and Hamilton, K. (2014). Waste, art, and social change: Transformative consumer research outside of the academy? *Journal of Macromarketing*, 34(1), pp. 80–86.

Tilley, F. and Young, W. (2009). Sustainability entrepreneurs – could they be the true wealth generators of the future? *Greener Management International*, (55), pp. 70–92, Greenleaf Publishing.

van Dam, Y.K. and Apeldoorn, P.A.C. (1996). Sustainable marketing. *Journal of Macromarketing*, 16(2), pp. 45–56.

Vargo, S.L. and Lusch, R.F. (2004). The four service marketing myths – remnants of a goods-based manufacturing model. *Journal of Service Research*, 6, pp. 324–335.

Veblen, T. (1898). *The theory of the leisure class*, reprinted 1998, Great Minds Series. London: Prometheus Books.

Walsh, J.P., Weber, K. and Margolis, J.D. (2003). Social issues and management: Our lost cause found. *Journal of Management*, 29, pp. 859–881.

Wagner, E.T. (2013). Five reasons 8 out of 100 businesses fail. *Forbes*. Available at: www.forbes.com/sites/ericwagner/2013/09/12/five-reasons-8-out-of-10-businesses-fail/[Accessed Jul. 2014].

Wang (2014). The elastic self: Understanding identity in social media [Online]. Available at: http://triciawang.com/updates/2014/1/26/new-talk-the-elastic-self-understanding-identity-in-social-m.html.

WHO (2019). World Health Organisation's framework convention on tobacco control (FCTC). Available at: www.who.int/fctc/en/ [Accessed 21 Jan. 2019].

Wired (2013). How to buy friends and influence people on Facebook, *Wired* [Online]. Available at: www.wired.com/2013/04/buy-friends-on-facebook/ [Accessed 2 Aug. 2014].

Wong, A. and Sohal, A.S. (2002). Customers' perspectives on service quality and relationship quality in retail encounters. *Managing Service Quality*, 12(5), pp. 424–433.

Wood, D.J. (1991). Corporate social performance revisited. *The Academy of Management Review*, 16(4, Oct.), pp. 691–718.

Wood, D.J. (2008). Corporate responsibility and stakeholder theory: Challenging the neoclassical paradigm. Academy of Management 2007 Symposium printed in Agle, B.R., Donaldson, T., Freeman, R.E., Jensen, M.C., Mitchell, R.K. and Wood, D.J. (2008). Dialogue: Toward superior stakeholder theory. *Business Ethics Quarterly*, 18(2), pp. 153–190.

Young, C.W., Hwang, K., McDonald, S. and Oates, C. (2010). Sustainable consumption: Green consumer behaviour when purchasing products. *Sustainable Development*, 18, pp. 20–31.

2 The Marketing Mix

Abstract

This Chapter will consider the tactical tools used by marketers, namely the Marketing Mix. All marketers must understand the fundamentals of communication if they are to gain insights into customers. Increasingly marketers must use communications approaches where they have less control. Customers want to have easy access to products and services and marketers must focus on convenience. The basics of product portfolio management will be addressed as well as considering how sustainability factors (such as the greening process) are changing marketers' approaches. Pricing is strategically important, highly visible to senior management, connects the customer to the supplier and conveys signals (e.g. about quality and exclusivity) to the market place. Pricing is primarily used operationally to generate the revenue required, to cover costs and to make profit. However, it can be used in a much more sophisticated sense, tactically and strategically; to gain entry to markets and to create barriers to entry for others. This chapter provides the key underpinning perspectives on pricing then considers the factors that shape pricing, pricing strategies/techniques and the role of technology. Consumers are more discerning and prepared to move if they are not satisfied with a service. Sometimes problems occur because of the perception of the service rather than the reality. Hyper-competition means that moving from one provider to another is easy. Competitive advantage can be obtained by delivering consistently higher quality service than competitors.

Learning outcomes

At the end of this chapter, students will be able to do the following:

- Discuss the nature of communications and be able to apply key models;
- Examine the nature of products and how they are managed;
- Assess how marketers make pricing decisions;
- Evaluate whether goods and services are distributed conveniently for the customer;
- Analyse how marketing services differ from marketing goods;
- Explain the impact of sustainable consumption on the marketing mix.

The key framework for tactical marketing is the marketing mix (hereafter the mix) traditionally featuring product, price, place and promotion. The mix was developed by Neil Borden, who initially identified 12 "ingredients"; however, recall that issues led to him reducing the number to four (Baker, 2009). The mix was originally aimed at helping goods manufacturers, and it can be argued that too much research relates to the traditional production view of firms rather than services. This manufacturing focus is looking increasingly outdated, as many countries continue their transition from being manufacturing economies to deriving most of their GDP from services.

Marketers have significant control over the mix and elements therein. Increasingly, however, concerns have been raised suggesting that the tools lack customer centricity. Hence, customer-centric variants are increasingly used, such as those that follow:

- Communications   (. . . promotion);
- Convenience   (. . . place);
- Customer benefits (. . . product);
- Cost   (. . . price).

2.1 Communications (aka marcomms)

The need to promote a brand is not new. The 19th-century entertainer, entrepreneur and icon of American spirit P.T. Barnum famously said,

> "Without promotion, something terrible happens: nothing!"

Marketers rarely use the term "promotion" these days, preferring comms or marcomms. Promotion is deemed to represent a monologue where the seller "talks at" the customer. It is one-directional and assumes the prospect or customer is listening, engaged or even interested. Communication suggests a dialogue where companies seek to sell, not tell. All good salespeople know that listening is more important than talking. An old cliché still applies: salespeople have two ears and one mouth, and these organs should be used in this proportion.

Schramm (1955) reflected on the different tasks that communication could perform: sharing knowledge, questioning or instructing. Ideally, marketing communication (hereafter marcomms) should be a simple process where the marketer sends a message that is received and understood unambiguously by the intended audience. In

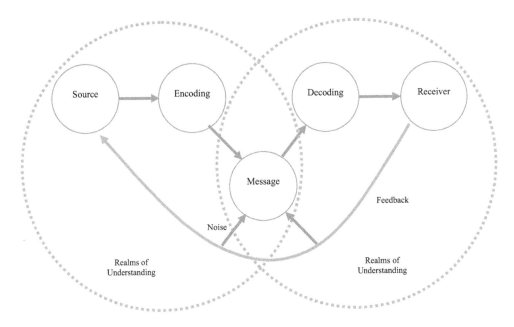

Figure 2.1 Linear model of communications

Source: adapted from Schramm (1955) and Shannon and Weaver (1949)

reality, this rarely happens. In Shannon and Weaver's linear model of communication (Figure 2.1), communication is seen as a linear process, where a sender "encodes" a message (using spoken or written language, images, signs or symbols) and is delivered via a source or medium to a receiver.

Before deciding on which communication tools to use to deliver the message to the receiver, there are a number of factors to consider that will inform the choice of communication tools and the configuration of the message itself. Marketers must identify the target audience/receiver. Research their lifestyle choices, reading habits, preferred TV shows or channels, their hobbies and their affiliations. The deeper the understanding of the receiver, the richer and more focused the encoding and the message being created.

Messages need to achieve clear objectives. Is the aim to raise awareness or to sell the benefits of the product, brand or service? Is the message designed to stimulate feedback or to increase sales and market share? With focused objectives, developing the message will be more straightforward and ultimately easier to convey. What does the brand represent? What is its personality? What are the values of the brand? Do they all need to be conveyed in the communication? (See Chapter 4.4.)

As a matter of course and practice, marketers should always be monitoring the competitive environment. The competitors' choices of communication tools (e.g. which ones they use, how often they use them and whether they are successful) will inform the decision – as will whether the communication and message relates to a product or service.

Noise

The receiver decodes the message to interpret meaning, but this can be affected by noise (Figure 2.1). Noise can be anything that affects how the message is received or distorts its original meaning. As previously discussed, consumers may be subjected to several thousand marketing messages per day. A key skill for marketers is to understand the nature of noise and create pieces of communication that can cut through the clutter bombarding the consumer. The aim is to create the key piece of communication that the receivers notice, recall and respond to. Marketers must seek feedback from the receiver to ascertain whether they had they received the message, understood it and responded appropriately. This can be achieved in numerous ways, such as by using music, animation, fantasy, imagery and memorable events. This is useful; however, it does not take into account other stakeholders and their realms of understanding. Terms such as CSR and sustainability can easily be misinterpreted

These messages can involve misinformation (i.e. messages that are accidentally incorrect) or disinformation (where the message is deliberately incorrect). Misinformation can arise from the oversupply of information about a product or service. Alternatively, it can result from language being used that is not easily understood by the consumer. Hence, noise can emanate from a marketer and/or the competition. It is no surprise that marketer-dominated sources are struggling to cut through the noise.

Communication can be inclusive or exclusive. Progressive, sustainable marketers should always practice inclusive communications. Some parties deliberately communicate in a way to exclude others. This is not new. Foucault talked at length about the use of communication as means of wielding power. Disinformation is also about wielding power. It is often covert, where the originator hides their identity. Sadly, governments and unscrupulous organisations practise such techniques.

Katz and Lazarsfeld (1955) noted that mass media communications often first reaches opinion leaders and opinion formers. An opinion former is somebody whom consumers trust because of their education, profession or expertise. They need to be perceived to be independent of the marketing organisation. Jeremy Clarkson of "Top Gear" is an opinion leader as he is perceived to be independent of the automotive industry. He is highly knowledgeable, indeed to such an extent that he can be argued to be a maven. Mavens have high levels of knowledge and can be deemed to be experts in their fields. Using an expert can help to build trust and credibility into marcomms activities and raise a brand's profile. Pharmaceutical companies promoting a new headache or hay fever tablet may use a chemist/pharmacist or doctor in their marcomms. By using an expert in their field, they hope to build trust and credibility into their communication activities and brand. The Product Adoption Process (see Chapter 2.3) is a useful model to illustrate how consumers can be influenced by others. Consumers adopt new products at different speeds and junctures. The adoption can be speeded up by using credible influencers.

> *Example* Before starting a module, most students do not know the books on the reading list; however, if one book is the core text, the students are more likely to purchase the recommended text. The publishers do not directly target the students when raising awareness of their products. Instead they target the lecturers and encourage them to build the text into the assessment or to incorporate it into the VLE. Larger publishers even provide materials for academics to use in the lectures and seminars. In this way, the publisher focuses on the hundreds of lecturers (in an institution) rather than the tens of thousands of students. An interesting dynamic arises when the academic adopts a self-authored book as the core text. Some students may see this as unethical – as a means of lining the academic's pockets. When the earnings of non-academic authors (e.g. J.K. Rowling) are in the millions, it can cause some confusion. Few academic authors make substantial money from their outputs. They largely produce texts to raise awareness of their research or to improve teaching in the classroom. In some cases, it is to correct poor practice carried out by their predecessors. See Chapter 3.4 and the rebuttal of the term "SWOT analysis" for an example of this.

Opinion leaders are not necessarily experts; rather, they are people whom consumers trust because of their social standing, closeness or general credibility. They can have a specific interest or passion, such as dining out, films, technology, video games, fashion or cycling (among many others).

Opinion formers and leaders will spread the message with their own interpretation and influence the receivers further down the two-step model of communication. When seeking to use such influencers, marketers must ensure that they are perceived to be credible, sincere and authentic. If this is the case, influencers may help to establish trust more quickly than without them.

Credibility can also arise from prospects and/or consumers seeing products being used by similar people. Advertisements designed to create awareness of a new pair of shoes for boys aged 13–16 would probably use boys of the same age. The message has been "encoded" in such a way that the receiver will respond positively. The same shoes on a middle-aged man would send a completely different message, even if all other factors were the same. The youth-oriented advertisement may not appeal to those over 30, but this is not problematic, because they are not the target receivers.

Single-step model

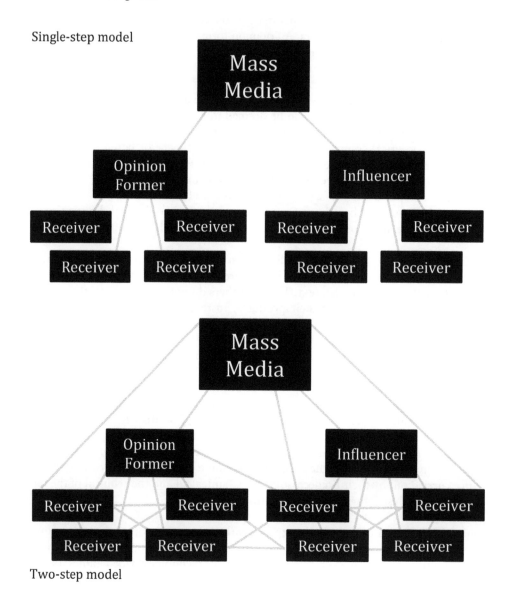

Two-step model

Figure 2.2 Single-step model of communication and two-step model of communication
Source: adapted from Lazarfeld and Katz (1955)

With young audiences, the message should be simple and repeated often. Humour is often used when seeking to grab the attention of younger audiences. Care needs to be taken when using humour, because it does not always translate across generations or beyond cultural boundaries.

Social communications, and marcomms, do not flow in logical, linear paths. Any model should consider the extra directions of communication between parties. In the multi-step model of communications, the receiver may communicate with the opinion leader, other "receivers" or the original sender of the message. Hence, rather than there just being one or two steps in the process, there can be a multitude of them, or what is known as many-to-many communication.

Word of Mouth (WoM)

Many linguistics experts argue that written words are more powerful than spoken words. Others insist that imagery is more powerful than text. Most marketers (academics and practitioners alike) believe that WoM is the most powerful means of communication.

Before making purchase decisions, consumers often seek online information. Particularly when making larger, riskier purchases, they need information to make better decisions and will often turn to those who offer impartial, credible advice. WoM has now morphed into Word of Mouse (eWoM). The latter captures how negative WoM and/or eWoM can pass around the world in seconds. Marketers must assume that their customers and prospects search online, where they can read "unbiased" peer comments before they make a purchase. The historical top-down approach is increasingly inappropriate, so marketers must design their Marcomms to make it easy to reach the influencers *and* the buyers.

Push, pull and profile strategies

A push strategy is used to "push" stock down through the marketing channels from one intermediary to the next. Therefore, in the case of a push strategy, the customer is often another business. A manufacturer may develop communications, such as encouraging a retailer to increase their monthly order for improved discounts and being willing to advertise it with posters, direct marketing or via their sales force.

A pull strategy is used to entice the end user to (first) create footfall and (second) encourage enquiries into (and purchasing of) goods and services. Therefore, in the case of a pull strategy, the customer is the end user. The aforementioned manufacturer may develop a second sales promotion aimed at the end user by advertising in store and on the packaging. It could suggest that if they buy one of the advertised products, they will receive a second free in store (BOGOF – buy one, get one free) or later (BOGOL – buy one, get one later).

Many organisations seek to communicate about issues other than their products and services. They may wish to communicate with key stakeholders or organisations identified as having a vested interest in the brand, the corporate personality, identity, image and so on. Therefore, in the case of a profile strategy, the receiver could be any (or even all) stakeholders.

Promoting companies' good ethical and ecological practices via social media sites can contribute to good WoM. This supports a personalised "pull" method, where users are encouraged to take active roles. With near global levels of networked people, the potential exists for (almost) everyone to communicate with each other. However, care is needed to avoid falling into the trap of thinking customers (and other receivers) are passive. Customers share, create and discuss ideas, using social media sites, blogs, fora, review sites and price-comparison sites. The advent of digital comms often overlooks that many customers and prospects still talk face to face.

Communication is and always will be a *social* process. It still "flows" in streams (or certain directions), but there is less acceptance of "push-based" communications, where customers are told what to buy or why. Consumers are less inclined to be told who they will "become" through consumption.

The Comms Mix

The traditional key tools of marketing communications (hereafter marcomms) make up The Comms Mix. It is useful to consider each tool.

Advertising

More traditional advertising activities are covered in detail elsewhere. Students could refer to texts by Shelley Rodgers and Esther Thorson or the one by Chris Fill. Driving the sustainability agenda increasingly uses the Internet and other technological developments. The Internet can support the delivery of a number of different types of advertisements (or adverts or ads): from the "classic" banner ad and (irritating) pop-ups to the increasingly common interstitial advertisements. Banner ads can also use other platforms and vehicles, such as mobile apps and mobile optimised websites.

Other areas for consideration are paid for display ads, via Pay Per Click (PPC) on search engines or targeted ads on social networks. These platforms offer more targeted, personalised content based on search behaviour and personal profiles. Search engines also provide the opportunity to advertise the brand against the competition through organic search results – hence the need for Search Engine Optimisation (SEO). Digital media can also be used to deliver (and support the sharing of) viral advertisements whose contents are more effective when funny, novel, entertaining and/or contemporary.

> *Example*   Former fee-paying newspapers are now been given away gratis, such as the *London Evening Standard*. This new business model relies on advertising fees. Free papers such as the *Metro* are increasingly popular with young consumers, despite largely recycling news stories and heavily relying on agencies such as *Reuters* and the Press Association (see www.pressassociation.com). Recent hard times saw long-established, esteemed companies such as Johnson Press struggling to find the right balance of online versus hard copy content. Monetising websites is a challenge for all newspapers. The *Guardian* asks each contributor to make a donation – effectively, a 21st-century honesty box for newspapers.

Advertising is going to become a major battleground where content suppliers will become increasingly protective. Increasingly, online material is catering to increasing streaming to handheld devices such as smartphones, tablets and smartwatches. Today, 15-year-olds to 21-year-olds spend more time online than they do watching TV. In future, they will get their news increasingly via their mobile phones. That said, it is not all plain sailing: many news-sharing sites are taking losses.

> *Example*   NewsNow (see newsnow.co.uk) is the UK's largest RSS site and has been aggregating links to Internet news since 1998. By 2019 NewsNow had links to tens of thousands of publications, from top news brands to top news publications. And it was visited by over 14 million unique monthly visitors, generating in excess of 120 million page views per month. Like many online organisations, NewsNow relies on a combination of advertising, sponsorship and subscription

revenues to fund its services. However, it has been caught up in a battle over revenues that continues to rage as companies adjust to life after Web 2.0. It accused News International (NI) of undermining freedom of access to public information having been informed by NI that it may no longer link to any NI sites.

This meant NewsNow visitors were no longer able to view content on the *Times* online site. The blocking was implemented using the robots.txt protocol, a convention for requesting search engines, web spiders and other web robots to refrain from asking for pages from all or part of a website. In December 2009, NewsNow pulled many of its links to national newspaper websites following attempts by The Newspaper Licensing Agency Limited (NLA) to impose a scheme that introduced the requirement to obtain permission and pay fees to circulate links to freely available webpages. The scheme was subsequently referred to the Copyright Tribunal. NewsNow.co.uk is the founding sponsor of the Right2Link Campaign (www.right2link.org/).

In 20–30 years' time, it is unlikely that licence payers will still fund the BBC. They have one of the world's most visited websites; however, their current funding means that they will be less able to compete with new technologies. The battle over whose site should be the gateway (and hence the major beneficiary) of advertising and click-through revenues will intensify.

Public Relations (PR)

Public Relations (PR) is about developing and managing relations with stakeholders. PR is often construed as being all about media relations: getting a brand in the newspaper, trade magazines, on radio or TV, whether at a local, regional or national level. PR is much more than media relations; it can be highly effective at improving relationships with stakeholders in the internal and microenvironments. Furthermore, it can support brands in times of difficulty or indeed crisis in these increasingly tumultuous times.

The CIPR (2019) defines PR as being

> "about reputation – the result of what you do, what you say and what others say about you. . . . Public relations is the discipline that looks after reputation, with the aim of earning understanding and support and influencing opinion and behaviour. It is the planned and sustained effort to establish and maintain goodwill and mutual understanding between an organisation and its publics".

PR practitioners refer to publics as being synonymous with stakeholders. Marketers use both terms, with *stakeholders* being engaged and *publics* have interest but no direct engagement.

Organisations can use digital media to share messages designed for wider stakeholder groups and publics. This could be via social media, their website, an intranet, their employees (and their personal online social media channels) or even corporate channels such as blogs.

Examples of negative PR can also be seen online, as complaints, poor customer or employee treatment, unethical practices (to name but a few) can be posted and shared online. They also have the potential to go viral and reach a much larger, sometimes global, audience that can cause significant damage to a brand. Messages can be shared very quickly and easily online, so crisis response communications can be optimised. Corporate websites can also add press relations sections, allowing journalists direct access to information, stories and contacts.

Traditionally, PR and marketing were seen as separate disciplines. PR academics and practitioners strove to be seen as independent from marketers. Marketers were always more open to PR. Some PR advocates argued that marketing is crude and transactional whereas PR is sophisticated, longitudinal and subtler than marketing with its use of (more expensive) advertising, sponsorship and so on. It is true that PR does not involve the higher above-the-line costs that advertising and sponsorship incur, and it is often used to complement these tactics. The reality, however, is that marketers have been using relationship-marketing tools for decades.

What is now questionable is whether PR should still be seen as a stand-alone discipline. The advent of Web 2.0 has seen a sustained increase in citizen journalists and other forms of User-Generated Content (UGC). Social media marketing has revolutionised the way clients want their accounts to be handled. They see PR as being a key tool within the extended Marcomms Mix. In most cases, PR agencies will be responding to briefs from marketers (directors and managers) who hold the budget. This industry shift has been reflected in universities as well, where more courses feature marketing *and* PR at undergraduate and postgraduate levels.

Sales promotion – A number of different types of sales promotion: coupons, online-only deals, time-limited discounts and so on can be delivered online and through channels. The various advertising and direct marketing channels available to marketers allow for targeted sales promotions through the use of customer data and analytics. The sales promotions can be delivered in a more timely, personalised manner and can be linked to loyalty schemes, of which the Tesco Clubcard is an exemplar. Marketers can use the companies' website, specialist voucher and coupon sites (e.g. vouchercloud), communities (e.g. moneysavingexpert.com), email, SMS, MMS and developing technologies targeting customers in stores (e.g. augmented reality apps like Layar).

Direct marketing – The key channels available to marketers to deliver direct communications are SMS (or MMS), email, Bluetooth, social media and display ads. However, some messages, especially those delivered via email and SMS, can be considered as spam if unsolicited or intrusive, in the same way that direct mail can be considered junk mail. GDPR legislation was introduced in 2018 to control aspects such as permission and opt-in and opt-out requirements. Previous legislation (Privacy in Electronic Communications Regulation – PECR) was incorporated into GDPR, and it will be interesting to see how unscrupulous marketers respond.

Personal selling – This requires at least two parties to be engaged, usually the buyer and seller. This can be done face to face with sales representatives visiting buyers in B2B markets or customer representatives interacting with consumers (think beauty consultants representing Clarins in retail outlets). Personal selling can take place virtually; however, this poses some challenges. During the engagement, the seller cannot reflect on other signals such as facial expressions or body language.

Organisations increasingly engage online with customers and prospects by using real-time communications such as online chats or live chats. These can be useful communications tools when used for high-involvement purchases online, and they aid in customer conversion. It can be used as a tool to offer support, whether customer driven through clicking on a link or via a pop-up box offering the option of a live chat.

Integrated Marketing Communications (IMC)

Credibility and trust are paramount in SM. Communicated messages based on facts and the credibility of the sender can influence whether customers adopt sustainable consumption. Consumers need to trust the brand whether they receive communications via newspapers or online or meet representatives at an exhibition. They increasingly want to engage in a mutually beneficial relationship. Mutual respect is the most effective way to develop a brand's reputation and build relationships with stakeholders, whether they are customers, staff, investors, suppliers, community groups and even activist groups who may oppose the activities of the business. Marketers must recognise that gaining this trust is important to building relationships.

Today, organisations can develop Marcomms campaigns by using many more tools than were originally envisaged in the comms mix. Figure 2.3 illustrates some of the tools available to marketers seeking to achieve their objectives.

The different comms tools do different jobs, and blending a selection of them in an effective campaign can be beneficial. Wider audiences can be reached and a consistent message can be delivered. This reduces the confusion of mixed messages while increasing the likelihood of cutting through the *noise* and being remembered.

Many companies will regularly use Marcomms techniques without fully understanding the impact of these individual activities, never mind the collective impact of using

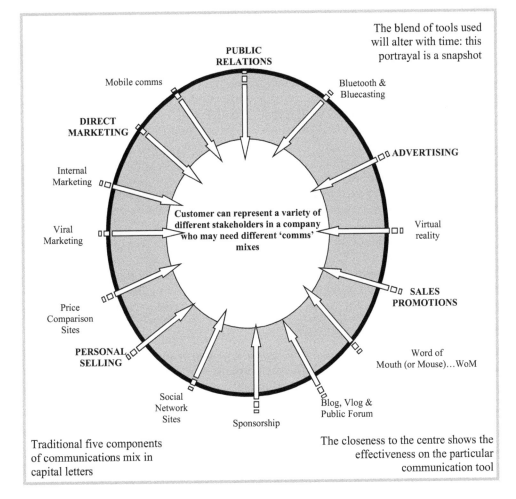

Figure 2.3 Expanded Comms Mix

Source: adapted from Fill (2006)

a range of tactics. Taking a strategic approach to marcomms increases the likelihood that the tactics used, from sending press releases to communicating with customers, prospects and other stakeholders are most effective. This is known as taking a coordinated marcomms approach, which can be delivered on a range of platforms.

An area of communication that has been dynamic in recent years is digital media. It has significantly increased the number of opportunities for marketers engaging with various audiences. The development of Relationship Marketing (see Chapter 4.1) had already led to improvements in communications between companies and their suppliers, staff and customers. This has been further improved with the use of two-way communications tools. However, the growth in such two-way communications has driven increasing demands and expectations (within companies and by customers) for more immediacy, transparency and personalised contact.

Digital media, predominantly enabled by Internet technology, provide opportunities, channels and platforms that can be linked to the comms mix.

Digital platforms

Mobile devices – Mobile devices allow marketers to interact with content in real time. Smartphones form Apple, HTC and Samsung (among others) are increasingly complemented by tablets. Tablets are still classed as mobile devices, and they provide a different experience from that of the smartphone.

At the other end of the scale, marketers increasingly communicate via wearable tech as comms technology becomes more embedded into glasses, watches and clothing. The key benefit of mobile marketing is that marketers can communicate with consumers who are (almost) always in possession of their smartphone, which itself is (almost) always on.

Gaming platforms – Gaming is the most profitable entertainment market in the world. There are a number of ways that gaming platforms are evolving, moving from being a niche activity to becoming central to home entertainment. Within gaming networks, such as Xbox Live and PlayStation Network, marketers can reach and engage with specific markets.

There is also the opportunity to deliver advertising with video games, say FIFA, or offer games for free in exchange for being exposed to advertising messages. As consumers increasingly adopt smartphone technology, there is a corresponding growth in "casual" gamers who can be reached by banner and/or in-game advertising. Some organisations, such as Audi, have even created branded "casual" games delivered via apps.

Indoor and outdoor kiosks – Kiosks are small, freestanding increasingly sophisticated structures that can provide independent (asynchronous) informational or transactional services. They can be used to provide information in cities or shopping centres, conduct research and provide facilities to purchase or order products. Kiosks can also incorporate a variety of different applications such as augmented reality or facial recognition making them more interactive and more effective.

Interactive signage – Digital out-of-home signage is another emerging development in the field of outdoor advertising. The traditional billboard is becoming more interactive as the technology allows for facial recognition. It is in its infancy, but age, gender and even emotions can be identified and then content delivered based on this. In 2010 Wall's used interactive techniques when their "Share Happy" vending machines dispensed ice cream to those willing to smile and have the pictures uploaded onto Facebook.

Other fixed connected platforms (e.g. smart TV) – There are a number of other platforms that are integrating connectivity. Smart TVs allow access to on-demand and online content. They are increasingly using voice commands and incorporating digital assistants such as Google Assistant and Alexa. TV service providers like Sky and Virgin also offer these services. One area of emerging interest relates to the IoT, where devices and platforms used daily can be connected, including cars, TVs, computers, fridges, freezers, cookers, thermostats, heating and so on. Marketers should work in a sympathetic, ethical way to improve the lives of individuals by providing the right control and the right content, at the right time and in the right place.

The use of Communications Agencies

The budget is a key determinant of the choices of communication tools available to marketers. Even the use or type of agency will be dictated by budgetary constraints. That said, many Comms consultants provide excellent services often at a fraction of the cost of a full-service agency.

The use of a Comms agency may be the optimal way to implement IMC and to achieve the objectives. There are two types of agency available to marketers. First, the large full-service agencies, such as Saatchi and Saatchi, who can create, develop, plan and execute any manner of Comms campaigns since they employ specialists in all aspects of communication, have vast resources and can therefore cross-coordinate all communication activities at a cost.

Alternatively, marketers can engage the services of an independent specialist agency. This choice would be generally cheaper, because they do not have the vast overhead to service. They will need to be briefed on other aspects of the IMC, though. Larger companies often employ multiple agencies – for example, one for design/creative, another for PR and one to cross-coordinate the campaigns.

Agencies can be costly, and marketers need to act quickly to avoid repeating any perceived mistakes. When using agencies, ensure that the agency analyse the campaign. The focus may fall on the brief itself. Was the agency given the appropriate information, direction and budget to achieve the objectives? It is the responsibility of the marketer to ensure the brief is "tight". Any wiggle room (or contingency) may be used by the agency to avoid being held responsible.

Measuring Marcomms

While today's technologies offer exciting communications choices, there are also challenges. Marketers can spend large amounts of time and money on marcomms activities, so they must know whether they are effective. Marketers are often expected to achieve a Return on Marketing Investment (RoMI) or a Return on Objectives (RoO). Whenever creating a Comms campaign (e.g. using PR, sales promotions, ads and direct mail letters), marketers must have a means to monitor the communications. Successful marcomms need to be "unpacked" so that lessons can be learned and changes adopted in future campaigns. Failing marcomms need to be dissected to ascertain the flaws: Is the message unclear? Is the medium chosen to carry the message working? Is there simply too much noise? Does the encoding work?

When Marcomms work well, they can provide considerable success for brands and companies. However, if they go wrong, they can have quite devastating effects. Not only can precious time, money and resources be wasted, but brand names, brand equity (the value of the brand) and the reputation of the company can all suffer. Because Marcomms activities are highly visible, key stakeholders may witness mistakes. Within any Marketing Mix, the Comms Mix (with its digital media and tools) should not be separated from the more traditional marcomms activities. Rather, it should be integrated and used to create value for customers.

2.2 Convenience (aka place)

"Place" has grown in importance over the years for a number of different reasons. Most organisations operate in highly competitive markets. Wherever costs are high, there is always potential for savings. If companies ship goods, they must establish the cost of transporting products from A to B. The goods must arrive at the right time, in the right place, in the right condition and with the right post-delivery support. This is particularly important when shipping goods overseas. They are expected to reduce their ecological impact (carbon footprint, pollutants, resource usage, etc.) while delivering the goods. Those who are incapable of performing to high standards and expectations are likely to lose customers to others who are more convenient for the customer. "Convenience" has replaced "Place" in the mix, as it is the benefit the customer gains. It links into their values. Simply put, focusing on "Convenience" can help companies to achieve a competitive advantage, and to understand it better, consider marketing channels and distribution logistics.

Marketing channels

In the context of distribution, a marketing channel is the route used to deliver goods (and services) to customers. There are a number of different ways that this can be done; hence, channel design is important. Factors affecting a marketer's choice include cost, convenience, customer requirements and control. Furthermore, decisions need to be made regarding distributing products directly or indirectly. If indirect, the optimal length of supply channel needs to be used.

Direct distribution uses a zero-level channel since no other businesses is involved in getting products to the customer. This does not include couriers or those delivering the goods. It refers to those who take a proportion of the sales price or profit and has been augmented by the use of technology to such an extent that a wide range of organisations now sell "direct". Recording artists are increasingly bypassing the retailers and shipping direct. This increasingly popular option moves the artist (and supplier) closer to the customer *and* retains a higher margin. The closer to the customer, the greater the likelihood of forming relationships, receiving timely feedback and, perhaps even more importantly, retaining control over how the product reaches the customer.

Websites can attract customers and increasingly support their purchasing, after which marketers must have effective postage and delivery systems to achieve complete satisfaction. Facilitating the ordering of their chosen products from the comfort of their home may be one key advantage, but if the delivery service fails to deliver on time and with their purchases in one piece, customer loss (or attrition) may result.

A one-level channel features one intermediary (another business) between the manufacturer and customer. The intermediaries (e.g. retailers, wholesalers, agents or franchisors) move the product from the manufacturer to the customer. They have established networks of outlets to reach certain target markets. Marketers should identify mutual marcomms opportunities with intermediaries and integrate each other's branding information into messages.

Two-level channels feature two intermediaries between the manufacturer and consumer. Some manufacturers will sell their products to a wholesaler, who in turn sells the products to smaller retailers and ultimately the end user. The longer the channel, the further removed the manufacturer becomes from the end user. Gaining immediate feedback from the consumer market becomes more complicated. Generally speaking, customers will return faulty or unwanted goods to the retailer. If the customer generates a complaint, this will cascade through the channel until it eventually travels back to the manufacturer.

Marketers will undertake consumer research to deduce the pricing needed or how the item should be positioned in the marketplace. However, it is difficult to dictate these points to intermediaries. In most contracts, when intermediaries pay for their order, they take title of the product and ultimately control.

The use of intermediaries

There are many reasons for using intermediaries: retailers and wholesalers already have established networks of outlets to reach certain customer segments. That is why many organisations, say Heinz, use retailers, such as Tesco, to sell their products. If Heinz had to reach the consumers directly, establishing their own network of stores would cost millions. Tesco has stores in most cities and towns in the United Kingdom. Their customers do not have far to travel to buy goods.

Convenience is more than simply location. Intermediaries break down bulk supplies and provide "allocation" and "assortment" – that is, they sort them into product groupings that the consumer find easier to recognise, such as the confectionery aisle in a store. Using existing retailers' resources provides customers with further convenience, such as dealing with post-sales services or returns. A large supermarket will stock 50,000 products, all of which have to be accessible, priced correctly and in good condition.

Manufacturers should concentrate on their core competencies and leave the distribution to the experts. Let wholesalers support the smaller retailers and concentrate on manufacturing the goods. This approach uses the manufacturer's skills, knowledge and resources to the best of their abilities.

Intermediaries offer great skills, resources, knowledge and expertise and can share risks. From a long-term perspective, they should be viewed not just as an intermediary but as a partner. Marketers must dedicate time and resources to developing and strengthening relationships. Trust and confidence should be central to long-term relationships, but in practice, this is not always achievable. Channel conflict must be avoided at all costs. One of the key sources of conflict is lack of communication and "stepping on others toes". So, the roles, terms and relationships need to be defined at the outset. When adopting a hybrid approach to distribution (using zero-level *and* intermediaries), it is always useful to create a supportive relationship with the intermediaries and to establish where responsibilities lie. This ensures that the channel runs smoothly and avoids conflict within the channel between intermediaries, which can lead to substantial problems.

Brick and/or click

Retailers can significantly influence manufacturers and customers. In the United Kingdom, the Cooperative have been highly proactive in addressing a range of social, ethical and environmental issues. There is concern that the size and price competitiveness of the major retailers can lead to a lack of consideration of sustainability issues, such as the working conditions of agricultural labourers or the environmental costs associated with products (cfsd, 2019). That said, most major retailers have at least a CSR platform and increasingly sustainability policies and procedures.

Many organisations sell online and via their own stores. For those selling in the real world (i.e. "brick"), the physical (or task) environment is important. The internal and external appearance of premises, waiting areas and equipment must be maintained. Customer-facing service deliverers must also pay attention to material aspects such as the appearance of delivery vans or staff uniforms. Those only using online delivery (i.e. "click") must ensure that their website is easy to find and navigate. Many providers are "brick" and "click" and have to decide whether it is beneficial to migrate "brick" customers to "click" (see Figure 2.4).

The simple answer is yes. However, the caveat is migrating customers only if their satisfaction can be maintained or improved. The decision to migrate existing customers to online depends on whether traditional and/or online provisions are offered.

Assume that a company has converted a prospect into a customer traditionally (A) or online (B). The first transaction (A or B) is fraught with risk, and the seller must ensure everything is done to get it right the first time. Once the customer has repeated their order several times, they will have developed a higher level of trust and will forgive the odd mistake. However, new customers are easy to drive off. Remember that responding to a mistake says more about a company than smooth transactions do.

Not all returning customer positions are equal; overheads are likely to be considerably lower online. Being pragmatic means having repeat customers in any form is "Preferred" to single transactions (hence the dashed migration from B to Preferred). Ultimately, whether through single (A or B to Ideal) or multiple migrations (A or B to Preferred to Ideal) opportunities exist to migrate customers to the "Ideal" position, where they are happy online and the seller enjoys the healthiest margins.

Market coverage

Marketers must consider the amount of market coverage needed for the product. Traditionally, the three choices of coverage are exclusive distribution, intensive distribution or selective distribution.

Exclusive distribution involves the deliberate restriction of product availability. This fosters a sense of exclusivity; for example, Aston Martin cars are usually sold in a single outlet in most major cities in the United Kingdom.

Intensive distribution is diametrically opposed to exclusive distribution. It is often used by Fast Moving Consumer Goods (FMCG) companies distributing convenience products such as toilet rolls, milk or potatoes. A widespread of distribution (intensive

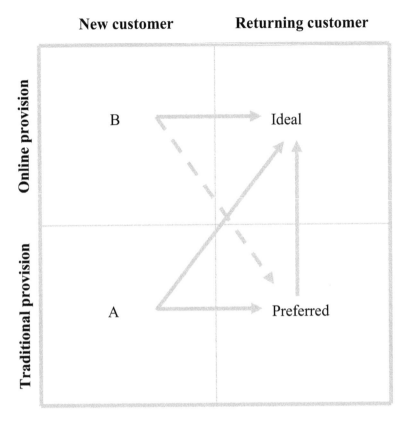

Figure 2.4 Brick versus click distribution

Source: Richardson, James and Kelley (2015)

coverage) is required, because customers require these products often on a daily basis. Availability and convenience are therefore key concerns.

Selective distribution is used where good coverage is required for a product but not to the extent of intensive approach (where horizontal competition may drive prices down) or limiting product availability with the exclusive approach. Herein a small number of select outlets are used. This maintains higher pricing and a degree of exclusivity.

Distribution logistics

Distribution logistics refers to managing the practical realities of physically moving products, often over great distances. The trend for manufacturing goods in the Far East and Pacific Rim is going to continue for the foreseeable future. Hence, the process of logistically manoeuvring the freight around the world to markets in the West has increased in importance.

Poor distribution can negatively affect customer satisfaction. From a B2B perspective, poor delivery may lead to attrition in key accounts as professional buyers seek alternative suppliers. Therefore, a number of issues need to be considered, as follows.

Products can be transported using airfreight, cargo ships, railways, lorries (semis), cars or motorbikes. Hence, careful consideration is needed regarding the mode of transport from one intermediary to another. Costs, convenience and capability all need to be taken into account.

The role of packaging is important, as complaints will often arise from goods damaged during transit. Therefore, the packaging needs to be robust enough to withstand the journey and mode of transport used.

Many organisations store products in warehouses, and as they receive orders, the products are picked out, put on board transportation and delivered to the customer. The number and location of distribution hubs is key. Again, this can be a costly venture. Many companies have received poor publicity resulting from dire working conditions in their warehouses. Indeed, some companies have been subjected to parliamentary scrutiny over perceived poor working practices.

In a B2B situation, an order processing system is often required. This system also wraps itself around inventory management. Stock is costly, particularly if it is finished goods sitting in a warehouse. Costs in terms of insurance and security start to increase at this stage. Stock needs to be converted into sales quickly, to create income and liquidity for the business.

However, managing stock is not an easy task. If a key client wants an order fulfilled quickly and the particular item is not available, the customer has little option other than to go to a competitor. Alternatively, the decision to hold extra stock to accommodate rush orders that may arise, particularly at peak periods, will lead to capital being tied up. Organisation and time management are crucial skills in this area, and marketers must work closely with the warehouse and production management teams.

Sustainable distribution

Distributing products is an area where much of the sustainability impact of products occurs through the burning of fossil fuels to transport products throughout global supply chains. There are also social implications to distribution in the accessibility of products, particularly in markets such as financial services where there are concerns about the exclusion of disadvantaged customers through the closure of bank branches and post offices (cfsd, 2019).

Sustainability needs to be viewed in terms of involvement within the wider context of stakeholder relationships. Reputations are easily tarnished by supply-side scandals with emotional and moral issues such as child labour. Hence, with organisational success often depending on suppliers, it is important to ascertain whether the supply network (a term preferred to "chain") operates in a sustainable manner. Retailers, for example, are undoubtedly interdependent networking organisations and will need to trust their partners. Trust can be shaped by previous experiences or cooperative efforts and on the more general reputation that firms build up. Sustainable marketers may also engender trust in like-minded consumers, and that trust can be grown, say, through PR as a means of promoting positive WoM.

When purchasing space on container vessels, wagons or trains, whatever the mode of transport, there are inevitable costs. Increasingly, customers are expecting suppliers to use green logistics. So a balance may be needed; for example, when shipping goods from China to the European Union, sea containers are cheaper and have a lower carbon footprint per item. However, it can take several weeks for the goods to arrive.

Using airfreight dramatically increases the carbon footprint and cost but dramatically reduces the delivery time.

> *Example*   The madness of thousands of tonnes of basic foodstuffs, whether chickens, potatoes or chocolate biscuits, passing each other in the sky, on the sea and on the roads, has been well documented. For example, in 1998, the United Kingdom exported 61,400 tonnes of poultry meat to the Netherlands and imported 33,100 tonnes of it from the Netherlands (**Howell, 2006**).

The notion of a return to greater local production is not new. In 1936 John Maynard Keynes (one of the greatest economists of the 20th century) said

> "I would sympathize with those who would minimise rather than those who would maximize economic entanglements between nations. Ideas, knowledge, art, hospitality, travel – these are the things that should of their nature be international. But let good be homespun wherever it is reasonable and conveniently impossible, and above all let finance be primarily national".
>
> (Keynes, 1936, cited in Porritt, 2005, p. 77)

Consumers and others downstream can develop different types of involvement with activities, objects, ideas and even social issues. Higher involvement results from stakeholders being committed to a cause or being affected, such as a local community. The term "local community" is somewhat nebulous as it covers suppliers who may profit from the service provided and those who may simply be affected. People belong to a local economy, which differs from the global economy and is extremely important to the welfare and quality of life in their locality (Tilley and Young, 2009). Sourcing locally is a clear way of acting in a more sustainably responsible way. Companies using local suppliers may engender trust in consumer communities *and* supplier networks.

Marketers must evaluate the extent to which they can trust the stakeholders in their network to act in recognisably sustainable ways (i.e. ethically or environmentally sound practices). Misplaced trust could pose a risk for companies, and the relationships need to be managed carefully. Retailers, for example, are often high-profile organisations that increasingly use social media to seek out customer feedback.

Larger organisations often reluctantly engage with communities. More-progressive companies seek to establish relationships with local firms, consumers and regulators. Rather than simply complying with the minimum expectations, marketers need to be more inclusive and sensitive to stakeholders. Doing so may improve PR with the community – not to mention improve the chances of success by favourably influencing the opinions of planners, who receive positive feedback from the local community.

Transparency is key to sustainable trade. Many companies are developing sustainability policies and practices and looking closely at their supply chains. The onus is increasingly

> "on companies to be proactive rather than reactive, to anticipate inevitable change, to fill the space available to them for much more environmentally and socially responsible actions, and to lobby government for faster change".
>
> (Porritt, 2005, p. 240)

Considering that "government" covers local, national and international government, it is safe to assume that marketers' remits are becoming increasingly complex. It is not enough for them to compete; they are expected to lobby as well.

2.3 Customer Benefits (aka Product)

Marketers often have direct or indirect responsibilities for managing products. It is a central task that can generate competitive advantage for companies. Baker (2009) argues that (for products) the mnemonic of AFB is useful:

- **Attributes** define distinguishing characteristics of an object.
- **Features** enable potential customers to differentiate between competing products.
- **Benefits** are customer centric – that is, solutions to the customer's problem.

Part of the challenge for marketers is that the competitors will always seek to replicate successful distinctive features. Always remember that the customer seeks value from the benefits that products offer. A common mistake is to simply list features in sales literature. This is not enough; marketers must sell the benefits and how the product solves customer problems.

At its simplest, a product consists of two key components:

1   **Tangible factors** – physical features;
2   **Intangible factors** – such as strength of the brand, quality of the materials and customer care. Customers cannot touch these factors, but they nevertheless enhance the "product offering".

Identifying these components can be difficult, because the emphasis placed on them differs from product to product.

> *Example* An Apple iPhone (being a strong brand) will probably have more emphasis and resource based on maintaining the brand integrity (intangible component) than, say, a Huawei equivalent. Huawei have manufactured mobile phones since 2003. In 2018 they launched their Mate 20 Pro as a direct competitor to Apple's iPhone X range. The Mate 20 Pro is packed with features, and their advertising directly contrasted these with the equivalent iPhone. In almost every measure, the Mate 20 Pro was ahead of the iPhone. The emphasis was on the features of the actual product (tangible components). The iPhone XR attracted new customers but was soon criticised on social media for suffering from charging problems. Image and usability are intangible attributes of the Apple brand that few can compete with. The tangible issue was addressed quickly; however, the intangible factors caused some damage to Apple's reputation.

A model used to develop a better understanding of products is the anatomy of a product (Figure 2.5).

Anatomy of a product

The core product refers to the actual function the customer derives from the product – for example, the core function of a car is transportation. This chimes with the aforementioned "attributes".

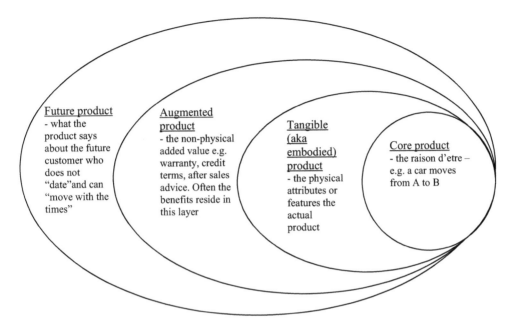

Figure 2.5 Anatomy of a product

Source: original diagram

The embodied (or tangible) product focuses on the physical features or delivered service. Marketers may refer to the Unique Selling Point (USP) of the actual product; for example, for a Dyson vacuum cleaner, the cyclone technology and the absence of needing a vacuum bag are all features of the product. Because products are highly visible, competitors may copy or imitate the physical features of a product. Companies may have to defend themselves with copyright protection. Dyson famously protect individual components and create three new patents per week. This is a prodigious effort.

The augmented product refers to the added value that customers take from products, such as the warranty, credit terms, after-sales advice and service. In many respects, this is a highly competitive level and requires much thought. Research has shown that 80% of failure to achieve repeat business from customers is attributed to factors at the augmented level. The augmented level is often where manufacturers seek to differentiate themselves. Think about Apple's image and perceived usability. These are sophisticated concepts and are therefore not easy to replicate.

The future product alludes to the wisdom of considering the future development of the product portfolio. Part of a marketer's responsibility is to consider the future, and as the customer needs and wants change, there is often a need to transform the existing product in a bid to "move with the times". Marketers must undertake research to gather feedback regarding the future level.

Applying the anatomy model provides a clearer view and understanding of the key issues that require consideration and resource. It is particularly useful when managing a portfolio of products and encourages marketers to reflect on the customer impact rather simply accepting a product and its features at face value.

Classifying goods

Marketers must understand how to classify their products. A better understanding of products can be used to support customers' reaching purchase decisions. The nature of decision-making varies, whether for individuals (B2C) or for organisations (B2B).

In the B2C market, products can be classified as follows:

- *Convenience goods* – require little time on the part of the consumer when purchasing them, owing to little risk financially, socially or personally associated with these goods: staple foods such as vegetables, bread, eggs and so on. The customer will usually purchase these products through "routine" or sheer habit.
- *Shopping goods* – require more time and effort by the consumer, because they incur an element of risk financially, personally and socially: a new kitchen suite, a new washing machine. This class of product would be associated with solving their "limited" problems (see Chapter 1).
- *specialty goods* – are often more luxurious goods for which consumers accept no substitutes. There is risk involved with these goods since they are often expensive. Branding is particularly important with these goods: designer clothing and expensive perfumes such as Chanel.
- *Unsought goods* – are goods for which consumers do not anticipate their needing them until either they are drawn to their attention (e.g. offers for double glazing being drawn to the attention of consumers via phone calls) or through unforeseen events: a flat tyre, burst pipes, a broken window and so on. These would be unsought goods, and customers will often be highly motivated to buy the goods quickly and may pay higher prices for a rapid solution of their problem.

In the business/industrial (B2B) markets, products are classified as follows:

- *Installations* – these are the central pieces of capital equipment, machinery or technology used in the production process. They are critical to the process and can be expensive.
- *Accessories* – These are also part of the production process but not necessarily central to it. They complement it and help create a smoother process – for example, office furniture.
- *Sub-assemblies* – These are the partly assembled products that B2B customers often want.
- *Raw materials* – Without these, consumer products would not be produced. The quality and timeliness of raw materials is incredibly important here. They are often supplied in large quantities.

Example   Nissan's Sunderland plant makes 500,000 cars annually and is regarded as one of the most efficient car plants in the world. They may want a supplier such as Hashimoto to supply a complete headlight assembly rather than the constituent components. This generates higher revenue and profit for Hashimoto; however, quality control is paramount here since any failures will affect the whole sub-assembly. Often original equipment manufacturers (OEMs), say the bulb manufacturer Lucas, will be happy to supply to the third party because the want to keep the end user (in this case Nissan) happy.

The Product Portfolio

Sustainable entrepreneurs who are founders often start a business with a single product. The entrepreneur can concentrate all of the marketing decisions on this product. Once the decision has been made to launch a second product, then new set of decisions are needed: which product is the most profitable and/or sustainable? At the other end of the spectrum are companies like Proctor & Gamble (P&G) who are a world-class provider of consumer products. P&G have no option other than to practice sound Product Portfolio Management.

The following are some of the key terms involved in product portfolios:

- Product mix – the total sum of all products and variants offered;
- Product line – a group of products that are closely related to each other, such as HP printers, laptops, desktop computers and so on;
- Product line length – the total number of items in the product line;
- Product line depth – the number of variants of each item in a product line;
- Product mix width – the number of product lines offered.

The details in Figure 2.6 were compiled from P&G's website, which is packed with useful information for the consumer. The brands are shown with the respective logos and a link is provided to each brand. Clearly, there are some interesting insights into P&G's portfolio. First, some product lines are obviously longer than others. Indeed, "Baby Care" features only one product: Pampers. The longest product lines feature six product ranges. Care must be taken in inferring from this that the Pampers provision is weak. It could be that it takes a substantial market share. Some products target different segments. Those that allude to luxury are targeted at socioeconomic groups with more disposable income. Some product lines have more cohesiveness: Feminine Care is tightly focused, whereas Personal Health Care ranges from pregnancy testing kits to fixing dentures and the long-established Old Spice. Old Spice is the only product range to feature in more than one product line. Clearly, P&G take a systematic approach to managing their portfolio. The benefits of this are being able to reduce or extend the portfolio in various ways:

- Introducing variations/models;
- Differentiating the quality;
- Developing associated items;
- Developing new products.

However, marketers must consider issues such as resource allocation, the expectations for each product, brand image and how to coordinate the marketing mix across the portfolio.

Product Life Cycle (PLC)

Professor Michael Baker argues that the Product Life Cycle (PLC) is a useful conceptual device that reminds marketing practitioners and academics of the inevitability of change (Baker, 2009). Indeed, the life cycle metaphor recognises that products, like human beings, are conceived, develop, are born, grow, mature, decline and ultimately

Product Mix Width

Beauty Care	Baby Care	Feminine Care	Fabric Care	Home Care	Personal Health Care	Grooming
Aussie Hair Care	Pampers Baby and Toddler Nappies/ Diapers, Pants/ Underwear and Wipes	Always Feminine Care Pads	Ariel Laundry Products	Ambi Pure Odour Eliminators	Clearblue Pregnancy and Ovulation Tests	Braun Personal Grooming
Head and Shoulders Anti-Dandruff Shampoo		Always Discreet Light, Sensitive Bladder Protection	Bold 2 in 1 Laundry Products	Fairy Dish Care	Fixodent Denture Adhesives	Gillette Razors and Skin Care
Herbal Essences Hair Care		Tampax Feminine Care Tampons	Daz Laundry Products	Febreze Odour Eliminators	Oral-B Toothbrushes and Dental Floss	Venus Razors and Shaving Gels
Olay Face and Skin Care			Fairy Non Bio Laundry Products	Viakal Kitchen and Bathroom Surface Care	Old Spice Hair and Skin Care	
SK-II Luxury Skin Care			Lenor Fabric Conditioner		Vicks Cough, Cold and Flu Relief	
Pantene Hair Care			Lenor Unstoppables In-Wash Scent Boosters			

Product line depth

Figure 2.6 Product line mix and depth applied to Proctor and Gamble

Source: adapted from P&G (2019)

die (ibid) – an honourable exception being Cadburys Dairy Milk, which has sold in largely the same format for over a hundred years. Therefore, it helps those managing product portfolios to understand how the stage of a product influences marketers' decisions regarding additional marketing-related activities.

Figure 2.7 shows a "generic" representation a PLC featuring five key stages:

Development: Marketers develop ideas or concepts and invest in them through research to see if they have any value. At this pre-launch position, there are no sales, but as can be seen, there is a financial burden resulting from investment in research, development, testing, communication, market analysis and building product prototypes. Meanwhile, the product is not generating any return on investment and is consequently running at a loss.

Introduction: If the research, testing and trials are successful, it may be decided to then launch the product into the marketplace. Post-launch, there are sales; however, they may be low initially since it often takes time for awareness of new products to filter through the marketplace. Some return is being generated; however, it is unlikely that enough products have been sold to cover the initial development costs.

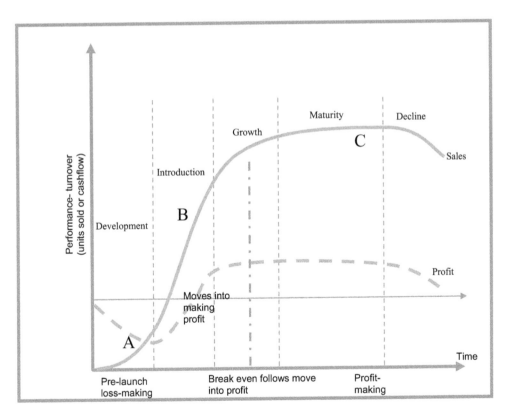

Figure 2.7 A generic Product Life Cycle (PLC)

Source: adapted from Rogers (1962)

Growth: As consumer awareness of the product grows, sales should increase at a higher rate. Herein, a profit is being generated, and the initial development costs are recovered until the product reaches the break-even situation. Growth cannot be assumed. Indeed, it will occur only if the consumer can take value from the product or service. Remember that value cannot be given. If enough customers take value, then the company should take market share. During *growth*, competitors will note its success and react by offering their own alternatives. There is always a reaction. If the product "has legs", the market may approach saturation where (akin to Darwinism) only those companies that can adapt will survive until the next generation is launched.

Maturity: Growth slows as the product approaches maturity. The market position can be maintained with reduced investment. The now-established product has a flatter sales line. The level of sales may still be high; however, newer, more contemporary, competitive products have entered the market. Profits, while still healthy, may be sacrificed to win sales. Many products spend most of their life in the maturity stage. Many marketing decisions relate to extending the maturity stage.

Example   Lucozade was traditionally a drink for children recovering from chicken pox and mumps and for ailing elderly people. Now rebranded with a re-launch featuring Daley Thomson and phrases such as "isotonic", it is a health drink for young athletes and sports people. This not only extended the maturity section but substantially increased sales. It is distributed intensively and is highly visible. Many vending machines on university campuses supply Lucozade, which would not have happened without the re-launch.

Inevitably, new variants or iterations will be needed since technological developments reduce the attractiveness of the original product, resulting in consumers switching their allegiance to the new offering. Care must be taken when launching the next iteration. Launching too early may lead to the cannibalisation of the current model; launch too late and sales may have dropped while opening the door for the competition.

Example   When Apple launched the iPhone X at $1000 per handset, eyebrows were raised as they were targeting a small, affluent segment with a PLC akin to a fad/fashion. Some thought this would open the door to competitors such as Samsung and Xiaomi. Clearly, Apple had enough demand to sell handsets at such premium prices. For several years, Samsung knocked them off the top spot; however, in mid 2018, Apple regained the global bestselling smartphone spot with the iPhone 8 (Counterpoint, 2018). Indeed, they were first (iPhone 8), third (iPhone X) and fifth (iPhone 8 Plus). In total, Apple had nearly 7% of the global market share but were by a long way the most profitable smartphone provider.

Smartphone manufacturers are increasingly working with systems integrators who incorporate the phone into their service. This is beyond a simple "app"; for example, medical instruments are increasingly using the mobile platform to enable practitioners to remotely monitor conditions such heart rate and blood pressure. This saves visits and patient stress by providing instant information.

Some marketers may try to extend the maturity stage, since their new products may not be ready to launch. There are a number of different ways to achieve this:

- Re-launch the product – update the product with, say, new colours or packaging to give it a renewed lease of life.
- Find new users for the product – rather than continuing to target a particular segment of customers, find any others, such as international markets. Many people now take aspirin because of its blood-thinning properties rather than simply curing a headache.
- Increase the usage/frequency of purchase – encourage consumers to use products more often by relating the benefits of repeatedly using the products (e.g. Sensodyne tooth paste claims that the more it is used, the greater the benefits).

Decline: As market conditions change, the product sales start to decline. In the face of stronger/younger/fresher/cheaper products, marketers must make several decisions:

- Whether to stay in the market (and strive to recoup more returns), which involves spending precious time, money and other resources on an old product;
- Whether to resource a newer, more competitive product;
- Whether to gracefully withdraw the product from the market.

The PLC as a coordinating tool

PLCs are getting shorter, and when launching new products, companies must penetrate the market as quickly as possible. There is little time to recoup development costs, break even or make a profit. Michael Baker argues that

> "the attraction of this diagnostic is that one can identify which elements of the marketing mix need greater or less attention in order to devise an effective marketing strategy for each stage of the life cycle".
>
> Baker (2009)

Indeed, the PLC can help coordinate other tools in the mix, such as marcomms. The comms mix will have to change as the product moves through its life cycle. Consider three scenarios, depicted in Figure 2.7:

Zone A A company is spending money developing and testing the product before releasing it. Here they would carry out research with prospects or users of existing models. For high-value products, the views of opinion formers could inform the early adopters. The research could be married to a mobile teaser campaign to raise awareness (while the research is ongoing).

Zone B A sports product has launched successfully, and the client wants to extend the rapid growth to recoup more R&D costs. Marketers could use social media or generate a mobile email campaign to involve users' clubs. Testimonials could help to explain the benefits that users reaped from the products.

Marketers could feed positive feedback via the mass media to inform their customer base (i.e. those clients who are still using their old models) of new developments.

Remember that advertising is expensive and that its impact may be diminished because people expect marketers to say good things about their own products. That said, they gladly accept the word of real customers or other opinion formers.

> **Zone C** It makes sense to maintain sales in the maturity section at high levels for as long as possible. This is known as extending the maturity section, and there are varying marcomms techniques that will help this. Marketers could use PR to explain the reliability of their products. Good feedback should be sought from third parties such social media sites, user fora or price-comparison websites. If possible, this PR should be seeded into the mass media, who are always eager to learn about a new angle.

To gain entry into a market with a brand-new product or indeed an existing product, marketers strive to recover the development costs and break even as quickly as possible before moving on to profitability.

> *Example*   A consultancy client who sells hubs and routers to the key UK Internet Service Providers (ISPs) argues that PLCs for his goods are now less than 12 months and approaching six months in some cases. This highlights the need for good relationships with clients based on regular, good-quality communications because a disgruntled client could simply skip a generation of products, with potentially devastating consequences.

Some alternative PLCs are shown in Figure 2.8.

"Staging" refers to knowing which stage the product is in and when it is moving from one to another. Marketers can check sales and profitability data, but there are many reasons for such increases or decreases. Consider a product that is subject to seasonality. As soon as the sales and/or profitability dip, this could be taken as a transfer from maturity to decline. But what if it is merely a seasonal blip? Marketers may take unnecessarily drastic action.

An underlying technology "wave" often supports a given product's PLC. The PLC of VHS recorders was irrevocably affected by the introduction of DVD, later by large-capacity internal hard disk technologies and most recently by web-based and streaming delivery. This creative destruction is discussed in more detail in Chapter 3.7.

In contrast, the delivery mechanism of toothpaste, the toothbrush, has evolved from manual to electric, vibrating and sonic, but many consumers still use paste-based products that their great-grand parents would recognise. The toothpaste market has fragmented from the basic product to include protection for gums, reduction in sensitivity and tooth whitening. These new lines have extended the maturity phase and also led to small growth curves in specific, specialised areas.

The PLC is not universally liked by marketers. That said, Michael Baker argues that it is a tool that can create Sustainable Competitive Advantage (SCA) and is still a useful theory, particularly for planning and analytical purposes. However, it does have a number of limitations:

- Every product is different, as is every related PLC.
- It is a gross oversimplification of the real life of a product.
- Not all products go through all of the stages.

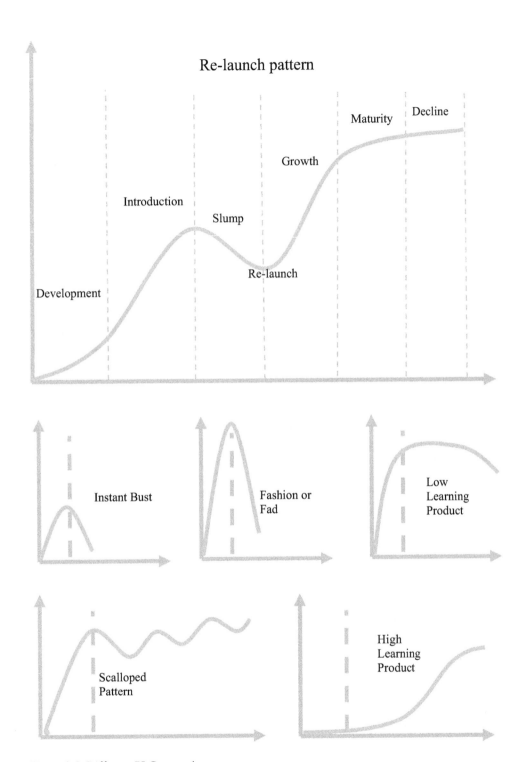

Figure 2.8 Different PLC scenarios

Source: adapted from Lambin (1996)

- A first iteration may receive a lukewarm reception, so version 2 may have to be rushed to market.
- Some products have short life cycles due to the input of further new technology into the product to update it, such as smartphones.
- It is difficult to understand when a product moves from one stage to another.
- It is somewhat inward and myopic since it neglects to consider external factors such as the macroenvironment, customers' changing needs and/or the competition.
- It cannot be used as a predictive tool.

Because the PLCs of many products are getting shorter, greater emphasis must be placed on good customer relationships based on regular, good-quality communications. Therefore, there is a need to penetrate the market quickly, raise awareness quickly and capture the hearts and minds of the customer before the competition does.

The Product Adoption Curve (aka the diffusion curve)

A technique that has helped marketing practitioners over the years is the product adoption process, sometimes known as the product diffusion curve (Figure 2.9).

This process attempts to explain how a product can be "adopted" or "diffused" (spread) throughout a marketplace efficiently. The process illustrates how consumers can be influenced by others and recognises that different types of adopters are not evenly spread out among society.

By adapting communications approaches, marketers could tailor their marcomms to use feedback from innovators to influence early adopters, who in turn influence the early majority. The innovators and early adopters could easily be knowledgeable opinion formers. Alternatively, early adopters could be opinion leaders, whose credibility could aid the diffusion of the message through networks and communities.

The discussion of product diffusion is largely B2C. The diffusion of new, disruptive technologies applies less in B2B segments. Geoffrey A. Moore in his enduring bestseller *Crossing the Chasm* indicated that the idea of different segments of the B2B market acting as advocates to the "next" group breaks down. This is what Moore calls "cracks in the bell curve".

Innovators (2.5%)	Early Adopters (13.5%)	Early Majority (34%)	Late Majority (34%)	Laggards (16%)
Young, professional, affluent, open-minded, risk taking and keen to experience new things. Opinion leaders and influencers. Highly motivated to try new goods.	Like innovators but with less social or technical standing and are therefore not as influential. Motivated to buy.	Slightly older demographic with less disposable income. Lower social standing and influence. Ambivalent.	Adopt products after accepted and tested by others. Risk averse. Lower disposable income or motivation to buy. Indifferent.	Oldest and most risk averse. Not risk takers. Tend to sit on the fence. Only buy products that are solidly tested and at lowest price point. Happy to wait or go without.

Figure 2.9 Product adoption curve or product diffusion curve

New Product Development (NPD)

Part of the repeating failure attributed to climate conventions (e.g. Copenhagen in 2009 or Paris in 2017) is largely due to a lack of understanding how consumers behave. The consumerism genie is out of the bottle and cannot simply be put back in. Western consumers are not ready or willing to make the changes necessary to return to pre-industrial levels of pollution or waste or by-products such as CO_2.

If products are not simply the toys of the well-off and are to permeate all societies, they need to be better, cheaper and greener. Technological advances may resolve many pressing issues (even global warming); however, there needs to be a shift towards replacing older, less-efficient products with newer, more-sustainable equivalents, whether they be cars, televisions, condenser boilers or mobile phones.

The world, the marketplace and customer needs are continually changing. Therefore, there is an ongoing need to create new products desired by consumers. Televisions today look very different and have many alternative features from those of 50 years ago. A 40" (100 cm) flat LED TV uses a quarter of the electricity of a 28" (70 cm) CRT equivalent. If companies produced the original version today, it would satisfy few customers. The same can be said of mobile technology. The first mobile phone (i.e. the Motorola Dyna TAC 8000X) was launched in 1983, weighing 1.1 kg, providing 30 minutes of talk time, taking ten hours to charge and costing nearly $4000. If mobile manufacturers from the 1980s still produced the same products today, they would not survive.

Conversely, a phenomenon with a different direction of travel was triggered by the 2007 global credit crunch. Companies adopted a back-to-basics approach, which targeted frugal buyers. Nokia re-launched their 3310 mobile phone in 2017. That said, it had new features such as a camera and a longer battery life and was nearly half the weight of the original, launched in 2000.

Some observers believe that the retail markets and subsequent buying habits have permanently changed. People are buying just enough rather than in excess. This notion of no frills "sufficiency" chimes with elements of sustainability. Tesco's introduction of its Harry's retail stores in 2018 is a direct consequence of the impact of the defection of their customers to discounters Aldi and Lidl. It is not just about FMCG. In the automotive sector, the Nissan-Renault's sub-brand Dacia has made a significant impact on Western European markets, so much so that the VAG Group (Volkswagen Audi) is actively considering launching its own sub-brand.

Some observers think that these "vfm" consumer durable brands represent a longer-term convergence of consumer needs and tastes that can be seen in developed and developing economies. It could be that consumers are no longer persuaded or driven by the promise of innovation in return for higher prices. Is this another side of "sustainable" consumption?

The first thing to remember about developing new products is that there are different risks associated it. Figure 2.10 shows how different types of new products can expose the company to different degrees of risk.

The following are some examples that fall onto the new-product risk continuum.

- **Innovative products:** The pharmaceutical/biotechnology-based industries are the key sectors where new products originate. Advances in mapping the human genome are leading to the development of new therapies. A great deal of research, development, testing, resources and time will have been spent on creating and developing these "new" products. They are initially high-risk ventures, but the

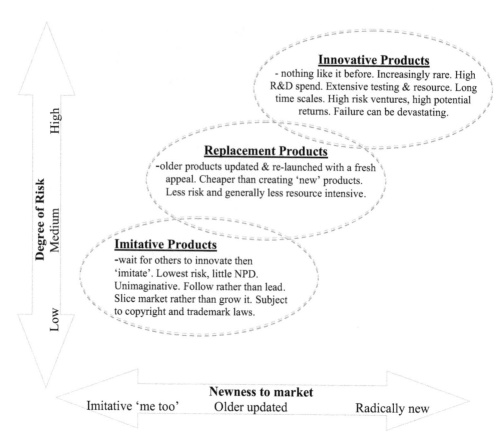

Figure 2.10 New-Risk Product Continuum

Source: Richardson, James and Kelley (2015)

returns can be phenomenal. Likewise, if they fail once launched into the market-place, they can have devastating effects on the investing organisation.

- **Replacement products:** Rather than perpetually creating new products, many companies update existing offerings. There is less risk associated with this approach and generally less resource demand. Manufacturers can take onboard comments from customers, stakeholders and publics.
- **Imitative products:** Dyson launched the first mass-market bagless vacuum cleaner with cyclone technology. Not long after, Hoover and Electrolux also launched respective bagless versions. Product-oriented organisations may wait for other companies to invest in their innovation and then imitate it post-launch. The inherent risk is that if the new product is successful, then rather than being the first to the market to capture the hearts and minds of the customer, imitative followers may be second or third and classed as a follower company. Being a follower can of course result in substantial sales – for example, in the energy drinks sector, Monster successfully followed Red Bull.

Being more systematic when developing new products should reduce risk and deliver products to market more quickly.

The NPD process

New products involve higher risks so in order reduce the number of failed "new" products, organisations have found it useful to create a systematic framework or process in which they develop them. This includes a number of steps, as shown in Figure 2.11.

Several issues arise from the NPD process. Focus groups are particularly useful in the product development stage because they can actually start to touch, use and feel the product as a physical prototype. Marketers can use "mocked up" pictures of products and ask the target audience what they think of the idea, shape, colour and design; how much they would be willing to pay for it; where they would go to purchase it; and so on. This feedback can be crucial to making the product launch successful.

At this stage and when developing the prototypes, marketers should be in advanced stages of designing the entire marketing strategy, the changes to the mix needed and how the changes will be controlled. All mix-related issues could be tested with focus groups, issues such as whether the product hit the correct price point, particularly when compared to the competition.

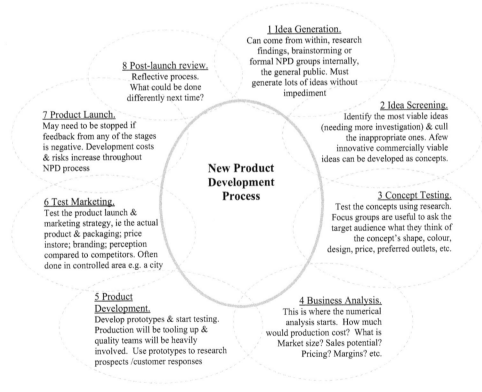

Figure 2.11 The NPD process

Source: adapted from Booz, Allen and Hamilton (1982)

If the target audience is unreceptive to the new idea, the options are to go back to the drawing board to redevelop the ideas or to abort the process altogether. Historically, some marketers, despite receiving negative feedback, pursued the development to the next stage because they believed they knew their brand better than the customer. Brand marketers are often subject to ritualistic or historical pressures: "We've always done it this way" (which is the refrain of many companies that go under).

Alternatively, for genuinely new product ideas, consumer "clinics" can produce false, negative results. The Sony Walkman was "new to the world" – that is, a game changer. However, in test marketing, consumers did not perceive a need for a portable music system which used headphones, so they reacted poorly to the concept. Sony ignored the results. Sony may be the exception to the rule, however. If prototypes are received warmly, marketers will have some sound data on which to move to the next step in the process.

The business analysis stage is typically the first-time price is seriously considered. Factors such as margins are considered and whether the new product is viable. Again, the choice is adapt or abort. The latter may be difficult, particularly if the prototype has been warmly received. Ultimately, throwing good money after bad is rarely a sound choice. However, if the new product seems commercially viable and marketable, continue to the next step.

Throughout the NPD process, marketers must be aware of the SPC (Standard Product Cost). Procurement and/or accounts teams should be involved in ensuring the latest costings are incorporated. The basic requirement of most pricing decisions is to cover the cost of the product. Furthermore, the marketer must liaise with senior management to ensure the margin of profitability fits with corporate objectives. This could be based on the individual requirement of the product or the product range, or it could be a historic judgement. Marketers must have a core understanding of all cost-related issues. The SPC is only one consideration; marketers must also consider the overall development cost and the payback period. As discussed earlier, the length of the PLC for many products is reducing, therefore creating less time to recover the initial development costs, cover the SPC and make a profit.

Test marketing is useful to "test" the entire marketing strategy in a controlled (i.e. less risky) fashion. Negative "test" feedback will provide room to address problems before launch. However, caution is needed because testing new products can compromise marketers if the competitors glean key information. They could tweak their own products, pricing or communications or even move a launch forward to steal some of the limelight.

Even though many companies use a process akin to NPD, many new products still fail in the marketplace. Kotler and Armstrong refer to research where of 25,000 new consumer food, beverage, beauty and healthcare products to hit the market each year, only 40% will survive five years. They cite another study that estimates that new consumer-packaged products (consisting of mostly line extensions) fail at a rate of 80%. New products fail for a variety of reasons.

NPD reduces risk, but launching a new product can never be a risk-free process. Every judgement call hinges on knowledge and skill. Using marketing agencies and consultants can often help in providing an objective perspective.

Moving through this process can take weeks, months and sometimes years to complete. Since the environment, marketplace and customers are constantly evolving, the goalposts are constantly moving, which creates a situation that is inherently difficult to manage.

Example   Lego Ideas is an online customer community where fans can submit ideas for a new Lego project. When over 10,000 members vote for the idea, Lego's marketing and design team assess whether it is a viable option. This is a unique take on NPD where fans provide not only the creative idea but also a degree of market analysis. Successful ideas become Lego sets and sell worldwide. Examples have included Lego Women of NASA, the TRON Legacy and the DeLorean from *Back to the Future*.

Although NPD is not easy to manage, it can be extremely rewarding if successful.

Barriers to good NPD

Many organisations fail to invest in research because it may be time consuming, resource intensive or expensive. Large organisations have the resources available, but many smaller organisations rely on intuition and current knowledge. To a certain extent, intuition should not be ignored, especially if the marketers have extensive experience in the field and marketplace. However, common sense also has to be used. Marketers must be wary when second-guessing decisions on behalf of potentially millions of customers. They must ensure that the research carried out throughout the process is collected and analysed correctly. If the data presented and analysed is flawed, the decisions based on this data also risk being flawed.

The failure to forecast and plan accordingly throughout the NPD process is a concern. Forecasting and projecting sales (among other things) is challenging, particularly when entering nascent, new or turbulent markets. Many organisations are overzealous with their future plans, offering wish lists rather than something predicated on sound research. Targets must be achievable. This is particularly problematic if investment is secured against planned targets.

Another key reason for NPD failure comes purely down to the mismanagement of the process. Many organisations lack the necessary systems for comprehensive NPD and stumble over one aspect to another. This may lead to (or indeed result from) communications breakdowns or misinformation. Management is based on knowledge, skills and attitude. Managers are often too proud to seek support from internal staff or third parties throughout the NPD process. Marketers must seek input from colleagues serving other functions, especially the sales department.

> *Example*　The advent of Web 2.0 has seen companies increasingly working together to develop new products. This has been based on shared communications, what some have called wikinomics. Companies such as Procter & Gamble, Oracle and Cisco seek user-generated feedback on products and ideas for new products. They increasingly use a mobile platform to enable dialogue. Cisco's I-zone encourages employees to submit ideas and even rewards non-employees with an I-prize for ideas. External perspectives can often remove hurdles when internal stakeholders cannot provide solutions.

Developing sustainable products

Sustainable ventures are often run by idealists, who may be more willing to launch innovative approaches and products (Hockerts and Wüstenhagen, 2010). The pursuit of sustainability ideals depends on the strength of the individual's intention to contribute to solving societal problems by realising a successful business (Schaltegger and Wagner, 2011). The development and launch of new sustainable products can generate success stories for organisations and create a real sense of achievement for those involved in its conception and development. Successful new sustainable products can do the following:

- Enhance an organisation's reputation and standing in the marketplace;
- Bring prominence to the brand;
- Increase revenues, profit and market share;
- Enhance customer satisfaction and build loyalty.

Choice editing

The shift towards sustainable consumption will influence the choices available to consumers. Choice editing increasingly takes place, which involves the manufacturers and/or retailers limiting the consumers' options. Manufacturers will be motivated to bias their product mix towards sustainability if they see long-term cost reductions or can access new ethical and/or green markets. Sometimes the choice editing will be imposed by government, as is the case with diesel cars being banned in the United Kingdom after 2030. Large manufacturers can develop hundreds of new products during the idea generation stage of the NPD process. These are reduced during the idea screening stage by using a range of filters. Sustainability has become one of these filters, with increasing significance.

Choice editing is not new. In 1995 the DIY store B&Q set a target for its timber to be certified sustainable by the Forest Stewardship Council (FSC) by 1999. Consumers at B&Q would be given the simple choice of buying sustainable timber (from B&Q) or shopping elsewhere. Some retailers prefer to offer sustainable and non-sustainable goods and leave the choice to the customer. This approach should not be denigrated, because in the long run, customers are becoming more ethical and green "savvy". In time, the non-sustainable options will be removed from the shelves. Sainsbury was among the first major retailers to offer pole and line caught tuna. The pole and line method inflicts much less damage on the marine environment and eradicates cast-off – that is, the catching of unintended fish that are returned to the sea, sometimes after perishing. Nowadays, most major retailers offer pole and line and often marine stewardship certification (MSC) as well.

Retailers have several motivations for choice editing. Markets fragmenting is one of the biggest challenges facing marketers. There may be hundreds of, say, domestic appliances, but a retailer may want to stock only the 20 bestsellers. Because electrical appliances are now rated for their power consumption, consumers are increasingly aware that their electricity bills can be reduced substantially over the lifetime of the product. Hence, retailers will increasingly stock A-rated appliances. Some of the shifts are driven by technology; for example, retailers made a conscious decision to stop stocking old-fashioned CRT televisions and adopted flat screen variants. These are easier to transport and display, and as a by-product, they use less electricity. DVD players have been dropped by most retailers as consumers increasingly use streaming services. Some may retain niche products such as Blu-ray recording units. These are high-value specialty purchases, whereas DVD players were low cost, almost routine purchases sought largely by laggards.

2.4 Cost to consumers (aka Price)

Cost (to customers) is preferred to "price", as customers experience sacrifices to buy goods. They understand what the cost is to them, seek value for money and often need to justify making a financial sacrifice. This represents a particular challenge for marketers, because there are many different factors to balance.

Pricing is an important variable of the mix for several reasons:

- It is the only variable in the mix that creates revenue.
- It is of strategic importance since it is highly visible to senior management.
- It connects the customer to the supplier.
- It conveys the quality and exclusivity to the marketplace.
- It is highly visible to consumers.
- Successful pricing can establish competitive advantages, whereas poor pricing can lead to customer attrition, poor profitability, longer break-even periods, reduced customer satisfaction and even reduced employee morale.

Pricing perspectives

Many academics refer to the three perspectives of pricing: the economist's perspective, the accountant's perspective and the marketer's perspective. These perspectives are credible from a professional point of view and illustrate how pricing can be viewed by different stakeholder mindsets.

The accountant's perspective: Pricing should fall under the domain of the marketing team; however, in some organisations, it is determined solely by accountants. The problem with this approach is that it requires long-term monitoring, but accountants do not monitor the marketplace, customer requirements/needs, the competition or wider environmental forces. Yet all of these affect the pricing of products and services.

That said, accountants play a key role in setting correct prices, and this is one of the challenges of creating a successful pricing policy. Indeed, good pricing may result only from involving other functions. Involving them in the process is preferable to alienating them.

The economist's perspective: This is founded upon the forces of supply and demand. Simply put, where demand equals supply, a price will be created. However, if supply and/or demand fluctuate, so will the price.

Example Petrol is always one of the most visible examples of pricing. Consumers see the price per litre every day and are sensitive to fluctuations in the petrol market. This sensitivity led to supermarkets entering the market and changing the dynamics of the petrol market. Petrol prices are "set" by the market – that is, the city. Prices (usually expressed in dollars per barrel) are affected by (perceptions of) the supply of oil and petrol, which can be affected by outbreaks of war, threats of terrorism, reduction of UK refining capacity and the malfunction of pipelines. While demand has levelled out in the United Kingdom, it is growing in countries like China. The price is inevitably being pushed higher. Meanwhile, in the United States, there has been an oversupply of gas due to their exploitation of shale gas. This has led to a dramatic fall in the price of gas for US consumers.

The marketer's perspective: Herein, the customer is the focus. How much is the customer willing to pay? Marketers undertake research to determine this issue, such as by using focus groups to show the prospective customer the product and its competition and asking them to determine the prices. It is often a useful way to gain insight into the mindset of the customer.

In reality, all three perspectives offer something of value. If organisations primarily use one of these perspectives, they may fail in the long term. Pricing is a balancing act, and elements of all three perspectives should be used. There are, however, a large number of balancing factors that come into play:

- Customers;
- Competitors;
- Costs;
- Corporate and marketing objectives.

> **Customers:** How much is the customer willing to pay? How much will they demand at a certain price? Marketers who have undertaken research regarding pricing will be better situated to set prices, particularly if the information is up to date and accurate.

In the B2B market, the situation is slightly different because marketers usually have a closer relationship with professional customers and because there are fewer of them. However, getting the pricing correct the first time is still important. Marketers must use research to focus on ascertaining the pricing points. However, as always, not all organisations have the time and resources to do this.

> **Competitors:** Marketers must reflect on how their brand compares to the competition. Can it command a higher price? Is the brand worth more to the customer than the competitor's? As part of a marketing audit (see Chapter 3), marketers will conduct a competitor analysis to take a holistic view of the market. They need to know how their brand is perceived by customers when compared to the competition.
>
> **Costs:** Creating a product or service incurs costs. Quite simply, marketers usually need to cover costs when setting prices. Costs are made up of fixed costs (e.g. capital, buildings, plant, leases, etc.) and variable costs (e.g. raw materials, casual labour, fuel, etc.). This necessitates marketers having a good grasp of costs to be able to offer ROI and Return on Capital Employed (ROCE) assessments (see Chapter 4).
>
> **Corporate and marketing objectives:** Pricing can be used strategically. Hence, the pricing of products and services should be compatible with corporate objectives. In a small company that is struggling to survive, perhaps there is a problem with cashflow and/or liquidity. Here manipulating the pricing can be used strategically, such as by setting it to just cover costs but still compete against and undercut the competition, creating a volume of sales and hence rapid cashflow and

liquidity for the business. Therefore, before creating actual price points, marketers must be fully aware of current organisational circumstances and objectives.

Trying to take all these factors into consideration is difficult. Imagine calculating all of the costs for a product or service and then analysing the competition, their offerings and setting a price accordingly. A sales price (e.g. £100) is set, and the margin being sought is 20% (or £20). But what if the customer is not willing to accept that price? What if they see less value in the offering and suggest lowering prices? If a marketer relents and lowers the price by £10, this does two things: First it puts the brand head to head with the established competition, which may be good from a positioning point of view. Second, however, assuming all costs remain the same, the new price has halved the margin. Questions would be raised as to whether the organisation should have launched a new product if the marketer anticipated only a 10% gross margin.

Once marketers have a sound understanding of the cost mechanisms, the competitive offerings, the requirements and willingness of the customer and the circumstances of the organisation, they need to decide on the pricing technique to be used to enter the marketplace.

Pricing techniques

There are a variety of techniques that can be used to price products/services accordingly. They each have advantages and disadvantages.

Cost plus pricing is a relatively easy and flexible technique to use. Calculate the total cost of producing one product, and add the required margin to calculate the price. Little or no skill is necessary to use this technique, but it is inwards looking, purely looking at the cost base of the product. What about the customer, environmental factors and the competition?

Going rate pricing is another easy and flexible approach to pricing. Analyse the competition and their offerings and prices. If a brand is as good as the competition's or f the marketer prefers to maintain stability in the marketplace, they may decide to take "the going rate" – the price charged by the competitor(s). However, if the offering is superior to the competition (e.g. a more powerful brand name with additional features and benefits), the decision may be taken to set the price above the competition's. This is called premium pricing. If after analysing the marketplace, the offering is perceived to offer less value than the competition's offering, then the decision may be to set a lower price. This is known as discount pricing.

Market skimming involves entering the market with a high price and then as the product/service matures and more innovative products move into the marketplace, the price lowers towards the going rate. Many "tech" products use this approach. Think about the PLC of a mobile phone: it is incredibly short because new technology is continually being used to update features. Therefore, the time that the manufacturer has to recover developmental and capital costs is short.

Market penetration is the opposite of market skimming. This is where an organisation chooses to price their offering lower than the competition to gain entry to the marketplace. As the brand becomes better known, the prices increase towards the going rate. This is a useful technique to use for new products, and the marketer is seeking to give the customer a reason to choose their product/service over the competition's, which may be more established. It is also a useful technique to sell large quantities. Market penetration also creates entry barriers to new entrants because of the relatively low price set.

As mentioned earlier, pricing is also a signal to customers and competitors about issues such as quality and exclusivity. It can therefore be assumed that pricing can influence customers "psychologically". Two such techniques are called "odd" and "even" pricing.

Even pricing involves customers' psychological perceptions about prices. They perceive even figures, such as £5, £10, £100, as being better quality than those set at "odd" prices, such as £1.99, £9.99, £99.99. Odd pricing is used because customers tend to round prices down when telling others rather than rounding up – for example, a new pair of jeans may have cost of £49.99 and people will often tell others they cost £40 rather than £50.

Quality providers (e.g. Mark's and Spencer's) generally use even prices to convey the notion of quality or at least the need to avoid such discount techniques. Pricing points need to be set carefully. Marketers will need to draw on a range of sources to be able to start creating the necessary price point. Ultimately, a price point is a judgement call, and prices must be monitored constantly. The nature of the monitoring will depend on the nature (and size) of the organisation, the marketplace and business environment.

Technology and pricing

Increasingly, smartphones are used as a means of payment. International payment provider Paysafecard was formed in 2000, and by 2007 it had accrued more than ten million first-time transactions. By 2017 it claimed to be used by over 650,000 sales outlets, in 26 currencies and 46 countries. In the United Kingdom, it teamed up with British Telecom to enable mobile users to buy online goods and services with the fee simply being charged to their mobile bill. This payment mode (and new entrants into the market) are likely to increase, particularly among the younger generations, who are becoming increasingly "cashless". Marketers should always make it easy for customers to spend their money, and such technology should be incorporated into marcomms messages and processes when appropriate.

Where there is little differentiation between products, consumers are increasingly using smartphone "apps" to make price comparisons. In scanning the Web, these sites may direct consumers to disreputable providers. Since security is an increasing concern, marketers need to ensure that their site is recognised as being secure and displays the padlock symbol. Prospects and consumers should be encouraged to engage with suppliers before buying, as this step will often be beyond the capability of unscrupulous providers. Some sites (e.g. www.trustpilot.co.uk) aggregate reviews into one score.

Vouchers and cashback

Increasingly, consumers are looking to online discount and voucher providers like myvouchercodes.co.uk. These sites offer promotional codes, often for online-only providers. The offers are often store-specific, not necessarily the cheapest and usually time stamped. Marketers must ensure that prospects and returning customers are aware of the benefits on offer as the competition prices may be lower but not necessarily better Value For Money (VFM).

Consumers will complement vouchers with cashback deals from sites such as www. quidco.com and www.topcashback.co.uk, which use sales from familiar online stores. The amounts clawed back vary, as do the times to payment (in some cases, it can be months). So again, make sure the product offer is well represented, and be aware of the negative publicity of cashback schemes that go awry.

Smartphone users are often involved with communities who generate a pool of advice that prospects and community members can access. For example, www.hotuk-deals.com is a case were "best" deals can be found supported by real-life advice, which is often up to date and impartial. At least, they are perceived to be more impartial.

Sustainable pricing

Developing a more-sustainable economy will require costs associated with sustainability being factored into markets and their prices. This can happen through voluntary actions or through additional taxation (such as a carbon tax on fossil fuels). Pricing can be used to "demarket" harmful products such as cigarettes or scarce or finite products like fossil fuels (cfsd, 2019). Developing more-sustainable markets may also require a switch in emphasis away from the purchase price of a product towards the lifetime cost of owning and using it. This would encourage the design, purchase and consumption of products with greater energy efficiency and longevity (ibid).

2.5 The Services Mix

One of the major world trends in recent years has been the dramatic growth of services. Services are now the major driver of many economies. This is due to rising affluence, more leisure time and the growing complexity of products that require servicing. The following are some examples of services:

- Teaching, tutoring and mentoring;
- Using price-comparison or cashback websites;
- Travelling;
- Renting a hotel room;
- Online banking;
- Legal representation.

Clearly, the core "product" is intangible.

Services marketing is based on the notion that there is more to service than being served.

Clearly, consumers seek benefits from service encounters (Figure 2.12). That said, some issues arise with services:

- Some (services) are "unsought" in that customers may be unaware of their need until a problem arises.
- Not all consumers can clearly articulate their needs and may become frustrated.
- A consumer cannot test (the service) before purchase, so there is a degree of risk.

Services take place in the "task environment", where specific attributes influence consumers' decision-making. The attributes can reflect tangible characteristics (such

Sought benefit	Factors to be measured
Reliability	Right the first time; consistency (billing, branding, timing)
Competence	Required skills; abilities
Courtesy	Respect; friendliness; politeness
Communication	Information; avoiding jargon
Credibility	Trustworthiness; believability; honesty; acting in best interests of client
Security	Risk; danger; doubt; uncertainty
Understanding	Leaning customer requirements; consistency
Access	Approachability; ease of contact; opening times
Responsiveness	Employee willingness; readiness; prompt service

Fig 2.12 Benefits sought in service encounters

Source: adapted from Parasuraman et al. (1985)

as spaciousness or layout) or more abstract psychological concepts (such as ambience, cleanliness and staff friendliness). Sustainable attributes can include standards, information, authenticity and environmental quality. These can create differentiation between competitors. However, consumer satisfaction is missing from many sustainability studies. The effectiveness of communicating standards or authenticity influences sustainable consumption.

All interactions or "touchpoints" (between service providers and customers) in the customer's "journey" provide opportunities to be perceived in a positive or negative way. Before the "journey" begins, the customer has already built up expectations, and after it, they reflect on the degree to which they were delighted. This reflection can seriously affect customer satisfaction, WoM, repeat business and so on. A "servicescape" comes into being when a heightened consumer focus is imposed on the (purely operational) task environment. Those who study the servicescape are concerned with the co-creating experiences between marketers, customers, prospects and consumers. Upon entering a servicescape, people immediately make judgements as to whether they feel welcome.

Services marketing versus marketing services

Companies often sell warranties for potentially long-lasting goods. The product is tangible, whereas the warranty is intangible and sold (often lucratively) to the client. This is marketing a service. Where the core "product" is a service, such as online banking, the company engages in services marketing. Online banking is worthy of mention as the Cooperative's "Smile" service consistently achieves the highest levels of customer satisfaction. Often just followed by First Direct. It is interesting that First Direct consistently out-perform their parent company HSBC in customer satisfaction.

Not all services have the same degree of customer involvement. A visit to a bank's ATM has a higher degree of involvement than accessing an account online. They are still relatively low involvement encounters. Buying a Groupon voucher for a massage is low involvement, whereas the massage itself involves a high degree of involvement. Clearly, the degree of involvement affects the level of customer expectations. This does not mean that customers are happy if the ATM is empty. And as Herzberg advises, refilling the empty ATM will not improve customer motivation. If something has gone wrong, simply putting it right does not automatically increase customer motivation. They expect it to be right in the first place. That said, those companies that strive to correct their mistakes and then deliver the expected levels of services may benefit from the service recovery paradox – that is, they may experience increased loyalty as customers have seen the lengths to which the company will go. To achieve this, it is necessary to consider the characteristics of a service.

Characteristics of services

Services have several characteristics that differentiate them from goods manufacturing:

- **Intangibility** affirms that services cannot be seen, tasted, felt, heard or smelled before they are bought – for example, people undergoing cosmetic surgery cannot see the result before the purchase.
- **Inseparability** alludes to services being inseparable from the providers, whether said providers are people (e.g. lecturers, hairdressers or doctors) or machines (e.g. cash dispensers).
- **Perishability** recognises that services, unlike goods, cannot be stored for later sale or consumption. A missed flight or doctor's appointment represents missed opportunities for both parties. Some doctors have started charging for missed appointments (with 250 million GP (family doctor) appointments in the United Kingdom each year, if even 1% of visits are missed, it can have a costly effect). So a key challenge for service providers is matching supply to demand.
- **Variability** (sometimes referred to as heterogeneity) acknowledges that the quality of the service depends on the person providing it and is therefore variable. This also extends beyond those delivering services to include when, where and how those services are provided. If a company suffers from unacceptable levels of variability, the solution lies in standardisation, motivation and/or training. Training is always essential, and marketers must pay particular attention to their relationship with their peers in HR. Recruiting, training and motivating staff is fundamental to marketing success. Employees need to be motivated to change their behaviour.
- **Ownership** – or, more accurately, non-ownership – refers to customers *not* owning services. Rather, they pay to secure access to the service. Car rental companies allow full use of the car but the ownership of the car remains with them. iTunes transformed music downloading by taking it to the masses. However, the consumer does not own the music; rather, they own the right to play the music under certain conditions.

The Extended Marketing Mix for services

Marketers increasingly use the extended marketing mix for services. where the traditional marketing mix is complemented by People, Process and Presence.

The extended marketing mix is widely accepted, and many commentators argue that the people element is the most important element therein. That said, the people element of the mix is problematic when interacting online. Marketers must avoid making the service too robotic, standardised and soulless.

With people being common to The Mix *and* the Triple Bottom Line, it is difficult to comprehend why sustainability has been largely ignored in the marketing domain for so long. Key sources of conflict include motivation, the lack of communication and "stepping on others' toes" or demarcation.

Although there are a number of internal influences in the DMP (see Chapter 1.5), the one that clearly is linked to people is motivation. It is wrong to assume that one approach to motivation fits all. After all, customers who are highly motivated will arguably pay any price. Jackson (2005) argued that people have several motivations:

- To know and understand what is going on;
- To learn, discover and explore;
- To participate and play a role in what is going on around them.

These states have several consequences that directly affect marketers:

- Customers hate being disoriented or confused.
- They prefer acquiring information at their own pace.
- They prefer answering their own questions.
- They hate feeling incompetent or helpless.

Clearly, the issue of communicating effectively with *people* is paramount. Consumers are not always willing actors in the consumption process, often finding themselves "locked into" making purchases beyond their control. This undoubtedly drives anti-marketing sentiments and unsustainable consumption. It is wrong to assume that consumers are passive. The sensible approach for marketers is to assume that consumers are free to choose and can easily switch suppliers.

Changes to regulations and legislation increasingly seek to make it easier for consumers to "switch". UK energy providers and financial services companies have had to react to imposed changes. Arguably, if consumers know they can switch service providers easily, they will feel more in control. Ironically, this could make them less likely to switch, all other things being equal. A way to avoid such dissatisfaction is to promote their sense of co-creating value or promote value seeking in customers. Either way, the consumer must feel *involved*.

Many service providers use *Process* to achieve a competitive advantage. They seek to make customers lives easier by providing services that are quicker, more flexible, safer, more consistent and easier and that come with lower risk. Process focuses on consumption in relation to services and digital technology, which have offered a lot in improving the customer experience. Governments are investing in *process* and are achieving considerable savings by moving online. In the United Kingdom, consumers no longer have to possess a physical TV licence. They pay online after the government sends a reminder before expiry. The cost and the carbon footprint of producing hard-copy licences have been removed.

Process *online* alludes to interaction and engagement with websites, social media, email and messaging. Marketers must consider the user experience (UX) when developing web content and the customer touch points, which must be (perceived to be) quick, easy and efficient. Marketers must ensure that their mobile site is easy to use. Smartphone users are demanding improved experiences, and sensible market-ers always aim to make it easy for customers to spend their money. Mobile sites are increasingly efficient, and marcomms are becoming more effective as users buy with-out delay. Many users have their phones with them 24/7, which has driven the growth of the Black Friday phenomena.

Operations are a key element of process. They have to keep pace with customer changes; however, some managers lack customer centricity and have elevated opera-tional effectiveness to being the key route to superior profitability (Porter, 1996). This is remiss, because without a clear understanding of customer needs, it may be impos-sible to make the necessary operational changes. What is needed is not change for its own sake but the *right* change, and many examples now exist of companies that have moved towards TBL practices (see DJSI, 2019).

Traditionally, The Extended Marketing Mix uses the phrase 'Physical Evidence'; however, it is inappropriate when considering the digital (i.e. virtual) nature of mod-ern marketing, where The term 'Presence' is preferred. A company's digital presence increasingly represents the company, its brands and its values to stakeholders. So eve-rything online (be it mobile, social, corporate website or anything else digital) must accurately represent the company and brand. Setting standards for logos, text, design, layout and similar facets all help to ensure a coordinated and seamless experience from the customer's perspective.

Example   After the ISPs and search engines, one of the world's most visited sites is the BBC. With their iPlayer service, they are able to stream shows around the world. "Banded" TV schedules are becoming a thing of the past. Look at the enormous amount of content streamed, by the BBC, of the Glastonbury festi-val. They send a team of over 300 people to Glastonbury and not only provide highlights on three terrestrial channels and cover it extensively on FM and digital radio stations but also stream every "set" in its entirety via iPlayer. They have moved inexorably towards offering a platform where voice, data, TV and mobile (known in the trade as quad play) interact seamlessly. This degree of interoper-ability is a sign of things to come.

All actions, communications and presence online provide a digital manifestation of the brand. All of the other elements of the mix must help to establish the presence. The following are some practical steps for websites to take:

- Segment contacts by heavy or light smartphone usage, time slots, information seekers and whether users can be identified as mobile email readers.
- Seek permission and use Bluetooth to highlight bargains when users are within range.
- Send time-related messages when most likely to complement their behaviour, such as when people are leaving work to remind them to stop on the way home.
- Keep messages short so that they are easily read on mobile phones.
- Provide notices, e-vouchers and regular (say monthly) newsletters, which must be suitable for computers, tablets and mobile devices.
- Be willing to provide support to extend the product's life, or provide information to repair/repurpose/recycle the product.

Service quality

Like value, service quality resides in the mind of the customer. Consumers' perceptions of how well a service meets or exceeds their expectations inform their decision-making. There are three elements that determine service quality experience: technical, functional and expectational (Gronroos, 1984). Technical alludes to aspects of the service, such as waiting times for trains; functional refers to how well the service is delivered, such as a friendly or professional delivery; and expectational refers to managing the expectations of the customer and staff delivering the service. Some customers have unrealistic expectations – some of which can be met, whereas others cannot. Malcolm McDonald warns against seeking to delight customers to such an extent that the company is no longer profitable. These elements are sometimes referred to as the triangle of quality perception.

Competitors can use service quality to differentiate their offering from their competitors' offerings. It can drive customer loyalty and satisfaction. Marketers must recognise that customer satisfaction and loyalty are not the same thing. Satisfaction is an attitude, whereas loyalty is behavioural. As mentioned previously, there is more to services than merely being served, particularly if companies seek to create loyalty.

Marketers must measure the service quality. There are two widely used models to measure service quality: SERVQUAL and EFQM.

Parasuraman et al. (1985) developed SERVQUAL (Figure 2.13) to identify customer service gaps between the management's and customers' perceptions of service delivery.

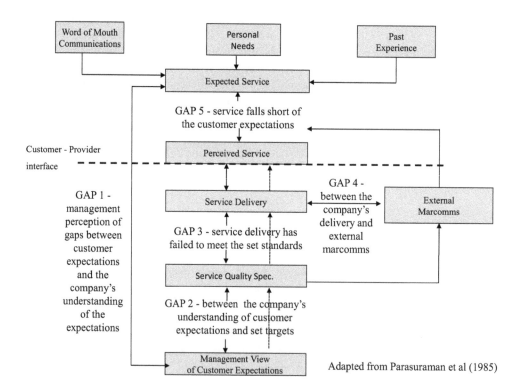

Figure 2.13 SERVQUAL: the gaps model of service

The gaps model of services encourages companies to develop organisational objectives and tactics in order to close the gaps (ibid). The following are some of the approaches to closing the specific gaps:

- **Gap 1** – hold regular team meetings and briefings to ensure they are customer focused;
- **Gap 2** – improve interaction between management and staff to establish realistic targets for staff;
- **Gap 3** – use internal marketing techniques to ensure customer-facing staff are clear on their roles, targets and expectations;
- **Gap 4** – service delivery standards need to be maintained and improved while managing customer expectations;
- **Gap 5** – ensure the highest levels of customer service are achieved and a customer-centric approach is adopted.

Service quality *can* be measured, but it is difficult. Being able to measure it will depend on learning more about the clients through marketing research, focusing on their expectations and perceptions. Marketers should adapt the mix to provide consistently high-quality services (Figure 2.14). Any changes to service design and delivery

Service Mix	SERVQUAL Components and Questions	Suggestions
Process	Reliability Can the company perform the service, accurately, dependably and consistently? Does the delivery "fit" the instructions given?	Set agreed, quantifiable, attainable standards for service delivery to create systems to measure and monitor success
People	Responsiveness Can the company offer a timely service that meets customers' expectations? Empathy Does the company focus on the individual? Assurance Does the company convey trust and confidence?	Establish clients' requirements Analyse internal implications – e.g. training needs, restructuring Develop training programmes Determine client care objectives Ensure adequate internal education and communication Consider performance-related pay and recognition systems Set up/revise systems for service delivery
Presence (Physical Evidence)	Tangibles Does the company project itself in a professional manner?	Ensure that the look and feel of tangible attributes (offices, cars, reception etc.) are excellent Create a culture where staff want to present themselves in the best possible manner Ensure online presence is easy to find, navigate and monetise

Figure 2.14 The extended services mix and SERVQUAL

Source: original diagram

should take place in a coordinated manner. Hence, it is appropriate to reflect on how such changes (among others) should be planned.

Top ten findings

1 Marcomms campaigns need to be developed with the customer journey in mind. The comms mix needs to be integrated into a seamless, consistent experience from the customers' perspectives.
2 The role of convenience is particularly important, involving getting the right products to the right place at the right time in the right condition. Failure to do so can result in customer dissatisfaction.
3 Key reasons for using intermediaries include their skills, knowledge and access to markets. Increasingly, organisations are seeking to green their supply network, such as by reducing carbon footprints, reducing waste, lowering emissions and so on.
4 Logistics includes decisions related to warehousing: number, size and location, transportation, internal ordering systems and so on.
5 A product is more complex than initially considered, and it is formed on the basis of both tangible and intangible factors. Consumer and industrial goods can be categorised.
6 The PLC is a traditional theory highlighting that products have lives. Although the PLC is useful, it has its limitations. The adoption/diffusion curve identifies subsets of customers who may help diffuse the product and support acceptance among the majority of potential customers.
7 Introducing new products can help organisations remain competitive, increase profitability, sales, market share, customer satisfaction and loyalty. Developing new products involves risks. The NPD process systematically guides marketers through a more-controlled and better-organised process of developing new ideas and subsequent products.
8 Customers experience sacrifices to buy goods and understand what the cost is to them. Pricing connects with customers' values, such as their value for money, quality, exclusivity and so on.
9 Many factors have to be taken into consideration when setting prices: the costs, the competition, customer motivation, corporate objectives and any legal and/or regulatory issues. It is easy to lower prices; however, raising prices presents marketers with one of their greatest challenges.
10 Service industries are growing and are a major driver for economic growth. Service quality can be used to achieve competitive advantage. Marketers must establish clients' requirements and then set internal standards for service delivery.

Ten activities

1 Search for press relations pages and different sites to see what types of information they provide and how they provide it. Here are a few examples:

- www.tate.org.uk/about/press-office
- www.bbc.co.uk/mediacentre/
- www.hsbc.com/news-and-insight/media-resources

2 Conduct some research online into social media "fails" – examples of organisations having tried to implement online campaigns via social media with no success. What brought about failure? Are there common mistakes? Hashtag campaigns on Twitter such as #McDStories can be a good starting point.

3 Imagine you are developing a newer, fresher version of a household product. Using the NPD process, write down what is involved in each of the steps.

4 Classify some recently bought goods. Are they convenience products, shopping goods or specialist goods? Were they unsought? How could the categorisation inform the DMP, as discussed in Chapter 1?

5 It is worth visiting exhibitions, seeing the products and taking part in seminars. One such UK show is the Technology for Marketing show (see www.t-f-m.co.uk).

6 Sketch out the PLC for a product, and consider the steps needed to extend the maturity stage. How could the tools from the extended marcomms mix be used?

7 The Sustainable Marketing Knowledge Network (Smart: Know-Net) is an online resource that exists to bring together the worlds of marketing and sustainability. As a business discipline, marketing has a tremendous influence over the environmental and social impacts of businesses and their products, policies and production processes (www.cfsd.org.uk/smart-know-net/).

8 Visit www.jeffbullas.com/2012/07/18/10-social-media-personas-understanding-personality-and-communication/ and consider the ten different social media personas. How accurate are they in their portrayal of real-life identities? What different types of communication approaches and messages would suit the different personas?

9 To learn about PR's role in marcomms, analyse information about practitioner responsibilities by studying the jobs pages of PR week and the media supplement of the *Guardian* newspaper. Both have websites with job advertisements and a list of specifications for practitioners as well as salary guides.

10 Representative bodies provide a wealth of information. The following have a PR focus:

- The Chartered Institute of Public Relations (see www.cipr.co.uk);
- The Public Relations and Communications Association (see www.prca.org.uk);
- MediaUK (see www.mediauk.com);
- The European Public Relations Confederation (see www.cerp.org/);
- The Science, Technology, Engineering and Medicine Public Relations Association (see www.stempra.org.uk/).

References

Baker, M. (2009). Aided Recall and Marketing Mnemonics Guest Lecture presented By Professor Michael Baker to Leeds Business School November 2009.

cfsd (2019). Pricing & distribution. Available at: www.cfsd.org.uk/smart-know-net/links/pricing.htm [Accessed 6 Feb. 2019].

CIPR (2019). Definition of PR. Available at: www.cipr.co.uk/content/about-us/about-pr. [Accessed 9 Feb. 2019].

Counterpoint (2018). Top selling smartphones – Apple regains the global best selling smartphone spot with the iPhone 8. Online article. Available at: www.counterpointresearch.com/global-best-selling-models-may-2018/ [Accessed 21 Sept. 2019].

DJSI (2019). Dow Jones Sustainable Indices website. Available at: www.robecosam.com/csa/indices/?r [Accessed 21 Sept. 2019].

Gronroos, C. (1984). A service quality model and its marketing implications. *European Journal of Marketing*, 18(4), pp. 36–44.

Hockerts, K. and Wüstenhagen, R. (2010). Greening Goliaths versus emerging Davids – theorizing about the role of incumbents and new entrants in sustainable entrepreneurship. *Journal of Business Venturing*, 25(5), pp. 481–492.

Howell, R. (2006). Global trade and sustainable development: complementary or contradictory? Paper for Corporate Responsibility Research Conference. July 2006. Dublin. Available at: http://crrconference.org [Accessed 20 Feb. 2008].

Jackson, T. (2005). Motivating sustainable consumption- a review of evidence on consumer behaviour and behavioural change; a report to the Sustainable Development Research Network January 2005. Funded by the Economic and Social Research Council's Sustainable Technologies Programme (STP).

Katz, E. and Lazarsfeld, P.F. (1955). *Personal influence: the part played by people in the flow of mass communications*. New York: Free Press.

P&G (2019). Brands – Iconic brands you can trust in your home. Available at: www.pg.co.uk/brands/[Accessed 26 Jan. 2019].

Parasuraman, A., Zeithaml, V.A. and Berry, L.L. (1985). A conceptual model of service quality and its implications for future research. *The Journal of Marketing*, 49(4) (Autumn, 1985), pp. 41–50.

Porritt, J. (2005). *Capitalism as if the world matters*. London: Earthscan.

Porter, M.E. (1996). What is strategy? *Harvard Business Review*, 74(6) (November–December), pp. 61–78.

Schaltegger, S. and Wagner, M. (2011). Sustainable entrepreneurship and sustainability innovation: Categories and interactions. *Business Strategy and the Environment*, 20(4), pp. 222–237.

Schramm, W. (1955). How communication works. In: W. Schramm, ed., *The process and effects of mass communications*. Urbana, IL: University of Illinois Press, pp. 3–26.

Shannon, C.E. and Weaver, W. (1949). *The mathematical theory of communication*. Urbana, IL: University of Illinois Press.

Tilley, F. and Young, W. (2009). Sustainability entrepreneurs – could they be the true wealth generators of the future? *Greener Management International*, (55), pp. 70–92, Greenleaf Publishing.

3 Sustainable Marketing Planning

Abstract

This Chapter will reflect on how marketing planning can be sed to drive the adoption of sustainable practices. It is wise to have a degree of structure when planning, hence some widely used frameworks are discussed. The steps taken in planning are common for many frameworks. Students need to be clear apropos the terminology e.g. the difference between objectives, strategies and tactics as this is the lexicon of marketing practitioners. The role of audits is considered with practical examples and many tools/frameworks are critiqued. Students are shown how to create marketing objectives and how to choose the appropriate strategy. Matters relating to implementation and control are addressed. The Chapter concludes by considering the barriers to adopting sustainable marketing planning.

Learning outcomes

At the end of this chapter, students will be able to do the following:

- Differentiate between objectives, strategies and tactics;
- Understand how planning can be applied to a variety of organisations;
- Examine the nature of the internal environments, microenvironments and macroenvironments;
- Assess which tools and frameworks are optimal for analysing the business environments;
- Appreciate how a SWOT summary provides the platform for a TOWS analysis, which is an objective-generating procedure;
- Evaluate the role of segmentation, targeting and positioning (STP);
- Identify the correct strategy to achieve key objectives;
- Explain how the implementation of the marketing mix can be controlled and monitored;
- Reflect on the barriers to implementing sustainable marketing planning.

Many managers struggle to adapt to the relentless changes in technology. If, as Marx suggested, the only constant is change, managers have no option other than to implement changes. The move to sustainable, customer-centric marketing should be one such change. Clearly, what is needed is not change for its own sake but the *right* change. Marketers must reflect on the changes needed to fully incorporate sustainability and customer centricity into their organisations:

- The balance between efficiency and effectiveness;
- Attitudes to and relationships with customers;
- The balance between "our" needs and "their" wants;
- Redefining customer satisfaction;
- Refocusing on the long-term objective rather than shorter-term objectives;
- Rethinking the value chain, such as "greening" the supply network and/or community;
- New corporate cultures.

A study by the Institute of Directors (the IoD – see www.iod.com/) found that 80% (of directors) believed they had the right strategies, whereas only 14% thought they were implementing them well. Drucker argued that efficiency is doing things right, whereas effectiveness is doing the right things. Clearly, organisations need to be efficient *and* effective if those at the IoD are going to raise that implementation figure and if they are to be more productive. When planning (potentially) years ahead, the issue of strategy arises. Companies must ensure that corporate strategies are working *in practice*.

Objectives, strategies and tactics

Too often terms are used loosely in marketing. Such poor use of terminology causes problems when implementing plans. Three common terms that marketers must understand are objectives, strategies and tactics. Objectives and strategies can be organisational or functional (e.g. marketing, HR, production etc.), whereas tactics are always a matter for the functions.

Larger organisations' corporate objectives are often set in terms of profit, Return on Investment (ROI) and/or Return on Capital Employed (ROCE), since these will satisfy the demands of governance and (usually remote) shareholders. With SMEs, it is usually the owner/manager who needs to be satisfied, and this is often shaped by their personality or attitudes. Objectives can be chosen only after an honest assessment of the company's attitude to risk: whether to speculate to accumulate or rather go for organic, incremental growth. Companies that are risk averse should not plan for "huge" growth, because it involves greater risk. Aggressive approaches may take the company away from its existing strengths and capabilities. The attitude to risk will shape strategic choices.

A range of corporate objectives and strategies can be directly affected by marketing:

- Supporting major change;
- Communicating executive and management messages;
- Communicating the business mission/vision/values;
- Raising awareness of business issues and priorities;
- Raising and maintaining the credibility of management;
- Motivating employees;
- Allowing staff to offer feedback;
- Improving the communications skills of management.

Hence, it is appropriate to clarify some of the key terminology about objectives, strategies and tactics. Simply put, a strategy is what an organisation uses to achieve its objectives (Figure 3.1).

The company's purpose or mission statement starts the process with corporate (and supporting marketing) objectives. The functions within companies (e.g. marketing, sales, HR, accounting, production, logistics) will have their own functional objectives.

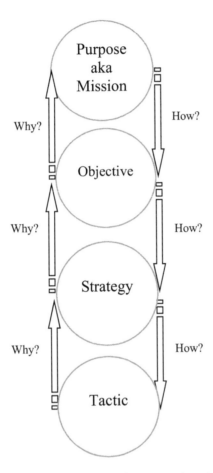

Figure 3.1 The POST model, featuring strategic, objective and tactical flows

In the vast majority of cases, functional objectives should support corporate objectives. To do otherwise is to adopt a maverick position. This is highly risky. Shareholders like mavericks when their schemes work; however, when the schemes go wrong and dividends are cut, it is a different matter. At this juncture, the maverick is sacrificed.

Three key corporate strategies are stability, expansion or concentration. A stability strategy seeks to maintain the status quo and make incremental improvements. This approach is good for low-growth, stable markets where opportunities are deemed to be minimal. It lends itself to companies who are risk averse or to industries where leaders struggle to develop alternatives. It can result from management wanting an easy life or other issues, such as organisational inertia. Such companies are not perceived to be "sexy", particularly by the city. Since the 1970s, the Japanese Kaizen approach has influenced manufacturing in Europe. Kaizen involves seeking small incremental changes across a wide range of metrics. It seeks to be 1% better at a hundred things rather than 100% better at one thing. If this approach is maintained over a period of time, dramatic changes can take place. The incremental change creates "buy-in" from stakeholders who may normally fear change.

Expansion strategies involve a degree of business redefinition. Managers seek to add services and products in order to satisfy their economic goals. Transformational leaders seeking dramatic returns and appeasing investors can drive this.

Finally, concentration strategies are based on low risk and seek to exploit existing resources. This often happens when the company has a relatively small market share. Simply put, they do not need to take risks to grow; they simply need to be better than the competition. This may involve reacting to competitors. While simply reacting to industry needs may reap short-term rewards, it may be more effective to take a lead, by being proactive.

Strategies may change with time as progress is made. The change may not be voluntary, though. No objective, strategy or tactic is cast in stone. Marketers must always reflect on their choices and actions and be prepared to make changes. A number of objectives can be achieved with a clear strategy; however, too many objectives (and strategies) can lead to confusion.

Marketers must reflect on whether a strategy helps them to achieve their objectives. Is this strategy the best fit? How will tactics be implemented to achieve the marketing objectives? Hence, corporate strategies achieve corporate objectives, and marketing strategies achieve marketing objectives. Marketing objectives and strategies are discussed in detail later in this chapter.

> *Example*   Netflix is one of the 21st century's most successful tech companies. That said, it had to change tack dramatically. Netflix's former marketing chief, Barry Enderwick, revealed that it originally planned to move into video-streaming using its own set-top box. Indeed, in "2007, we were so far down the path with the Netflix-branded streaming device that we were shooting promotional videos for it. . . . Then the handbrake was pulled – and hard". Netflix elected to stream its services via other hardware platforms. This successful strategic shift was recognised when Netflix temporarily overtook Disney (in 2017) as the world's most valuable entertainment company (LinkedIn, 2018).

The tactics are the short-term measures adopted to achieve the objectives and subsequent strategies. Tactics reside within the functions. In marketing, the tactics involve changes made to the Marketing Mix (i.e. the 7Ps, as detailed in Chapter 2).

3.1 Planning frameworks

Plans can be short term, say based on a specific event or a long-term programme of activities affecting the whole business. Good planning will improve the understanding of why the change is necessary and how implementation will occur. Planning encourages marketers to do the following:

- Prioritise – ensure that time is not wasted on unnecessary activities;
- Avoid unplanned activities – justify the need to avoid unnecessary activities;
- Be cohesive – in short-, medium- and long-term activities;
- Reflect – on activities that will influence achieving objectives;
- Be cost-effective – use RoMI to demonstrate past achievements;
- Engage stakeholder groups – identifying their needs and potential to contribute;
- Control the agenda – work proactively to identify issues and corrective actions.

Marketing planning ultimately involves having a longer-term view on how to market a company. *Planning horizons* often feature durations of years, not months. Some commentators consider the following to be reasonable guidelines:

- Short term   1–3 years
- Medium term   3–5 years
- Long term   5+ years

Marketers must question whether these horizons apply to their industry/business. If PLCs are crashing, it may be prudent to consider a shorter planning cycle. Volatility in the Macro environment, whether political, economic or legal, will shorten planning horizons. The important thing is to look as far forward as is sensible and then consider the different scenarios that may apply.

Scenario planning

A successful marketing plan will consider the problems that might occur and make appropriate preparations to deal with them, should the need arise. This is central to the ability to respond to change. The what-if approach serves well here, with examples:

- What if the oil price hits $200 per barrel?
- What if Turkey joins the European Union?
- What if female representation at board level becomes mandatory?
- What if our competitors start to incorporate graphene into their products?

What-if scenarios are diverse. Clearly, the spread of possible outcomes of each of these scenarios is equally wide. Given the definition of strategy and assuming that marketers know where they want to be, the next key decision involves how to get there. The use of a planning framework can make it easier to implement a plan. Kotler (1967) introduced the notion of planning to a wider business audience. Since then, a number of corporate planning models have been offered (Figure 3.2).

This list is not exhaustive. In reality, no framework is any better than any other. The REACH NEW framework tries to frame planning in a way that is more appropriate for the 21st century, by using better language. such as nurturing, collaborating and so on. There is, however, no one-size-fits-all option. Marketers must identify which plan is better and may have to adapt a plan to suit their circumstances. There are similarities across corporate and functional (e.g. marketing) planning frameworks. Ultimately, they can be distilled into the following steps:

1 Goal setting – mission (or vision) statement, corporate objectives and gap analysis
2 Situation review – the internal (micro)environment and external (macro) environment
3 Strategy formulation and tactical implementation
4 Resource allocation – monitoring, evaluation and control

Goal setting

A mission statement generally expresses a company's overall purpose. They vary widely, from a few lines to comprehensive statements concerning wide-ranging factors, such as why the company exists, how it operates, what sort of company it purports to be.

APIC Planning Framework	Parallel Corporate Strategy Model	Sequential Marketing Strategy Framework	SOSTAC Sequential Marketing Strategy Framework	Sequential Corporate Strategy Model	Reach New Framework
Analyse (Environment, resources, expectations, objectives and culture)	Strategic analysis (Environment, resources, expectations, objectives and culture)	Situation review (Marketing Audit, SWOT Analysis)	Situation analysis	Environmental analysis (e.g. marketplace, customers) Resource Analysis (e.g. human, financial)	Reflection • the role of technology and your company • your orientation and readiness to change • your approach to marketing
Plan (generation and evaluation strategic options; forecasts)	Strategic Choice (generation and evaluation of options)	Goal setting (mission, corporate objectives)	Objective setting	Vision, mission and objectives	Enabling change • by recognising and removing barriers to adoption of good marketing practices • by putting sustainability into your marketing mix
Implementation (resource planning, Tactical implementation)	Strategic implementation (resource planning)	Strategy formulation (objectives, plans and mixes)	Strategy	Strategy development	Actively communicating • by engaging with stakeholders in in a considered manner • using tools and techniques that help your customers • by getting your staff to "buy into" promoting internal change • your brand to your customers by tailoring your communications tools to be fit for purpose
Control (ROI, KPIs*, budget)		Resource allocation and monitoring	Tactics	Strategy implementation	Considering your situation • so that you know your strengths and weaknesses • and will be able to exploit future opportunities • to understand how those around you can help (or hinder) your progress

Actions

Harvesting knowledge
- to know you're achieving what you want
- to identify where you want to be

Nurturing growth
- by acquiring and satisfying new customers
- by developing relationships and partnerships

Control

Embracing coordination
- by planning your marketing campaigns
- by monitoring your success in reaching your goals

Where you stand
- On the key issues of sustainability, namely ecological and ethical concerns
- When technology keeps changing

Figure 3.2 Planning process models and frameworks

*KPIs: key performance indicators

Source: adapted from Kotler (1967), Johnson and Scholes (1999), McDonald (1999), Smith et al. (1999), Lynch (1999) and Richardson (2010)

Often (most importantly) they define the customers and the benefits offered. Some sustainable organisations have replaced mission statements with purpose statements, which they believe are more aligned to their ethical and environmental cultures.

Ideally, mission statements should fit the values and expectations of key stakeholders. A worry for managers is that companies that lack clarity in what they seek to achieve (i.e. their mission) often have employees who lack direction. Employees need to engage with a progressive, aspirational, grounded vision of the company if they are to be fully motivated to drive through any changes.

The core elements of a mission statement are as follows:

- Raison d'être, essence or purpose;
- Long-term views on strategy;
- Area of company involvement in products or services;
- Core competences and key strengths;
- Benefits to customers;
- Policies, standards and attitudes, such as CSR;
- Value systems, such as fair trade, green, sustainability.

The danger of providing a list is that it can be misconstrued as one size fits all. For it to work, marketers should strive to influence mission statements to serve the company's interests *and* to inform the customers of the value being created for them. Mission statements that are not customer centric need to be treated with caution, if not contempt. They need to be reviewed and revised periodically to ensure that they are still relevant.

Jones et al. (2017) lay out the following the key influences on mission statements:

- Corporate governance;
- Whom the organisation should serve;
- Accountability and a regulatory framework;
- Stakeholders;
- Business ethics;
- Cultural contexts.

Vision statements tend to be somewhat nebulous, offering direction but often without specifics. This text is concerned with providing practical guidance, so measurable components such as mission statements and corporate objectives are preferred.

A common way to start the planning process is to carry out a gap analysis to illustrate the brand's current position and extrapolate (or forecast) the target point after a set period of time. In larger companies, this is often measured in terms of turnover, but do this with caution. If turnover is up 50% in three years, this may trigger delight; however, if the market has grown 100% in the same timescale, the company has lost market share, which could have dramatic effects. Growth in profit is often safer (than turnover), but market share is better.

This applies to most companies, irrespective of their size and whether they are profit making, third sector or charity. Some marketers measure success against other criteria, such as brand awareness or customer satisfaction. These *can* be measured, but some skill is needed.

Gaps have to be addressed if the organisation is to achieve its potential. This means considering alternatives: to reduce the objectives or to seek to raise performance (i.e.

over-deliver). The latter can be achieved by reviewing the opportunities available to your company. Gaps can be either operational or strategic.

Operational gaps can be filled by methods such as improving organisational productivity, reducing costs or increasing prices. This links to discussions on extending the maturity stage of the PLC (see Chapter 2.3), where marketers would seek to stimulate sales or find alternate uses of existing products.

To decide where to focus these operational methods, the company's core competencies should be determined. A core competence should significantly contribute to the perceived customer benefits, should be difficult for competitors to imitate and should provide potential access to a wide variety of markets. Core competencies are where managers link internal skills with resources such as technology in such a way that employees can react efficiently and effectively. Much valuable work was undertaken in this area by Prahalad and Hamel.

Strategic gaps can be addressed by finding new user groups, entering new segments, expanding geographically, developing new products and/or diversifying. When addressing strategic gaps, the company's attitude to risk must be considered. The strategic choice of selling new products to new markets (known as diversification) carries higher risks, as was illustrated painfully during the financial crisis of 2007–2008 in the United Kingdom (Northern Rock) and the United States (Lehman Bros).

3.2 Situation review

Technology has accelerated the rate of change in ways that have affected consumers' lives beyond recognition. Before marketers can identify strategies, they need to assess the foundations that will provide a springboard for any decisions:

> "By comparing our strengths and weaknesses with the threats and opportunities that face us we hope to identify an area where we have an SCA or "sustainable competitive advantage" . . . the likelihood of success will depend very much upon the quality of the manner in which we carry out each of these evaluations".
>
> Baker (2009)

Marketers have to continually monitor the factors that are operating externally and internally, to ensure organisations change with the times. These internal and external factors constitute marketing environments (Figure 3.3), which influence a company's ability to transform its inputs (think ITO models) into outputs that create value for customers.

External factors are beyond the control of the organisation; these are known collectively as the macroenvironment or the situational environment. With macro-analysis, marketers always look to identify future trends

Internal factors are specific to particular industries or organisations where an organisation, to a degree, has control. These factors reside in the internal environments and microenvironments and feature recent and current strengths and weaknesses among, say, the company, target segments, marketplace and so on.

Too little detail will lead to a lack of action, whereas too much could lead to analysis paralysis. A lack of skills and resources are key factors that lead not only to poor marketing planning but also to ineffective implementation. A key component of most planning frameworks (see Figure 3.2) is the audit.

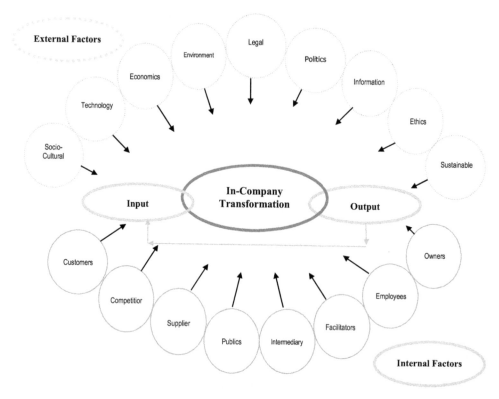

Figure 3.3 Marketing environments influencing value creation

Marketing audits

Environmental scanning can be done with a marketing audit, which should have the following characteristics:

- Comprehensive;
- Apolitical;
- Structured;
- Timely.

CAST is a useful mnemonic because of its structure; however, it leaves a number of matters to be judged: How comprehensive? What degree of structure? Is an apolitical audit achievable without external input and the timing of audits? What is the appropriate timescale for the organisation to implement changes? Each of them needs careful consideration.

All audits are inherently political. They can suffer from clashes within organisational power bases. The findings may not be palatable to non-marketers; however, the focus on the customer should be unrelenting. This underpins the need for healthy dialogue between the functions. Otherwise, those carrying out the audit may be exposed to hostility. Ultimately, the message has to be conveyed that it is the customers who count.

It is not enough to carry out a marketing audit and then fail to act on the findings. This risks the audit simply becoming a ritual, an onerous task, which is unlikely to have the required impact.

The internal marketing environment

SM involves engaging with communities whether inside or outside of the organisation. Communities are groups of people that come together due to a common interest. The larger the organisation, the more likely it is that numerous communities will reside internally and in the microenvironment. Each may have different interests and roles. Some may be hostile, antagonistic groups, whereas others may be supporters or advocates. Some communities may be special interest groups, interested in, say, customers, processes or design. Marketers must consider the role of internal communities and the benefits they can offer as they can create value and bring many benefits. Organisations have the most influence over internal staff and less so with key external "micro" stakeholders.

Internal environment analysis tools

A wide range of internal and micro-tools or micro-frameworks is available. No one tool is sophisticated enough to capture the data, whereas using, say, ten tools creates as many problems as it solves. Marketers should select the best three or four and create a blend that really suits the circumstances. The following represents some of the more popular internal tools/frameworks.

McKinsey 7S framework

Waterman et al. (1980) created the 7S framework (Figure 3.4) to assist managerial analysis by portraying the company's interconnectedness between its strategy, structure, systems, skills, staff, style and share values.

It was one of the earlier frameworks seeking to use academic research to inform managerial practice. Its aim was to act as a change catalyst by promoting organisational change and shaping new strategies. Waterman et al. suggested, if nothing else, that the framework could be a checklist:

> "to understand how organizations really operate or to design a truly comprehensive change program. . . . At its most powerful and complex, the framework forces us to concentrate on interactions and fit. The real energy required to redirect an institution comes when all the variables in the model are aligned".

The 7S framework helps marketers take a holistic view of the organisation and reflect on how each factor may be affected. It can also be used as a framework in mergers and acquisitions, where companies have a structure to make comparisons. This is also the case with Porter's Value Chain Analysis (VCA).

The 7S framework has advantages and disadvantages (Figure 3.5); however, it is still one of the few tools that differentiates between hard and soft factors. Using it promotes "taking seriously the variables in organizing that have been considered soft, informal, or beneath the purview of top management interest". Style, systems and

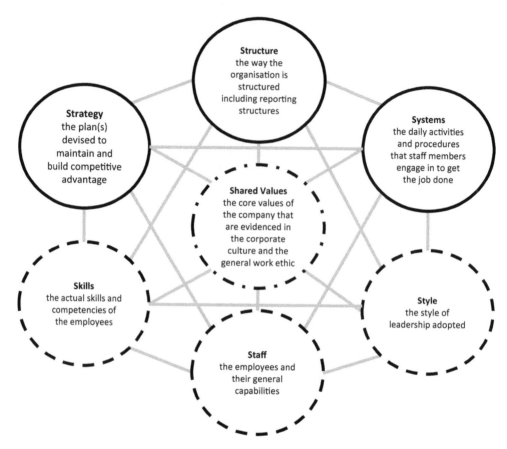

Figure 3.4 McKinsey 7S framework

skills "can be at least as important as strategy and structure in orchestrating major change; indeed, they are almost critical for achieving necessary, or desirable, change" (Waterman et al., 1980, p. 26).

Waterman and colleagues concluded that businesses that have these seven elements aligned and mutually reinforced are more likely to achieve competitive advantage.

Core Competence Framework

In 1990 Prahalad and Hamel introduced the idea of the core competence of organisations. They suggested a company's competitiveness derives from its core competencies and core products (the tangible results of core competencies). Core competence refers to an organisation's (collective) knowledge, skills and attitude. Does it have the ability to learn when coordinating diverse skills and technological platforms (Prahalad and Hamel, 1990)? Those wanting to understand more about *learning organisations* should seek out the work of Burgoyne and/or Sprenger and ten Have. Prahalad and Hamel's paper, while seminal, focused on large, manufacturing companies. This has

Advantages	Disadvantages
Comprehensive internal review of how companies operate	May not consider SBUs* where gaps in strategy conception or execution may occur
Highlights the need to consider soft and hard factors	Little practical support for the model, particularly with SMEs
Underpins how strategy implementation is shaped by other factors, which in turn influence each other	Difficult to properly assess the degree of fit; relies on judgement calls; and works only within a blend of other tools
Develops historical overreliance on considering only strategy and structure when reviewing organisational effectiveness	Does not provide solutions to improve implementation and control
Emphasises coordination and planning	It is a static model in an increasingly turbulent environment
Early model linking academic research with managerial practice	Although interlinked, not all are equal and will be subject to the usual politics
	Neglects external stakeholders and macroenvironmental concerns

Figure 3.5 Advantages and disadvantages of the McKinsey 7S framework

*SBUs: strategic business units

often been the case in marketing. Clearly, core competence has to be extended to services.

Core competencies involve promoting behavioural changes to create value for customers. Value-creating behaviours should become the foundation for the company. Ideally, companies should adopt a set of behaviours that apply to all stakeholders. They can be values based and, if so, should reflect the core values and culture of the organisation. Marketers must communicate the competencies to all key stakeholders across organisational boundaries.

There may be more competencies within an organisation; however, "chunking" (see Chapter 1) applies to stakeholders in a company as much as to consumers involved in decision-making. Too many competencies will lead to confusion and inertia. Too few would suggest a lack of reflection on the organisation. The competencies must be memorable, and many commentators suggest a portfolio of (no more than) five competencies, where each is broken down into (a maximum of) five behaviours. As is the case with product portfolio management, competencies are a key resource and will have to be "managed". These limits make the successful implementation and control of the core competencies more likely.

Core competencies should be chosen with care. They should meet the following criteria:

1   Provide potential access to a wide variety of markets;
2   Create value for customers and prospects;
3   Differentiate the organisation and remain difficult to imitate;
4   Reflect the values of the organisation;
5   Cross organisational boundaries internally and externally via collaborations;
6   Resist diminishing over time.

Figure 3.6 juxtaposes core competencies for a large organisation with those of a smaller marketing agency. Ultimately, marketing students will work either client side or agency side. The large company would build on the strengths that derive from its size, structure and resources. Leadership is crucial in large companies. The agency would look to use its strengths, deriving from its ability to service niche markets, its speed of response and its being able to adapt to create value. For example, its digital marketing expertise could be used to exploit growing social media opportunities since it has lower overheads. Akin to the notion of Unique Selling Points (USPs), core competencies are unlikely to be unique to all companies. Many will share similar behaviours, as is the case in Figure 3.6. In both cases, the core competencies should be tested against the aforementioned six criteria.

Core competencies are the engine for NPD (see Chapter 2.3) and thus should be nurtured. This necessitates "buy-in" from senior management, as does marketing planning in general. Each competence (and the behaviours therein) will have to be measured and monitored over a long timescale. Indeed, Prahalad and Hamel suggest competences can take decades to develop, in a process of continuous development. That said, companies seeking to refine their competencies could see immediate benefits on the first steps of their "journey".

	Core competencies	*Measurable behaviours*
Client side	Leadership	Communication; clarity; foresight; commitment; values
	Conscientious	Focus; detail; efficiency; resilience; initiative; excellence
	Service	Responsiveness; reliability; credibility; courtesy; consistency
	Collaboration	Advocacy; flexibility; representativeness; compliance; personal development
	Professionalism	Understanding organisational purpose; environmental awareness; knowledge of structure, process flows, profit centres and cost controls
Agency side	Digital expertise	Social media management; direct marketing skills; content design; control measures; lead conversion
	Marketing experience	Branding; CRM skills; segmentation analysis; positioning knowledge; marcomms abilities; internal marketing
	Procedural	Project management; accountability; reporting; brief creation; presentation
	Insightfulness	Customer centricity; feedback opportunities; tailoring service; creativity; responsiveness
	Tenacity	Self-motivation; resilience, problem-solving; adaptability; flexibility

Figure 3.6 Core competencies – client versus agencies

Source: original diagram

A product is not a core competence; rather, it is the output (of core competencies). Apple should not see itself as an iPhone or iMac *manufacturer*. It has a proven ability to also design, develop and launch (successfully) highly stylised devices. Design, development and marketing are among their core competencies. First Direct offers bank accounts, credit cards and mortgages; however, its competencies relate to its award-winning customer-centric services featuring ease of use, 24/7 access and a sector-leading use of technology. Many online banks have call centres, apps and online facilities, but few can replicate the long-term customer satisfaction garnered by First Direct.

Prahalad and Hamel also refer to competence carriers, who are effectively the champions of the concept. These people should be supported by senior management and operate across functions. They should create core competence communities. By travelling regularly, talking frequently to customers, and meeting with peers, competence carriers may be encouraged to discover new markets (Prahalad and Hamel, 1990).

Competence is not a permanent state; it can be lost. Competencies are based on the knowledge, skills and attitudes of people. Companies that suffer from staff turnover will lose much of the tacit knowledge when the employees leave. Wherever possible, this knowledge should be made explicit – that is, recorded in a format than can be communicated in future. The costs of losing competencies can be substantial and only partly calculated in advance (ibid). Hence, it is prudent to consider some of the barriers to applying the concept, as follows:

- Not all competencies are equal and to be effective they must interact.
- Different competency sets may be needed for different groups of people.
- Those in rigid SBU structures may be unwilling to partake in sharing best practices and resources;
- Identifying a set of competencies that will still be relevant after five to ten years is subjective and challenging.

Even now, how to build core competencies is deemed to be ambitious by some commentators. Many managers make easy decisions, such as changing company structures. In reality, it is much easier to change structure than culture and behaviours. That said, if core competencies are identified at a corporate level, marketing objectives and strategies should seek to offer support.

Boston Control Group (BCG) matrix

In Chapter 2.3 the merits of the PLC were discussed. The PLC is an internal tool: it has no consideration of stakeholders outside of the company. The PLC acted as a springboard for the Boston Control Group's widely used BCG matrix. In 1970, BCG's founder, Bruce Henderson, suggested

> "A company should have a portfolio of products with different growth rates and different market shares. The portfolio composition is a function of the balance between cashflows. . . . Margins and cash generated are a function of market share".
>
> (Henderson, 1970)

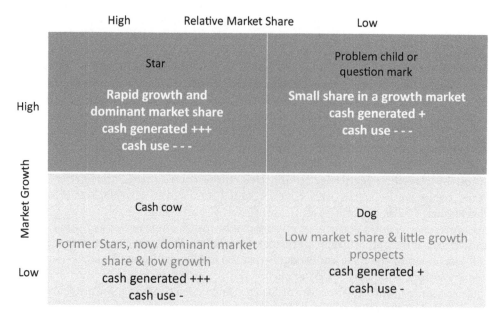

Figure 3.7 Boston Control Group (BCG) matrix

Clearly, Henderson's views were shaped to be assumptions that were valid at the time. It was assumed that marketing investment would create product growth and that in turn greater market share would lead to increased profit. Products had longer PLCs, and thus profit could be made during the maturity stage. In those days, brands sought to dominate their competitors, and the growth stage was optimal for creating a dominant brand. Managers believed that profitability and cashflow increased with larger Economies of Scale (EoSs) that resulted from greater market share. So they invested more working capital into increased production capacities and diverted more revenue towards promoting their products. These were the inwards-focused, top-down behaviours of product- and production-oriented companies (see Chapter 1.2).

Many of these assumptions have been subsequently updated to recognise the different nature of 21st-century markets. It is possible that such tools could have led large manufacturers to prematurely abandon product ranges. Prahalad and Hamel (1990) discuss how American and European TV manufacturers largely abandoned the market, thus opening the door to Japanese, Korean and Chinese entrants.

The accepted wisdom is that marketers should invest in Stars to achieve growth. This growth may be at the expense of profit. Question Mark (a.k.a. problem children) should be evaluated to ascertain whether they could grow into a star or a cash cow or decline and become a Dog. Some commentators argued that the optimal cashflow is from cash cow to question marks. Cash Cows should have enough investment to maintain their market share and to provide the investment in other categories. "Overmilking" the cash cows can lead to them being unnecessarily weakened. Dogs, weak cash cows and unpromising question marks may need to be harvested or culled if they threaten the company excessively. Such decisions can be problematic; for example,

Dogs may be able to generate decent profits if not starved of investment. Hence, it is sensible to consider some of the limitations of the BCG matrix.

First, it is a somewhat simplistic tool that sees products independently of their peers in the product portfolio. To an extent, it ignores related accessories – for example, laser printers may have a different BCG matrix to toner cartridges. Being an internal tool, it does not overtly factor in external matters, such as the role of competitors and practices such as predatory pricing or "dumping". Any successful product will provoke a reaction from competitors, including new entrants. Unless clearly differentiated from the competition, this often leads to lower prices and profits. The BCG's reliance on cashflow neglects the critical issue of profitability. It lacks customer centricity, and customers may choose other brands if their preferred product is lost. Sometimes an adaptation of the product can be enough to cause customer attrition, as was the case when Apple removed the 3.5 mm jack from their iPhone range. Some customers wanted the facility of the plug-in socket. Finally, a common challenge for product portfolio tools is whether it should be used at the product, product-group or SBU level. Analyses undertaken at the SBU level may conceal significant underlying differences or ignore synergies between SBUs or products.

Directional Policy Matrices

In the 1970s, General Electric (GE) commissioned McKinsey & Company to develop a portfolio analysis matrix. The GE McKinsey matrix or GE matrix evolved from the BCG matrix. Rather than using single measures of success – that is, market growth rate and relative market share – the GE matrix, often known as a Directional Policy Matrix (hereafter DPM), uses a multivariate approach where market growth rate is replaced by market attractiveness and relative market share by business strength.

A DPM, like many simple tools, provides useful insights for marketers. Simple tools are more likely to be used when implementing changes. A DPM has two uses: first, it assesses a product's position in a company's portfolio, and second, it can be used as a positioning tool to map key competitors.

If the DPM merely portrays a current snapshot, it is purely descriptive. To be an analytical tool, it should offer not only the current product positions but also their positioning at the end of the planning period. This way, a DPM can identify which products need more support. The criteria include a range of factors (Figure 3.9).

Proctor (2008) insists that market attractiveness and business strengths are Critical Success Factors (CSFs). The content of each of these sets of CSFs depends entirely on the organisation and the competitive environment. Market attractiveness and business strength should be measured by the key criteria marketers must get right to succeed. Business strengths should enable a comparison to be made relative to the major competitors. Some commentators have proposed weightings for the criteria (Figure 3.10).

This is useful in suggesting that marketers prioritise their selection of criteria. Beyond that, it raises many questions. In focusing attention on market share and differentiation, it downplays brand image. Clearly, it could be argued that the brand image is more valuable to the organisation than the 10% weighting suggests. Tools that refer to markets suffer the problems of (market) definition. Some markets have many similar products with little differentiation. Markets can be niche or widely spread among many small competitors. Niche markets can offer real potential for growth and developing new brands. Markets can be growing, static or declining.

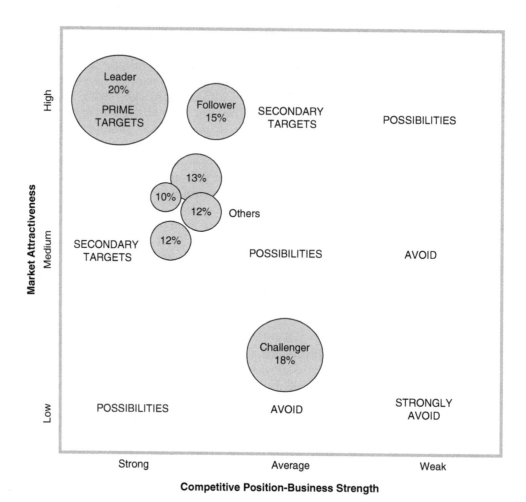

Figure 3.8 Directional Policy Matrix (DPM)

Industry attractiveness	Business strengths
size	size
market growth	growth
pricing	share
market diversity	position
competitive structure	profitability
industry profitability	margins
technical role	technical position
social	strengths/weaknesses
environment	image
legal	people
human	size

Figure 3.9 DPM criteria – industry attractiveness versus business strengths

Source: adapted from McDonald (1999, p. 189)

		Market Attractiveness Criteria			
		Profit Potential	*Market Growth Rate*	*Market Size*	*Strength of Competition*
Business Strengths Criteria	Market share	60%			
	Potential for differential advantage		20%		
	Potential cost advantages			10%	
	Brand image				10%

Figure 3.10 Weightings for DPM criteria

Source: adapted from Megicks et al. (2009)

They can be monopolistic, duopolistic, oligopolistic or competitive. A company can be a market leader, challenger or follower. Young markets may be subject to rapid growth that will plateau at an (as yet) unknown level. Products and services may target nascent markets where growth estimates are little more than educated guesses. All of these factors (among others) can shape the application of internal tools (PLC, BCG and Directional Policy Matrices) and Micro environments tools (e.g. 5Ms and Porter's Five Forces).

As the DPM does not rely on income-related measures for assessing the various services on offer, it seems to offer more to public sector organisations than the Boston matrix (Proctor, 2008). Indeed, there is sufficient flexibility in the approach to use whatever measures appear to be most appropriate. However, it has limitations:

- The circle sizes may not reflect the true situation since the visuals are quite simplistic.
- Positions are often chosen on the basis of subjective elements.
- Market growth is not a good description for overall industry attractiveness.
- It may fail to take into account strong buyers and low entry barriers.
- Market share is an inadequate description for relative competitive strength.
- Other factors, such as location and degree of vertical integration, may need to be considered.

Value Chain Analysis (VCA)

In 1985, Michael Porter introduced a generic value chain model that comprised a sequence of primary value-creating activities common to a wide range of firms. The primary (value-creating) activities provide a "value" flow through the organisation, and ultimately, value is "given" to the customer in a way that generates profit. Like many of the tools used today, it drew on the experiences of large manufacturing companies and was shaped by the economic situation of the 1970s and 1980s, where strong competition and relatively stable market structures endured. It can be applied to SMEs; however, there are limitations (see Chapter 4.7).

The constantly changing market conditions facing marketers today are turbulent if not tumultuous. Market fragmentation, globalisation, hyper-competition, oversupply, regulation and disruption are among the watchwords of marketers in the 21st century. Porter's models rely on being able to know an organisation or being able to predict behavioural outcomes of third parties. The more dynamic the environment, the more the organisation needs to collaborate internally; hence, internal marketing (see Chapter 4.2) plays an important role.

That said, Porter's Value Chain Analysis (hereafter VCA) has a role in the modern marketers' environmental analysis toolkit. Johnson et al. (2017) suggest that VCA (Figure 3.11) describes the activities within and around an organisation that together create a product or service. They describe how the primary activities are linked to support activities. Indeed, it is the interaction between the value-creating activities that determines the success of achieving organisational objectives. The interaction of the activities should create value and differentiation for customers.

The nomenclature is problematic. To say that marketing and sales are primary whereas procurement and/or HR are secondary is questionable. These are professional functions with their own bodies (CIPS and CIPD respectively). Clearly, all of the functions have to be customer centric if the organisation is to prosper. Internal barriers can affect the ability to satisfy customer needs. A common issue for a number of the tools in this chapter is that they have separate "elements" to be benchmarked. These "elements" are not isolated, and issues arise from how they interact. In the case of VCA, sales and marketing are integrated, whereas in reality this is not always the case. Marketing is separate from HR, whereas in reality, the role of HR is crucial for

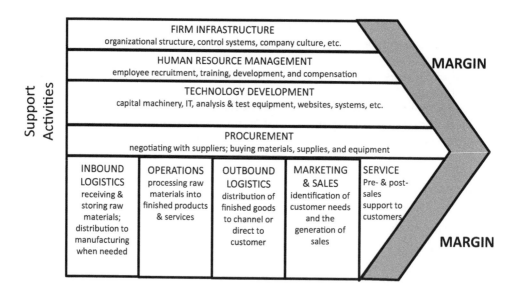

Figure 3.11 Porter's Value Chain Analysis

Source: adapted from Porter (1980)

marketers. They must recruit, train, motivate and reward the marketing and/or sales teams. The relationship with "buyers" is important internally and externally. Internal buyers can help identify and manage relationships with key suppliers. They can also gather relevant competitor intelligence from suppliers, trade bodies and so on.

That said, a number of areas for potential inter-functional conflict (with marketing) exists. The production function wants to standardise products and demands accurate forecasts. They are often risk averse and resist the demand to change products. Procurement will want to influence product specifications. They can have a short-term mentality and see necessary spending as "costs" rather than investment. The finance function sets corporate budgets and may measure the Return on Marketing Investment (RoMI) through a short-term lens rather adopting a longer-term perspective. Many of these arguments have merit; however, none of the other functions have the insights from the customers. Value can be created only in the mind of the *customer*. It cannot simply be added up and given. This is a key flaw in VCA.

VCA is essentially an internal framework; however, it can be used to assist in micro-environmental analysis. It can be used to compare and contrast organisations or SBUs. This can support strategic decisions, say regarding mergers and acquisitions (M&A) or internal restructuring. Managers would seek to identify synergies, overlaps or gaps when comparing the two bodies.

The "Micro" marketing environment

Marketing channels represent all of the organisations involved in delivering goods and services to customers (see Chapter 2.2). There can be several intermediaries between a manufacturer and the customer. Porter recognised that value can be created (or destroyed) at each of the interfaces between upstream suppliers and downstream channels and customers (Figure 3.12).

There are issues with the value system, though. Clearly, there needs to be feedback reflecting on the interactions. The term "chain" is problematic, first because it alludes to companies being chained to their customers, which is anachronistic; second, modern companies use a network of suppliers, many of whom can provide similar services and products. The structure of the organisation will also play a role. Those with high degrees of vertical integration may be better able to coordinate upstream and downstream activities. Those with little vertical integration will still have access to a vast, global online array of potential suppliers. Manufacturers often encourage their

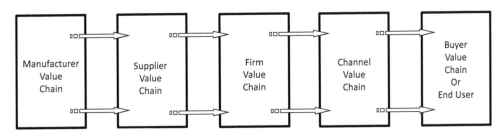

Figure 3.12 Porter's Value System

Source: adapted from Porter (1980)

suppliers to be in the same proximity in order to improve the creation of value. Being closer suggests improved communication (including feedback), reduced lead times and more-progressive inventory management approaches (e.g. Kanban). Kanban is a supply approach in lean manufacturing systems. The suppliers often play an active part in stock management, taking responsibility for monitoring stock levels and automatically replenishing inventories. This has seen the increased use of one-stop shopping by manufacturers. The supplier must be local and have access to all of the necessary items. This is a highly integrated value system where some boundaries are becoming blurred.

Traditionally, commentators argued that a company's Sustainable Competitive Advantage (SCA) derived from its own value chain and its ability to manage the value system. This suggests a degree of control, which is often illusory. Many product recalls have resulted from a lack of control. Mattel famously had to organise global recalls of children's toys because their manufacturing sub-contractor used lead-based paint.

The microenvironment involves those stakeholders who can directly or indirectly influence the extent to which a company achieves its objectives. The degree of influence varies from stakeholder to stakeholder. The single most important stakeholder is the customer, followed by those who influence them. Marketing is about not only satisfying customers but delighting them. It is about creating the scenario where customers seek and take value from what is offered.

Businesses have to meet increasing public expectations and to address legal obligations around environmental and sustainability issues. The need of business to make profit can, at times, conflict with its stated ethical aims and objectives. Hence, conflicting stakeholders with different needs, rights and obligations have to be managed.

Customers who have positive experiences will create positive WoM. If it is a bad experience, it is likely that they will create negative WoM on an even larger scale. This applies now more than ever since the advent of Web 2.0, which has seen an exponential increase in the use of smartphones to access websites, blogs and social media sites.

Marcomms (see Chapter 2.1) provide the tools to promote internal marketing *and* the adoption of sustainable practices internally. People (after a key foundation of TBL is), and there are hundreds of studies that demonstrate the benefits of treating people well. Those interested in such studies should seek out the works of Pfeffer. The crucial area of internal marketing is discussed in more detail in Chapter 4.2

Customer behaviour is constantly changing as technology enables quicker, easier decision-making. For example, consider the role of cost-comparison websites in shaping consumer behaviour. Consumers clearly use a range of social networks for different purposes. Some may be purely "social", whereas others may be more professional, such as LinkedIn. Indeed, businesses and professionals are increasingly using social networks as part of their online research activities and to form new links and partnerships.

As customers change, their desires, needs and wants also change and companies that fail to adapt will increasingly fail to offer value and will suffer customer attrition (i.e. losses). This underpins the need to coordinate marketing, especially marcomms activities. Ultimately, marketers are seeking to change consumers' behaviour by influencing their decision-making process (see Chapter 3.1). TV still has importance in marcomms, but it needs to be more interactive and involved. The process of engaging in conversations and finding more information must be simple and quick. Also, identities are being formed and/or shaped by, say, reality TV shows. Consumers form thoughts, attitudes and opinions and also influence how others consume media. Marketers must think creatively and combine invention with relevance in their marcomms. The battle now is for content, style and timeliness.

Communities and networks in the Micro environment

Communities come together and communicate using tools such as websites, social networks, email, messaging apps and even text messages. They develop around a shared, collective purpose or interest, whereas networks may not have that shared purpose or identity. Communities are inherently based on trust and shared values. Social media can be used by marketers to link various communities of stakeholders into networks.

All communities are networks of individuals who come together, but not all networks are communities. Essentially, networks are a series of connections formed between participants, which can be used to coordinate different communications campaigns, such as ethical communities with environmental communities in campaigns. This often happens with large political events, such as the opposition to the third Heathrow runway or G20 meetings (e.g. Copenhagen, 2009).

Networks are equally capable of influencing the business environment. Networks of communities can exist, where each community represents people with a shared purpose that then connects with other communities to achieve a mutually beneficial objective. A network may form between, say, Greenpeace supporters who are concerned about the environment and union representatives who are concerned about workers' rights. They are often sympathetic towards each other's causes.

Communities provide opportunities for marketers to undertake research, generate insights, test new ideas and/or engage in dialogues. Marketers should ensure that members of the community are enthused and passionate, given information and supported to further develop the community, who should feel embraced, valued and rewarded. Benefits will accrue from the community's influencers and advocates, opinion leaders and innovators.

Chaffey and Ellis-Chadwick (2012) suggest that organisations can develop four different types of communities: purpose, position, interest and profession. These provide a degree of structure for marketers to ascertain whether the community is part of the brand's audience:

- Has the community been developed for a particular *purpose*? If so, impartial advice and support can be offered.
- Does the community exist for people in the same *position*? For example, people at the same life cycle stage (new parents for example) or health issues are in the same position.
- Is the community there for people with a common *interest*? This could involve a shared hobby, passion or enthusiasm for an activity. Marketers could seek to improve their experience by providing knowledge, information or even reward.
- Has the community been built for a particular *profession*? These communities may relate to specific industries. The Chartered Institute of Marketing, however, has a community of marketing practitioners across all sectors. Content for professionals could include useful information regarding jobs opportunities, roles, skills or current issues.

If all of these criteria are met, then marketers can be confident that they are aligned with the community. The key theme here is based around providing the right communities with useful content and information, that is helpful to them, that offers specific benefits to meet their current needs – being customer centric.

Different communities have different rules. Marketers must understand the culture of the communities and seek out opportunities for conversations. It presents opportunities to intervene if there is negativity towards the brand and provides opportunities to find a mutually agreeable resolution. Marketers cannot control a community and must not seek to shape it into something else. The community exists in its own right and for its own purpose. A community is not a sales platform; rather, it provides an opportunity to develop awareness and positive sentiment with those who may want to take value.

Online communities

Facebook has billions of users who log on daily. When people connect on Facebook, they use specific pages, groups and communities. Marketers use Facebook pages to develop relationships with their target market – that is, those identified as perceiving the brand positively. There are several hundred million Facebook groups, each of which can be public, closed or secret. They are designed for people to connect with others who have shared interests, affiliations and activities. People can be members of many Facebook groups and can use a tag to see them in one location. However, the practicality is that people usually join at least two or three groups. Facebook group traffic is not uniformly spread, with midweek peaks in the early afternoon. Marketers should factor this into their decisions regarding communications.

When people search for information from online communities, they trust their opinions on companies, brands and products. This is an established phenomenon where marketer-dominated information (say advertisements) generates less trust than non-marketer generated information, such as WoM.

> *Example*   Mumsnet was conceived in early 2000, and by 2019 it was "the UK's biggest network for parents, with over 14 million unique visitors per month clocking up over 128 million page views" (Mumsnet, 2019). While it is not overtly political (i.e. party political), it is a lobby group and has instigated a number of campaigns that have influenced retailers such as Primark, Next, Tesco and John Lewis to change practices in relation to selling clothes that sexualised young girls and to move magazines with overtly sexual covers out of children's eyelines in stores. This is just one online community, but a powerful one that has developed significant influence within the marketing environment. Have no doubt that somewhere online your customers will be actively using social media and quite possibly in a community relevant to your market or product.

Tribes

Godin (2008) takes this idea of online communities a little further: he considers the communities as "tribes" and focuses on an important role in a tribe, that of the leader. Communities, or tribes, are no longer local. Using the communications tools provided by developments in technology, marketers are privy to new social behaviour on a global scale. There are only two requirements to turn a group of people into a tribe: a shared interest and a way to communicate (ibid).

Hierarchies exist within online tribes. Communities brought together through shared interests may have leaders. Members of the tribe can be opinion leaders for outsiders, and the leaders can be opinion leaders within the tribe. Marketers must recognise that tribes are not there to be "sold to" or "talked at". Instead, marketers should identify the values within the tribe and whether they see value in the brand. If these values align, marketers can try to become part of the tribe's narrative.

Creating networks and communities

Social networks and online communities are mutually exclusive, all competing for online time, searches, clicks and patronage. Because of this, the audience may be spread across a number of platforms, with some individuals on several platforms. Marketers have several options on how to interact with communities:

1 Marketers can strive for an omni-channel presence: being present on every platform.
2 Marketers can adopt a multi-channel presence: being present on key platforms that the majority of the target audience use.
3 Marketers can build their own community.

Marketers could use combinations of these three approaches. Most use options 2 and 3. Existing social networks offer marketers the ability to easily create their own managed community. There are hundreds of millions of local business pages on Facebook covering SMEs, places, large organisations, brands, products, public figures and more. Facebook is regarded as an essential tool for marketers, whether targeting audiences directly as a B2C company, building awareness and preference as a B2B or even facilitating new channels such as C2B, G2C or G2B (i.e. Government-to-Business).

Twitter allows organisations to build positive profiles of the organisation, brand or product and then build audiences of interested followers with whom they can engage. Engagement is a key, if underused, concept in marketing. The followers can form an invaluable community who choose to follow and are interested and potentially passionate about the brand.

YouTube is the second largest search engine after Google (also owned by Alphabet Inc). It allows marketers to create branded channels that deliver broadcast video content as well as comment and discussion. YouTube viewers spend a short amount of time on the site (often less than four minutes) and visit numerous pages. Therefore, YouTube content needs to quickly engage by entertaining, encouraging user input related to content rather than overtly about the brand. This must be done regularly to attract subscribers and ultimately to build a community.

Facebook, Twitter and YouTube are just three examples; there are many more communication platforms out there through which marketers could build communities or networks. Alternatively, they could build their own platform. SmartInsights (2012) offered five reasons why organisations should develop their own online community platforms:

1 It can improve the quality of engagement.
2 It can increase ideation and better support crowdsourcing.

3   It can add value to other digital assets.
4   The organisation retains ownership of the platform and content.
5   ROI can be better measured.

Marketers who invest resources into engaging with communities will be expected to provide a RoMI. This is challenging because much of the interaction is qualitative in nature. Marketers can use analytics tool (such as Google Analytics) to track where traffic originates and whether it is coming from the communities. Furthermore, in-page pop-ups could be used that ask a question such as "How did you hear about us?" These small pop-up questions often appear in the bottom right-hand corner of the screen and provide a choice of options. These options can include the communities and shared posts or information to assess their impact and relevance.

Microenvironment analysis tools

Porter's Five Forces

In 1979 Michael Porter introduced a model based on the five forces to be evaluated when assessing competitive environments (i.e. Microenvironment) (Porter, 1979). Since then, it has become widely used by marketers when evaluating an organisation's industry structure. Porters model (hereafter P5F) is based on the insight that a corporate strategy should meet the opportunities and threats in the organisation's microenvironment. In particular, competitive strategy should be based on an understanding of industry structures and the way they change (ibid).

The evaluation of these features is subjective, and again, marketers will have to make judgement calls. Where possible, use credible sources of information, and remember that competitors are unlikely to provide the information willingly.

Hamel and Prahalad were fairly critical of P5F. They argued that the core competencies of a company should not be underestimated and suggested that "in the long run, competitiveness derives from an ability to build core competence, at lower cost and more speedily than competitors" (Prahalad and Hamel, 1990).

Competition does not equal substitution; in days of old, some academics argued that a steel supplier from China entering the UK market would be a substitute for the incumbents. This was an example of flawed logic. All marketers are global marketers. Chinese steel (or American steel, for that matter) is a competitive rivalry force. Substitution is akin to creative destruction, where a new paradigm is created. See Figure 3.14 for some substitutes.

Within some of the substitute categories, existential competition can take place. In video tapes, VHS succeeded where Betamax failed, despite the latter using superior technology. Substitutes may have first-mover advantage; however, they will have to react to a competitive response. Sky were hugely effective at rolling out their technologically inferior analogue satellite dishes while BSB toiled to perfect their digital alternative. In the end, Sky won the battle and BSkyB emerged from the battle. Of course, today all of the satellites are digital, so while BSB were the visionaries, Sky had the better marketing plan.

> *Example* Uber represented a substitute for traditional taxis and car-hire companies. Their rise has been controversial, with some local government authorities citing issues regarding vetting drivers and the use of illegal immigrants. Their use

Forces	Distinguishing features	Impact (H/M/L)	Positive or negative	Rank
New Entrants	Economy of scale (EoS) Differentiation Switching costs Convenience for customers Cost leadership Market type (duopoly, oligopoly, fragmented, etc.) Capital requirement			
Supplier Power	Differentiation Switching costs Availability Status Attraction to competitors			
Buyer Power	B2B or B2C Differentiation Switching costs Profitability Loyalty Scale One-off or repeat			
Substitute Products or Services	Switching costs and risk Approvals Reputation Quality Lead times Post-sale support			
Competitive Rivalry	Concentration Nature (aggressive, collaborative, etc.) Sector characteristics (growth rate, profitability, etc.) Diversity			

Figure 3.13 Porter's Five Forces table

Source: adapted from Porter (1979)

Incumbent	Substitute A	Substitute B	Substitute C	Substitute D
Cigarettes	Chewing tobacco	Nicotine patches	Vaping	
Vinyl record	Cassette	CD	MP3	Streaming
Cinema	Video tape	DVD/Blu-ray	MP4	Streaming
Television	Satellite	Cable	Streaming	Podcasts

Figure 3.14 Original offerings and related substitutes

Source: author

of dynamic pricing has also created negative publicity, which is odd since it is a fundamental part of the business model. The BBC alluded to the "Indian taxi-hailing giant Ola" moving into the UK as it continues to challenge Uber globally. Ola was founded in 2011 and by 2018 had 125 million customers and operated in 110 cities. Unlike Uber, it will offer a choice of private hire vehicle or black taxi. Ola claimed to be working with local authorities across the UK as it sought to provide nationwide coverage.

(BBC, 2018)

Whether cigarettes predate chewing tobacco or vice versa is a moot point. Both have been around for centuries. Some cigarette substitutes are regional; for example, Snus is a form of chewing tobacco that has been used in Scandinavian countries since the mid 19th century. It's popularity rose dramatically in the 1970s. Users place a pea-sized portion under their top lip. All tobacco products are carcinogenic, and Snus is no different; however, it seems to be popular among younger Scandinavians. It has not gained a foothold in the United Kingdom. Traditional chewing tobacco is still used in parts of the United States. In regions of South Asia, variations of chewing tobacco include Betel quid (used in India) or paan (Bangladesh), where tobacco is blended with areca nut and flavourings. Chewing tobacco use may be higher than for cigarettes because of cost and relative lack of regulation compared with cigarettes. In England the highest self-reported use of chewing tobacco products is among Bangladeshi women, followed by Indian men, Pakistani men and Pakistani and Indian women (Longman et al., 2010). This presents a challenge for social marketers, who want to promote healthy lifestyles.

Some substitutes evolve from posing an existential threat to being complementary; for example, cinema production companies shortened the gap between a films' release and the launch of the DVD. This was done to maximise the impact of the marketing campaign for the original film on DVD sales, which are now deemed a major income generator.

> *Example*   In the music industry, record companies now release on multiple formats, accepting that there are segments who want to buy vinyl (often at substantial prices) and others who want to buy CDs for convenience. Increasingly, vinyl albums include a code for downloading the MP3 versions of songs. Vinyl has seen a resurgence built on marketing events such as Record Store Day. That said, vinyl sales will never recapture their prominence during the 1970s. Streaming is a greener option, with a lower carbon footprint and no use of materials; however, there are ethical issues around whether all artists are paid fairly for their creative content. Artists are increasingly adopting marketing tactics such as having "merch" stalls at every gig and providing substantial opportunities to buy products via websites.

5Ms

There are many tools and frameworks based on the number 5 (e.g. Porter's Five Forces, the 5Cs of the individual change process, the 5Ss); however, only the 5Ms has more than five factors. 5Ms is one of the CIM's preferred microenvironmental tools; however, many cite it as having Money, Men, Machines, Materials, Markets and Minutes. Despite this, it is still referred to as the 5Ms. The inherent sexism in the M that stands for "Men" must be addressed. It is an old model, which really should be gender-neutral; however, four Ms and a P (for people) may reduce its memorability. Another problem with the term "men" is that it is duplicated with HRM in Porter's VCA and staff in McKinsey's 7S framework. For those who (rightly) object to the use of the term "men",

Materials	• Imports dog grooming products, so no manufacturing materials needed
	• Biffy has a weaker brand than its biggest competitors, as they are a younger company who entered the market later (Biffy US, About Us).
	• Graphic design company provides a range of services, including photography, videos and the production of literature for new products
Money	• Biffy have experienced a 33% growth in turnover between 2016 and 2018, which is projected to rise further to 38% in 2020, despite the Brexit instability (Confidential Report 1, Biffy)
	• Due to increased turnover pressures GM percentage has declined from 21% (2014) to 18% YTD 2018 (Confidential Report 2, Biffy)
	• Despite the growth of sales in most product categories, some areas are behind budget for 2018. (Confidential Report 2, Biffy)
	• Sales targets have increased by 24% between in 2016 and 2018 (Confidential Report 3, Biffy)
Markets	• Biffy are now launching more new products than any of its competitors (Biffy Market Research Report, 2018)
	• The oligopolistic market in which Biffy operates does not have a clear leader
	• Due to the extensive competition and well-established brands, new entrants selling quality products are sporadic
	• Biffy do not currently undertake any audits to assess the marketing environment
	• A recent customer survey suggested Biffy needed to provide a better range of Dog Shampooing Aids (Biffy Customer Survey, 2015)
Machines	• Biffy do not use SEO for the website to analyse web traffic on new products
	• Telecommunications are used when launching new products within the market to increase sales quickly and recoup initial investment costs
	• MkIS suffers due to a lack of functional integration and information sharing due to departmental silos
	• More than 41% of UK companies, including Biffy's competitors, are using social networking sites to win new business

Figure 3.15 5Ms as applied to Biffy, a fictional importer of dog grooming products

they should use these alternatives when they create an internal environment/microenvironmental blend. There is no place for sexism in marketing, nor anywhere else.

Figure 3.15 shows how four of the 5Ms could be applied in an audit. Assume that the others have been captured elsewhere or are deemed irrelevant. Finding information on competitors is never easy. Markets are not always easy to define, and their behaviour cannot be predicted. No economist can predict a recession several years in advance. That said, Figure 3.15 clearly provides insights that would complement those of the other tools (and vice versa). These can be mapped to core competences.

Mendelow grid

The concept of mapping stakeholders was introduced in Chapter 1. The Mendelow grid, while less useful than the approach used in Figure (1.4), is more widely used. While mapping tools such as this (Figure 3.16) are merely snapshots, they can provide insights into relationships and can contribute to refined stakeholder communications.

Power sources may be identified (Figure 3.16); however, relationships may not be evident from the grid. It is preferable to consider where the stakeholders may be in the

		Interest	
		Low	*High*
Power Sources of power: • Positional power • Resource power • System power • Expert power • Personal power Within organisations • Hierarchy – formal power • Influence – informal power • Possession of knowledge and skills • Control of human environment • Involved in strategy implementation	High	A	B
External power sources • Control of strategic resources – materials, labour, money • Through internal links • Possession of knowledge and skills • Involved in strategy implementation	Low	C	D

Figure 3.16 Mendelow grid, featuring sources of power

Source: adapted from Megicks et al. (2009, p. 26)

future and (be prepared to) act accordingly. However, stakeholders may have interest in only certain aspects of an organisation's activities, say a project.

Balanced Scorecard

In 1992 Kaplan and Norton introduced the business community to the Balanced Scorecard framework. It was specifically designed to not only link objectives with performance measures but also provide a more holistic view than merely financial measures (Kaplan and Norton, 1992). The Balanced Scorecard combines qualitative and quantitative measures to evaluate the different expectations of stakeholders and relate assessments of performance to strategic decisions (Johnson et al., 2017). It is a useful tool because it challenges the hegemony of the financial functions. It makes the company look beyond the traditional bottom line. In other words, it makes accountants think about customers and marketers think about accounts. Simply put, if applied meaningfully, it can identify hidden, complex inter-functional relationships. It does this by reviewing the organisation from four perspectives (see Figure 3.17).

Companies use the Balanced Scorecard to set (more consistent) objectives and to focus on how organisational operations interact. Hence, it can provide a platform to monitor the effectiveness and efficiency that results from the objectives. Furthermore, it can go beyond monitoring corporate performance to include those in the supply networks. Like all tools and frameworks, it is useful only if it helps to create value that the customer is willing to take.

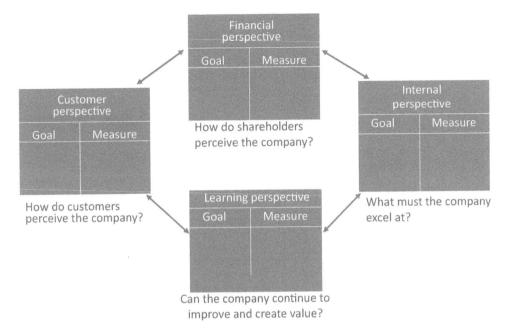

Figure 3.17 Balance Scorecard

There should be clear links between any control measures and the objectives (Figure 3.18). This should engender improved employee engagement. The Balanced Scorecard requires involving employees, which should improve employee "buy-in" to strategic objectives and measures. Any inter-functional synergies within organisations can have only positive effects on value creation internally and throughout the supply chain.

Although the Balanced Scorecard offers a platform to measure and monitor the organisational functions, it has limitations. It can be difficult to operate in practice because objectives are set in different functions, at different levels and with different timescales. (Imagine trying to compare the Balanced Scorecard of Virgin Trains with that of Virgin Mobile.) While it has a customer-centric component, it only tacitly recognises the influence of other stakeholders. It is the most complex microenvironmental tool to use. Companies must invest sufficient soft and hard resources for it to be used effectively. It will have to reside in the Management Information System (MIS) because it has to access functional systems (e.g. the MkIS for customer insights). This limits the extent to which some staff will be allowed to engage. It is predicated on complementing financial returns (ROI) with other Returns on Objectives (RoO). This will meet with some resistance, say from institutional investors. Companies with weak marketing departments or no marketing representation at board level may see the customer insights marginalised.

Finally, the balance scoreboard shares a common flaw with all internal and microenvironmental analysis tools and frameworks: it ignores the impact of the turbulent, tumultuous, uncontrollable macroenvironment. Hence, it is appropriate to reflect on this.

Perspective	Strategic Objective	Strategic Measure	Information Source

Financial	Profitability
	Managing key
	  stakeholders
	Return on capital
	  cashflow
	Organisational growth
		Net profit margin; %
		  of turnover; ROCE;
		  Cashflow (suppliers,
		  clients); organisation
		  growth vs industry
		  growth.
			Annual audited
			  accounts;
			  management
			  accounts; industry
			  information;
			  publications;
			  benchmarking using
			  industry standards;
			  competitor analysis;

Customer	Value for money
	Willingness to pay
	Competitive pricing
	Client satisfaction
	Supplier satisfaction
	Tender to success ratio
		Satisfaction survey;
		  pricing index;
		  mystery shop ratings;
		  client meetings;
		  customer attrition;
		  recommendations;
		  % repeat business;
		  % of new business;
		  non-payments/late
		  payments.
			satisfaction survey;
			  marketing
			  information; review
			  of competitor
			  pricing; complaints;
			  customer ranking
			  survey; competitor
			  benchmarking; social
			  media analysis.

Internal	Operations
	  management
	Service development
	Employee Motivation
	Accountability
	Ownership
		Low work duplication;
		Effective MkIS system;
		effective cooperation
		  between
		  departments; client
		  feedback; client
		  engagement time;
		  staff churn; level of
		  responsibility and
		  ownership
			Departmental function
			  updates; work
			  schedules; CRM
			  system; account
			  management
			  meetings; HR
			  database; job
			  satisfaction survey

Innovation and
  learning
	Time to market
	Creative workforce
	Learning organisation
	Forward looking
	Transparent
		NPD cycle time; enabled
		  and empowered
		  workforce; 360-degree
		  reviews; continuous
		  environmental
		  monitoring; staff
		  input valued.
			Research in NPD –
			  focus groups; idea
			  generation from shop
			  floor; can unlearn old
			  habits; clear strategic
			  horizon; employee
			  motivation.

Figure 3.18 Balanced Scorecard showing typical strategic objectives, measures and information
        sources

Source: adapted from Kaplan and Norton (1992) and Megicks et al. (2009)

3.3 External environmental frameworks and analysis

The Macro environment

The Macro environment is volatile and ever changing and can profoundly affect companies. Marketing objectives, strategies and tactics are subjected to these external forces. Hence, marketers must identify trends today that will continue into the future, which is when (after all) new products or services will be launched.

Macro forces do not operate in isolation. They can constrain or energise each other. Businesses need to take advantage of any opportunities that arise and steer clear of any threats – unless of course the threats provide a radical new direction for your company. At some point, someone at Apple (at the time a computer hardware/software manufacturer) saw the potential for portable music players even though the company had little experience in the sector. It can be argued that the diversification towards the iPod laid the foundations for much of Apple's subsequent success.

Identifying future trends

Too many managers do not spend enough time looking to the future. They stay within their comfort zones by focusing on internal rather than external issues. This is understandable, since thinking about how markets will develop over the next ten years is challenging. They often fail to meaningfully consult with colleagues in order to build consensus on the shape of future markets. Those that do tend to look two to three years into the future rather than ten to 20 years adopt the simple approach of predicting the future by reflecting on current situational trends that (they hope) will continue into the future. Marketers do not have this luxury; they must consider short-, medium- and long-terms changes to the market. They should seek to understand, better than their competitors, the macroenvironmental trends (and disruptions) that may transform sectors and create new opportunities.

Remember that a trend is a phenomenon that (over time) maintains the status quo, increases or decreases. Once identified, marketers must identify whether the trend is gathering momentum. Furthermore, marketers must establish whether the trend is neutral or has a positive or negative effect on achieving objectives.

A range of frameworks can provide structure for the assessment of future external trends.

Macro-frameworks

PEST has acted as the springboard for most commonly used frameworks (Figure 3.19).
There are some aspects worth considering before choosing a framework:

- The CIM's preferred framework is PESTEL.
- Some use educational as one of the STEEPLE variants; however, this could be covered by informational, which refers to knowledge and knowledge management.
- Charities, not-for-profits and QANGOs could use STEEPLE's ethical component.

Political/legal	S	P	S	E	S	P
Economic	Legal	E	T	P	T	L
Sociocultural	E	S	E	Informational	E	Access
Technological	P	T	E	S	E	T
	T	Environmental	P	T	L	Finance
		L	L	L	P	Ores
			Ethical	E	I	Regulations
					E	and reform
					Sustainable	Manners

Figure 3.19 PEST and other macro-frameworks

Source: adapted from Gosnay and Richardson (2008) and Stead et al. (2003)

- New technology companies would deem information to be key and thus use EPISTLE.
- Only STEEL PIES covers all of the factors and specifies the increasingly important sustainability.

PLATFORM was developed by Richard Stead in the 1990s. Although it is not widely used, it may be useful for those who seek access to raw materials in other countries. Many of these raw materials are depleting and irreplaceable. Their depletion presents problems for future generations. Helium, for example, is not only used for party balloons; it is also a key component in MRI scanners. Another way to audit the use of raw materials (including ores) is to use the materials aspect of the 5Ms framework.

The Chinese government has courted many African nations, offering substantial developments in infrastructure developments while making agreements to access sources of ores for decades to come. The host nation sees it as an opportunity to boost their economies by using infrastructure as an economic multiplier. Sustainability is covered in depth elsewhere, so it is prudent to reflect on key "Macro" factors by using the EPISTLE framework

Economics

Economics covers factors such as national growth/decline, interest rates, exchange rates, inflation rate, balance of trade, wage rates, minimum wage, working hours, unemployment (local and national), credit availability, cost of living, levels of disposable income, import tariffs and many others. Combinations of these factors can have a substantial impact on consumer confidence. With an estimated world turnover of $88 trillion, economic factors will always feature when analysing the business environments. A country's economic performance is traditionally measured using gross domestic product (GDP) growth, which itself is increasingly under scrutiny. In 1948 Simon Kuznets introduced the concept of GDP as a means to compare the economic wealth of nations (Kuznets, 1949). Since then, GDP has been used extensively as the key yardstick for economic growth. However, the underlying factors are complex and include many unsavoury contributors. A sad reality is that war often boosts GDP for some countries (though not necessarily those involved in the conflict). No sane person would advocate war as a means of economic growth.

Furthermore, headline GDP figures hide wide variations within countries. Consider the potential impact on GDP from Brexit. There are only two absolutes regarding the economic impact: first, there will be winners and losers economically; second, the impact will not be spread uniformly across the United Kingdom.

Many factors that shape GDP are beyond the control of national governments. After the global credit crunch of 2007–2008, the UK GDP reduced by 7% in the biggest fall in living memory. The UK economy technically "recovered" most of the losses by 2013; however, by 2018 wages (when allowing for inflation) were lower than pre-crunch. Around the same time, the members of the IoD were asked if they had the appropriate strategies for their organisations. Over 80% responded that they did. When asked if they believed that they implemented their strategies well, the figure plummeted to 14%. This raises major concerns about the United Kingdom's productivity and organisational effectiveness; however, it is beyond the capability of government to address these issues.

Large swathes of the media have a built-in scepticism towards "business". Inflated executive pay is a matter that is revisited many times, though arguably not always fairly.

Example The year 2018 saw the CEO of Persimmon Homes tender his resignation. There had been a media furore stimulated by a BBC reporter who ambushed the CEO regarding the bonus he had received. The bonus was large (approximately £100 million); however, it had been approved by the shareholders in 2012. What was wholly ignored was that the CEO had overseen the company's share value (and therefore company value) increase from £6.57 in 2012 to £26.27 by the end of 2017. During this period of 400% growth, the shareholders received generous dividends. Undoubtedly, Persimmons had benefited from the UK government's "help to buy" equity loan scheme (FT, 2017); however, this also benefited all of their competitors.

Questions should have also been asked of the shareholders and the Non-Executive Directors (NEDs) who are supposed to monitor such mechanisms. In 2011 the Cass Business School produced a report titled Roads to Ruin. The report found that poor corporate governance led to many organisational failures. The NEDs were found to be unwilling or unable to monitor and control the activities of those at board level – that is, the executives. In part, this inability resulted from nepotism – that is, NEDs had existing connections or relationships with the CEO. Alternatively, some of the NEDS simply lacked the knowledge and skills necessary to perform their duties in a meaningful manner. This was demonstrated by the organisation's core values and/or principles being ignored in practice. Some of the companies had adopted a groupthink mindset where directors and employees conformed to the expectations of the CEO. Some conformed because they did not know better, they benefit from it or they feared sanctions for non-compliance.

In the 1960s, the typical CEO earned 20 times that of the lowest-paid worker. By 2019 this figure has risen to 300, with no appreciable evidence that the inflated CEO salaries have left companies (and society) proportionately better off.

Organisations such as the OECD are seeking more meaningful ways of measuring economic growth. Their Better Life Index (see www.oecdbetterlifeindex.org) compares well-being across countries using 11 measurements considered essential regarding material living conditions and quality of life. The measures clearly correlate with sustainability, and in future, GDP will have to be complemented (or replaced) by such approaches

Example The 2007–2008 credit crunch may have been triggered by poor decision-making in the financial services sector, but major economies slowed and fell deeper into recession in 2008–2009 because of falling consumer confidence and hence reduced spending. Simply put, in most Western economies, consumer spending fuels growth. The downturn provided opportunities and threats to businesses and their activities. Businesses were forced to look at ways to maintain or indeed increase their income while continuing to provide customer satisfaction in effective and efficient ways. Sales promotional activities (see Chapter 2.1) both traditionally and through more contemporary digital media were used more frequently to stimulate consumer behaviour and incentivise consumers.

Example   Mobile telecoms companies such as Vodafone paid huge sums to acquire the licences and hence actively drove the promotion of text and MMS technologies, which in turn increased the traffic on their networks. Some commentators thought that the sums paid for licences in the United Kingdom (£23 billion) acted as a serious brake on the development of the 3G market. The 4G revolution presented if anything even greater opportunities for consumer change; however, the politicians only forecast £3.5 billion (in a similar auction in 2013). Ultimately, the National Audit Office (NAO) investigated the government's sale of the "super-fast 4G mobile phone spectrum" after the money raised (£2.3 billion) was £1.2 billion less than the amount the chancellor said it would raise.

Politics

There are three levels of politics: local, national and international. The three levels cover areas such as tax policy, employment laws, environmental regulations, trade restrictions and reform, tariffs and political stability. The European Union, for example, may introduce a new environmental law to cover all member states. These will be enshrined in UK law by the national government in Westminster. However, when it comes to policing the implementation of such laws, it falls to local government officers. A local government has enormous power; suffice it to say, those who transgress are much more likely to be prosecuted (and jailed) by local government representatives. It is not all about illegality, though. Companies seeking to physically expand will need planning permission, which is provided through local government facilities. At times, there are tensions between the different political levels.

Example   The coalition government elected in 2010 gave property developers the opportunity to challenge the findings of local councils by appealing to a central government department. This led to local objections being overturned by those in Whitehall. A by-product of this was a dramatic increase in the number of houses built on "green belt" land compared to the previous government.

Example   In 2013 the UK government announced its intention to redesign its digital services to make them so straightforward and convenient that all those who can use them prefer to do so (see www.gov.uk for details). Many companies were business-to-government (B2G) suppliers and needed to be aware of this development, particularly as the aim was to make savings of £1.7 to £1.8 billion each year.

Governments have a direct impact on marketers' activities and intentions. Change, or potential change in governments (after or in the run-up to a general election), brings uncertainty, a change in emphasis or, on occasion, a dramatic reversal in policy. Many governments are accused of "greenwashing", because they claim to be green and yet reduce support for renewable micro-generators such as solar panels (Ethical Consumer, 2018). These political decisions have provided businesses with greater opportunities to target users and convert them to customers. Governments make many policy decisions that affect current and future marcomms activities.

That said, "government action is not necessarily as effective as we would like" (Tadajewski and Hamilton, 2014, p. 81). This has to be seen in the context of post-credit crunch austerity programmes, where many national governments (often at the behest of central banks) are cutting social budgets in response. Increasingly, national governments are abrogating their responsibility and devolving social causes to the third sector. Hence, marketing is inherently political, though not necessarily party political. Local governments, along with communities, institutions, and individuals, may need to take part in longer-term, sustainable marketing projects to create society-wide changes.

A degree of hubris would suit many marketers who seem to think they are in control. Ultimately, marketers are allowed to ply their trade as they have the blessing of society expressed through its elected representatives. Indeed, van Dam and Apeldoorn (1996), who first coined the phrase "sustainable marketing", argued that market and individual consumer self-correction is unlikely to happen without government involvement and oversight.

Example   In 2011 the Welsh government introduced a 5p charge on plastic bags issued by retailers. This was followed by Northern Ireland (2013) and Scotland (2014). The English government was somewhat sluggish in that it introduced the tax only in 2017. No doubt they were test marketing the policy in the devolved countries. An estimated nine billion plastic bags were taken out of circulation. Between the implementation and 2018, the number of plastic bags handed out by retailers fell by 86%. In England the "average person" (whatever that means) now uses 19 bags per year compared to 140 before the charge. The bag levy raised £58 million in 2017 alone, and this was given to good causes. Subsequent studies suggest plastic bag–based marine litter has reduced by 50% around the UK shorelines. Other single-use plastic items are now under scrutiny, such as plastic straws, stirrers, cotton buds and coffee cups.

Example   Since the 1960s, many of the green initiatives that have been adopted globally have started in the United States, specifically California. Take automobiles, for example: California was at the forefront of introducing legislation on zero-emissions vehicles (ZEVs) and creating an infrastructure for hydrogen as an energy source. A dozen other US states adopted the Californian initiative, constituting a third of the US domestic car market. President Trump challenged the autonomy of the individual states to set their own emission targets. Indeed, in 2018 California was one of a 17 states to file a lawsuit challenging the US Environmental Protection Agency, who had declared the US vehicle emissions to be inappropriate. This coincided with President Trump ending US participation in the 2015 Paris Agreement on reducing GHGs. Whether this was right or wrong is beyond the scope of this book. Irrespective of who is in the White House, the Californians will continue to develop and adopt new green products.

Information

Information provides the basis of effective decision-making, and therefore, its availability and content accuracy are issues for managers and leaders alike. Information clearly resonates with communication (see Chapter 2.1). Technological change has enabled changes in communication; for example, Web 2.0 has created an explosion of accessibility to information and for an increasingly wider audience. Smartphones provide access via social media to brands and enables improved communication with users. Reading blogs and general information on, say, RSS sites (see www.newsnow.

co.uk for an example) provides an additional dimension to information. Marketers can gain key insights from bloggers and users. This should improve the encoding of messages to better support consumers and customers in their decision-making.

> *Example*   Google had a stand-off with the Chinese government over the issue of censorship and dissemination of political messages. Google resisted pressure from the Chinese government to agree to political censorship. That said, in the long run, Google may win as the desire for greater openness among young Chinese citizens increases with every generation. In 2018 Google relented and agreed to create a search engine for Chinese citizens that allowed a degree of censorship.
>
> *Example*   The GDPR recommends using approved codes of conduct (ICO, 2018). These will reflect the needs of different processing sectors and micro, small and medium-size enterprises. Trade associations or bodies representing a sector can create codes of conduct to help their sector comply with the GDPR in an efficient and cost-effective way. Signing up to a code of conduct is voluntary. However, if there is an approved code of conduct relevant to your processing, you may wish to consider signing up. It can also help show compliance to the Information Commissioner's Office (ICO), the public and your business to business relationships (ibid).

Sociocultural

A common mistake made by those undertaking marketing audits is to confuse "sociocultural" with "social". Indeed, "social" trends may be of interest; however, they represent only one facet of this huge diverse area. Sociocultural includes cultural norms and expectations, health consciousness, demographics (e.g. population growth rate, age distribution, family size, life cycle, divorce rates, etc.), career attitudes, safety, attitudes to global warming, lifestyle choices, and hobbies, to name but a few.

Marketers must remember that such trends transcend national borders. Because of film, broadcast media and, of course, the Internet, attitudes, fashions and pastimes are continually evolving. This is as evident in Europe as it is in the United Kingdom, where the influence of the United States remains particularly strong.

Sociocultural attitudes evolve, so what is deemed unacceptable now may not always be the case. Alternatively, things tolerated in the past are no longer acceptable. An example is racism in football. Behaviour that may have been allowed in the 1970s is simply not acceptable in the 21st century.

Another positive example would be the change of attitude to drink driving, which is now seen as unacceptable. How long it will take for drivers to accept that using a mobile phone without a hands-free kit is just as morally wrong? It is difficult to predict to what extent media consumption habits will change in the future. Younger generations are already reading fewer hardcopy newspapers, preferring to get their news online. Similarly, television-viewing habits are changing with more on-demand options becoming available. In the United Kingdom, an ageing population and a shrinking youth market has seen businesses adapting their targeting accordingly. In ten to 20 years' time, when the current youngsters are the captains of industry, it is hard to imagine that they will see newspapers as their first-choice communications channel or "media vehicle". Smartphones and tablets will increasingly provide opportunities to access different media.

Smartphones can store personal biometric data such as finger prints and retinal scans. These features, complemented by voice recognition, enable secure transaction billing, and consumers increasingly use smartphones to make small contactless purchases. This increases the responsibility of suppliers to handle such data securely. Marketing organisations who process payment card data are obliged to comply with the Payment Card Industry Data Security Standard (PCI-DSS), which outlines a number of specific technical and organisational measures that the sector considers applicable whenever such data are being processed. Although compliance with the PCI-DSS is not necessarily equivalent to compliance with the GDPR's security principle, if marketers process card data and suffer a personal data breach, the ICO will consider the extent to which measures that PCI-DSS requires have been adopted, particularly if the breach related to a lack of a particular control or process mandated by the standard (ICO, 2018).

> *Example*   The major mobile phone companies (e.g. Ericsson) launched a payment system called Payforit. The Payforit scheme provides a safe, trustworthy environment for mobile content purchases. The Trusted Mobile Payment Framework rules define how merchants, accredited payment intermediaries and operators cooperate to make mobile payments a secure and seamless process. Further to developing trust in mobile payment, Payforit aims at creating transparency and ease of use for consumers. A set of "screen style" rules govern how payment pages look and function, simplifying and securing how users purchase content via a standardised interface presented on their mobile phones. Similar schemes already exist; for example, consumers in Alaska can pay for household goods by mobile. This trend could ultimately challenge the need for carrying credit cards, as it would provide considerably more security and ultimately reduce fraud.

Ultimately, it is hard to see how the credit card industry can survive (in its current form) as users will increasingly use their mobiles as their preferred choice of payment device. The banking industry will increasingly incorporate smartphones that provide greater security, into their processes. The Chip'n'Pin development dramatically reduced credit card fraud. eBay's purchase of Paypal was undoubtedly a shrewd business acquisition. Their auction business may have peaked; however, online and mobile payment is going to grow. Marketers must ensure that goods and services can be paid for (easily) using a mobile platform to reflect the sociocultural changes of the younger segments.

Technology

Marketing has at times struggled to keep up with the pace of technological change. If anything, change is *accelerating*, and marketers need to be aware of how "new" technologies can help to achieve their corporate and marketing objectives. The Internet is not a "new" technology. It's established and embedded in marketing for nearly all companies. Clearly, there are some important trends that will continue to shape marketing in the future.

Samsung, Panasonic and Sony launched Internet-enabled TVs in 2009. Around the same time, in the United Kingdom, Channel 5 announced that most of its key outputs were to be shown on YouTube, thus creating a virtuous circle of converging technologies. This interoperability continued with Netflix and Amazon (among others) commissioning and offering exclusive TV shows "online". Top movie directors such as Joss Whedon offered mini-films online "direct" to the audience. Musicians such as Bjork provided projects (e.g. Biophilia) where an app was integral rather than merely complementing the usual formats (e.g. CD, download, streaming, etc.). Where the creative industries lead, traditional businesses often follow.

> *Example*   The next generation of 5G phones will have more functionality. The bandwidths will be substantially better, the processing power and storage will continue to double every 18 months and downloads will take place at up to 100 MB per second. New ranges of applications will make the most of these developments, particularly based on video, which at times still struggles under 4G. Vlogging, where the users use their mobile sets in situ rather than sat at a desk, will increasingly replace traditional blogging. Mobile-enabled videoconferencing will become commonplace as the camera and microphone technologies improve. Hence, marketers will be able to have more, better-quality interactions with remote stakeholders or customers while reducing their carbon footprint.

Video-sharing sites will increase dramatically, similar to the picture-sharing sites such as Pinterest, which are still popular. The reduced time to download video will see a corresponding increase in piracy. South Korea has led the way in broadband speeds, with 100 MB being common when most of the United Kingdom was at 4 MB. When it only takes a couple of minutes to download a film, the tendency for illegal copying and sharing increases hugely. This was the case in South Korea.

3D printing will become more significant in the future as the technology becomes more accessible and affordable. There are specialist stores that already offer 3D printing services (e.g. Home Depot in the United States). Consumers will have the ability to print in plastics, powder (achieving a much higher resolution), resin, metal, ceramic and even foodstuffs. Future marketers and customers will be able to produce their own custom products. Manufacturers may have to evolve from making goods to providing the blueprints (or at least printing instructions) and raw materials for smartphone cases, simple toys, clothes or even food. Marketers are already using 3D printing to produce custom gifts and direct marketing content. 3D printing has the potential to be something more than a novelty or a gimmick, but it depends on people's acceptance (and use) of the technology. Scientists have already used 3D printing technology to create functioning human organs and tissues. The technology is in its infancy, and consumers will undoubtedly be more sophisticated with 3D printing in future. If a product breaks or a part is lost, it could be printed and replaced locally, having a significant positive impact on the longevity of the product and its environmental footprint. It could make a major contribution to the circular economy.

Legal

Legal frameworks exist to regulate business and ensure it operates legally, ethically and fairly. A number of Acts of the UK Parliament have provided a framework for marketers within which to operate both legally and ethically. The Libel Act of 1792, the Data Protection Act 1998, the Freedom of Information Act 2000 and the Privacy

Law of 1987 are crucial to protecting the activities of many practitioners, and they act as a boundary for ethical practice.

The EU Directive on Information and Consultation of Employees (2004) gives employees of "undertakings of 50 or more employees" rights to be informed and consulted about issues that affect their employment and the prospect of the business. This has in turn increased the need for employers to embrace internal marketing (see Chapter 4.2) in order to communicate more effectively with staff via internal communication strategies that are increasingly designed and delivered by marketers rather than HR departments. Other forms of legislation allude to employment, access to materials, quotas, resources, imports/exports, taxation, pricing and more.

In 2004 the United Kingdom saw a major shift in the regulation of marcomms when the Advertising Standards Authority (ASA) was designated as the self-regulating body for advertising content regulation in both broadcast and non-broadcast advertising. In 2013 the ASA's remit was broadened to regulate online content. There will likely be more regulatory activity in social media. This may feature disclosures of interest, copyright protection for creative artists, codes of practice, the protection of minors and the removal of offensive material.

GDPR

A case where technology and legal meet is the GDPR legislation introduced in 2018. Marketers now have access to a staggering amount of information from watches tracking calories and sleep to apps for managing finances or messaging friends. Historically, the legislation (e.g. the Data Protection Act) saw protection provided for institutions often at the expense of individuals. In 2016 the European Union passed legislation to create the GDPR and to harmonise privacy laws across Europe commencing May 2018. GDPR was introduced to reverse the institutional bias and to give individuals more control over how organisations use their personal information or data.

The GDPR set out seven key principles:

1   Lawfulness, fairness and transparency;
2   Purpose limitation;
3   Data minimisation;
4   Accuracy;
5   Storage limitation;
6   Integrity and confidentiality (security);
7   Accountability.

Marketers have no excuse for misusing data, because the GDPR principles are broadly similar to the principles in the Data Protection Act 1998. It is likely that marketers will face more requests for personal information about consumers. Marketers need to ensure they act in accordance with GDPR and have the correct systems and procedures (Figure 3.20).

Personal information means anything that could identify a living person, directly or indirectly, including their name, address, location, phone number, IP addresses and even Internet cookies. It also includes data classed as "sensitive" (under GDPR), such as DNA, ethnicity, sexual orientation, religious beliefs and trade union membership.

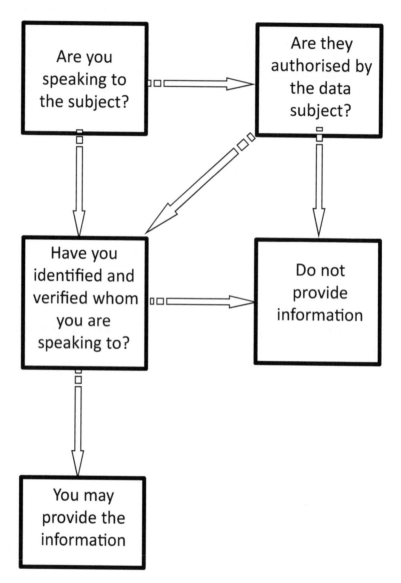

Figure 3.20 Flowchart for information requests under GDPR

Source: adapted from ICO (2018)

Such "sensitive" data is expected to be given more protection, and any breach must be reported within 72 hours. The year 2018 saw regular reporting of breaches (e.g. Facebook, Uber and MyFitnessPal). The breaches were extensively covered in mainstream media and led to reputational damage.

Subjects must actively opt in to having their data used, and they can withdraw consent at any time. They can request information regarding the nature of data being collected and how companies use their data and why. Companies must respond in language that is easy to understand. Subjects have the right to be provided with a copy of the information – as well as the rationale for collecting their personal data and who has access. The response must be provided pro gratis, in an accessible way and within 30 days. Upon receipt of the information, subjects can insist on inaccurate data being corrected.

Under GDPR, there are two key stakeholder groups: data "controllers", who determine how and why personal data is processed, and "processers", who collect the data.

Larger companies (i.e. have more than 250 employees) who sell into the European Union will have to comply with GDPR irrespective of where their HQ is located. They must document all of the data they are processing, including why, how customers opted in, who has access and a description of their security measures.

The regulation also applies to sole traders, entrepreneurs and SMEs. Indeed, any organisation, no matter how small, who, say, collects customers' email addresses needs to comply. SMEs need only to document sensitive data or data that is used regularly.

Online GDPR

People now have the right to be forgotten, which means they can ask for their personal data to be deleted at any time, assuming it is no longer relevant. An employer can reasonably hold relevant information, such as emergency contacts. This applies online and offline. Companies who may share data are obliged to inform others that the subject has requested the right to be forgotten. The data, links to the data and copies of the data must be deleted. Social media companies will have to delete any posts made when the subjects were children.

The GDPR allows the ICO to issue fines to anyone failing to comply, up to £17.5 million, or 4% of a company's global turnover, whichever is higher. Fines can be issued for misusing data, data breaches or failing to process an individual's data correctly. GDPR rules will continue to apply after the United Kingdom leaves the European Union. The government's Data Protection Act means that GDPR rules will be replicated in UK law.

Environment

For the purposes of macro-analysis, the term "environment" refers to the broader, ecological environment. Environmentalism has traditionally received less coverage in the key marketing texts despite a widening range of issues becoming increasingly important to UK consumers. As consumers take a greater interest in the environment, driven by the media and better education, the need for marketers to consider the environment in a friendly and sustainable manner is important. All things being equal, where consumers have a choice, they choose green. Consumers have changing expectations, and they are increasingly discerning – that is, willing to change their spending patterns. Many people buy tinned tuna from Sainsbury's, which was the first grocery retailer to guarantee the fish were caught with pole and line. The price was higher than the net-caught alternatives, and yet it has proven to be a successful product line for Sainsbury's.

> *Example*   Pressure is increasing on companies to act sustainability. There are 1400 environmental pressure groups in the United Kingdom alone. Any one of

these could go to the press and create a bad news story for a marketer to manage. The 13 largest green groups in the United Kingdom have over five million members who may exert pressure through lobbying, PR campaigns and direct action. Regarding plastic bags, in 2018 Friends of the Earth (FoE) argued that "A 5p charge may not have sounded like much, but the plummeting number of single-use plastic bags demonstrates the difference that can be made by effective legislation. Companies and governments must do more. It's time that legislation was extended to cover all other unnecessary single-use plastics, from straws to coffee cups". Similarly, Greenpeace insisted that "the success of the plastic bag charge shows that a smart and well-aimed government intervention can change behaviour, . . . but we need to go further, faster".

Reduce, recycle, repair, repurpose and reuse

Many activists believe that modern business practices advocate "selling more", while "sustainability" is about consuming less. Marketers may need to adapt their marcomms to address stakeholders' concerns, by inviting them to ask questions that can be answered. It is sensible to inform the local media of any good news stories that result from these dialogues. Sustainability is not simply about damage limitation; rather, it's an opportunity to promote good practices. Business as usual cannot continue, and the good news is that companies and even countries are changing their behaviour. For example, in 2014 copper use in China featured 80% use of recycled metal. This was driven by increasing copper prices; however, it illustrates how changes can be made, such as the use of fuel, recycling and waste.

These changes in expectations have coincided with the public's increasing cynicism towards environmental claims, leading to increasing accusations of "greenwashing". Merely stating green credentials may no longer be enough.

Ethical

Consumers' changing expectations and spending patterns are repeated with ethical purchases; for example, the Cooperative is the largest seller of fair-trade wine in the United Kingdom. Undoubtedly, fair-trade wines cost more, and yet sales grow year by year. Attitudes to ethics are sociocultural in origin; however, they are often intertwined with environmental concerns.

> *Example*   A common practice is to leave links in the comments pages of blogs and other social sites. This is known as "link spam" and is deemed by some observers to be unethical. Organisations such as Automattic (see http://automattic.com/) provide software that "catches" over 21 million spam comments per day. Cases have been cited where digital marketing agencies have targeted up to 500 blogs to promote their client's services. Automattic estimated that 83% of all comments are spam, which (if true) is ultimately self-defeating for marketers because customers (or prospects) having to trawl through irrelevant and/or misleading information can only deter them from engaging with social sites, fora or blog.

Some argue that such "link-building" techniques are legitimate components of SEO marketing; however, misinformation due to spam is simply another form of noise for marketers to overcome. The line between legitimate blog commenting and blog spamming seems blurred for too many parties, and this can ultimately only lead to a breakdown of trust in networks and/or communities.

Privacy campaigners are concerned about the implications of the data and information available on mobile platforms downloaded from sites, intranets, confidential meetings and so on. Increasingly, technology is enabling unethical behaviour (e.g. upskirting, clandestine audio/video recording, etc.). While most commercial technology is used respectfully, the information could be used in an unethical manner for commercial and profitable purposes. Many professional bodies provide codes of conduct to address such behaviour.

> *Example*   In 2014 Facebook courted controversy over research undertaken by two US-based universities into users' attitudes. Clearly, Facebook's intention was to use information gleaned from their users for commercial purposes. The problem is the users were not aware that their dialogues were being listened to and analysed. No permission had been granted by the respondents. This breaks arguably the single most important rule in research: to respect the respondents. Generally, marketers should seek the permission of those being observed. In response to the backlash, Facebook quickly reviewed their plans and launched a PR campaign to counter the negative publicity.

As stated, the ethical issues surrounding social media are prevalent. But herein lies the issue: what is considered ethical and what unethical? It is a grey area. The need for ethical behaviour is paramount, so marketers must use sound judgement.

Issues with the environmental tools and frameworks

There may be some debate regarding where Macro factors reside in a framework. Clearly, there are areas of overlapping factors – for example, increasing disposable income (economic) and leisure time (sociocultural) have changed the platforms used to communicate (technological).

Not all Macro factors are of equal weight. An example would be a business undertaking a marketing audit and changing its comms activities to reflect the macro trends by increasing its use of social media sites. Social media continues to evolve, particularly in the youth market, and marketers must monitor these sites to be able to respond to opportunities or threats that arise. Quick responses are necessary as online customers and prospects can be fickle, and the "trend" of the moment can soon evaporate. To be able to respond, marketers must be able to prioritise the issues.

Marketers must assess the organisation's strengths and weaknesses before implementing any marketing-related changes. The tools are not sacrosanct and can (or even should) be adapted. Many involved in SME marketing have amended VCA to include entrepreneurialism or the characteristics of the owner-manager. The following are some of the issues relating to the internal, Micro and Macro tools:

- They have different degrees of complexity – for example, the 5Ms tool is easier to apply than, say, undertaking a balance scoreboard exercise.
- Larger organisations work in SBUs that often have different markets to address (think of the Virgin empire and its enormous range from music to trains to planes

to credit cards, all of which have markets that differ in terms of size, type and condition). Hence, consideration has to be given to how corporate level objectives 'translate' when creating objectives at the SBU level.

- Information is not easily available from competitors. Look for trade bodies to give a market overview.
- With matrices and grids (e.g. Mendelow, BCG, DPM), the findings rarely fit neatly into a pigeonhole.
- With staged models (e.g. the PLC), it is not always easy to know which stage the product is in or when it should move from one (stage) to another.
- Far too many micro-tools lack customer centricity.

Marketers should not be fooled by the vast array of internal and/or micro-tools compared to the simple PEST analysis. The external analysis is vital and must be carried out diligently. Also, all tools have strengths and weaknesses, and marketers must choose the ones best suited to their organisation and market.

The SWOT summary

A SWOT summary juxtaposes the internal analysis/micro-analysis in the form of recent strengths and weaknesses (SWs) with future macro opportunities and threats (OTs). It should be detailed and include trends rather than snapshots (Figure 3.21).

SWs reflect the organisation over recent years and up to the current time. They provide meaningful information that alludes to the organisational core competences. OTs represent the marketer's perception of the issues that may affect the company over a given planning horizon. Having carried out a meaningful SWOT, marketers should be in a better position to create marketing objectives. Figure 3.22 illustrates how the components of the SWOT affect one another. Some findings arguably go in different sections. For example, a strength of a competitor could go into another company's weakness section – that is, unless the competitor has opened a new market. Apple did not invent tablet computers or MP3 players. However, their iPad and iPod were game changers that opened markets. They certainly benefited from first-mover advantage; however, the competitors (e.g. Samsung and Huawei) soon caught up.

The SWOT can inform strategic planning (e.g. acquisition opportunities, entering new markets, investment opportunities, etc.) or marketing planning (e.g. product development and launches, research, etc.). It can be from departmental or individual perspectives, looking at what is delivered, to whom and how. To be effective, it needs to be regularly undertaken so that organisations may spot trends before others, thus providing competitive advantage. Always remember that SWOT summaries are snapshots taken at one specific time.

Students often produce SWOTs with single words of short phrases, such as "disposable income". The phrase is meaningless unless qualified. That is, is it increasing, decreasing or staying the same? In short, trends are needed rather than snapshots. Ideally, a SWOT should feature findings from recognised, reputable sources. If it is made up of guesses, the credibility of the exercise diminishes. Finally, a key flaw in a SWOT summary is that it does not offer solutions or (specifically) marketing objectives. Hence, it is time to consider the start of the analytical stage.

Strengths (Internal/Micro)
Resources, assets, people
Experience, knowledge, data
Financial reserves, likely returns
Market reach, awareness
Innovative aspects
Location
Price, value, quality
Accreditations, qualifications
Processes, systems, IT
Cultural, attitudinal, behavioural
Management qualities
Market developments
Competitors' vulnerabilities
USPs
Tactics – surprise, major contracts
Business and product development
Information and research
Partnerships, agencies

Weaknesses (Internal/Micro)
Gaps in capabilities
Lack of competitive strength
Reputation, presence and reach
Financial strength
Timescales, deadlines, pressures
Continuity robustness
Effects on core activities
Reliability of data
Morale, commitment, leadership
Accreditations
Processes and systems, IT
Competitor intentions
Market demand
Sustaining internal capabilities
Insurmountable weaknesses
Loss of key staff
Sustainable financial backing
Volumes, production, economies
New or niche target markets

Opportunities (Macro)
Industry or lifestyle trends
Technology development and innovation
Global influences
Geographical, export, import
Seasonal, weather, fashion influences

Threats (Macro)
Political effects
Legislative effects
Environmental effects
IT developments
New technologies, services, ideas
Economy – home, abroad
Seasonality – weather effects

Figure 3.21 Generic SWOT summary

3.4 Generating useful SM objectives

The final part of the "review" section is the production of the SWOT summary. It is often wrongly called a SWOT analysis, which is a misnomer as so far no analysis has taken place. All that has happened is the collection of findings. The analysis starts by judging where the Micro (S&W) fit in with the Macro (O&T) in such a way that marketers can create marketing objectives. Figure 3.22 shows the SWOT findings for a restaurant chain that is thinking of diversifying into opening vegan outlets. In a form of test marketing, they are investigating Leeds as a potential first location. The success of the first flagship store could provide the platform for expanding across the country.

As discussed, a SWOT does not provide answers but rather informs the creation of objectives. Identifying "key" objectives provides a platform for achievable marketing goals; they are most effective if they are few in number, concise and prioritised. Generic areas for marketing objectives may include raising a brand's profile, shaping the opinions of key stakeholders or increasing the market share. Many commentators suggest objectives should be SMART:

- **Specific** – Avoid being either too vague or too tightly focused.
- **Measurable** – Ensure objectives can be measured and compared with previous results. This raises the credibility of marketing objectives in other functions.

Strengths	Weaknesses
1. High customer/prospect population 2. Strong Core Competency among staff 3. Premier facilities available in Leeds. 4. Strong marketing expertise 5. Experienced serial entrepreneur with good attitude to risk 6. Leeds has a substantial student population with 5 degree awarding institutions 7. Parent company has strong track record of digital development for start ups	1. No existing corporate presence in Leeds 2. Millenials harder to target as predominantly seek information online 3. Entrenched/outmoded working practices of many suppliers/retailers 4. Increasing red tape when starting businesses 5. Potential partners have poor online footprint, i.e. website or social media presence 6. High city property rates and rents
Opportunities	Threats
1. Obesity is on the rise with the UK having one of the worst rates in the EU 2. Graduates can't get on the housing ladder so increasingly living with non-vegan parents 3. Leeds is the 3rd largest city in the UK and will grow to nearly 1 million over next 20-25 years 4. Yorkshire has increasing demand for vegetarian and vegan enterprises 5. The trend for increasing fragmentation of the food market is set to continue 6. Consumers are increasingly demanding healthier foods and choosing to 'eat out'	1. Vegans perceived by some to be "tree huggers" & obsessed with worthy causes 2. Vegans attracting negative perceptions due to death threats being issued 3. Vegans associated with aggressive pressure groups/extremists 4. Increasing conflict between consumer perception of taste and health concerns when food is deemed desirable (taste) and undesirable (high calorie/fat content of meat) 5. Reducing funding from government agencies, including councils 6. Economic uncertainty after Brexit

Figure 3.22 SWOT summary for a restaurant chain opening a vegan outlet in Leeds

Source: original diagram

- **Accurate** (or aspirational or achievable) – Do not set unachievable targets (aka a wish list), because imposing targets that cannot be met demotivates staff.
- **Realistic** – Will the objective deliver the required changes? Will senior management "buy in"?
- **Timely** (or targeted) – Are the resources available to achieve the objectives in the timescale? Is the objective targeting the appropriate segment?

Not all elements of SMART are equal. S&M are fundamental because objectives must be specific (not vague) and measurable. Marketers are often persuading colleagues from other functions who may be sceptical. Hence, offering measurable objectives, which can be judged, goes some way to defusing inter-functional objections.

TOWS analysis

Marketing objectives often incorporate two key areas namely product and market development. A TOWS analysis is a creative process that can easily generate 20–30 marketing objectives. These 30 potential objectives need to be evaluated in terms of probability (that senior management will buy into the idea), urgency and impact on client perception. The factors (urgency, impact and probability) are widely used; however, others may be incorporated.

Using the aforementioned vegan restaurant, the key objectives have been ranked in a TOWS analysis (Figure 3.23). Ultimately, the TOWS must be customer centric. As discussed, marketers must prioritise the marketing objectives. The marketing objectives in Figure 3.23 have the following characteristics:

- Spring from the SWOT (by identifying the specific SWOT factors);
- Are ranked and therefore prioritised;
- Are SMART, at least S&M;
- Have timescales.

Remember that marketing objectives do not stand in isolation. Having identified SO_1, SO_2 and ST_1 (see Figure 3.23) as the key marketing objectives, the marketing consultant must ensure that they fit with the corporate objectives and would need to identify which components in the mix (i.e. the 7Ps) need to be adapted. It is useful to map the marketing objectives against the mix (Figure 3.24).

Figure 3.24 should act as the springboard for control tools such as KPIs or Gantt charts, which are useful for detailing implementation.

TOWS	Marketing Objective	Urgency	Probability	Impact	Total
SO1 (S1S4O3O4O6)	Create a profile in the local media over the next 6 months	3	3	3	9
SO2 (S2S7O2O5O6)	Offer discounted vegan meals to students in existing branches to test recipes by year end	3	3	2	8
ST1 (S1S4S7T4T6)	Start teaser campaign with advertising hoardings around Leeds over next 6 months	3	2	3	8
ST2 (S1S4T3T4T6)	Create a mobile platform to engage with vegans in Leeds in the next fiscal year	2	2	2	6
WT1 (W1W2T3T4T6)	Develop social media campaign to target existing customers in region by the end of the quarter	2	2	1	5
WO2 (W1W4W5O3O4O6)	Buy an existing vegan restaurant and rebrand by year end	2	1	1	4

Figure 3.23 TOWS analysis with detailed objectives for vegan restaurant

Source: original diagram

Mix	Marketing Objectives		
	SO1	SO2	ST1
Customer benefits (aka Product)	●	●	●
Cost to customer (aka Price)			●
Convenience (aka Place)	●	●	●
Communications (aka Promotion)	●	●	●
People	●	●	
Process	●	●	●
Presence (physical evidence)	●	●	●

Figure 3.24 Mapping the mix against marketing objectives from the TOWS analysis

Source: original diagram

3.5 Strategic SM choices (i) – Sustainable Segmentation, Targeting and Positioning

The next step is to reflect on the strategic decisions necessary to achieve the prioritised marketing objectives. Before implementing changes to the mix, marketers must, first, establish the Segmentation, Targeting and Positioning (STP) and, second, choose the correct marketing strategy for the marketing objectives.

Segmentation

Any assessment of the segment undertaken during the audit stage of a marketing plan will have to be revaluated. Marketers cannot assume that the original segment (whether B2C or B2B) will be appropriate for marketing objectives developed in the TOWS. Furthermore, the means of communicating the segment may also need to be reviewed.

Two well-known segmentation frameworks are "DAMP" and "MASS". DAMP is an acronym for distinct, accessible, measurable and profitable:

- *Distinct* – each segment should be unique and may need a tailored marketing mix;
- *Accessible* – the marcomms campaign must be able to access the buyers, whether B2B, B2C, B2G and so on;
- *Measurable* – marketers need to know the size of the segment in order to assess the success of their campaign, which is not always easy;
- *Profitable* – the segment must be able to generate revenue and profit now and in the future, which may not always be the case, such as for a one-off project like the Olympics.

MASS shares the measurable and accessible criteria and adds specific and sustainable:

- *Measurable* – marketers need to know the size of the segment in order to assess the success of their campaign, which is not always easy;
- *Accessible* – the marcomms campaign must be able to access the buyers, whether B2B, B2C, B2G and so on;

- *Specific* –close to the meaning of distinct, this means that the segment is easily identified and differentiated from others;
- *Sustainable* – this means long-lasting and has no association with the TBL or sustainability in the sense of ecology and/or ethics, though such use of nomenclature is problematic.

Segments must be used; however, they have to be applied judiciously when considering the multiple values and motivations of individual consumers. There is more to being a sustainable consumer than is covered in the traditional segmentation frameworks. Hence, Figure 3.25 offers an SM segmentation framework.

Segments may be split into sub-segments. These sub-segments still have to be large enough to target. Using the aforementioned proposed vegan restaurant, the marketing consultant would undertake research and identify sub-segments (Figure 3.26).

Having identified the sub-segments, the marketers could apply the framework in Figure 3.25 to identify those worth targeting. The mix could be tailored for each

Factor	Comment
Accessible	The marcomms campaign must be able to access buyers/prospects/influencers, whether B2B, B2C, B2G or other.
Profitable	The segment must be large enough (or in small segments, the customers must have sufficient disposable income) to provide revenue and profit or to achieve other objectives. Profit is not necessarily financial – e.g. charities may seek to recruit volunteers.
People and Planet	The segment must be willing to pay for products and services, where some profit is invested in people- and planet-related objectives
Return	Marketers should differentiate consumers by their profitability and their involvement in a category. That helps to prioritise investments in business actions intended to promote segment growth. For instance, two consumer segments may both be highly involved in a category in terms of attitudes and volume of purchases. One may value time over savings and typically pay full price, whereas the other may be sensitive to price
Opportunity	The segment must have long-term prospects unless it is for a specific project. Opportunity also considers the frequency or depth of use, knowledge or expertise and the amount of money spent (or available). It takes into account the time they spend thinking, researching, learning, talking about and shopping for brands.
Values	The degree to which consumers consider a product category important given their needs, emotional makeup, attitudes, perceptions, values and interests needs to be assessed.
Estimable	Each segment should be measurable and distinct. It will need a tailored marketing mix.
Size	Relevant to market needs, marketers need to know the size of the segment in order to assess the success of their campaign. This is not always easy.

Figure 3.25 APPROVES – a sustainable segmentation framework

Source: adapted from DAMP and MASS frameworks and BCG (2008)

Segment	Comment
Fruitarian	Lives mainly or exclusively on fruits. May eats only fruit that has fallen
Ultra-vegan	Eats, wears, uses no animal-related products under any circumstances
	Like voluntary simplifiers will actively seek information to ensure they abide by their principles
	Accepts limited choice as way of life
Vegan	Eats, wears, uses no animal-related products largely – will compromise occasionally
Vegetarian	Eats no animal-related products under any circumstances but may consume dairy products
Flexitarian	A plant-based diet with the occasional addition of meat
	Sometimes referred to as flexible vegetarianism, casual vegetarians or vegivores
Omnivore	Eats meat and vegetables with little distinction
Conscious consumer	Eats meat and vegetables but insists on minimal animal suffering or damage to the environment
	May take vegan option when offered
	Subscribes to notion of sustainability, i.e. the triple bottom line
Carnivore	Predominantly consumes meat as part of a high-protein diet

Figure 3.26 Segments for those who eat meat versus those who do not

Source: adapted from Flexitarian (2018), Fruitarian (2018), Vegan Society (2018) and Vegsoc (2018)

segment in order to attract most of the sub-segments to the restaurant, though probably not the carnivores. Marketers cannot keep all of the people happy all of the time.

Segments and sustainability

Segmentation is important; however, some marketers insist on reducing everything to data sets. They think marketing is a science, whereas in reality it is as much art and philosophy as it is science. Consider that, typically, 90% of new FMCG products fail within two years. Surely a scientific approach (to segmentation) would be able to address this. However, consumers are often emotional and irrational when buying goods. They are often driven by their values, which are not easy to segment. Many marketers use behavioural segmentation to consider attitudes, lifestyle choices and motivations. It is much harder to segment on the basis of such soft subjects compared to hard metrics – for example, age, occupation or income. Many of the values attributed to sustainability change from generation to generation.

> *Example* Generation Z includes those born since 1995. They are "digital natives" and are constantly connected online. They use the mobile platform extensively and use smartphones as a hub for supporting social connectivity. To access this segment, marketers must develop credible digital identities, through a branded website or social media. Generation Z is considered to have short attention spans and are easily distracted. Previous studies have suggested attention spans to be less than six minutes (Campaign Monitor, 2019). Hence, more targeted sustainability strategies need to be developed, providing information, entertainment and other

valuable content when and where it is needed. Gamification, bringing game-based mechanics such as leader boards, competition and reward to interactions, is a useful approach. When dealing with minors, confirmation and support from parents is essential.

Generation Z often display high levels of environmental and/or societal concern. As discussed in Chapter 1, consumers who are concerned about sustainability issues can be mapped and thus segmented. Figure 1.13 provides a basis for value-based segmentation and mapping. Companies seeking to self-identify as sustainable may not necessarily prioritise the pursuit of growth; indeed, many sustainability start-ups prefer to keep standards undiluted and demanding. Being supported by idealistic stakeholders strongly committed to the sustainability mission, they may prefer to keep their niche at a size that is not attracting undue interest from mainstream incumbent competitors (Hockerts and Wüstenhagen, 2010). Such attitudes to risk are *not* captured in Figure 1.13.

> *Example* In 2008 the UK government Department of Food, Environment and Rural Affairs (DEFRA) developed a green segmentation that was based on self-reported public behaviours. The aim (of the segmentation) was to better understand and then drive green or pro-environmental behaviours. It received wide media coverage and was used by various organisations. Threeworlds (2014) refer to a follow-up survey by CDSM (see www.cultdyn.co.uk). This time, CDSM were to apply values mode segmentation to the DEFRA segments. These are based mainly on behaviour, standard demographics and social questions. The aim was to give a guide towards a more effective strategy for engagement and behaviour change because it is motivational. The analysis also revealed that some of the segments were not "real" segments at all – in so far as they represent people with a variety of fundamentally different, even opposing, unconscious motivations – and that any attempt to treat these people as a homogenous group based on common behaviours or standard demographics would likely not work.

Ultimately, to meet the needs, desires and expectations of customers, marketers need to map how and where value is created: does it reside in the customers, or in the co-creation of a service?

Figure 3.27 shows how four possible behaviour patterns of festivalgoers enable segmentation based on their approach to minimising the ecological impact of attending music festivals. It equally demonstrates the possible strategies each interested party may support. Each option presents government, business and society with possible scenarios. The left side, labelled *sacrifice*, suggests some stakeholders will have to give up something in order to behave as they wish. Some consumers will *pay as they burn*, accepting financial disincentives (say higher duties, tolls, vehicle tax). Where governments bring in such "taxes", a criticism is that it allows the wealthy to behave as they please, whereas those with less disposable income will have to change behaviours. The *sustain* quadrant shows the most radical option for the highly motivated sustainable citizen wishing to avoid the impacts of car usage as much as possible. This behaviour chimes with highly committed groups such ecowarriors and voluntary simplifiers.

So segments can be used but have to be applied judiciously when considering multiple values and motivations of individual consumers. Customers and consumers are the

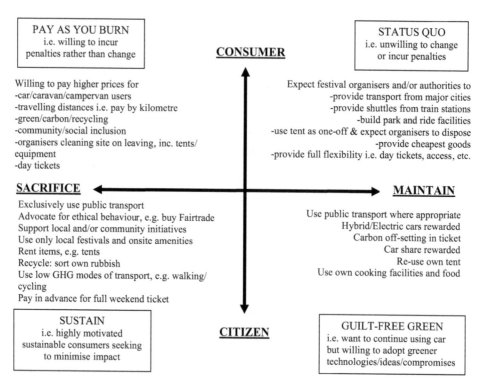

Figure 3.27 Possible sustainability behaviours of consumer versus citizen segments attending festivals

Source: adapted from Emery (2012) and Richardson (2015)

most important stakeholders in your professional life, followed by those who directly service them.

As good as a segmentation effort might be, its value will be wasted unless the whole organisation embraces it. Too often, critical insights are not realised, because of a lack of senior management buy-in. Furthermore, other functions that are not directly involved may feel disconnected and could lack engagement.

Targeting

Oddly, some texts refer to targeting as identifying the target market or segment. This seems like a duplication of effort, since clearly the task of segmentation is to identify the people or companies to approach. Targeting simply refers to the intended means of communicating the benefits on offer so that the customer can take value.

There are four traditional modes of targeting:

1   *Undifferentiated* – this is seen as a mass market. For example, think of British Gas servicing 22 million homes in the United Kingdom. They do offer different levels of service; however, on the whole, their communications are targeted using undifferentiated means.

2   *Differentiated* – here the market can be broken down into clear segments to target. For example, Toyota has Hilux trucks, family saloons, green cars (e.g. the IQ and the Prius), all of which will need a different marketing mix and hence communications.

3   *Concentrated* (some say niche) – this can be in the luxury end of the market. For example, in 2014 Astbury launched unique bejewelled hand-bags for a select audience who were invited to the London store. At over £3000 per bag, it was a bold attempt to target a niche market. Some companies, particularly SMEs, may use a niche strategy because they simply don't have the resources. After becoming more established, their targeting may evolve into another mode.

4   *Focused* (some say customised) – in B2B markets, a company will provide a service level agreement (SLA) for a specific customer. This comes with a high degree of risk if the customer is let down. In B2C markets, custom solutions can be targeted in this way. For example, artisan wood carvers will make a piece of furniture to given specifications.

Good targeting will help a company to achieve its positioning – that is, how it is perceived by the customers and prospects. This clearly involves communication (rather than segment identification).

Ethical targeting

As discussed in Chapter 1.7, CRM systems are widely used, and this is a key challenge for marketers when complying with GDPR. Marketers should adopt a default position where data protection is designed into all systems. ICO (2018) refer to seven principles of privacy by design. These should underpin targeting.

1   *Proactive, not reactive; preventive, not remedial*: Evaluate the risks by anticipating privacy issues rather than waiting for them to arise. Use good systems design to embrace a culture of "privacy awareness" across organisations.

2   *Privacy as the default setting*: Design any system, service, product and/or business practice to protect personal data automatically. With privacy built in, the individual does not have to take any steps to protect their data and their privacy remains intact.

3   *Protection as the default setting*: Embed data protection into the design of any systems, services, products and business practices. Ensure data protection becomes integral to all systems and services.

4   *Full functionality – positive sum, not zero sum*: Seek win-win scenarios rather than trade-offs. Seek privacy *and* (rather than *or*) security. Incorporate all legitimate objectives while ensuring compliance with obligations.

5   *End-to-end security – full life cycle protection*: Introduce strong security measures from the beginning, and extend this security throughout the "data life cycle" – that is, process the data securely and destroy it securely when no longer needed.

6   *Visibility and transparency – keep it open*: Ensure that all practices and technologies operate accordingly. This needs to be independently verifiable. Individuals need to know what data is processed and why.

7   *Respect for user privacy – keep it user centric*: Keep the interest of individuals paramount in the design and implementation of systems or services. Offer strong

privacy defaults, provide individuals with controls and ensure appropriate notice is given.

> *Example* A marketing director plans an advertising campaign, where choices have to be made regarding which customers to target, what method of communication and the personal details to use. In this case, the marketing director cannot also be the company's Data Protection Officer (DPO) since that would pose a potential conflict of interests between the campaign's aims and the company's data protection obligations. The marketer makes the decisions regarding the processing of the data, whereas the DPO ensures information rights are complied with.

Positioning

Positioning alludes to how consumers, customers and prospects perceive the position companies adopt in comparison to competitors. Products and services can be positioned by focusing on specific factors which themselves can be subject to different positioning approaches (Figure 3.28).

Features can be used when they provide differentiation, such as the bagless Dyson devices. Problem-solving is at its best when a company has a unique selling proposition (USP). All toothpastes will clean teeth; however, Sensodyne took market share by stressing the use for sensitive users. Competitive positioning can be linked to class positioning to gain market share by implying similar quality: think how Lexus is compared to Mercedes Benz. Alternatively, it can be linked to cost leadership (see Huawei's advertisements comparing features with the iPhone X). Once a marketer has established the factors needed, they must then choose which approach to adopt. A single approach is always the preferred option.

To determine the strategic position of brands, marketers often use mapping devices. Some were discussed earlier (e.g. DPM). A common approach is to use perceptual mapping featuring "plots" with two axes. The commonest format is plotting price versus quality. This is useful; however, it can be misleading, as price is clearly not the same as value-for-money. Some products may be the cheapest in their category and

	Positioning Factors					
	Features and design attributes	Benefits, problems and solutions or needs	Specific usage and applications (or occasions)	Competitive positioning against another product	Class association	Cost leadership
Positioning approaches	Distinctive – a clear, unambiguous brand position					
	Unoccupied – where the competition is absent, under-represented, under-performing, inefficient or generating dissatisfaction					
	Repositioning – products and services may need to be adapted, which may involve finding new uses for products					

Figure 3.28 Contrasting different positioning factors and approaches

Source: author

yet deemed of poor value. Conversely, the owner of an Aston Martin may consider it extremely good value for money despite its six-figure cost.

Ultimately, four attributes underpin positioning:

1   *Credence*: Any claims must be credible. Damage to credibility can taint the whole organisation, as was proven in the Diesel Emissions scandal of 2017, where VW Audi lost $30 billion from false environmental claims.
2   *Competitiveness*: Where possible, the value taken from the product or service should be unique – that is, not imitated by competitors. Rolls Royce cars have a unique position in the luxury car market that derives from a hundred-year history of satisfying their clients. Kotler's competitive positioning strategies (Figure 3.29) is often cited as a useful tool.

As with all such tools, care has to be taken when using labels. Super-bargain may be difficult to differentiate from, say, bargain in the customer's perception. Furthermore, only a minority of companies will be able to adopt a premium positioning strategy.

3   *Consistency*: The Cooperative Retail organisation has consistently promoted ethical behaviour and is the United Kingdom's largest seller of fair-trade products.
4   *Clarity*: Companies must be transparent in their dealings with the public and other stakeholders. Increasingly, companies are accused of greenwashing, where their environmental claims do not stand up to scrutiny. Sustainable consumers will increasingly avoid such companies.

Sustainable positioning

Individuals consider and/or adopt the attitudes, beliefs, opinions and values of others. This influences their decision-making. Companies need to appreciate how they are perceived with regard to sustainability. To build sustainable brands that consumers associate with social and environmental values, challenging decisions have to be made involving sustainability brand positioning (Belz and Peattie, 2009). Historically, the track record of many companies has been dubious. They have lacked transparency and credibility regarding adopting sustainability. Governments have failed to legislate, preferring to delegate responsibility for sustainability to largely voluntary organisational mechanisms such as CSR. This has contributed to consumer awareness of greenwashing and scepticism regarding ethical claims.

		Price		
		High	*Medium*	*Low*
Quality	High	Premium strategy	Penetration strategy	Super-bargain strategy
	Medium	Overpricing strategy	Average Quality strategy	Bargain strategy
	Low	Hit and run strategy	Shoddy goods strategy	Cheap goods strategy

Figure 3.29 Positioning strategies using contrasting price and quality

This assumes CSR is central to organisational culture and beliefs, but some maintain that it may simply be an "add-on" feature to their business operation, an afterthought (Jones et al., 2009) or deemed voluntary in nature (Barkemeyer, 2009). Gordon (2002) referred to the flagrant violation of societal standards in the corporate scandals of "recent years". Sadly, in 2019 this comment still resonates (e.g. Libor rate fixing and the Volkswagen "defeat device" debacle). It questions whether society and stakeholders can trust organisations.

Trust can be shaped by previous experiences and cooperative efforts and based on the more general reputation a firm has built up through its earlier behaviour (Haberberg et al., 2010). Adopting sustainable practices may engender trust in consumers, which can be grown, say, through positive WoM. For an organisation to trust its suppliers, it must assume that they will comply with its sustainability policies. However, suppliers comply for a range of reasons – for example, being enlightened, coerced or mimetic, among others (ibid). Organisations that are highly motivated may adopt idealistic CSR stances or even ones of enlightened self-interest, whereas stakeholders on whom they rely may do so only when coerced.

Hart's *Beyond Greening* introduced sustainability positioning by offering the environmental sustainability portfolio (Figure 3.30).

	Internal	External
Tomorrow	**New environmental technologies** Many organisations that have made good headway in pollution prevention and product stewardship are still limited by existing technologies. To develop fully sustainable strategies, they will need to develop new technologies.	**Sustainability vision** The company's products and services, processes and policies must evolve and what new technologies must be developed to get there. This vision of sustainability provides a framework for pollution control, product stewardship and environmental technology.
Today	**Pollution prevention** Pollution prevention involves more than pollution control – cleaning up waste after it has been created means eliminating or minimising waste before it is created, i.e. "green marketing" programmes – but also developing ecologically safer products, recyclable and biodegradable packaging, better pollution controls and more energy-efficient operations.	**Product stewardship** Product stewardship involves minimising not just pollution from production but all environmental impacts throughout the full product life cycle and all the while reducing costs. Many companies are adopting design for environment (DFE) practices, which involve thinking ahead in the design stage to create products that are easier to recover, reuse or recycle. Not only does DFE help to sustain the environment, but it can be highly profitable.

Figure 3.30 Hart's environmental sustainability portfolio

Source: adapted from Hart (1997, p. 74) and Kotler et al. (2009, p. 90)

Most companies focus on the lower-left quadrant of the grid, investing largely in pollution prevention (Kotler et al., 2009). This may indeed be the case for large manufacturers. Some progressive companies practice product stewardship and develop new environmental technologies; however, few have well-defined sustainability visions, which may be owing to the inherently product-oriented nature of Hart's portfolio. It lacks customer centricity, which critical marketers, including Kotler, suggest applies to many marketing stalwarts.

There is some debate on how to implement SM practices. Some suggest SM practitioners will need to challenge existing assumptions and alter traditional marketing practices. Others argue that SM has evolved from the marketing orientation and largely uses the same frameworks and tools as conventional marketing (Richardson et al., 2015). To address this paradox, Armstrong and Kotler (2013) positioned SM in relation to other concepts (Figure 3.31).

This is problematic because it implies that companies adopting the marketing concept are interested in only the now and not the future. Companies that adopt the marketing concept are deemed to be marketing oriented and are clearly interested in the future needs, wants and desires of customers (and prospects). The grid lacks detail, as is often the case with such positioning tools, and also limits discussion of stakeholders to the business and its customers, thus ignoring key actors, such as the local community.

Kotler counters the legitimacy of the grid, arguing that marketers cannot rely on the behaviour of consumers to provide the market signals to shift to SM. He says that some

> "are committed to ethical consumption and many enjoy the warm glow of doing good when they buy, but consumers are confused and there is little sign that they will buy ethical products that cost more or perform less well than the norm. It is a free-rider problem: most wealthy consumers are enjoying being free-riders where their immediate descendants and the world's poor pay".
>
> (Kotler et al., 2009, p. 112)

Kotler's framework provides no indication of how organisations should move from one orientation to another; it simply acts as a positioning tool rather than a benchmarking framework.

As service providers need to be able to position themselves within their markets in order to make effective decisions, it is prudent to assume that they (knowingly or otherwise) are located on the Sustainability Continuum (Figure 3.32). Organisations need

	Business needs (now)	*Business needs (future)*
Customer needs (now)	Marketing concept	Strategic planning concept
Customer needs (future)	Societal marketing concept	Sustainable marketing concept

Figure 3.31 Sustainable Marketing grid

Source: adapted from Armstrong and Kotler (2013, p. 509)

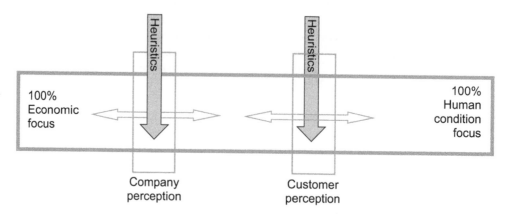

Figure 3.32 Sustainability Perception Continuum, influenced by heuristics

to be aware of how customers perceive their sustainable position. Those not aware of changing consumer attitudes, such as the increasing consumer demand for green and ethical practices (Ethical Consumer, 2018), risk alienating customers.

The continuum illustrates the influence of heuristics on the company and the customer. Marketers understand that customers use heuristics to simplify decisions and ultimately perceive companies in simplistic terms – for example, good company versus bad company or sustainable versus unsustainable. This diagram improves positioning in that it highlights how decision-making is simplified for companies and consumers alike. Prioritisation must take place: whether to invest in people and/or planet and to what extent?

Two issues arise from the sustainability continuum. First, does profit allude to the company's profitability or rather to the profits being reinvested in the people and planet foci? Second, do outputs or perceptions should be benchmarked?

Plotting the three foci of TBL onto a single axis may not be easy, so Figure 3.33 provides a matrix akin to the Mendelow grid (Figure 3.16). It assumes that profits must be reinvested. Companies must not only reinvest profit but must also be seen to do so. The degree of reinvestment depends on the company and its circumstances.

Consider three scenarios. First, a company is profitable but invests only a small amount of profit into people (position C). It could simply invest more to improve its social/ethical position. Second, a company invests a high amount of its profit into green projects, but nothing in people (position D), in which case it could maintain the status quo, by investing some profit into people or investing more into its existing green projects. Third, a company invests profits into people and planet, with a bias towards green projects (position B/A), in which case it may want a more balanced sustainable positioning and thus may sacrifice some green projects to invest in ethical alternatives. The options suggested for the scenarios are far from exhaustive.

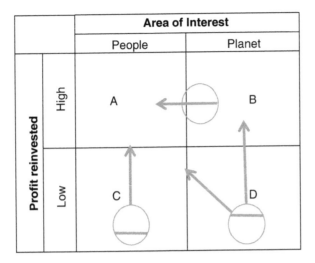

Figure 3.33 SM positioning grid

3.6 Strategic SM choices (ii) – choosing a strategy to achieve SM objectives

Since the advent of TBL, sustainability has gained credence and acceptance among academics, consultants and practitioners. Sustainability represents a nascent branch of social science that some consider a form of creative destruction, which could ultimately render the traditional ways of operating businesses redundant. Alternatively, others suggest organisations find their strategic intentions may be deflected (Mintzberg, 1990) by failing to react to changes in consumer values – for example, the growth in demand for ethical and/or green goods or services. Hence, it is sensible to consider these two schools of thought.

Schumpeter's Creative Destruction

"Creative destruction" describes the process where incumbents' competences and perceptions are challenged by new paradigms (Schumpeter, 1950). Some argue that sustainability represents a step change in how businesses are expected to operate and the advent of TBL is Schumpeterian (Sandberg, 2010). To be Schumpeterian, TBL's step change would have to have fundamentally changed service providers' knowledge base, leading to new opportunities and in turn market growth. Market boundaries would be redefined as companies sought to differentiate product offers or to create and target new segments. New entrants to the enlarged market would have a greater incentive to innovate. Sustainable entrepreneurs may discover new opportunities and stimulate change in society, whether this be a production method, technological development, product/ service, distribution system or even a new organisational form (Tilley and Young, 2009).

A key point is that sustainability and its subsequent potential for creative destruction applies to services as much as to the production of goods; however, in services, the innovation is in process. Some warn that the fears formed by the innovation resulting from

> "the entrepreneurial process of "creative destruction" can bring out the worst among the "modernisation losers" (industries that are intrinsically unsustainable). This conflict with vested interests can affect non-innovative people and organisations leading to resistant, evasive and disruptive behaviours".
>
> (Tilley and Young, 2009, p. 82)

Studies have identified a significant increase in the media coverage of (corporate) sustainability-related concepts since 1990 (Barkemeyer et al., 2009). This increase seems to be of an incremental nature rather than distinctly associated with a certain number of events. This evidence could be used to argue against those in the Schumpeterian school.

Mintzberg's deflected and realised strategies

Simply put, Mintzberg argues that due to the turbulent business environment, companies cannot foresee impacts on their strategies. They will be reacting to events, adapting to create "realised" strategies rather than those originally intended. A risk is this could lead to strategic drift (Mintzberg, 1990).

Figure 3.34 illustrates how strategic drift may result from failure to adopt or react to emergent elements of TBL, macroenvironmental changes and/or changes in consumer values – for example, growing demand for ethical or green goods. To militate against such outcomes, organisations may need to be measured on their sustainability. As discussed in Chapter 1, consumers consider many of society's problems to be beyond the capacity of government alone to solve. They expect companies to contribute significantly to solving these problems, many of which those companies have

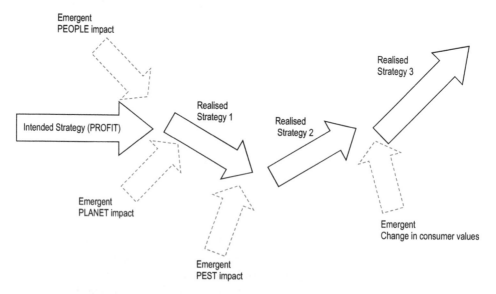

Figure 3.34 Mintzberg's realised versus intended strategy

Source: adapted from Mintzberg (1990)

aggravated. However, inertia or fear of change is often cited as a reason for businesses to be conservative or risk averse.

Strategy formulation

Marketers may identify a wide range of strategic options; hence, they will need to prioritise which ones best suit their company. Porter's work has influenced much of the debate on strategy.

Porter's Generic Strategies

Porter proposed three strategic choices: cost leadership, focus and differentiation (Figure 3.35).

This has since evolved into a straight choice between cost leadership and differentiation. The customer should regard the brand as offering good Value For Money (VFM) or should be able to take value that justifies paying more. Good value for money is offered rather than simply saying "the cheapest", which is simply not the case. Consumers rarely buy the cheapest product available. They do, however, constantly strive to find the best value for their money.

British retail is recognised as being world class. The choice is wider than ever, and the high street is under pressure from changing consumer behaviour and macro influences such as Brexit. Figure 3.36 shows how some retailers could be mapped using Porter's generic strategies. Some have broad segments, whereas others are cost leaders

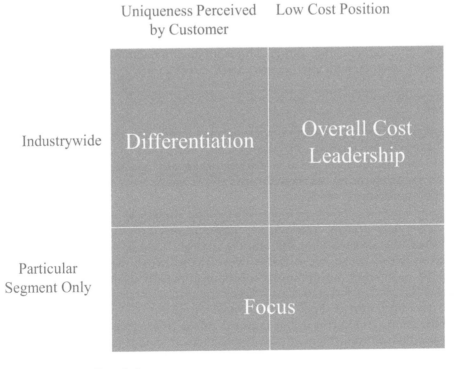

Figure 3.35 Porter's Generic Strategy

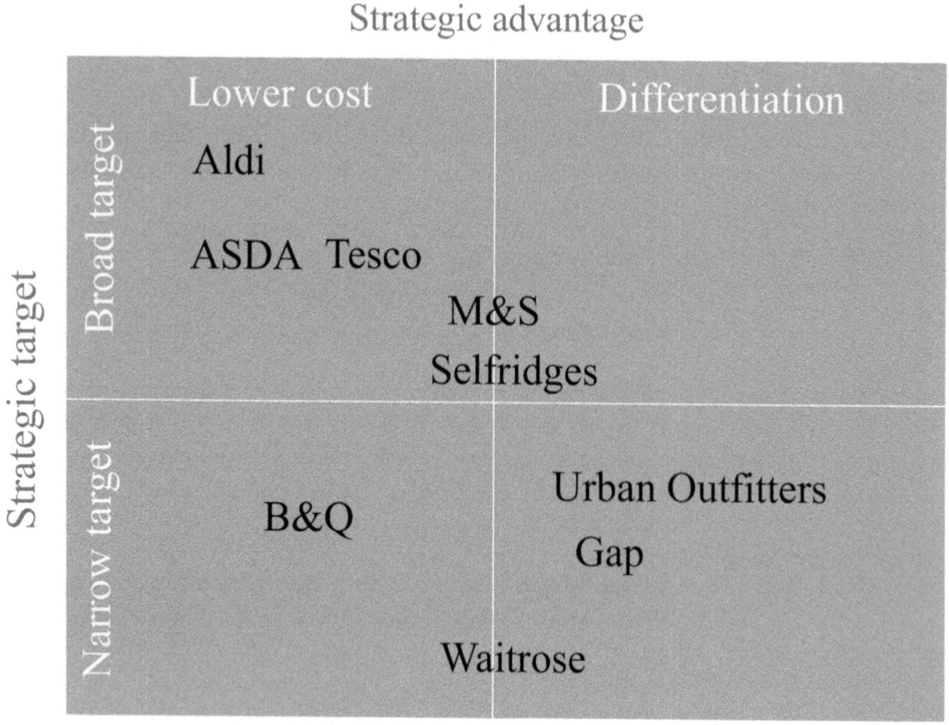

Strategic advantage

	Lower cost	Differentiation
Broad target	Aldi ASDA Tesco M&S Selfridges	
Narrow target	B&Q	Urban Outfitters Gap Waitrose

(Strategic target — label on left axis)

Figure 3.36 Porter's Generic Strategy

with narrow segments (e.g. B&Q). This is useful at a corporate level but limited for marketers who are, naturally, concerned with products and markets.

Ansoff

Ansoff (1957) recognised that company growth is linked to the relationship between products and their markets. He proposed that companies should reflect on whether new or existing products are to be delivered in new or existing markets. His strategy matrix for products and markets (Figure 3.37) is widely recognised as a useful tool in choosing a marketing strategy.

Ansoff's matrix is preferred to Porter's Generic Strategy by many commentators as the former links strategy to the two key marketing areas: product and markets. It also introduces the recognition of risk into the strategic decision. If (as in Figure 3.37) a company is risk averse (e.g. a charity or social enterprise), then diversification (with high risk) is probably not appropriate. Seeking growth by selling more to the existing market (i.e. market penetration or concentration) is the strategy for many companies who have small market shares and/or limited resources.

If the company culture is inclined towards taking risks (e.g. growth through aggressive mergers and acquisitions or even simply highly resourced) then immediate diversification is an option. Think of Microsoft spending $3 billion developing the first Xbox

	Old Products	New Products
Old Markets	Market Concentration Low risk: seeks increased sales for its present products in its present markets through more aggressive promotion and distribution	Product Development Medium risk: seeks increased sales by developing improved products for its present markets Can lead to diversification if product taken to a new market
New Markets	Market Development Medium risk: seeks increased sales by taking its present products into new markets Can lead to diversification if followed by a new product	Diversification High risk: seeks increased sales by developing new products and new markets. Can be achieved by • Concentric diversification • Conglomerate diversification • Vertical or horizontal integration

Figure 3.37 Ansoff's strategy matrix

Source: adapted from Ansoff (1957)

knowing they would never recoup the investment. Those in the middle ground (i.e. willing to take some risks but, analysis suggests, in the long run need to diversify) have two options. They can take the following two-step approaches:

1   Market Penetration → Market Development → Diversification
2   Market Penetration → Product Development → Diversification

These strategies are not mutually exclusive. Indeed, research by Baker and Hart (1989) into competitiveness in British industry established that the most successful firms pursued some two-step strategies in parallel and that following combination of new products and new markets frequently resulted in diversification (Baker, 2009).

Ultimately, theory without implementation is futile. Marketers need to translate corporate objectives into marketing strategies that can be implemented – that is, that are practical. Many directors think they have the right strategies; however, most think they are poor at implementation.

Practical steps towards Sustainable Marketing (SM)

What is needed is not change for its own sake but the *right* change, and many examples exist of companies who have benefited by moving towards adopting TBL. Third-party codes of conduct can be useful. They provide credibility to the argument for being more sustainable while acting as valuable sources of information in their own right. The FTSE4Good index, for example, includes human rights criteria. Marketers can sell the concept of sustainability to cynics by highlighting how the public's mounting concerns are partly driven by the following factors:

•   Growth in prosperity;
•   Expansion of media coverage;
•   Notable disasters;

- Greater scientific knowledge;
- Longer-term cultural shifts;
- PR and celebrity endorsements.

Most of these have increased as a direct result of increasing use of social media. With 1.7 billion Internet users worldwide, avoiding reputational damage is increasingly difficult. The following are increasing on a daily basis:

1   Levels of environmental awareness/concern leading to demand for eco-friendly products, the adoption of green product substitutes, reusing/redesigning/recycling products;
2   Shifting consumer values, from consumption to conservation;
3   Demand for less pollution from industry, with more conservation of resources and energy saving;
4   Greater regulation by government, with businesses charged for the environmental impact of their activities;
5   Demand for, and availability of, information on environmental issues, with companies expected to conduct and publish ecological audits;
6   Opportunities to develop ways to protect of the natural environment, animal rights and endangered species.

There has been a sea change in consumer opinion regarding TBL, and it is likely that marketing academics are trailing consumers, progressive organisations and other disciplines. Kotler now argues that marketer's lives will become more complicated. Meeting planet-related costs may necessitate raising prices. This does not automatically mean that the product will be harder to sell; however, the focus will need to be on the benefits and value for the customer. Increasingly, companies will need to reflect on their position on the sustainability perception continuum (Figure 3.32) and the extent to which they are willing to adopt sustainable practices.

3.7 Issues of control and measuring value

Throughout the ensuing implementation of changes to the marketing mix, there should be scheduled opportunities to reflect on the plan's effectiveness. All stakeholders should be aware of the timescales and the need for feedback. Marketers must act on these reflections.

Simply put, a marketing plan without control is not a marketing plan. The issue of control is key. There must be a period to measure and review any marketing plan. Controls must be established to assess how well it is being put into practice. The following are key factors to consider:

- Objectives must exist.
- outputs must be measurable (some use Key Performance Indicators – aka KPIs).
- A predictive model of the outcomes is required (to enable measurement).
- Capability to take action must exist.

Key Performance Indicators (KPIs)

On KPIs, the most important element is "key". Far too often, companies produce dozens of KPIs and then are puzzled when they underperform. KPIs should be few in number and sufficiently important for all stakeholders to buy into achieving them. There are many examples of frivolous KPIs, often where the company culture promotes managerialism or ticking boxes rather than genuine innovation.

The controls should reflect the organisation's culture. Hence, scenario planning and forecasts for an organisation with an aggressive growth culture should reflect this. Simplistic sales analysis, such as actual versus budgeted turnover, is only the first step. Further analysis (e.g. by product/service type, region, customer, etc.) may be needed. In a hotel, marketers should identify the activities needed to support each guest by category and the cost drivers of these activities. Thus, the cost of a one-night midweek stay by a businessperson could be distinguished from that of a one-night stay by someone visiting a cultural event.

If analysing market share, it must be done in context – that is, related to the market type (duopoly, oligopoly, etc.), condition (static, growing, declining), size and role (e.g. market leader, challenger or follower).

540-degree feedback

The organisation's capacity to react to changes needed to get the plan "on track" should have been considered during the internal audit. There should be scheduled opportunities to reflect on the plan's effectiveness. Marketers must recognise the need to get feedback from staff. Sustainable marketing involves undertaking 540-degree feedback. Whereas 360-degree feedback features staff providing feedback on their line managers, the 540-degree alternative encourages inviting consumers, customers, suppliers and other stakeholders to provide inputs. They will provide key insights into areas such as a lack of staff knowledge, training, vision, skill or security.

Twitter provides a means of gathering feedback while having a low environmental footprint. Marketers can use resources such as www.tweetstats.com and www.twitterholic.com to see the volume of tweets by week, day or even hour. Using them allows marketers to incorporate retweets and replies. By doing so, key internal trends and potentially new issues can be identified. Stakeholders in the microenvironment can also voice their concerns regarding the organisation's performance. They will potentially provide insights into areas such as a lack of staff knowledge, training, vision, skill, security and so on. In short, 540-degree feedback should go beyond monitoring and become a platform to promote learning within organisations.

Hard and soft controls

Controls can take many forms. They can be "hard" (i.e. number based) or "soft", which is to say qualitative. The following are some examples of hard (quantitative) metrics:

- Cost level;
- Units produced per week – sales levels and costs;
- Delays in delivery time;
- Zero defects/returns;
- Customer service complaints;
- Market share – market penetration by product/service type;
- Customer retention and acquisition.

One of the key benefits of digital marketing is the ability to quickly review marcomms campaigns by using hard data (Figure 3.38).

The effectiveness of a campaign can be viewed in real time and, if necessary, amended. Reports can be produced in a simple spreadsheet and can cover key metrics.

The following are some examples of soft (qualitative) metrics

- Brand image, awareness and perception;
- Employee motivation and welfare;
- Customer satisfaction;
- Social responsibility performance.

To be clear, there is no ranking between hard and soft; they are equally important. Many companies will use a blend of hard and soft metrics.

Budget

In a sustainable marketing plan, there should be a detailed budget for the first year. The budget should follow the SMART objectives. Indeed, budgets need to be related to what the whole company wants to achieve, which makes the resulting budget more likely to be realistic. The results can be broken down into the different market segments, so that how well the marketing mix has worked on specific target sectors can be analysed. Ideally, the company should use the budget to contribute to knowing the RoMI. It makes sense to know the marketing costs associated with different strategies.

Many costs are driven by customers (delivery, discounts, marketing, after-sales service, etc.). Costs and targets must always be measured against operating conditions.

> *Example* A company has a corporate objective to boost its profitability by attracting new business. The TOWS generates a key marketing objective of using direct marketing. After the audit, the strengths and weaknesses lend themselves to using mail as against telesales or personal selling. The marketing function posts 10,000 mail-outs at a cost of £1000. This seems to provide good value at a cost of £0.10 per mail-out. The mail-out has a 5% response rate (which is considerably better than the industry norm), generating 500 responses. Typically, the pipeline suggests converting 25% of the responses. Each sale generates a net profit (surplus) of £12. Hence, you have a profit of £12 × 125, or £1500.

Metrics	SMS	MMS	WAP
Messages sent	☺	☺	
Messages delivered	☺	☺	☺
Messages bounced		☺	☺
Stop messages	☺	☺	☺
Replies	☺	☺	
Downloads and value		☺	☺
Opens and click throughs		☺	☺

Figure 3.38 Key mobile metrics

This generates a number of metrics that may be useful for control/evaluation purposes:

- Cost per response – £1000/500 responses = £2 per response
- Cost per sale – £1000/125 sales = £8 per sale
- ROI – (£1500 – £1000)/£1000 = 0.5 which equates to a 50% gross ROI

Whether these metrics are acceptable depends on a number of factors, both internal (aims, objectives, etc.) and external (competitors, market share, market growth, etc.).

Larger companies use more complex feedback control indicators, such as the return on capital employed (ROCE). ROCE factors in the use/depletion of capital assets to give an overview of the whole company, not just the sales/marketing functions. ROCE has problems, however:

- It is <u>justifiably</u> different in different parts of the supply chain.
- It is impacted by geography.
- It is influenced by the age of a department/division (and, thus, its assets).
- It is inappropriate to products early in their PLC.
- It drives (short-term) investment in old products rather than new (and more productive) assets.

Naturally, operations have to keep pace with customer change, and the move to SM could be one such change.

A sustainable marketing benchmarking framework

Benchmarking can be used to instil best practice into companies across a range of issues. It should be a continuous, iterative process that measures gaps between the *marketer's* perception of what the brand offers and the *customers'* perceptions of the offering. Benchmarking compares and contrasts perceptions of value(s) with recognised competitors. As previously discussed, value can be created (or destroyed) by anyone in the value system. Hence, benchmarking should be applied to all aspects of the value-creation process across departments, suppliers and distributors. If done in a meaningful (rather than tokenistic) manner, it will provide the springboard for planning and marketers must address the issues highlighted within the benchmark report. To promote the adoption of SM practices for companies of all sizes and types, marketers can use a sustainable marketing benchmarking framework (Figure 3.39).

This framework deliberately chimes with Mintzberg's realised/deflected strategies (see Figure 3.34). Marketing strategies, like any other strategies, can be deflected. It clearly shows the areas to be benchmarked and the areas where marketers must scan (i.e. the macroenvironment and other disciplines). The factors portrayed can affect multiple TBL elements; for example, adopting a CSR policy could impact on people and profit. Most of the benchmark areas are self-explanatory.

Marketers may use outside support from environmental or sustainability consultants or agencies. They can be employed on a one-off or ongoing basis. Sustainable marketing is a long-term orientation, and changes may take time. Having carried out a sustainability audit, social media can be used to publish the results in a format that is easy for people to assess (Figure 3.40).

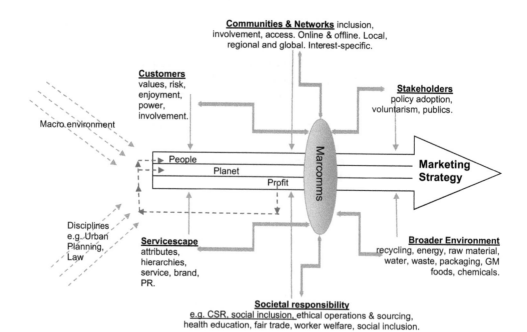

Figure 3.39 Sustainable marketing benchmarking framework (Richardson, 2015)

Source: adapted from Gosnay and Richardson (2008)

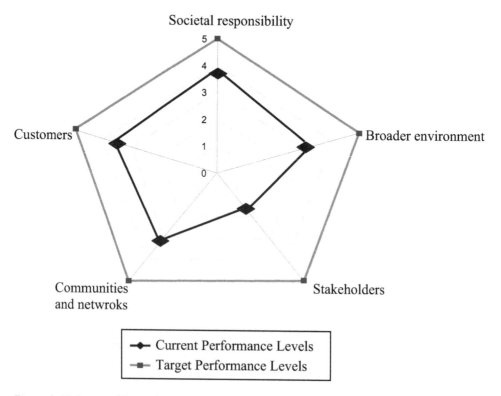

Figure 3.40 Sustainable marketing polar diagram

New measures may satisfy more than one element of People-Planet-Profit i.e. the TBL. For example, reducing the carbon footprint by holding meetings and/or conferences virtually. Hence, these meetings could be a considerable environmental improvement undertaken at little cost and greater convenience for the stakeholders.

> *Example* A useful online tool is offered by B Corporation (see https://bimpactassessment.net), which are a US-based not-for-profit organisation. Their approach is built around *assess, compare, improve*, which is not too far from Kotler's APIC, discussed earlier. It provides limited options regarding choosing the sector; for example, users are asked to choose service with minor environmental impact or service with major environmental impact. This is a judgement call, and some stakeholders in organisations may not know the answer unless directly involved in environmental auditing. It poses questions on governance, workers, community, environment and customers. Again, these are limited – that is, there is little on suppliers. That said, it is a useful tool if US centric and really more suited to large manufacturers. This is a common complaint; indeed, far too many marketing texts make the same mistake. That said, some of the questions it poses should make marketers think about their relationships with the community and the environment.

3.8 Barriers to adopting Sustainable Marketing Planning

As discussed, the newer idea of SM needs to be adopted more widely and with more conviction. However, many companies fail to implement successful marketing planning without the added challenge of adopting sustainability. Size is often cited as a justification; however, many studies have noted the positive link between having a marketing plan and business performance in SMEs. Also, many large well-resourced organisations fail to plan or fail to implement well as a result of their planning. Certainly, organisational culture (rather than size) has a lot to do with successful planning.

One of the key causes of corporate failure is *bad management*, and this also applies to marketing planning. This malaise can take the form of weak direction from senior management. A simplistic forecast and a resulting unachievable target will cause problems. THE sales target is too often a wish list: "it's where we need to be".

In future, marketers will need to operate in an increasingly sustainable fashion and will need to identify and remove barriers to adopting sustainability (Figure 3.41).

The REACH NEW framework (see Figure 3.2) should support those undertaking an SM plan. That said, it is appropriate to consider some of these barriers in detail.

Focus

Many managers have chosen operational effectiveness over customer-centred strategies, particularly in scenarios like retail, where constant improvement is often seen as the route to superior profitability. This may be because of having a disproportionate internal organisational focus rather than external factors such as customers and competitors. Retailers like Toys "R" Us, Woolworths and Maplins did not react to external changes and consequently lost their fight for survival.

Responsibility for ownership

Sustainability "ownership" can be fuzzy in some companies and hotly contested in others. Ethical matters (e.g. CSR) are often controlled by Human Resource departments.

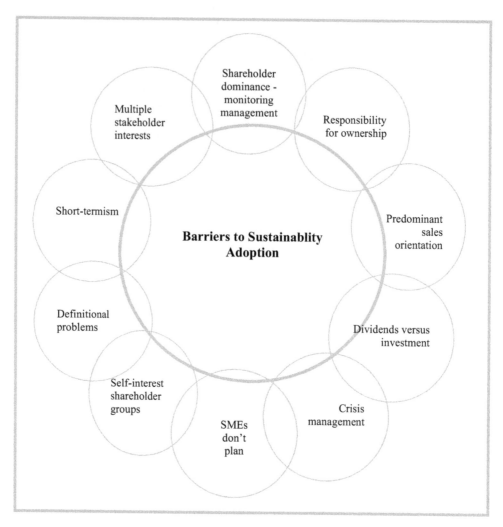

Figure 3.41 Barriers to (sustainability) adoption

Some organisations recognise the importance of CSR, as seen in elements of their mission statements (a strategic management decision), which may include green issues (possibly a quality control issue), ethical supply policies (the purchasing department) and charitable links (all of the above). This corporate disagreement is reflected on the larger stage, where proponents of sustainable development differ widely in terms of emphases – for example, what to sustain or to develop and when. In B2C sector responsibility lies with the service provider, the consumer, the community, the regulator and/or even the government. An example of governmental influence is the Companies Act (2006), which heavily impacts CSR. Increasingly, the environment will be used as a launch pad for governmental initiatives and legislation. Marketers must use a blend of comms tools to inform the different parties and manage their expectations.

Undoubtedly, when things are going well, everyone wants to stake their claim; however, when something goes wrong, where does responsibility lie? Recent studies have discussed CSI, where CSR is abused by organisations seeking competitive advantage through misinformation. It is no wonder why consumers are increasingly sceptical of environmental claims, which has led to the rise of accusations of greenwashing. Ultimately, marketers must act ethically and communicate transparently with the stakeholders.

Shareholders

Principals (i.e. shareholders and institutional investors) are aware that agents (i.e. directors and managers) may act out of self-interest and position the company in such a way as to reduce returns and share value. Hence, the principals incur the cost of monitoring the directors via annual audits, which are obligatory for all UK PLCs. Too often, agents communicate only with their shareholders in the run-up to the Annual General Meeting (AGM). This approach should be avoided and replaced by engaging shareholders in the same way as customers – that is, by using digital comms to build relationships, keep stakeholders informed, build loyalty and enhance shareholder satisfaction.

In larger companies or those with "active" shareholders who seek maximum returns on their investment, there are many tensions, some of which are exacerbated by the (mis)use of the word "sustainability" itself. For some, shareholder sustainability is the main corporate driver, featuring returning dividends and maximising share value for owners. Principals demand regular stable dividend payments; however, funds needed to pay dividends detract from the agent's ability to undertake new (sustainable) projects; principals want to sustain dividends to maintain market value. Shareholders concerns (having funded the company through investment) should be acknowledged in conjunction with those stakeholders who enable the company to continue and thrive. Progressive managers should naturally cater for the lives and well-being of its microenvironmental stakeholders (e.g. employees, suppliers and the community) in which the company is located. Hence, for most commentators, shareholder sustainability does not equate to "sustainability".

In some companies, principals (aka shareholders) were deemed to be key in that they had influence; however, they were largely deemed to be passive. Increasingly, shareholders actively participate in the running of the AGM. Some acquire shares specifically to affect the running or direction of the company, which would usually be the domain of the agents (i.e. directors and managers). This may lead to strategic shift and/or drift not to mention the potential for diminishing returns. Recently shareholders have formed well-organised pressure groups to maximise their influence on corporate policy. These groups are often adept at using PR and digital comms to promote their agenda.

Multiple stakeholder interests

It may be stating the plain and the obvious but the terms used so far – that is, "business", "company" and "organisation" – are somewhat nebulous. There are many different types of multi-stakeholder businesses – for example, single proprietorships, partnerships, cooperatives, non-profit enterprises, social enterprises, private limited companies and public limited (PLC) enterprises. Each of these differ in terms of their aims, objectives, visions, culture, structure and so on.

Organisations do not exist in isolation, which renders Friedman's philosophy somewhat redundant. Simply put, companies affect the lives and well-being of their stakeholders (see Chapter 1). Managers have to interact with employees, unions, suppliers, intermediaries, governments and most importantly customers. Each of these may have agendas and/or be motivated by self-interest. In business schools, we often preach the mantra of improving customer perceptions of value; however, shareholder "value" may come at the expense of customer "value" and satisfaction. Companies could certainly use digital comms to address issues such as diminished job security, higher unemployment and poorer (perceived) products and services.

At a higher level, it is a concern that *customers* rarely feature in sustainability models discussed at the highest levels – for example, the United Nations, the European Union, UNCTAD and so on. Many of the contributors lack an understanding of consumer behaviour.

Short-termism

The economic difficulties of 2008/2009 clearly illustrated that many financial institutions do not operate in a free market where they can do as they wish. Governments will bail out financial institutions if the alternative is economically damaging. Cases such as Northern Rock should serve as an invaluable lesson about the danger of short-term approaches. In Northern Rock's case, the business model was changed (after demutualisation) to a more aggressive model, which strove for higher returns than had been the case in the company's long history as a mutual "friendly" society.

In some cases, managers may wish to adopt policies beyond those demanded by legislation or regulatory bodies, such as being listed on the FTSE4Good index. This could incur costs that diminish market value or returns. Such action is often watered down if not prevented outright by fear of overreaction by the short-termist markets. Hence, those with vested interests (such as institutional investors and free marketeers) encourage managers to ignore investments in longer-run drivers of success such as sustainability. Many of these investors lost substantial funds in Northern Rock, which (ironically) could have had a different trajectory if they had adopted a more-sustainable approach.

Predominant sales orientation

Having discussed orientations in Chapter 1 it is worth recognising (here) the perception of sales oriented companies. A popular misconception is that marketing promotes the (short-term) selling of products to the target groups. Such sales orientations are now cited as contributing to consumers' increasing awareness of greenwashing.

SMEs don't need to plan

Marketing planning is an essential activity; however, many SME owners deem it unnecessary. They regard marketing as something more relevant to large organisations. If in doubt, SMEs should seek external advice: their local business school will often be able to provide cost-effective assistance.

It is impossible to apply a single rule to all SMEs, because they are simply too diverse. Many exhibit entrepreneurial behavioural patterns while having little structure, whereas others are long-standing and well established, with structures comparable to larger companies. Whatever the scenario, the small nature of SMEs will affect their approach to marketing (see Chapter 4.8).

Crisis management

Marketers cannot plan for all identifiable eventualities (e.g. fire, flood, contract breaches, financial mismanagement, disrupted customer services, etc.). Hence, it is prudent to consider crisis as a risk element that can be either anticipated or not.

Managers are often judged on how they deal with crises. Many marketing and PR agencies provide crisis management support to organisations that may suffer reputational damage. Marketers can take steps to plan for a crisis; for example, they can run simulations and test different scenarios. If a damaging scenario is flagged, it can inform senior management's strategic decision-making.

Any stakeholder mapping analysis will shift dramatically during a crisis. Dormant stakeholders may become active, and consideration must be given to whether they will be a positive or negative influence and what degree of influence they may have. It is better to *proactively* communicate with key stakeholders rather than wait until they read about the problems elsewhere. Ignoring some stakeholder groups could result in extending or escalating the crisis.

Too many organisations adopt the unethical stance of denying any wrongdoing and demanding proof. They refuse to acknowledge the story until sufficient time has passed that (when raised again) they can dismiss it as "old news". This leads to further scrutiny, but the media (and other audiences) will be more sympathetic to the brand if the response is sincere, sympathetic and authentic. Demonstrating sincerity may require further evidence that not only is the issue being addressed but also measures are being implemented to ensure it does not reoccur. In crises, brand reputation is limited if the company is open and transparent.

Overcoming barriers to adoption

In future, marketers will need to operate in an increasingly sustainable fashion while being able to identify and remove barriers to adopting sustainability (see Figure 3.41).

The following are the key issues in overcoming these barriers:

- Costs;
- Technical and organisational;
- Conflicts between objectives;
- International implications;
- Lack of visibility;
- Timescale;
- Lack of certainty about the nature of the problem;
- Concerns regarding proposed remedies;
- Tokenism;
- Moral fatigue.

These can prevent adoption, particularly because some issues, say costs, can combine with others (say timescales) to generate inertia. What is needed is a marketing campaign that regularly updates stakeholders with measurable evidence of improvements. Do not expect them to make huge leaps in the dark. Instead, gently nudge them over a period of time, and steady progress will be made.

As well as codes of conduct, a range of "standards" are available to assist in measuring sustainability – for example, ISO 20121 (based on BS 8901:2007) provides a specification for a sustainable events management system. Since service industries make up approximately 85% of UK GDP, it is fair to assume that some of the support materials for the event management sector will chime with other areas.

ISO 14001 is an internationally accepted standard that provides organisations with a planned set of criteria required for implementing an effective environmental management system (EMS). Trade bodies and special interest groups will have their own codes.

Top ten findings

1   Marketing is most effective when it is considered, planned and evaluated continuously. There must be a period of measurement and review of any marketing plan.
2   Efficiency is doing things right, whereas effectiveness is doing the right things. Clearly, sustainability involves being efficient *and* effective.
3   A strategy is used to achieve organisational objectives. A marketing strategy (e.g. Ansoff) is the means of achieving specific marketing objectives. Marketing objectives must "fit" with corporate objectives. Objectives (whether corporate or marketing) must be specific and measurable.
4   Mission statements should be customer centric and, like objectives, need to be reviewed and revised periodically to ensure that they are still relevant.
5   The situation review must feature 540-degree feedback from consumers, customers, suppliers and other stakeholders. A gap analysis can show where the company may be after a set period of time. Internal marketing can facilitate marketing planning *and* the adoption of sustainable practices. It is not enough to carry out a marketing audit and then fail to implement changes. If it has simply become a ritual, an onerous task, then it's unlikely to have the required impact.
6   Customers should be at the heart of *all* business and marketing decisions and activities. Organisations should be both inwards and outwards focused to truly understand and react to changing customer needs and trends. Marketers must continuously scan all business environments.
7   Networks are series of connections between different people, but a community is a network with a shared interest or purpose. Online communities (i.e. those already within organisations) can offer value in terms of research and gathering insight as well as supporting value co-creation. Tribes have power and influence since they have significant credibility in their area of interest and can function as highly influential opinion leaders.
8   The SWOT summary audits micro and macro findings. Too little detail will lead to a lack of action, whereas too much could lead to analysis paralysis. However, it is the TOWS that generates marketing objectives.
9   A marketing plan without control is not a marketing plan. Benchmarking is a practical and proven method to help measure (sustainability) performance against

competitors. KPIs should be few in number and sufficiently important that all stakeholders "buy into" achieving them. There is a wealth of good advice that is freely available in the codes of conduct of various bodies.

10 There must be "buy-in" from senior management. A lack of skills and resources may lead to poor marketing planning and ineffective implementation.

Ten activities

1 To drill down into marketing planning, access the various outputs from Malcolm McDonald. Although not without critics, he has written more on the subject than anyone else and has made a substantial contribution.

2 For an overview of core competences, see Prahalad and Hamel's *Harvard Business Review* article (http://hbr.org/1990/05/the-core-competence-of-the-corporation/ar/1).

3 For more detail on the benefits of treating staff well, seek out the works of Pfeffer from Harvard, Michael Armstrong and the CIPD in the United Kingdom.

4 The Information Commissioner's Office (ICO) is responsible for enforcing the GDPR in the United Kingdom. It has published a 12-step guide (ICO, 2018) on how businesses can get ready.

5 See Chaffey's thoughts on why organisations should develop their own online communities (www.smartinsights.com/customer-engagement/customer-communities/social-engagement-for-business/ [Accessed 01/08/2014]).

6 To be better placed to sell the benefits of sustainable marketing reflect on the following sources:

  • The Dow Jones Sustainability Index (www.sustainability-index.com/);
  • The FTSE4Good index (www.ftse.com/Indices/FTSE4Good_Index_Series/index.jsp);
  • The Global Reporting Initiative (www.globalreporting.org/Home).

7 Those who want to develop their benchmarking skills can access the following resources:

  • The Benchmark Index – formed by the DTI in 1996 and run through Business Link. Compare your businesses with others (www.benchmarkindex.com/);
  • Best Practice Club – an organisation to facilitate cooperation and information dissemination on benchmarking and best practice (www.bpclub.com/);
  • Director's Briefing on benchmarking – Quick guide to what it is, what it can mean for your organisation and how to plan/implement benchmarking (www.bizhot.co.uk/files/St4bench.pdf).
  • BuyIT – best practice network for the ICT and e-business industry. Has links to actual best practice guidelines and case studies (www.buyitnet.org/).

8 Access the following "standards" to identify useful information and practices relevant to adopting sustainability:

  • ISO 14001:2015 Environmental management systems – Requirements with guidance for use (www.iso.org/iso/home/store/catalogue_tc/catalogue_detail.htm?csnumber=60857 [accessed 20/11/15]);

- ISO 20121:2012 Event sustainability management systems – Requirements with guidance for use (www.iso.org/iso/home/store/catalogue_tc/catalogue_detail.htm?csnumber=54552 [accessed 20/11/15]);
- ISO 26000 – Social responsibility (www.iso.org/iso/home/standards/iso26000.htm [accessed 20/11/15]).

References

Ansoff, H.I. (1957). Strategies for diversification. *Harvard Business Review*, 35(5), pp. 113–124.

Armstrong, G. and Kotler, P. (2013). *Marketing: An introduction*. 11th ed. Pearson: Boston.

Baker, M. (2009). Aided Recall and Marketing Mnemonics Guest Lecture presented By Professor Michael Baker to Leeds Business School November 2009.

Baker, M.J. and Hart, S.J. (1989). *Marketing and competitive success*. London: Phillip Allen.

Barkemeyer, R., Figge, F., Holt, D. and Hahn, T. (2009). What the papers say: Trends in sustainability – a comparative analysis of 115 leading national newspapers worldwide. *Journal of Corporate Citizenship,* (33)(Spring), pp. 69–86.

BCG (Article II) (2008). Consumer segmentation – a call to action. Online article. Available at: www.bcg.com/documents/file15287.pdf. [Accessed 1 Feb. 2019].

Belz, F.-M. and Peattie, K. (Article III) (2009). *Sustainability marketing – A global perspective*. Chichester: Wiley & sons.

Campaign Monitor (2019). The ultimate guide to marketing to Gen Z in 2019. Online article. Available at: www.campaignmonitor.com/resources/guides/guide-to-gen-z-marketing-2019/Z in 2019 [Accessed 22 Sept. 2019].

Chaffey, D. and Ellis-Chadwick, F. (Article IV) (2012). *Digital marketing: Strategy, implementation and practice*. 5th ed. Pearson Education: Harlow.

Ethical Consumer (2018). Ethical consumer markets report. Available at: www.ethicalconsumer.org/research-hub/uk-ethical-consumer-markets-report [Accessed 9 Feb. 2019].

Flexitarian (2018). The flexitarian website. Available at: https://theflexitarian.co.uk/the-flexitarian-diet/ [Accessed 10 Feb. 2018].

Fruitarian (2018). What is a fruitarian. Available at: www.fruitarian.info/#fruitarian [Accessed 10 Feb. 2018].

FT (2017). Persimmon chairman resigns over £100m CEO bonus. Available at: www.ft.com/content/c9f88bf8-e175-11e7-8f9f-de1c2175f5ce [Accessed 26 Jan. 2019].

FTSE4Good. Available at: www.ftse.com/Indices/FTSE4Good_Index_Series/index.jsp [Accessed 20 Feb. 2018].

Godin, S. (2008). *Tribes: We need you to lead us*. London: Penguin.

Gordon, J.N. (2002). What Enron means for the management and control of the modern business corporation: Some initial reflections. *University of Chicago Law Review*, 69, pp. 1233–1250.

Haberberg, A., Gander, J., Rieple, A., Martin-Castilla, J.-I. and Helm, C. (2010). Institutionalizing idealism: The adoption of CSR practices. *Journal of Global Responsibility*, 1(2), pp. 366–381.

Hart, S.L. (1997). Beyond greening: Strategies for a sustainable world. *Harvard Business Review*, 75(1) (Jan/Feb), pp. 66–76.

Henderson, B. (1970). The product portfolio. Available at: www.bcg.com/publications.aspx [Accessed 3 Feb. 2019].

Hockerts, K. and Wüstenhagen, R. (2010). Greening Goliaths versus emerging Davids — Theorizing about the role of incumbents and new entrants in sustainable entrepreneurship. *Journal of Business Venturing*, 25(5), pp. 481–492. doi:10.1016/j.jbusvent.2009.07.005

ICO (2018). Guide to the general data protection regulation (GDPR). Available at: https://ico.org.uk/for-organisations/guide-to-the-general-data-protection-regulation-gdpr/ [Accessed 13 Aug. 2018].

Johnson, G. and Scholes, K. (1999). *Exploring corporate strategy*. 5th ed. London: Prentice Hall.

Johnson, G., Whittington, R., Scholes, K., Angwin, D. and Regnér, P. (2017). *Exploring strategy: Text and cases*. 11th ed. Harlow: Pearson.

Jones, B., Bowd, R. and Tench, R. (2009). Corporate irresponsibility and corporate social responsibility: Competing realities. *Social Responsibility Journal*, 5(3), pp. 300–310.

Kaplan, R.S. and Norton, D.P. (1992). The balanced scorecard- measures that drive performance. *Harvard Business Review*, January-February Issue.

Kotler, P. (1967). *Marketing management: Analysis, planning and control*. Englewood Cliffs, NJ: Prentice Hall.

Kotler, P., Wong, V., Saunders, J. and Armstrong, G. (2009). *Principles of marketing*. 5th European ed. Harlow: Prentice Hall.

Kuznets, S. (1949). Suggestions for an inquiry into the economic growth of nations. In: *Problems in the study of economic growth*. New York: National Bureau of Economic Research, pp. 3–20.

LinkedIn (2018). Available at: www.linkedin.com/pulse/how-copy-netflix-barry-enderwick/ [Accessed 18 Oct. 2018].

Longman, J., Pritchard, C., McNeill, A., Csikar, J. and Croucher, R. (2010). Accessibility of chewing tobacco products in England. *Journal of Public Health (Oxford, England)*, 32, pp. 372–378. doi: 10.1093/pubmed/fdq035.

Lynch, R. (1999). *Corporate strategy*. London: Prentice Hall.

McDonald, M. (1999). *Marketing plans: How to prepare them, how to use them*. 4th ed. London: Butterworth-Heinemann.

Megicks, P., Donnelly, R. and Harrison, G. (2009). *CIM coursebook: The marketing planning process*. London: Butterworth-Heineman.

Mintzberg, H. (1990). The design school: Reconsidering the basic premises of strategic management. *Strategic Management Journal*, 11, pp. 171–195.

Mumsnet (2019). About us. Available at: www.mumsnet.com/info/about-us. [Accessed 28 Jan. 2019].

Proctor, T. (2008). *Public sector marketing*. Harlow: Pearson Education.

Porter, M.E. (1979). How competitive forces shape strategy. *Harvard Business Review*.

Prahalad, C.K. and Hamel, G. (1990). The core competence of the corporation. *Harvard Business Review* (May-June), pp. 79–91.

Richardson, N. (2010). *A quick start guide to mobile marketing: How to create a dynamic campaign and improve your competitive advantage*. London: Kogan Page.

Richardson, N.A. (2015). The adoption of sustainable marketing practices within the UK music festivals sector. PhD thesis. Available at: http://etheses.whiterose.ac.uk/13578/1/The%20 adoption%20of%20sustainable%20marketing%20practices%20within%20the%20 UK%20music%20festivals%20sector.pdf.

Richardson, N., James, J. and Kelley, N. (2015). *Customer-centric marketing: Supporting sustainability in the digital age*. London: Kogan Page.

SmartInsights (2012) [online]. Should you create your own online community? Available at: www.smartinsights.com/customer-engagement/customer-communities/social-engagement-for-business [Accessed 1 Aug. 2012].

Sandberg, M. (2010). The Greening of the Swedish Innovation System Paper to be presented at the International Schumpeter Society Conference 2010 on innovation, organisation, sustainability and crises Aalborg, June 21–24, 2010.

Schumpeter, J.A. (1950). *Capitalism, socialism and democracy*. 3rd ed. New York: Harper & Bros.

Smith, P.R., Berry, C. and Pullford, A. (1999). *Strategic marketing communications: New ways to build and integrate communications*. London: Kogan Page.

Stead, R., Curwen, P. and Lawler, K. (2003). *Industrial economics: Theory, applications and policy*. London: McGraw Hill.

Tilley, F. and Young, W. (2009). Sustainability entrepreneurs – could they be the true wealth generators of the future? *Greener Management International*, (55), pp. 70–92.

Tadajewski, M. and Hamilton, K. (2014). Waste, art, and social change: Transformative consumer research outside of the academy? *Journal of Macromarketing*, 34(1), pp. 80–86.

Threeworlds (2014). Online article. Available at: http://threeworlds.campaignstrategy.org/?p=74. [Accessed 15 Jul. 2014].

van Dam, Y.K. and Apeldoorn, P.A.C. (1996). Sustainable marketing. *Journal of Macromarketing*, 16(2), pp. 45–56.

Vegan Society (2018). What is a vegetarian? Available at: www.vegansociety.com/go-vegan/definition-veganism [Accessed 10 Feb. 2018].

Vegsoc (2018). What is a vegetarian? Available at: www.vegsoc.org/definition [Accessed 10 Feb. 2018].

Waterman, R.H., Peters, T.J. and Phillips, J.R. (1980). Structure is not organisation. *McKinsey Quarterly In-house Journal*, pp. 14–26.

4 Marketing themes in the 21st century

Abstract

This Chapter directs students' analytical work into important themes within the tumultuous business environment. It contributes to the achievement of the overall philosophy, aims and objectives of the book by facilitating students' analysis of the contexts, scenarios or themes in which the theories outlined in Chapters 1–3 may apply.

> **Learning outcomes**
>
> At the end of this chapter, students will be able to do the following:
>
> - Discuss the rationale and benefits of relationship marketing;
> - Examine the role of internal marketing;
> - Assess the nature of sustainable entrepreneurship;
> - Evaluate the application of sustainable brands;
> - Analyse how sustainability informs global marketing;
> - Discuss techniques to manage digital marketing;
> - Explain alternative marketing approaches for SMEs, charities and not-for-profit organisations.

4.1 Relationship Marketing (RM)

Historically, marketers have focused on transactions. Ultimately, however, the survival and success of organisations depend on repeat purchases. Repeat purchases suggest the development of confidence and trust leading to a relationship between buyers and sellers. Companies must balance (finite) resources when either acquiring new customers and/or retaining existing customers. Both are crucial but need different approaches: acquisition requires a company to undertake research to gain information about potential customers, assess their value to the company and allocate resources to attract those with the greatest long-term value. Retention, by contrast, requires maintaining relationships with existing customers on the basis of their long-term value.

Defining RM

As discussed in Chapter 1.3, marketing deservedly has its critics. Indeed, many marketers identify with being critical marketers, and their work has sought to keep marketing honest. Since the 1970s, marketers, especially the Scandinavians, have developed the notion of Relationship Marketing (RM) in a deliberate move away from transactional practices. That said, there is still much confusion regarding the nature of relationships.

Berry (1983) developed RM against the background of the rapid growth in services marketing in the 1980s. He argued for the need to move beyond the one-off-sale transactional sales-oriented model of marketing (see Chapter 1) to the development of longer-term relationships between supplier and customer.

This featured the concept of customer Lifetime Value (LTV), which simply means the value of the business that a company would gain during the time that the customer bought products or services from it. The following questions need to be asked at this point:

- Can a company pursue the same level of relationship with every customer?
- Will all customers want the same level of relationship with their supplier?

There is not a simple yes or no answer to either question. Customer engagement (whether B2C or B2B) varies from customer to customer and by type of product or service. RM in B2C marketing is desirable despite the lower level of engagement with most customers, contacts that are more routine and less opportunities for personalisation. Financial services companies, typically, use the value of a customer's business or size of bank/savings account or size of shareholding to determine the level of service that they will provide. The highest-value customers – typically representing the smallest proportion of clients – receive a highly personalised service (Figure 4.1).

Customers lower down the pyramid receive lower levels of contact/support. A distinction has to be made between frequency of transactions and their profitability. Furthermore, expectations still have to be managed.

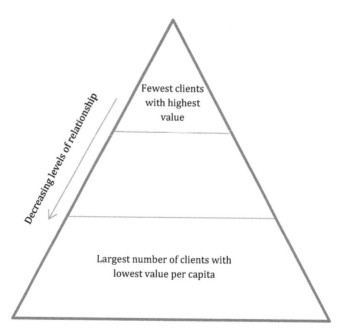

Figure 4.1 Customer value pyramid

Marketers must monitor the monetary value of their customers' purchases/use of services to identify changing levels of activity, which could trigger higher/lower levels of promotion or service and, thereafter, of RM management. In B2B marketing, the number of customers (and companies supplying them) is smaller than in B2C marketing. B2B features a greater emphasis on the importance of supplier relationships (or preferably partnerships) in terms of technology, quality and reliability. That said, the trend for companies rationalising (i.e. reducing) the size of their supplier base is set to continue, as is the adoption of one-stop shopping. These developments have strengthened the importance and value of relationships. That said, not all organisations treat their suppliers fairly and equitably.

CRM and RM

There is a debate whether CRM is the same as RM or whether it refers to the adoption of technology to implement RM. A meta-analysis by Rababah et al. (2011) concluded that some saw CRM as a philosophy (akin to RM), while others simply saw it as a technology. Most saw CRM from the perspective of IT-related strategies. With the advent of Big Data (data trawling, user-generated data, etc.) the picture has become less clear. Having a substantial database of prospects and clients is pointless if they do not value what is offered. Value resides with the customer only, which is why many companies fail despite having substantial client databases. Michael Baker insists, even now, that the stress on CRM "suggests an imperfect understanding of the nature of relationships. Attempts to manage relationships are inevitably doomed to failure; far better to concentrate on CSM or Customer Satisfaction Management" (2009). Hence, it is prudent to recognise that CRM alludes to the use of technology to support the adoption and practice of RM.

Loyalty

Online services represent a challenge *and* an opportunity for marketers to generate customer loyalty. Loyalty is not just an attitude towards a product or service; it also implies changing behaviour patterns – that is, the repeat(ed) purchase of products or services (Dick and Basu, 1994). Worryingly, few companies have a working definition of what loyalty means (Aksoy, 2013).

Nigel Piercy shaped many of the discussions around RM. He developed a useful way of understanding behavioural loyalty (what customers or prospects do), namely the loyalty ladder (Figure 4.2), which aids in segmenting customers according to their levels of loyalty. Harridge-March and Quinton (2009) applied similar principles to social media sites.

Loyalty ladders have several characteristics. The fundamental idea, beyond segmenting the actual or potential customer base, is to remind marketers that they should try to move customers up the ladder. There are problems, however:

- It is not clear how to move customers up one or more rungs.
- Suppliers cannot have the same depth of relationship with each customer.
- It is not possible to push every customer up the ladder.
- It doesn't specify how to identify suspects, prospects or lurkers before they have engaged.
- Different marketing approaches will be needed for the different categories.

Traditional	Social Media	Sustainability
Advocate – actively promotes brand to others	Evangelist – actively promotes social site to others	Sustainable stakeholder – an advocate of brands that reinvest profits in people and planet and seeks to influence others to adopt sustainable practices
Supporter – an influencer rather than a customer	Lead members or celebrities – highly active and may influence others	Pro-eco/social – regularly buys brands that reinvest profits in people and planet
Client – a customer who makes repeat purchases	Insider – seen as expert in specific topics and post regularly	Pro-eco – regularly buys brands that reinvest profits in planet
Customer – an individual who purchases your product or service	Devotee – contributes regularly and are beginning to develop social ties	Pro-social – regularly buys ethical brands that reinvest profits in people, such as fair trade.
Prospect – finds the company's offer interesting	Mingler – mature tourist, perhaps, who posts comments but without any regularity or frequency	Social – is committed to the notion of improving the human condition and critical of commerciality.
Suspect – researches a brand but is not interested	Newby – an individual who has just started to post comments	Dark green – ecowarrior or voluntary simplifier who is wholly committed to a green lifestyle
	Tourist – posts comments but lacks engagement with the network	Libertarian – believes in small government, thinks tax is theft, and wants to buy everything at point of sale.
	Lurker – observes and may join the network	

Figure 4.2 Traditional, social media and sustainability loyalty ladders

Source: adapted from Piercy (2009); Harridge-March and Quinton (2009); Richardson et al. (2015)

The sustainability ladder (drawing on the stakeholder mapping in Figure 1.13) presents other challenges. The Piercy ladder and Harridge-March and Quinton ladder assume that those at the bottom of the *social media* ladder (e.g. suspect or lurker) are uncommitted, perhaps indifferent or ambivalent, about the brand or site. Whereas those at the bottom of the *sustainability* ladder (e.g. libertarians) may have principled reasons for their attitudes and behaviours. Someone who is dark green may be an ecowarrior or voluntary simplifier. They may choose to value ecological considerations above all else. Marketers may simply not be able to move these up the ladder to the ultimate sustainable stakeholder. That said, as is often the case, the middle ground could be fruitful. If consumers are found to be pro-social, sustainable marketers should seek to encourage environmentally friendly behaviour to migrate these consumers to pro-eco/pro-social. If they are satisfied and demonstrate loyalty to brands that are committed to ethical and environmental causes, they may in time evolve into sustainable stakeholders.

Loyalty versus satisfaction

Clearly, issues such as loyalty and satisfaction need some consideration. Piercy warned marketers against confusing loyalty with satisfaction. He identified a number of states that could apply (Figure 4.3) and insisted that marketers should be precise in their use of language.

Customer Loyalty

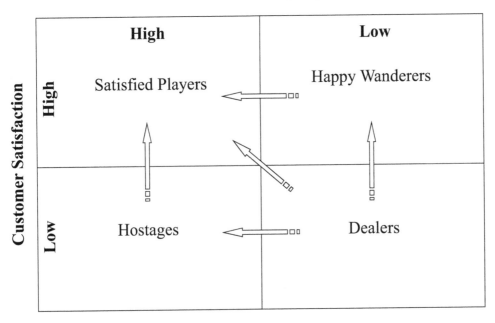

Figure 4.3 Customer satisfaction versus customer loyalty matrix

Satisfaction is "the emotional state that occurs as a result of customers' interactions with the firm over time" (Verhoef, 2003). This suggests that genuine satisfaction can come only after repeated experiences (purchases); however, there is still no clear link to creating loyalty. Academics generally agree that satisfaction is a matter of comparing expectations with experiences.

Loyalty starts with customer acquisition – that is, converting suspects to prospects to customers. A number of tools can generate leads (a common first step in online customer acquisition) from real time, say live chat, through to the forms used to capture user information – that is, names and email addresses. Permission must be obtained to allow cookies and if retargeting, such as providing advertisements on products previously browsed elsewhere.

The challenge is persuading customers that there is value in a continuing relationship, which can only happen after dialogue. Marketers must sell the benefits and not simply list the features. Customers want to know how their problems can be solved. The oft-used metaphor is marketers are not selling drill bits; rather, they are helping customers to drill accurate holes easily, repeatedly and safely. Hence, the value comes from reduced risk, lower costs, greater accuracy and quicker completion. Loyalty will result from implementing this customer-centric approach if meaningfully supported by senior management. The right-first-time approach is customer centric and sustainable (in reducing waste of energy and materials).

Measuring and monitoring online loyalty

Good communications and engagement are key to the implementation of RM. Aksoy (2013) identifies the following loyalty measures:

- Indicators of customer perceptions and attitudes (customer satisfaction and commitment);
- Indicators of customer loyalty behaviours (retention, share of wallet, frequency);
- Customer financials (value of purchases, profitability, LTV);
- Indicators of loyalty intentions (repurchase intention, recommendation intention, net promoter score).

This list shows areas of focus and measurement, some of which (e.g. commitment, repurchase and recommendation intention) may be difficult to measure and/or predict accurately. Information can be gathered using tools (e.g. Google Analytics or Radian6) to improve understanding of online behaviour through social media sentiment analysis. These insights into media consumption, customer needs, wants and desires (as well as considering competitor activity and future trends and emerging technology) allow marketers to support value-seeking customers and establish (or maintain) a competitive advantage.

Reaching and acquiring prospects/customers may involve migrating existing customers to an online platform (see Figure 2,4). This must be done only if satisfaction is maintained or enhanced. Marketers must understand customer behaviour – that is, where they go online, which sites or platforms are used, browsing patterns and the most common search terms.

Digital media channels have different advantages and disadvantages. The blend of channels being used must be economically viable and suitable for the customers. Furthermore, good content can increase the "stickyness" – that is, dwell time on sites and promote repeat visits. Good content must be relevant, useful, unique (if possible) and current.

Marcomms should be designed to encourage customer "action", whether buying for the first time, signing up for a newsletter, downloading content or taking part in a competition. Ultimately, marketers must monetise online provision in an ethical way. It is useful to consider the concept of conversion funnels. Google offer a funnels visualisation service via their analytics programme.

Customer acquisition is expensive and risky (until trust has been thoroughly developed), so marketers must prioritise customer retention and convert them into clients who "repeat". As long as customers are happy, marketers want them returning again and again. This may involve incentives or offers (sales promotions), or it may simply mean making them feel valued through dialogue and excellent customer service. Whatever the reason, marketers must focus on both acquisition *and* retention. If this is the case, clients will ultimately become advocates and will spread positive WoM, which is still the most potent form of communication.

Benefits of RM

The implementation of RM should see increased trust and more equitable treatment of stakeholders. This clearly resonates with sustainability. Trust is central to the idea of loyalty and is built on reliability, consistency, transparency, commitment and being treated fairly (with equity). Equity is particularly interesting in that research tends to undervalue its importance.

Loyal customers may be less sensitive to price levels than those who are first-time customers. Harris and Goode (2004) recognised that while perceived value, satisfaction and service quality are important requirements in relationships, trust is the central factor without which loyalty cannot be assumed.

> *Example*   An illustration of trust is music festivalgoers' willingness to pay for the following year's festival during the current event despite not knowing the lineup of performers and having no idea how the weather will behave in a year's time. This has two benefits: first, the cashflow is improved and, second, it leads to more commitment from festivalgoers, who are given the opportunity to nail their colours to the mast and come back next year.

RM can lead to higher levels of repeat purchasing based on increased customer satisfaction. Whether the most loyal customer is the most profitable customer is another matter. Loyal, satisfied customers who trust their suppliers behave in specific ways:

- Can increase a company's income;
- Purchase additional products and services;
- Generate more business through WoM (and Word of Mouse);
- Help to reduce costs because they are less expensive to make deals with;
- Allow companies to set the cost of sales and marketing against the revenues generated during the period they deal with the client (think CLTV) rather than a single transaction;
- Represent a source of competitive advantage that is difficult to copy.

In the B2C arena, the sheer number of consumers make interactive marketing (Figure 4.4) and having identical one-to-one relationships with *every* customer difficult. Social media has allowed companies to improve their customer engagement and has encouraged customers (users and influencers) to exchange views about brands. This has added both complexity and opportunities since customer relationships are influenced by not only external marketing but also interactive marketing and interactions with others (e.g. other consumers, influencers and commentators).

The ideas for building relationships can also be applied to internal stakeholders who have power, ideas and insights. It is wise to engage with them and to better understand their interests and needs.

4.2 Internal Marketing (IM)

This subchapter is heavily influenced by the research of Ruth M. Gosnay. She has a clear insight into Internal Marketing (IM) that many marketing academics and practitioners lack. IM (see Figure 4.4) is essential, and despite being a long recognised concept, it is often poorly practised. Marketers *must* repeatedly sell the benefits of IM to their colleagues. Companies focus largely on managing their reputation externally, such as via the corporate website, and sometimes neglect conflicting messages made public by employees and other stakeholders. Sometimes gaps exist between organisational

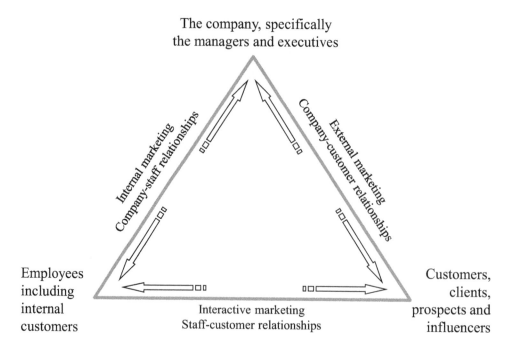

Figure 4.4 Kotler's service profit chain applied to Relationship Marketing (RM)

Source: adapted from Kotler et al. (2009)

attitudes and behaviours. Those who claim to offer ethical and/or green brands will suffer more reputational damage should poor practices be exposed.

Defining Internal Marketing (IM)

There is no single definition of IM; indeed, Yu-ting and Rundle-Thiele (2014, 2015) cite 43 definitions over the past 30 years. Furthermore, most studies in IM have neglected the views of employees, which is a serious omission given the nature of the research (ibid). The following definition is one widely cited by key authors:

> "a planned effort using a marketing-like approach to overcome organisational resistance to change and to align, motivate and inter-functionally coordinate and integrate employees towards the effective implementation of corporate and functional strategies in order to deliver customer satisfaction through a process of creating motivated and customer oriented employees".
>
> (Rafiq and Ahmed, 2000, p. 454)

HR guides often identify expectations of behaviour and advise employees of the consequences of, say, misusing the Internet during work time or posting negative messages about the brand. Negative comments should not be dismissed as the act of a curmudgeon or ne'er-do-well. Some negative comments could result from whistleblowing, where a company claims to operate in a certain way and the employee feels compelled to dispel any misrepresentation, especially if these concerns have been ignored through formal internal channels.

> *Example*   In 2018 the CEO of Ted Baker was cited on Organise. An online petition garnered 2500 signatures; however, it is not certain how many of these were Ted Baker staff. Whether guilty or not, investors sold Ted Baker shares, resulting in a 15% drop, which is the equivalent of wiping £123 million off its market value. It is safe to say that when a company's reputation is brought into disrepute by disgruntled employees, management will be faced with a challenging situation: how to deal with negative comments appearing publicly and how to deal with the employee.

User-Generated Content (UGC) often appears above a company's website in search engine listings. Clearly, organisations are no longer able to control the messages or brand-related discussions. They must engage with online debate or disgruntled employees to overcome any challenges. This may include refining internal communications and making fundamental changes to the company's modus operandi.

Most organisations fail to use IM at a strategic, tactical or operational level in an explicit manner despite the benefits that can accrue. Many non-marketing functions undertake IM on an ongoing basis. Consider the role of modern IT departments that increasingly talk about satisfying internal customers.

There is a degree of conflict in academic circles as to what IM involves and represents. This can cause confusion and may explain why such practices are limited in business today. IM is worthy of consideration for several reasons:

- It identifies a key stakeholder group missing from most texts, namely internal customers.
- It underpins the adoption of a market orientation and a sustainable marketing orientation.
- It advocates using marketing techniques to motivate staff and increase internal "buy-in" or involvement.

The concept of the internal market and internal enterprise (i.e. the internal market, decentralisation and the establishment of profit centres) relates to IM. This intrapreneurship necessitates the application of marketing management knowledge and techniques.

Internal supplier–customer relationships

In large, highly structured organisations such as supermarkets, large, complex networks of internal supplier–customer relationships operate daily. The CEO may visit various supermarkets on a regular basis but will rarely work on the shop floor. The board of directors are responsible for leadership and strategic management led by the CEO. And area managers (who report to the board of directors) and store managers have department heads reporting to them. Clearly, there are many layers of staff who have other employees as internal customers. The internal customers of senior management teams are the staff members they line manage. The personnel rely on the board's strategic ability and skills to lead the organisation. Store managers may have heads of departments report directly to them, and so there is an internal supplier–customer relationship. Store managers supply their managerial skill and knowledge to the heads of departments – the internal customer, who in turn supplies their supervisorial abilities to the staff members who come into contact on a daily basis with the external customer. There are internal supplier–customer relationships throughout organisations.

In SMEs and micro-enterprises, the structure will be flatter; however, internal supplier–customer relationships will still exist. For example, a creative design agency employs a designer, a copywriter and an account manager (AM). The copywriter and designer rely on the skills and abilities of the AM to win accounts and brief them correctly on customers' requirements. Hence, the copywriter and designer are internal customers to the AM (the commercial supplier). Likewise, the AM (the internal customer in this scenario) relies on the ability of the designer and copywriter (the creative suppliers) to fulfil the design requirements of the client's brief and to ensure that the AM has the proofs of work ready to enable meeting the required deadlines at the agreed-on points in the brief's development. To enable this internal chain of events to unfold in an effective and efficient manner, effective systems and processes are required.

Internal Marketing (IM) and the marketing mix

To better understand IM, consider how it influences the interpersonal aspects of the marketing mix, specifically people, process and communications.

People: organisational success is usually predicated on the way the internal stakeholders perform. An organisation is an intricate web of functions that marketing transcends in its inter-functional approach. Within those functions, people strive to fulfil their role and the overall strategic objectives of the organisation. Marketers must be willing to ask several questions:

- Does the staff feel valued by the management, and to what extent?
- How motivated are they to fulfil their role to the best of their ability?
- Does the organisation reward their staff well?
- How does the company measure up against the sector on delivering rewards for employment and the exchange of skills and knowledge?

Many managers struggle to answer these questions and are surprised when staff surveys generate negative outcomes. Those who advocate IM recognise their colleagues not just as employees but as valued *internal customers*. Once this change in perception is established, the attitudes and responsibilities of senior management must change. In larger highly structured organisations, it is easy for the management team to become divorced from the "shop floor".

In marketing and market-oriented companies, the customer should be placed at the heart of all key management decisions. This also applies to internal customers, particularly in services where *people* are the key component of service marketing. Hence, the recruitment, training, motivation and rewarding of staff are critical to ultimate success. Even with product-based marketing, the role of the staff involved in its development, testing, production, marketing, distribution and post-sales support are all central to success. Marketers must ensure that internal customers are satisfied

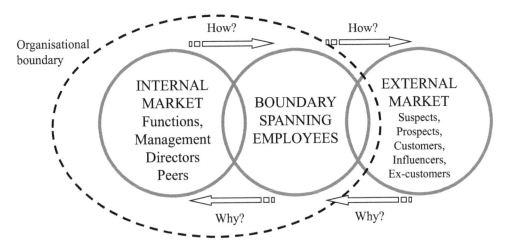

Figure 4.5 Boundary-spanning employees at the internal–external markets interface

Source: adapted from unpublished research into IM by Ruth M. Gosnay

and focused on creating value particularly those that work on the boundary with the external customer.

These boundary-spanning employees often work daily with external customers, and every touch-point or interaction provides an opportunity to portray the organisation in a positive or negative light. Therefore, senior management must reflect on how boundary-spanning employees create value, while the staff should always reflect on why value must be created. This applies at the boundary-spanning employee as customer interface and the boundary-spanning employee as colleague interface. Internal feedback is not solely the responsibility of the HR department; marketing has a unique inter-functional responsibility that transcends formal structural boundaries. The need to train or inform staff throughout the organisation should drive the creation of value and improve the external customer's perception of the brand and thus internal feedback relevant to the marketing team. Marketers should inform decisions made by the HR function when recruiting staff.

Process: to facilitate internal supplier–customer relationships, systems and operations should be designed to enable and empower the *people* performing their duties within a company and throughout the supply network. Marketers must identify the internal supplier–customer relationships that are formed, developed and used on a daily basis. This can ultimately affect the quality of the final product or service that reaches the external customer. Fang et al. (2013) argue that there must be active, responsive IM activities within organisations that seek, gather and disseminate information from and to employees.

Communications: good engagement takes account of staff views and suggestions. Marketers can influence the comms media and messages used to inform, persuade and gain support of internal customers for the marketing plan. The message and language will have to be adapted to the needs, concerns and understanding of the target audience.

A key concern of staff (particularly in larger organisations) is that they have not been made aware of major issues. This could relate to the strategic objectives, mission or values of the organisation as a whole. Marketers must reflect on the effectiveness of the organisation's internal communication processes and be willing to speak truth to power regarding how the senior management team communicate. How well do middle managers communicate? Even in a small business, how well do the core internal customers cross-coordinate and communicate? The following are some of examples of communicating tools and approaches:

- Face to face;
- Internet;
- Emails;
- Newsletters;
- Video/podcasts;
- Conference calls;
- Teleconferencing;
- Annual staff conferences;
- Team meetings;
- Suggestion boxes.

Naturally, the other mix ingredients should also be viewed through the prism of IM. When changing the benefits of a *product*, internal customers (especially boundary-spanning employees) must have input into the marketing plan, objectives and strategies. They have valuable insights into customer values, attitudes and behaviours. Changes in customer perception of the value available from a brand can be shaped by pricing. There may be costs and benefits for internal customers who may be asked to make sacrifices as a result of a new marketing plan (e.g. lost resources, lower status, new (harder) ways of working). Changes to the convenience of the service consumption can influence whether marketing objectives are achieved. Marketers must choose the most effective way to engage with the internal customers, directly or indirectly.

IM and segmentation

Marketers are experienced in developing techniques to target and obtain feedback from external customers. However, senior management rarely use this expertise to secure feedback from their internal customers on how well they, the management team, are performing. All marketers understand the concept of segmentation (see Chapter 3.6) and should be capable segmenting internally (Figure 4.6).

Figure 4.6 draws on the work of Peck et al. (1999) and Jobber (2007). As with external marketing (Figure 4.4), research should be undertaken and each target segment should have a tailored mix applied. Particular emphasis should be placed on communications and process. Companies like First Direct have happy customers and (unsurprisingly) happy staff. It is a yin and yang situation where they both feed into each other to the benefit of all parties.

Benefits of Internal Marketing (IM)

Research has demonstrated that effective IM practices increase business performance overall. Fang and colleagues (2013) identified a strong link between effective *internal*

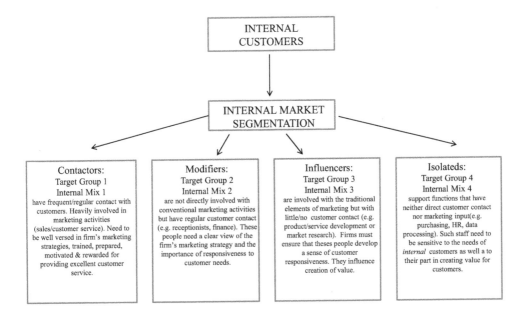

Figure 4.6 Internal marketing: segmentation

Source: adapted from Peck et al. (2002) and Jobber (2007)

marketing and effective *external* market capabilities in what they term "market sensing" – that is, finding out what the dynamics of the marketplace and external environment are – and "customer linking" – that is, analysing current and prospective customer behaviour and building relationships ("bonding") with customers. This analysis supports the view that the marketing function should lead to the situation in Figure 4.7.

If internal customers are engaged, they are more likely to be motivated and satisfied; they will feel valued, which in turn leads to increased work output, higher quality and attention to detail in their work. This therefore can lead to more positives:

- Increased sales and market share;
- Improved reputation and brand integrity;
- Greater employee knowledge, satisfaction and retention;
- Better trained, motivated staff being more involved with corporate objectives;
- Breaking down "them and us" cultures and reducing of the silo effect;
- Improved communication and organisation;
- Product/service innovation from internal customers;
- A competitive edge that is hard to "imitate".

Satisfying internal customers increases the likelihood of creating value and satisfying external customers, which leads to the improved business performance indicators (Figure 4.7) – particularly in a service-based organisation, where boundary-spanning employees are in direct contact with the external customer on a daily basis. That said, good customer service needs constant reinforcement. An additional benefit of internal

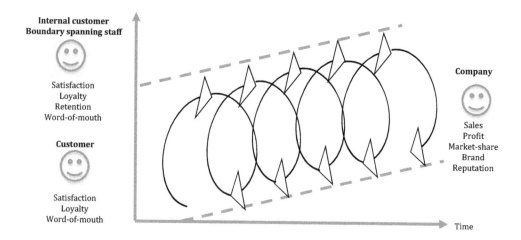

Figure 4.7 Benefits of IM expressed as organisational performance indicators

marketing practices is a reduction (if not eradication) of the silo effect. Many employees, particularly in large organisations, complain of the lack of joined-up thinking in terms of inter-functional operations and communications. As an organisation grows and functions and employees become more formally structured, quite often into formal departments or functions, the cross-functional links between these departments can fracture. Job descriptions and general responsibilities often do not formally recognise the inter-functional collaboration that is required. Since IM is based on viewing the internal customer as part of the internal supplier and customer process, it generally starts to bond employees and managers at all levels across and throughout the organisation in a much more robust manner, creating much better cross-functional relationships and operational efficiencies.

Key criticisms of Internal Marketing (IM)

One of the key criticisms of IM is the general diversion of resources, time and attention away from the external marketplace and external customer.

- IM can create subservient internal relationships with power struggles arising throughout and across various functions of the internal market.
- It can develop internal euphoria – when the internal customers become so cohesive as a unit, it is to the detriment of the external customer relationship.
- It can lead to inter-functional conflict, with power struggles being created as a result of shifting internal responsibilities and resourcing.
- It can highlight many internal aspects of managerial weakness, particularly from operational, resource and communication perspectives – which is inherently political.
- It can create problems for managers who may prefer to preserve the status quo, who are resistant to change or who are not well versed in change management.

Practical steps towards implementing Internal Marketing (IM)

Research into best IM practices undertaken by the North Western University (NWU, 2006) advocated for several actions:

- Creating an efficient and collaborative work environment where employees feel involved and/or motivated to work;
- Giving positive reinforcement of proactive work;
- Communicating the brand promise to employees across the most relevant channels and motivate employees to deliver on that promise;
- The HR function playing a vital role in developing strategies that synchronise with marketing and business development;
- IM encompassing all employees;
- Horizontally integrating and involved all functions and levels;
- Showing leadership initiative, support and "buy-in";
- Taking a formal approach to IM, including research and planning.

IM can be implemented (or at least introduced) by adopting the following practices:

- *Generate information* by ensuring that the organisation is providing timely and accurate information to all staff.
- *Communicate* relevant information to the correct internal customers in a timely manner.
- *Reflect* on how well the company responds to its internal market's needs. Are internal customers well rewarded for their skills, time and abilities? Are you a competitive organisation in relation to pay, pensions, holiday entitlement? Or do you lose valuable staff due to your lack of competitive ability in this area?
- *Gather data* from performance reviews. Too many managers merely appraise staff in a top-down manner. However, internal customers, particularly those on the front line, should ideally be providing meaningful feedback on their line manager's ability to provide them with resources, skills, time and rewards. Performance reviews should involve 360-degree (and ideally 540-degree) appraisals.
- *Act* on the findings. To be effective, IM needs "buy-in" from senior management, which sadly does not always happen. Too often, marketing audits (whether internal or external) are rendered ineffective by the lack of management's commitment. Changing structure within organisations is often easy, as is evidenced in the early days of new senior management appointments. A cultural shift is often required, which can take time, skill, resilience and resources. However, the benefits that can be achieved both internally with a greater number of satisfied, motivated and skilled internal customers will inevitably affect their ability to create value for the external customer and achieve key performance metrics for the organisation.

Marketing's role in supporting the organisation's market orientation

Kohli and Jaworksi suggest that intelligence gathering cannot be the sole responsibility of the marketing function, but it *is* logical for marketing to be responsible for collating data, processing it into information and disseminating this across the organisation.

Fang et al. (2013) argue that there must be an active, responsive internal marketing activity within organisations that seek, gather and disseminate information from and to employees. Their research suggests that marketing can be seen as an internal service provider for other functions/departments because of several factors:

- Marketers act as a catalyst for change by communicating changing customer needs.
- IM helps disseminate corporate culture (see Chapter 4.2).
- Marketing can brief HR on the skills required for customer service.
- Marketing liaises heavily with all functions (or departments), such as regarding product launches.

4.3 Sustainable entrepreneurship

Little research on entrepreneurship and sustainability appears in the academic literature. Many writers view entrepreneurship as the engine of sustainability, expecting that its innovative power will bring about a more-sustainable future. That said, entrepreneurs face disadvantages when pursuing "costly" sustainable actions, so costs may not be borne by competitors (Pacheco et al., 2010). Hence, it is appropriate to consider the nature of sustainable entrepreneurship (SE).

Traditionally, an inherent large firm focus exists in the corporate sustainability literature; however, entrepreneurs and SMEs play a vital role in managing global environmental and social resources (Moore and Manring, 2009). Sustainable entrepreneurs can bring skill sets to bear quickly and even more competitively than larger incumbents (ibid). They seek to maintain the balance between social, environmental and economic dimensions, requiring a specific orientation for guiding the venture design process (Munoz and Dimov, 2015). SE embodies those who holistically integrate these goals into an organisation that is sustainable in its goal and in its form of wealth generation (Young and Tilley, 2006).

There is increasing interest in SE as a phenomenon and a research topic (Shepherd and Patzelt, 2011). SE research has traditionally focused on small firms, sometimes down to the level of the individual entrepreneur (Hockerts and Wüstenhagen, 2010). SE promotes sustainability through the realisation of successful businesses (Munoz and Dimov, 2015). Factors that drive SE are related to the individual entrepreneur and the context in which the behaviour occurs, such as social norms, the openness of the business context to sustainability practices and the nature of the value-creation goals (ibid).

Creating sustainable value may be subject to time constraints or may be impossible given resource allocations. Specifically, while some may immediately implement sustainable practices, others may need to accrue the resources to initiate changes (Pacheco et al., 2010). Not all activities to improve environmental or social performance can be characterised as SE. There is some debate as to what constitutes a sustainable entrepreneur because those who have no intention to broaden their impact on a wider market may be categorised as

"incrementally innovative and hence not sustainable entrepreneurs. . . . [They] often come from the voluntary sector and sometimes tend to be opposed to

consumerism and growth. They worry that mainstreaming requires them to abandon their ideals".

(Hockerts and Wüstenhagen, 2010, p. 484)

These positions allude to organisational and personal values, norms and motivations.

Values, norms and sustainable entrepreneurs

Entrepreneurs must quickly align their values with changing consumer perceptions
and engagement. They must also engage with a diverse range of stakeholders, such
as suppliers, consumers, facilitators and other stakeholders in the microenvironment.
Entrepreneurial perceptions of value are not limited to financial profit or economic
wealth creation but instead reflect personal and wider generalised value systems. The
entrepreneurial process is therefore embedded in a given social context. As social contexts, values and rules change, so do the entrepreneurial opportunities (Tilley and
Young, 2009).

It is worth considering whether values influence behaviours and whether special
efforts are needed by those who want to successfully commercialise sustainable innovation. As Hockerts and Wüstenhagen (2010) ask, how do they convince consumers
that the product offering is not only good for society but also good for them? Such
desired value creation pertains to the value that sustainable entrepreneurs aim to create, both for their business and for society, by articulating a holistic value proposition predicated on intertwined social, economic and ecological value (Munoz and
Dimov, 2015). Limitations of the notion of value propositions have been considered
elsewhere.

Co-creation of value counters the idea of giving or proposing value by suggesting it
is mutually created. The notion is not new; indeed, Freeman (2008) suggests that people have been creating value and trading with each other since long before there were
corporations. Hockerts and Wüstenhagen (2010, p. 485) argue that SE is "a combination of economic, social and environmental value creation". Freeman (2008) insists
that entrepreneurs are creating value, making our lives better and changing the world.

What sets sustainable companies apart is their pronounced value-based approach
and their intention to effect social and environmental change in society. They seek to
change market equilibria and in the process change the playing field for everybody by
asking customers to pay a premium for socially and environmentally superior products (Hockerts and Wüstenhagen, 2010).

A key point is that value is not a permanent state; rather, it can be created or
destroyed. Cohen et al. (2006) identified elements of sustainable value creation,
including economic performance, socio-efficiency, stewardship and eco-efficiency.
These are consistent with Elkington's TBL, which sets the standard to identify a form
of business value that delivers simultaneously economic, social and environmental
benefits (Munoz and Dimov, 2015). The pursuit of such desired outcomes prompts
the elaboration of business strategies and practices capable of tackling pressing challenges (ibid).

Individuals who attend to the social or ecological environments are more likely to
recognise changes therein and the opportunities that arise. Therefore, compared to
individuals more focused on the economic bottom line, those individuals are more

likely to form beliefs about opportunities for sustainability even if they show no intention to personally pursue such opportunities (Shepherd and Patzelt, 2011).

Values and motives that give rise to SE may result in specific organising tensions that have the potential to challenge the viability of the enterprises (Munoz and Dimov, 2015). Sustainable ventures, often run by idealists, are less likely to be caught in a specific technological mindset and more prone to try out innovative approaches (Hockerts and Wüstenhagen, 2010). The pursuit of sustainability ideals through entrepreneurial means depends on the strength of the individual's intention to contribute to solving societal and environmental problems (Schaltegger and Wagner, 2011). Entrepreneurs may be motivated for a number of reasons – for example, being acquired can free the founding entrepreneurs to continue to develop new firms and to pursue other synergistic alternatives (Moore and Manring, 2009). Motivations associated with increased economic return may be deemed most important, whereas those based on altruistic concerns for society or the environment may be less effective since institutional change is generally a costly endeavour (Pacheco et al., 2010).

Entrepreneurs exist within a history or stream of ongoing action that gives meaning to and orients their behaviour (ibid); for example, by acting as buyers, entrepreneurs can exert more pressure for sustainable supply chain management (Moore and Manring, 2009). SE transforms institutions by altering and/or creating norms. Examples of norms developed in the realm of SE include codes of behaviour, partnerships and third-party certification programmes (Pacheco et al., 2010).

Norms exist in a given social setting to the extent that individuals often they find themselves "locked into" unsustainable patterns of consumption by social norms that lie beyond individual control (Jackson, 2005). In addition, norms (which are not exclusively related to monetary issues) can bring uniformity to behaviour, as their introduction encourages conformity. A variety of industries have witnessed the intervention of entrepreneurs in promoting self-enforced cooperative norms. Entrepreneurs may be forced to rely on a sanctioned third-party to devise and enforce industry norms (Pacheco et al., 2010). Not all companies adopt normative notions of doing what is perceived to be right (Jackson, 2005).

Hockerts and Wüstenhagen (2010, p. 484) suggest that

> "sustainable entrepreneurial firms do not only see sustainability as central to core business activities, but at the same time aim for mass-market transformation beyond the eco-niche".

Sustainable enterprises must be robust and resilient in the face of anticipated and unanticipated economic, environmental and social challenges (Moore and Manring, 2009). The central idea is that the activities performed by entrepreneurs in the pursuit of gains must not undermine ecological and social environments and (when necessary) must restore or nurture such environments towards recovering the balance between nature, society and economic activity (Parrish, 2010). A number of forces underscore the emerging opportunities to proactively adopt sustainable practices, including networked communications, extended (and interconnected) supply chains and rapidly changing markets (Moore and Manring, 2009).

Sustainable entrepreneurs in the community

Within service economies, entrepreneurial action can be found in various organisational settings; however, Spedale and Watson (2014, p. 760) argue that attention to context in mainstream entrepreneurial studies remains inadequate. Some sustainable actions are undertaken intuitively; however, intuition in itself may not be enough when promoting behavioural changes among stakeholders. This conscientiousness chimes with those critical of wealthy consumers enjoying being free-riders, where their immediate descendants and the world's poor pay (Kotler et al., 2009).

Traditionally, the notion of community refers to those locals who host (or live near) events (Vestrum and Rasmussen, 2013). Traditionally viewed as a public (interested but no engagement), communities can evolve into "engaged" stakeholders. The idea of community can be used to foster good relations or a supportive atmosphere. A benefit of this approach is that it improves involvement. Involved stakeholders are often committed to supporting the community beyond the entrepreneurial activity itself. These entrepreneurs often highlight the importance of welfare and quality of life in their locality (Tilley and Young, 2009). However, awareness of activities in the locale should not be assumed. Community engagement varies: after all, the people in a community are heterogeneous, and their needs vary. Some communities overlap and evolve, which can provide opportunities for entrepreneurs who may seek to develop interdependence with different sectors of the community (Vestrum and Rasmussen, 2013).

Social inclusion is an ethical objective for some entrepreneurs. Social inclusion should not be seen as purely altruistic, because those included can make positive contributions. This chimes with the idea of enlightened self-interest (Haberberg et al., 2010); however, there is a caveat to social inclusion: organisations often make social investments in the face of compelling economic reasoning not to do so (Margolis and Walsh, 2003).

Ownership and sustainable entrepreneurship

Stakeholders often see ownership of sustainable practices as a value, where involved consumers may take responsibility across a range of aspects of the exchange. This ownership can be linked to incentives; for example, some music festivals incentivise litter collection (e.g. Boomtown offer an eco-bond in which at the end of the festival, consumers receive a £20 refund on their ticket if they collect a specified amount of litter). Ownership is linked with the co-creation of value; for example, "safety" concerns are more likely to be addressed if, say, parents at an event think their peers will help care for the children onsite. Furthermore, the emergence of consumers as co-creators of value has been harnessed by firms in the creative industries (UNCTAD, 2008). It is always worth remembering that stakeholder theory is a simple idea about how people create value for each other (Freeman, 2008). Hence, entrepreneurs and consumers can develop different types of engagement with activities, objects, ideas or even social issues.

Growth

Growth is often a key concern for entrepreneurs; however, the different modes of growth have risks, which may ultimately lead to increasing dissatisfaction among customers. The age of the enterprise will shape the attitude to risk, and some entrepreneurs may not feel comfortable increasing their risk by taking on board "extra" costs of sustainability. This fits with Fussler (1996), who insisted that most firms are not actively pursuing SE as a strategy to create market share. Ultimately, as consumers become increasingly sustainable with every passing generation, it will be easier for entrepreneurs to treat sustainability as an investment rather than a costly risk. Indeed, the argument may in time evolve to become, how can entrepreneurs afford *not* to adopt sustainable practices?

Growth can result from SE activities that represent disruptive, rather than incremental, innovation (Hockerts and Wüstenhagen, 2010). This does, however, raise the question of what is being disrupted. Entrepreneurs may not be overtly "sustainable", whereas some in their supply network may be so. For the smallest, youngest organisations, the pursuit of growth is a key objective. It is difficult to survive when constrained by low turnover and cashflow. Such enterprises are subject to the capricious nature of business environments. Many small companies failed during the financial crisis of 2007/2008, whereas most multinationals were able to ride out the storm. Indeed, the FTSE 100 index rose because most incumbents were considered to be global and thus beyond the ramifications of local turbulence.

Some organisations will implement SE practices immediately, whereas others will accrue the resources (or economy of scale) to initiate changes (Pacheco et al., 2010). The growth may lead to specific SE tensions with the potential to impede the enterprises (Munoz and Dimov, 2015) – for example, whether to charge for car parking at an event, provide transport, include the socially excluded and so on.

For some sustainable entrepreneurs, motivations that are associated with increased economic return, while deemed important, are not of the highest priority, because growth is not universally sought, contrary to Hockerts and Wüstenhagen (2010). A challenge for sustainable entrepreneurs is that growth is deemed by some to be the antithesis of sustainability. As they grow, they may become more commercial and may lose their attractiveness for those interested in sustainability. Hence, many sustainable entrepreneurs are happy to achieve a stasis where they are financially resilient but not dependent on growth. Resilience, of course, takes many forms.

Environmental resilience

Sustainable entrepreneurs seek to attract mainstream consumers, which may explain why so many are just focused on niche green consumers. The notion of resilience is key for many sustainable entrepreneurs. Sustainability is often seen to represent the regenerative use of resources. Indeed, many studies have found that individuals have a connectedness with the broader environment. Their environmental interaction features emotional commitments, which can affect their patronage decisions. When discussing sustainability, stakeholders are often confused by the vastness of topics – for example, recycling, energy saving, water saving or being environmentally friendly. The range of terms used may in itself be problematic when seeking to engage consumers. This may, to some extent, explain studies that that identified increasing sustainability rhetoric but little progress in addressing environmental and social problems facing society (Tilley and Young, 2009).

Jackson (2005) identified the need to change behaviour in relation to transport modes, eating habits and leisure practices, in order to reduce the damaging impact on the environment and on other people. These offerings fit with a "biospheric" value orientation (ibid) and align with Young et al. (2010), who found that the environment was a key driver during purchasing decisions.

Attitudes are linked with pro-environmental behaviour, which flows from pro-eco and pro-social values. Hence, stakeholders, like consumers, have a range of competing values that lead to dissonance when making a decision. A wide body of research has found that consumers are increasingly willing to pay a premium for socially and environmentally superior products. Hence, their values are based on altruistic concerns for society or the environment, and while potentially costly, they're worth the investment. SE values may influence stakeholder engagement as they are not averse to the notion that the green and societal endeavours are not just good for *society* but also good for *them* (Hockerts and Wüstenhagen, 2010).

Consumers often see and interact with "sustainable" entrepreneurs, who are essentially local, micro-enterprises, many of which feature single individuals, including "founding entrepreneurs" (Fisher et al., 2014). Entrepreneurs adopt ad hoc approaches to engagement and exhibit diverse sustainability orientations.

4.4 Sustainable branding

Branding is a contentious area in marketing. Branding specialists insist that it is the be-all and end-all of marketing; however, they are often at a loss to explain why so many brands fail.

To start, de Chernatony et al. (2011) describe brands as clusters of functional and emotional values that promise stakeholders a particular experience. It must be assumed that brands fail primarily because customers and stakeholders do not take value form the particular experience. Brand loyalty is a measure of a consumer's attachment to a specific brand. It is a function of several factors such as perceived quality, values, image, symbols, visual messages, nonverbal messages, emotional intelligence, the trust placed in the brand and the commitment the consumer feels towards it (ibid).

If, as Jackson (2005) suggests, consumption is socially constructed, then sustainable branding represents a social construct involving the brand, its ecological footprint and any ethical impact on society. This presents the marketing versus sustainability dichotomy (see Chapter 1). Consumers may have positive attitudes towards sustainability; however, this is no guarantee of changes in behaviour. Some consumers are reluctant to pay more for sustainable brands, whereas others see sustainability as an essential part of their social status.

Organisations not only sell brands but are also brands themselves. An organisation's brand is an amalgam of its reputation, product branding and image. Such branding helps to establish the positioning of products and companies. That said, positioning is perceived from the perspective of customers and stakeholders. Organisational branding can support IM and the marketing of the brand itself. All employees, especially those who are internal customers, need to buy into the *brand promise*. If the brand values, which are extolled externally, are not experienced internally, there is a risk of employees feeling they are merely a "channel to market". Rather than the brand values being at the heart of the culture of the organisation, employees may perceive them as being superficial, which in turn may lower motivation and morale.

Thomson et al. (2010) identified the importance of communicating brand values to employees and suggest that employees generally use a mixture of sources to draw on information about an organisation's brand values. Brand performance is enhanced when employees are aware of their organisation's brand strategy and values. For this to happen, both functionally, intellectually and emotionally, the brand values and message need to be communicated clearly and consistently (ibid). Senior management are responsible for building a brand's identity and must create a culture of open communication throughout the organisation. Seeking 540-degree feedback will encourage more fluid horizontal and vertical communication that involves all stakeholders.

Marketers must work diligently and intelligently in order to build and maintain sustainable brands that form part of sustainable consumers' social constructs. A sustainable brand management process will increasingly enhance an organisation's ability to acquire and retain customers. An added benefit is that it may also foster relationships with sustainable tribes, communities and networks.

As discussed in Chapter 2, service and product marketing are related but different. Service brands require greater emphasis on IM because they rely on boundary-spanning, customer-facing employees who are subject to the different characteristics of services. Branding can play a key role in building trust among service customers and stakeholders. Customers will trust a brand that they perceive can provide consistent quality over a period of time. That said, markets are often subject to hyper-competition, oversupply and fragmentation. In these circumstances, brand differentiation is harder to achieve.

Brand personalities

In the 1950s, Gardner and Levy (1955) became the first to suggest that brands had personality characteristics. Aaker (1997, p. 347) defined brand personality as "the set of human characteristics associated with a brand". Consumer decision-making is informed by their perceptions of the product's functionally and on the basis of brand personality perceptions. Indeed, consumers associate distinctive and relatively enduring characteristics with specific brands and these associations help (consumers) form relationships with specific brands (Aaker, 1997). Carlson and Donavan (2013, p. 196) develop this suggesting "brand personality is a dynamic amalgamation of unique attributes (i.e. brand adjectives) working together to create an overall personality for a brand". In tumultuous times, all marketing activities must be dynamic rather than static. Introducing the link between human personality traits and brands was a significant contribution to brand management.

Aaker (1997) developed a brand personality framework (Figure 4.8) that has been applied widely in branding research. Criticisms of the Aaker framework related to the lack of negative terms in the dimensions and attributes. Some attributes include degrees of overlap, and clearly language and culture will shape perceptions. This raises questions regarding how the framework applies across international boundaries. A number of scholars have produced adapted frameworks to suit their scenario. One of which was Geuens et al. (2009). While their dimensions do not overtly refer to ethical or ecological matters, responsibility, simplicity and emotionality could be argued to resonate with sustainability. These could be developed so that the values within sustainable brands can be communicated (Figure 4.8).

Aaker (1997)		Geuens et al. (2009)		Sustainable Brands	
Dimensions	Core Attributes	Dimensions	Core Attributes	Dimensions	Core Attributes
Sincerity	Down-to-earth Honest Wholesome Cheerful	Responsibility	Down-to-earth, Stable Responsible	Responsibility	Down-to-earth, Durable Stable Responsible Collaborative
Excitement	Daring Spirited Imaginative Contemporary	Activity	Active Dynamic Innovative	Activity	Dynamic Innovative Accountable Willing Collectivist
Competence	Reliable Intelligent Successful	Aggressiveness	Aggressive Bold	Transparent	Communicative Listening Open Bold
Sophistication	Classy Charming	Simplicity	Ordinary Simple	Contentment	Committed Long-term oriented Simple Voluntary
Ruggedness	Masculine Tough	Emotionally	Romantic Sentimental	Compassionate	Caring Considerate Honest Sentimental

Figure 4.8 Brand personality frameworks

Source: adapted from Aaker (1997) and Geuens et al. (2009)

Kapferer developed a brand identity prism in which he considers a brand as a speech flowing from a sender to a receiver (Kapferer, 2008).

Figure 4.9 illustrates how the identity prism could be applied to an organisation wanting to open a vegan coffee shop. The brand identity dimensions (physique and personality – human personality traits) imagine the sender. Reflection and self-image represent the receiver, whereas culture and relationship connect the sender and the receiver. The identity prism is largely judgement based; however, it can provide insights into how a segment could be supported.

Brand equity

Aaker (1991) suggested that brand equity occurs when brand associations are complemented by brand awareness, perceived quality and loyalty.

Brand awareness relates to the level of consumer familiarity and recall. Marketers should not infer that this means the brand is "superior". Consumers often have high levels of brand awareness and knowledge; however, this does not necessarily shape their decision-making.

Perceived quality reflects how the consumer perceives the brand quality when compared to the competition. In high-quality markets, a strong brand identity and

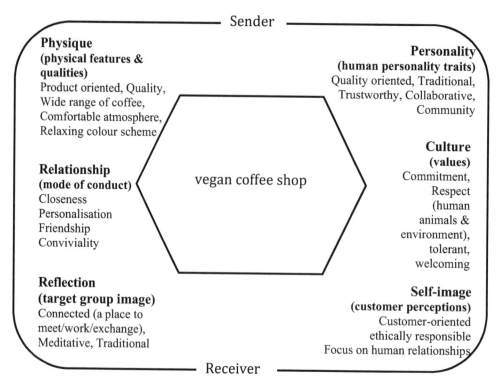

Figure 4.9 Kapferer's brand identity prism applied to a vegan coffee shop
Source: adapted from Kapferer (1997)

personality are essential. This applies to markets with low differentiation. The iPhone is the most profitable smartphone ever, not because of its features, which are broadly similar to Huawei's and Samsung's respective mobile phones, but because of its identity and personality.

Brand loyalty starts at an early age and can be both attitudinal and behavioural (Russell-Bennett et al., 2007). Children have been found to be increasingly aware of charitable campaigns and specific charity brands and events. Targeting children is one of the most contentious marketing activities. Any research must comply with rigorous ethical standards (see the MRS code of conduct).

Brand loyalty is also an important outcome for many social marketing programmes, where it is highly desirable to change behaviours. Recycling programmes, for example, encourage people to regularly separate their paper and food products for recycling, while healthy-eating programmes focus on increasing the number of people who sustain healthy-eating habits.

Brand positioning

Product positioning was previously discussed regarding products (see Chapter 2.3). Brand positioning develops this by building on the brand's equity and characteristics.

However, the need for customer centricity still applies. Brand positioning is positive only if the *customer* perceives it that way. A brand achieves competitive advantage only if *customers* think they are more likely to take value from the brand than from a competitor.

Kapferer (2008) offered a positioning framework based on four questions (Figure 4.10).

Sustainable brands need to counter the idea that some customers perceive such items as "costly". Marketers must acknowledge the limitations of brand positioning. The statements help because in competitive markets, brands have to be able to position themselves against the competition, who may not burden themselves with ethical or green practices.

Brand communities

SM is inclusive and often seeks interactions with communities. Brand communities are groups of consumers with shared enthusiasm for a brand. They have well-developed collective identities (in-group, out-group) and engage in in-group activities to achieve common objectives. Furthermore, they often share a common consciousness of kind, moral responsibility for one another. They are akin to tribes in that they participate

Positioning Statements	Scenarios		
	Sustainable Music Festival	Sustainable Marketing Agency	Environmentally Friendly Stationery Manufacturer
A brand for what?	A festival based on the rock music genre	Internal, B2B, consumer and crisis communications	Personalised celebratory stationery
A brand for whom?	All professionals with interests in rock music and going to events	Sole traders, small budget charities and larger companies looking for regional and national brand exposure	Professionals with an inclination towards entertaining and/or sentimental products
A brand for when?	Annual event for people to come together and enjoy rock music	Permanent projects or short-term consultancy work	Special occasions of friends or family
A brand against whom?	Hedonistic festivals with high eco and social impacts.	Agencies seeking to boost client profitability with no investment in social and green concerns Unethical PR agencies offering spin	Non-green suppliers of generic off the roll gift wrap Those who promote single-use wrapping

Figure 4.10 Kapferer's positioning model applied to three sustainable scenarios

Source: adapted from Kapferer (2008)

in shared rituals and/or events associated with the brand while co-creating value for each other.

Brand communities differ from standard brand relationships since the focus is on the inter-consumer relationships rather than between the consumer and the brand. Sustainable marketers will benefit from developing long-term relationships with brand communities. SM uses relationship-marketing techniques predicated on long-term dialogue and considering the customer's LTV, societal impact and carbon footprint. The synergies within the brand community will align with the brand, which should create stronger bonds. The advent of Web 2.0 and user-generated content has enabled international brand communities to flourish, often overcoming linguistic and cultural barriers. Marketers have to understand the structure within a brand community, as some may be hierarchical. This should be coupled with an appreciation of sustainable segmentation (see Chapter 1) since community members have different degrees of commitment and motivation.

A consumer using two sustainable brands at a similar time is not necessarily a sign of disloyalty. Rather, sustainable consumers have a "repertoire of brands" (de Chernatony et el, 2011). For example, buying Fairtrade goods in one category, MSC items in a second category and Soil Association goods in a third category. This will be welcome news to sustainable brands that do not necessarily want to ferociously compete with each other if their customers demonstrate multiple brand loyalties.

> *Example*   Unilever had 1 million likes of Marmite on Facebook in mid 2014. They also had user-generated content via Recipe of the Day and other measures. The Marmite brand community provided an alternative to the traditional "push" form of marcomms. However, care must be taken in suggesting that the community activities caused sales to increase.

Sustainable brands often subscribe to building the "sustainability pie" rather than engaging in a race to the bottom to seek a bigger slice of the "pie". They regard each other in a complementary fashion, which is appreciated by the brand communities. This reflects the concept of equifinality. The old adage is that all roads lead to Rome. Regarding sustainability, there are many ways to reach the ultimate destination of sustainable consumption. Every truly sustainable brand helps along the way.

Reputation

A benefit of SM is that it may generate improved organisational and brand reputations. A reputation is generally what is said or believed about the character of a person, brand or organisation. With social media increasingly shaping marketing efforts, reputations can be the sum of the stories that people tell about a person (or organisation). Urban myths can be associated with brands, which can be difficult to shake off. The old adage "never let the truth get in the way of a good story" often applies. Brands can be "trolled" online and often have little recourse. That said, libel and slander laws apply whether online or in print. Companies are increasingly concerned about reputational damage inflicted by their own employees. Bringing an employer into disrepute can lead to the rapid termination of a contract. That said, progressive employers understand the benefits of a sincere whistleblowing programme. Reputations vary depending on whose perspective is being used – for example, family, friends, employers, customers or suppliers. When does a strong manager become a bully? These can be fine lines. That said, bullying is never acceptable.

> *Example* Reputations can have sub-reputations and constituent parts. The reputation of a city such as Leeds comprises the reputation of its people, its buildings, its location, its music, its history, its sporting teams and major events. Sometimes branding needs serendipity. Sir Gary Verity almost singlehandedly brought the Tour de France's Grande Depart to West Yorkshire in 2016. Two of West Yorkshire's finest athletes (the Brownlee brothers) have been hugely successful in triathlon events at the highest level. They have brought triathlon events to Leeds. These two different events have seen the reputation, for sporting events, of the city of Leeds enhanced on the world stage. Credit is also owed to the local authorities that supported these new ventures.

Trust in a brand is no longer just in terms of doing "what it says on the tin". Consumers increasingly want to be able to trust the people behind the product. They want to believe the brand represents the sort of people who do the right thing. Sustainable brands can build win-win relationships, create a bigger sustainability cake and share the benefits of the best suppliers, partners, investors and customers. In treating people decently and ethically, they build a reputation for being good people with whom consumers can work. Some commentators are more cynical. Kotler et al. (2009) suggested that

> "Ethical consumption is perhaps the biggest movement in branding today. [However,] . . . consumers are confused. The public is not sure what an ethical brand actually is. There are so many angles to being ethical. . . . The more optimistic British thought that supporting ethical brands could help make companies more accountable but were wary that ethical brands were for 'people with money'".
>
> (2009, pp. 94–95)

This view is becoming increasingly outdated as brands align themselves with the social and ecological values of consumers. Consumers are indeed more green and ethical (Ethical Consumer, 2018). Sustainable marketers must engage by communicating the brand's value and character. A key to many branding campaigns is (and probably always will be) WoM. Ultimately, power is largely a matter of perception. The mightiest of companies can be brought down by reputational damage caused by unethical practices (see Bell Pottinger for an egregious example). If marketers want consumers, prospects and influencers to see them as a powerful, sustainable brand, they need to act like credible leaders. Brands have evolved beyond their original role as a tool for sales-oriented transactional companies. Branding needs to become a management tool that creates clear, credible value for those who want to take it.

4.5 Global Sustainable Marketing

In the 21st century, all marketers are global marketers who source goods, service customers and face global competition. There are many push-and-pull factors relating to trading internationally (Figure 4.11).

Push Factors	Pull Factors
Oversupply and hyper-competition in domestic market	Nascent and developing markets
Future economic recession or low GDP growth	Weaker competition
	Strong economic growth
Unfavourable demographics – ageing population	Increasing disposable income and living standards
Fragmentation of market	Favourable demographics – younger age profile
High operating costs	Pro-business governments and bodies
Excessive shareholder power	Lower fixed and variable costs
Short-termism – government, city	Geographical spread of trading risks
Lack of differentiation in mature markets	Positive attitude towards newness and innovation

Figure 4.11 Push-and-pull factors for Global Marketing

Source: author

Clearly, the global business environments must inform marketing objectives, strategies and tactics. The marketing mix may need to be tailored to suit international customers. Furthermore, different methods of entering overseas markets exist, and companies must adopt suitable entry strategies. Hence, marketers must be able to analyse aspects of the business environment beyond the confines of their domestic market.

Key factors in global marketing

In the mid 20th century, two key organisations were created: the International Trade Organization (ITO) and the World Bank. Under their auspices, 22 countries signed up to General Agreement on Trade and Tariffs (GATT) in 1947. GATT covered goods and the principle of Most Favoured Nation (MFN) and included a commitment to rounds of negotiations to reduce tariffs. Founding members of GATT (predominantly rich countries) participated in many rounds and consequently have very low tariffs. The first 25 years of GATT coincided with the most prosperous years in history. Rapid growth fostered liberalisation, which stimulated further growth. GATT evolved into the World Trade Organization (WTO) in 1995. A key WTO function is to prevent the exploitation of Intellectual Property Rights (IPRs) within set timescales. Sometimes the long-term IPRs can conflict with short-term public policy initiatives; for example, the South African government deliberately and justifiably violated pharmaceutical IPRs in order to better treat citizens with AIDS.

Substantive developments are associated with "rounds" trade talks in specific locations:

- Paris: patents, trademarks and designs;
- Rome: recording and broadcasting;
- Berne: copyright;
- Uruguay: anti-dumping measures, export and general domestic subsidies.

Uruguay saw the acceptance of Trade-Related Aspects of Intellectual Property Rights (TRIPs), featuring IPRs, to do the following:

- Protect copyright, databases and computer programmes (50 years);
- Trade marks (seven years);
- Industrial designs (ten years);
- Patents (20 years);
- Trade secrets (indefinite).

Developing countries have ten years' grace. TRIPS strengthens the protection of IPRs almost worldwide with disputes subject to WTO dispute settlement procedures. Dispute procedures feature

- Panels of experts;
- The automatic adoption of reports;
- Time limits;
- Permitted retaliation.

The United Nations–based World Intellectual Property Organization (WIPO) administers the "rounds" and generally promotes IPRs. WIPO is (allegedly) a neutral forum (drawing on experts from government and industry) with arguably less political bargaining than the WTO ministerial conferences. The matters under discussion are complex and ever changing; consider e-commerce, artificial intelligence, genetically modified foods, biodiversity, and/or environmental considerations

The WTO seeks to harmonise measures such as product standards, packaging provisions, marking or labelling requirements and assessment procedures. The agreements allow for some national flexibility; however, the aim is to reduce impediments to trade.

The Uruguay round enshrined anti-dumping measures that resonate today. Countries using anti-dumping measures – for example, President Trump's United States – are open to charges of protectionism. Two broad types of subsidies are allowable: export and general domestic subsidies. Uruguay provided a RAG (traffic light) system for subsidies as follows:

- Red – any that seek to enhance exports or that promote local content in preference to imports;
- Amber (actionable) – any action that injures another country's exports;
- Green (non-actionable) – such as areas of high unemployment.

Foreign Direct Investment (FDI)

Foreign Direct Investment (FDI) occurs when an entity, located in one country, takes a long-term interest in and/or control of an entity in another country. The minimum proportion of equity that is needed is 10%.

The 2018 World Investment Report (UNCTAD, 2018) found that in 2017 global FDI flows fell by 23%, to $1.43 trillion. Half of the top ten host economies are developing economies; however, the United States received the most FDI inflows ($275 billion), followed by China, who had record inflows of $136 billion (ibid). This was a central plank of President Trump's 2016 platform, in which jobs would purportedly be relocated to the United States. That said, it is highly unlikely that, say, Apple will relocate the manufacture of its devices to the United States rather than China. President Trump has tacitly acknowledged this by imposing import tariffs on Chinese goods. These tariffs are effectively a tax on the US consumers, who show no signs of wanting to stop buying goods manufactured overseas. An irony is that the largest seller of smartphones (by units) is Samsung, who are South Korean and as such are not involved in the escalating tariffs.

The fall in FDI is in stark contrast to the accelerated growth in GDP and trade. FDI flows to developing economies remained stable at $671 billion, with (developing) Asia receiving $476 billion (UNCTAD, 2018). In 2002 the United Kingdom was in the top seven recipients of inward FDI investment. By 2017 it was not in the top 20, but it had the fourth largest FDI outflow (ibid). It is hard to imagine that Brexit was not a factor in this development. Normally, a period of reduced inward investment would lead to serious economic impacts such as a poorer balance of payments, higher inflation and unemployment. Such a prognosis cannot be made at this juncture. Only two things are certain regarding Brexit: first, there will be winners and losers; second, the impacts will not be uniform across the United Kingdom.

Vulnerable states

Sustainable Marketing is predicated on ethical decision-making. This is particularly the case when supplying goods and services to vulnerable states and countries. Worryingly, UNCTAD (2018) identify the following investment trends:

- FDI flows to Africa slumped to $42 billion in 2017, a 21% decline from 2016, representing a ten-year low.
- FDI inflows to the LDCs as a group declined by 17%, to $26 billion, representing 4% of FDI flows to all developing economies.

Marketing decisions will be influenced by the characteristics of the host economy. Strategies and tactics may alter if the host is a large developing country as against being developed. Marketers targeting states with weak institutions will have to be wary of corrupt practices, particularly in the post-Sarbanes-Oxley Act world.

Countries with great dependence on natural resources, say oil, are more likely than others to suffer poverty, civil war, dictatorship and corruption. Sachs and Warner (1995) found that 97 natural resource–dependent nations had slower economic growth than the rest of world. The drivers for this were economic, as the drive for oil revenues took resources from other export sectors and corruption as politicians received money from outside sources rather than taxpayers and were subjected to little scrutiny. These resulted in conflicts, deprivation, poor investment and high levels of debt.

Marketers can potentially export to over two hundred countries. For the 2019 fiscal year, countries are categorised using GNI per capita (aka income per head):

1	High-income economies	$12,056 or more;
2	Upper-middle-income economies	between $3896 and $12,055;
3	Lower-middle-income economies	between $996 and $3895;
4	Low-income economies	$995 or less in 2017.

World Bank (2018)

Clearly, the term "high income" is relative. Marketers must recognise that the United Kingdom median salary is substantially higher than $12,506, despite some UK citizens living in poverty. Seeking to change international consumer behaviour may be challenging because it involves paying a premium for "costly" sustainable actions. Other characteristics that distinguish high-income economies from the rest of the world are growth trends, birth rate, average family size, infant mortality rate, disposable income levels, debt and the share of GDP coming from agriculture.

Most vulnerable states would welcome FDI; however, the scale of benefits will be dictated by the incoming company's approach. If it is static it may

- Not develop link ages with the host community;
- Limit or stop future investment;
- Not increase local economic value added;
- Be susceptible to sudden departure;
- Lead to a race to the bottom;
- Cause job losses in local firms.

If, however, the incoming company is dynamic, it may

- Continually upgrade facilities and infrastructure;
- Increase economic investment;
- Raise economic value added;
- Create linkages with local communities and institutions;
- Have positive spillover into the host business sector.

International marketers operate in Micro and Macro environments. The Micro environments alludes to stakeholders in the host country – for example, labour markets, creditors, customers, competitors and forces therein, such as the cost of capital or export restrictions. The Macro environments refers to the situation where the organisation has little control – that is, strategic decisions have no effect on economic, financial, political, cultural and technological factors. Some organisations straddle the micro/macro divide, such as the United Nations, OPEC, the European Union and so on. It is sensible to reflect on these environments.

Global marketing and the Macro environments

Initial assessments of a country are physical (e.g. location, climate zone, natural resources, population size and rate of growth). These complement the macro factors in PEST, which was adapted by Richard Stead into PLATFORM (Figure 4.12)

Aspects of the PLATFORM macro-framework are useful because they focus on natural resources eagerly sought by countries and companies worldwide. Marketers can often cherry-pick the best elements within models and frameworks to produce the optimal analysis. Economic factors, while not reflected in PLATFORM, are significant when dealing with international markets. Economic factors can include

- Different rates of growth;
- Changing balances of payments;
- Varying fiscal and monetary approaches;

Macro Factor	Questions Posed by Factor
Politics	What is the political structure? Are government's powers limited? Is a constitution in place? Is there meaningful opposition? Is there a tendency for rapid (or inadequate) governmental change?
Legal	How does the legal system operate? Are companies fully accountable or protected by the government? Do tariffs and/or quotas apply? Are there issues with product liability? Is there "home country" legislation – think of the US Sarbanes-Oxley Act.
Accessibility	Is the potential industry public or private sector? Is it easy to access and assess government data? Do monopolies or other restrictive practices exist?
Technology	Does the government allow private sector competition with the public sector? Does the government control the infrastructure, including the media? Will foreign companies be forced to share IPR? Does the government fund pure and/or applied technology research?
Finance	Is capital available locally? Does the stock exchange have sustainability indices? Can NGOs support inward investment? If the target sector is private, will it be going public? Or vice versa? Is the government hostile to foreign capital? Is the tax regime benign?
Ores	Does the country have abundant, accessible natural resources? Are these resources unique or in high demand? Will infrastructure need to be developed to access these resources? Is there a renewable alternative?
Regulations and Reform	How does the government control private enterprise? What contributions does the government expect from the private sector?
Manners	Are foreign companies regarded as threats to national sovereignty? Is populism or nationalism rising? Do regions seek independence and/or recognition?

Figure 4.12 PLATFORM macroenvironmental analysis framework

Source: adapted from Stead et al. (2003)

- Inflationary/deflationary GDP trends;
- Price and/or wage controls;
- The business cycle;
- Rate of domestic and foreign investment;
- Level of personal consumption;
- Variations in unit labour cost;
- Disposable income per household (or per capita).

Marketers need to make research-informed decisions. There is a wealth of data held by many relevant international bodies; however, care is needed as they may have conflicting data. Within the European Union, the euro binds member states' currencies together to reduce exchange rate fluctuations and supposedly create stability. Internal trade with/from the European Union should be stable and therefore more attractive to marketers. The United Kingdom retained the pound sterling, and thus, marketers need to understand that the depreciating value of currencies can influence cashflow. However, foreign countries may have benign tax regimes, and global marketers can benefit by declaring profits overseas. Larger companies can gain a competitive advantage over domestic-only competition by borrowing internationally, where monetary policy is looser. Care has to be taken, though, because reputational damage can result from negative WoM relating to tax management schemes. Apple have a vast amount of money banked offshore that does not generate tax for the US government. Amazon had to change their European arrangements as politicians and pressure groups noted that their original Luxemburg headquarters meant little or no tax was paid where the profits were generated. The pressure will only increase on large global marketing companies (Facebook, Apple, Amazon, Google, etc.).

Increasing investment in Sustainable Development

Policies and instruments designed to promote investment in sustainable businesses are an increasingly important feature of the global investment landscape. Market innovations related to sustainable development continue to attract interest from portfolio investors, and the positive track record of sustainability-themed products is reinforcing asset managers' views that environmental, social and governance (ESG) issues are material to long-term investment performance. As these sustainable investment trends take root and expand, they can have a stronger influence on the operational policies and practices relative to sustainable development (UNCTAD, 2018).

By Q1 2018, there were 38 stock exchanges in the world that were providing voluntary guidance on ESG disclosure (up from 32 at the end of Q1 2017) and 14 exchanges where ESG disclosure was a mandatory rule (up from 12 last year). The United Nations Sustainable Stock Exchanges (SSE) initiative now includes 72 exchanges (up from 63 at the end of Q1 2017); these exchanges collectively list over 45,000 companies, with a market capitalisation of over $80 trillion (ibid).

Sociocultural factors

Host countries and their consumers may resent the cultural imperialism of foreign marketers. Hence, cultural training and sensitivity are essential. The following are some simple steps to follow:

1   Be culturally sensitive and prepared;
2   Adopt the local language and customs;
3   Respect the host country's values;
4   Avoid ethnocentricity;
5   Recognise local complexities – do not stereotype;
6   Consider different approaches to time – that is, Westerners are monochronic, whereas the hosts may be polychronic;
7   Set realistic objectives;
8   Be willing to unlearn, and be open to new experiences.

> *Example* Hollensen (2007) describes how Guanxi is deeply rooted in Chinese culture and is basically a tool to get business and a way of getting things done. It may take considerable time (possibly years) to establish Guanxi. Exporters and importers must establish and maintain close relationships with their Chinese counterparts and relevant government agencies. Exporters must encourage strong Guanxi between their Chinese representatives and customers. A web of strong personal relationships can often help ensure expedited governmental

procedures and the smoother development of business in China. Guanxi has been associated with corruption and bribery scandals, however, and it can be argued that Guanxi is not the cause of bribery and corruption, but rather an enabler (FT, 2012). Guanxi can help a company more efficiently accomplish what it needs to, but at the same time, it explains why many overseas companies fail in China. It is an uneven playing field for international companies in China, because they have not had as long to cultivate business relationships as their local counterparts (ibid).

Gender balance

There is no room in marketing for sexism, nor for any of the isms for that matter. In 2018 the CIM reported that women hold most UK marketing manager roles. At this juncture, men still held most marketing director roles; however, it is only a matter of time until women also hold the majority of these positions. At the end of 2017, women held an average of 22% of board seats in the top hundred global MNEs, and five corporations had a female CEO. Board representation is slightly better than the S&P 500 average and compares favourably with national averages in almost all countries in the world.

The MNEs with the most diverse boards are from Europe, where some countries have introduced quotas and targets, followed by North America, where the appointment of women is not regulated. Among developing economies, South African corporations have a comparable share of women on their boards of directors. Companies in other developing economies, along with Japanese corporations, lag significantly behind their Western and South African counterparts.

Technology factors

Marketers must evaluate whether using technology can generate return. Knowledge-intensive companies tend to be highly profitable and are more willing to take risks and diversify. This can be done via M&As, where companies can use in-house expertise in new markets. They can exploit outputs of their earlier research, developed by in-house R&D. Alternatively, companies can develop overseas R&D facilities where the host country benefits from technology transfer and diffusion into the local institutions and markets. Sometimes local subsidiaries or partners can buy or licence the technology. That said, some countries are taking a more critical stance towards foreign takeovers, in particular when they relate to national security or the sale of strategic domestic assets and technology firms (UNCTAD, 2018).

Global marketing and the Micro environments

A Transnational Corporation (TNC) takes a long-term interest in or control of an entity in another country. It holds at least 10% of the shares. If it holds the majority of the shares, it moves from being an affiliate to being a subsidiary of the parent company. In developed countries, incoming TNCs often pay higher wages while the outgoing TNCs shed jobs.

TNCs play a key role global marketing and impact the host economy's trade performance directly (injecting capital, technology and/or management know-how) and indirectly (with spillovers to local suppliers who have improved market access and can establish reputations on a larger platform). They can imitate the TNCs and recruit their staff while using infrastructure and institutions (created by the TNC).

TNCs seek entry to markets using "greenfield" opportunities or M&As. The following are three modes of entry into global markets:

- Indirect – use of domestic agents;
- Direct – use of overseas agents, licensing, distributors;
- Direct investment – joint ventures or wholly owned foreign enterprises (WOFEs or Woofies).

To enter into a global market, they have to reflect on whether their marketing mix can simply be adopted or whether it needs to be tailored to the new market.

Global Marketing and the Marketing Mix

In global marketing, branding involves much more than product name selection. All Comms vehicles must be appropriate, for the target market, including social media, websites, print media, packaging and documentation. Figure 2.1 in Chapter 2 shows the communication model and refers to realms of understanding. In global marketing, one realm represents the context of the Country of Origin (CoO). The other realm represents the context of the foreign market. Linguistic and cultural mistakes are easy to make when seeking to move into new markets or simply refreshing the brand in an existing international market. Marketers must recognise that the brand name may mean something undesirable in another language and should undertake research to avoid faux pas in gestures, expressions and even dialect. Consumers of tech-related products prefer to have domestic support, including service centres and local representatives. Consumers prefer to have catalogues and user manuals in their mother tongue. Some global marketers (e.g. IKEA) have worked tirelessly to produce wholly graphical assembly manuals with little or no written language.

Colours play a significant role in marketing materials; however, they are not consistent across international boundaries and cultures. In some cultures, red is used to represent danger, whereas others use green or black. In some, white is the colour of funerals, whereas others use it for weddings. To avoid (accidently) sending inappropriate messages, marketers must understand how colours are perceived in host countries.

The advent of new technologies is driving the latest wave of globalisation with the increasing adoption of free market styles of management. This presents marketers with key decisions, namely whether to adopt or adapt their marketing mix for the new foreign market. Figure 4.13 illustrates how product and comms could influence each other.

Marketers must choose which option will have the highest likelihood of success. As previously discussed, new FMCG products have a high failure rate. In Figure 4.13 higher-risk options would involve adaptation or launching a new product into a new foreign market. The question of adopt versus adapt presents different challenges when coordinating changes across the whole marketing mix. Adoption, sometimes referred to as standardisation, will create economies of scale. Since the same product is adopted in different markets, companies will benefit from improved inventory management, shorter replacement lead times and less capital tied up in goods. Marketers may simply use this approach as CoO may be well received by the customers.

		Product		
		Adopt	*Adapt*	*NPD*
Comms Mix	Adopt	Sell to new market using existing product and comms mix (Lowest risk)	Sell to new market using next iteration of same product and existing comms mix (Medium risk)	Develop and launch new product with new comms mix (Highest risk)
	Adapt	Sell to new market using existing product with a new comms mix (Medium risk)	Sell to new market using next iteration of same product and adjusted comms mix (Medium-high risk)	

Figure 4.13 Adoption, adaptation and NPD in global markets

Source: author

Sustainable distribution

As discussed, the overlap between functions can determine the success of the organisation. One such overlap is between marketing, sales and logistics regarding international shipping. Goods can be shipped by land, sea or air, and in each, terms need to be clearly communicated between stakeholders. Incoterms have become the global standard for international trade and have been translated into more than 30 languages (Figure 4.14).

Table 4.14, while not exhaustive, is produced so that marketers can at least be aware of the rules for any mode or modes of transport. Whenever goods are transported internationally, seek advice from experts, say in the chamber of commerce. They are often involved in producing documentation for exports. As a matter of interest, the incoterms for using ships and/or boats applies to sea-based and inland waterway transport.

4.6 Digital marketing in the sustainable age

It is appropriate to look to the future challenges facing marketers. The advance of digital technologies presents challenges but also opportunities to operate in a more-sustainable fashion. The following are some important current and future digital trends:

- Mobile marketing;
- The Internet of Things (IoT);
- Digital Out of Home (OoH);
- Virtual and augmented reality;
- Personalisation and customisation;
- Digital marketing research.

Incoterm	Seller's responsibilities	Buyer's responsibilities
Ex Works (EXW)	Deliver the goods to the buyer at the seller's premises or at another named place.	Load the goods onto collecting vehicle and clear the goods for export (where needed).
Free Carrier (FCA)	Deliver the goods to the carrier or person nominated by the buyer at the seller's premises or another named place.	The parties are well advised to precisely specify the point within the named place of delivery, as the risk passes to the buyer at that point.
Carriage Paid to (CPT)	Deliver the goods to the carrier or another person nominated by the seller at an agreed place. Arrange and cover the costs of carriage to deliver the goods.	Collect the goods from a nominated person or at the named place of destination (after the seller unloads).
Carriage and Insurance Paid to (CIP)	Deliver the goods to the carrier or another person nominated by the seller at an agreed place. Arrange and cover the costs of carriage to deliver the goods. Insure against the buyer's risk of loss of or damage to the goods during the carriage.	Under CIP the seller is required to obtain insurance only on minimum cover. Should the buyer wish to have more insurance protection, it will need to take appropriate actions.
Delivered at Terminal (DAT)	Deliver and unload goods for the buyer at a place of destination (e.g. a quay, warehouse, container yard or road, rail or air cargo terminal). Bear all risks involved in bringing the goods and unloading them.	Collect the goods at the terminal at the named port or place of destination (after the seller unloads).
Delivered at place (DAP)	Deliver the goods ready for unloading at the named place of destination. Bear all risks involved in bringing the goods to the named place.	Collect the goods at the named place of destination (after the seller unloads).
Delivered Duty Paid (DDP)	Deliver the goods when cleared for import and ready for unloading at the destination. Bear the costs and risks involved in delivering the goods, provide export/import clearance, pay duties and undertake all customs formalities.	Collect the goods at the named place of destination (after the seller unloads and has cleared the goods for export/import, paid any duties and carried out all customs formalities).
FAS Free Alongside Ship	Deliver the goods alongside the vessel (e.g. on a quay or a barge) nominated by the buyer at the named port of shipment. The risk of loss of or damage to the goods passes when the goods are alongside the ship.	Collects the goods at the named place of destination (after the seller unloads).
FOB Free on Board Ship	Deliver the goods on board the vessel nominated by the buyer at the named port of shipment.	Bear all costs and responsibilities once the goods are on board a vessel. The risk of loss or damage to the goods passes when the goods are on board.
CFR Cost and Freight Ship	Deliver the goods on board the vessel. Pay the costs and freight necessary to bring the goods to the named port of destination.	The risk of loss of or damage to the goods passes when the goods are on board the vessel in port.
CIF Cost, Insurance and Freight Ship	Deliver the goods on board the vessel. Pay the costs and freight necessary to bring the goods to the named port and insure against the buyer's risk of loss of or damage to the goods during the carriage.	Under CIF, the seller is required to obtain insurance only on minimum cover. Should the buyer wish to have more insurance protection, they will need to take appropriate actions. The buyer collects the goods on board the vessel in port.

Figure 4.14 Incoterms for all modes of transport

Source: adapted from ICC (2019)

Mobile

Over half of the world's Internet access uses the mobile platform. Mobile traffic, and mobile Internet access, is affecting consumer behaviour in a number of ways. For example, showrooming emerged as a threat to traditional high-street stores. Ultimately, marketers need to take note of the change in search behaviour. As networks and handsets improve, the immediacy of location-based searching will become increasingly important, so marketers can let those searching know what the brand represents. Marketers can now send messages, rather than wait for searches, in store via (i)Beacons, Bluetooth LE and via NFC tags.

By the end of 2018, 20% of all UK spending in the Christmas period was online, much of which was via the mobile platform. This represents a significant behavioural change, as consumer search, locate, evaluate and then buy products via their always-on, always-with, always-connected smartphones. Mobile buyer behaviour, security and privacy risks, the mobile user experience and location and interests are of increasing importance.

The Internet of Things (IoT)

The IoT is powered by sensors integrated into devices, whether in the home, the organisation or elsewhere. These connected, communicating devices will increasingly generate data for marketers to analyse.

> *Example* Honeywell launched a thermostat, Lyric, to compete with the Google-owned Nest. The Lyric thermostat connects to an app, so it can be controlled and set, but interestingly, it can independently adapt its setting depending on whether anyone is at home. Through geo-fencing, the thermostat can identify who is out and change its settings automatically. When re-entering the geo-fence, currently 7 miles for the suburban types, the heating will come back on to create a pleasant environment for the user.

Such connected devices will collect data about their users, their habits, their behaviour and actions, making homes, workplaces, leisure time and travel more connected. Improved aggregation of (what should be) anonymous data could deliver further value through insight.

Out of Home (OoH)

Digital out of home (or outdoor) advertisements were introduced in 1978, but new digital techniques now offer even more OoH possibility. The film *Minority Report* showed outdoor advertising delivering targeted messages via iris scanning. It's an interesting idea, but it's impractical because it is restricted by the limitations of the scanners themselves.

Interaction with outdoor advertisements is being enhanced through NFC and beacons, allowing access to promotions, free content, directions, opportunity to purchase, links to social media and downloading information.

Facial recognition is also becoming a part of OoH advertising. Tesco has facial recognition software in screens present in petrol forecourts that can estimate age and gender and deliver targeted advertising. Technology similar to that of Xbox's connect, which recognises movement, is also being trialled – allowing for outdoor advertising content to be controlled, changed and interacted with via gestures.

Virtual Reality (VR)

Virtual Reality (VR) is increasingly used to deliver interactive brand experiences. Coca Cola recently offered a 2014 World Cup experience where groups of visitors, among others things, got to use Oculus Rift headsets to enter the Maracanã locker room before walking onto the pitch to the roar of the crowd and playing a game of football in which they scored the winning goal, all the while being exposed to subtle Coca Cola advertising in context (i.e. hoardings and billboards in the stadium). Facebook bought Oculus Rift for $2 billion, with Zuckerberg (2014) himself saying

> imagine enjoying a court side seat at a game, studying in a classroom of students and teachers all over the world or consulting with a doctor face to face . . . just by putting on goggles in your home.

Augmented Reality (AR)

Augmented Reality (AR) has the potential to deliver targeted messages to mobile consumers, via specific devices. Information such as special offers, directions, product reviews and more could be presented as layers, augmented onto the reality seen by the wearer. This does not just have to be via wearable devices: apps such as Layar are already popular.

Personalisation and customisation

Suppliers will increasingly seek to personalise their full and mobile websites to improve the user experience. iGoogle enables the creation of a personalised homepage that contains a Google search box at the top and the user's choice of gadgets. They can have access to several parts of the online experience:

- Gmail messages;
- headlines from Google News and other news sources;
- weather forecasts, stock quotes, movie showtimes, etc.;
- stored bookmarks while "mobile", providing quicker access to the sites when revisited.

The trend for customisation will continue on a number of fronts. Increasing miniaturisation means the trend of embedding technology has been extended to clothing. Bluetooth motorcycle helmets are now commonplace.

Digital marketing research

The platforms, channels and tools made available through continued developments in technology offer marketers access to phenomenal amounts of data, information and potential insights. This is in itself an issue as the amounts of data can be overwhelming.

Furthermore, 90% of the world's data have been generated since 2011. Individuals, organisations, communities and networks continue to generate data at an increasing rate, including areas such as behaviour, communications, interests and purchases.

The challenge for marketers has moved from gathering data to analysing and interpreting them, in order to generate valuable insights and support effective decision-making. Only recently are tools and processes being developed to make sense of the mountains of data available to marketers. There are two broad categories of data that marketers can consider: onsite and offsite.

Onsite versus offsite data

Onsite data are data gathered by analytics tools specific to the organisation, such as Google Analytics, that track behaviour and actions specific to websites – traffic, journey, conversions and similar. Offsite analytics are much broader and focus on the potential audience, the wider population of interest, sentiment, buzz and the share of voice.

Analytics

Analytics refer to the digital tools available to marketers that help gather, store, interpret and analyse online data. They are increasingly important, and modern marketers see analytics as key for digital marketing research, worthy of investment and capable of generating a Return on Marketing Investment (RoMI).

Big Data

Effective decision-making is almost always underpinned by relevant data and analysis. The focus on data has increased in recent years, facilitated by the innovations presented by the digital marketing environment. There is an increasing number of categories, including product data, mobile data, campaign data, website data, funnel data, engagement data and customer data, among others. One classification is increasingly recognised and talked about in relation to more effective marketing, namely Big Data. The key points are that Big Data

- Use increasingly large data sets recorded and stored using technology;
- Are generated at speed and requires timely responses to exploit the opportunities it presents;
- Are complex, coming from many different sources and in various formats.

Big Data also present challenges to marketers:

- Identifying which data are relevant, which data actually matter.
- Being able to analyse, form insights and react quickly.
- Bringing all of these "quant" and "qual" data from different platforms together in a cohesive, coherent format.

The task of taking a variety of data sets, from a variety of data sources, with varying degrees of relevance, accuracy and validity and giving it structure through matching, cleansing and linkage is daunting. Marketers increasingly use visualisation software to shape the huge volumes of data into meaningful results. These visual representations can highlight patterns and trends that can support decision-making.

Kelley's 3S approach: Search, Site and Social

Neil Kelley proposed the following 3Ss:

- Search (search engine analytics and behaviour);
- Site (website analytics and visitor behaviour);
- Social (social media behaviour).

The aim of search engine marketing is *not* to focus on search engine optimisation (SEO) and pay per click (PPC) per se but instead consumer behaviour during consumers' online "journey". Customers using a search engine are often in the early stages of buyer behaviour (see Chapter 1.5). They have a problem deriving from a need or want and require a solution. Those searching online are becoming more sophisticated in their searching, using longer search terms, or more "long-tail" keywords that are highly specific to their needs. As sustainability covers a multitude of terms and has various definitions, these insights are valuable to marketers seeking to support sustainable consumers.

It is important to know where and when they search. Historically, most searches were in a fixed location; however, increasing use of smartphones, coupled with improved availability of broadband (or 5G), will create always-connected customers. The most widely recognised analytical tool is Google Analytic with alternatives being KISSmetrics, Adobe, Clicky or Open Web Analytics, among others. These tools provide insights into digital areas such as the performance of advertising, conversion rates, content performance and preference, interactions and flow of traffic. Marketers' decisions must be informed by knowing where the traffic originates (so what inbound links and search engine terms are effective) and where consumers go when they leave the site.

Also worth investigating are what platforms they use (desktop, laptop, tablet, phablet, smartphone, TV) and what browser. Marketers can evaluate which times of the day are more popular for visitors to the site. Are there trends? Can patterns in behaviour, with certain platforms, or geo-demographics, be identified? This can help develop a more in-depth profile of the customers based on their online behaviour and preferences for technology.

Furthermore, it is important to identify and understanding what visitors do when they arrive on the site. What is the bounce rate? How many leave straight away? Which pages are the most popular? Do they relate to interesting or valuable content? What are their entry and exit points?

Regarding social media, marketers must pose similar questions to those in the previous sections of their data, even drawing on offsite data like Facebook insights, Twitter Analytics and/or Social Mention. The data can start to build a psychographic picture of the customer. Marketers can identify common interests, sentiment in relation to brands, purchases and experiences, even the stage of family life cycle and lifestyle choices. What is also useful to analyse in relation to social media are the frequency of posts, how active they are on different networks, and how much influence they have. Do people ask questions of them about purchases? Are they opinion leaders or influencers?

Listening

Sustainability is built on ongoing, continuous dialogue with stakeholders. This dialogue is an essential part of progressive, customer-centric sustainable marketing. Marketers should be holding conversations, providing relevant content, posing questions on social media and creating discussions facilitated by hashtags. Social media and communities provide ideal opportunities to "listen" to communities. Reading and giving consideration to online communities should improve the co-creation of value that consumers seek through their decision-making.

Bernoff and Li (2011) refer to this online environment, controlled by customers, as the groundswell. The groundswell is a social trend, along communities and networks, with individuals sharing information they want and need with others – avoiding organisations, advertising and other forms of marketing messages. Bernoff and Li recommend brand monitoring and listening to the Internet. Who's saying what, where, to whom and (more importantly) why? They developed this into a five-step plan:

1   *Who are your customers?* Make sure you have knowledge of who your customers are, where they go online and where they post.
2   *Who are the creators and critics?* Who are the more vocal customers? Who has influence and impact?
3   *Start monitoring key areas – brands, products and service encounters.* Start small, focus on key areas and begin to grow your listening and monitoring as you become more confident.
4   *Draw on experience and skills internally, and outsource if needed.* Use skills inside the organisation: who knows the customer and who understands social media and online conversations?
5   *Have a skilled a dedicated interpreter.* Ensure that there is someone responsible for turning the data gathered into insight: what do these conversations mean, and ultimately, how should marketers respond?

4.7 SMEs and micro-enterprises

The United Kingdom has over 2.5 million enterprises, of which 99% are small to medium-size enterprises (SMEs). The SME sector's annual turnover exceeds £1 trillion, representing over half of the United Kingdom's private sector economic activity. They are major providers of employment and often provide the platform for new ideas (think technology spinoffs from universities). Clearly, they are vital for the economy and will play an increasingly important role in future.

The EC definition (2003/361/EC) states that SMEs should be "independent" and employ fewer than 250 people. Further to this, companies who have nine (or fewer) employees are classed as micro-enterprises.

Large and small firms play different roles, and it is largely agreed that SMEs (hereafter including micro-enterprises) are more flexible and can react more quickly to changes in the marketplace than larger competitors can. SMEs have characteristics that dictate their approach to marketing:

- The inherent characteristics and behaviours of the owner/manager;
- Size limitations and the stage of development;
- Limited resources (such as finance, time, marketing knowledge);
- Lack of specialist expertise (owners tend to be generalists);
- Limited impact on the marketplace.

(Gilmore et al., 2001)

Marketing planning is an essential activity for all organisations; however, many SME owners deem it unnecessary. SME service providers need to train their staff to minimise variability; however, they traditionally undertake less formal marketing training than their larger counterparts do. They regard marketing as something more relevant to large organisations. Furthermore, the financial restrictions faced by many SMEs, coupled with the time demands of the owner/managers, undoubtedly contribute to the lack of coordinated marketing therein.

It is, however, impossible to apply a single rule to all SMEs, because they are simply too diverse. Many exhibit entrepreneurial behavioural patterns while having little structure, whereas others are long-standing and well established, with structures comparable to larger companies (Figure 4.15).

These suggest an interesting paradox: as larger SMEs, they could be in a win-win scenario having the benefits of SMEs and larger companies; they could be in a lose-lose scenario, having only weaknesses; or they could have a combination of both. Whatever the scenario, it will impact on their approach to marketing. All SMEs should engage in PR (see Chapter 2.1) and networking. PR has many benefits and few downfalls for SMEs. Support is available from a wide range of third parties, from agencies to consultants to the local business school. One of them will be able to help on an affordable budget.

Regarding networking, there are many events suitable for SME managers, such as those run by the chambers of commerce. Furthermore, online networking sites are increasingly useful in helping SMEs to grow while adopting sustainable practices. Facebook and LinkedIn are generic networking sites widely used by SMEs. Increasingly, SMEs are using Instagram to promote their brand. More specialist sites, such as Gurgle (Mothercare's social network site), are gaining credence.

	Weaknesses	*Strengths*
SMEs	Poor finances Weak market presence	Flexibility Speed of response Independence
Large Enterprises	Inertia Politicised Slow response	Strong brand Financial stability Economy of scale Professional management

Figure 4.15 Attributes in relation to company size

The Decision-Making Unit (DMU)

Traditional marketing has always stressed the need to understand the role and influences within The Decision-Making Unit, or DMU. A problem with the DMU in larger organisations is that passivity is implied; that is, the stakeholders tend to *react* to events. In SMEs, the DMU may be smaller; however, different stakeholders often share roles – for example, initiator and user but not buyer. SME stakeholders in the DMU have little option other than to multitask – that is, fill a range of roles. It is unlikely that they will have dedicated HR or procurement teams, relying on consultants and agencies instead.

While online buyers are typically younger, increasing social inclusion will feature providing services to all sectors of society. Interestingly, over half of eBay's buyers are over 45. Silver surfers (i.e. those over 55) are increasingly visible online. eBay also attracts a wide variety of sellers. Originally, sellers were consumers selling unwanted goods to other consumers in a classic C2C sense.

Some SMEs look to share resources either through working collaboratively or using portals. For example, SME booksellers use Abebooks as a portal (see www.abebooks.co.uk/) to sell their wares globally. Others use eBay or Etsy (among others) to sell their goods to consumers and other businesses. While eBay was originally a C2C platform, it now features predominantly B2C and B2B sales, with B2B sales growing faster than C2C. People and business have always bought from governments (i.e. G2C and G2B). Now local government departments are saving money by buying items from sellers on eBay (i.e. B2G and C2G).

SMEs and sustainability

SMEs (including micro-enterprises) have significant environmental impacts. Walker and Preuss (2008) suggest that SMEs may be responsible for up to 70% of all UK industrial pollution. They have significant social impacts, with behaviours and characteristics that are important in the evolution towards adopting sustainability. They may, however, tend to focus on their societal and environmental behaviours internally, rather than engaging with stakeholders in the supply chain (Moore and Manring, 2009). Kerr (2006) argues that SMEs should develop strategies that incorporate sustainability and that the resulting skills would guide them to act in a sustainable way.

The benefits of sustainable strategic plans for micro-enterprises are different from those offered to larger competitors (Moore and Manring, 2009). Many sustainability studies focus on larger manufacturers; however, micro-enterprises have different characteristics and can act more nimbly to fill local, specialised or niche markets.

SMEs' sustainability barriers

There are some barriers to SMEs adopting sustainability:

* Lacking awareness of sources of assistance – for example, grants;
* Perceiving the necessary skill problems as barriers;
* Believing their company size is too small to have a meaningful affect;
* Thinking "costly" sustainable actions are unaffordable;
* Believing it incompatible with existing in-house systems.

Tools and frameworks

Historically, key marketing texts have concentrated on large organisations, and they have arguably failed to provide SME managers with meaningful marketing guidance. Certainly, many of the tools and frameworks are not easy to apply.

Consider Porter's Value Chain analysis (See Figure 3.11). In a micro-enterprise, it is highly unlikely that they will have both inbound and outbound logistics in their primary activities. Regarding the support activities, the firm infrastructure is less of an issue because SMEs are flatter and more flexible. McLarty (1998) recognised the role of entrepreneurial drives in small firms. These are shaped by the characteristics and behaviours of the founding entrepreneur, the owner or the manager.

In small firms, managers have to be leaders as well. The have to be creative and pragmatic. They have to deal with the current and the future development of the company. The number and nature of their resources will shape their ability to grow. Often a key factor will involve the resource structure. Finally, SMEs and micro-enterprises are limited when it comes to technological development.

It is sensible to adapt VCA when applying it to SMEs and micro-enterprises. In VCA the analysis of management is often subsumed within the operations or infrastructure activities, which may be more appropriate for larger more structured enterprises than for SMEs. McLarty (1998) developed this concern, suggesting that the model also failed to recognise that entrepreneurial drives play a leading part in stimulating growth and specifically the owner/manager's role as the driving force within an SME. The traditional definition of support and primary activities were too limiting for his study. Imaginatively, he redefined the support activities:

- Entrepreneurial drives;
- Management capability;
- Resource infrastructure.

McLarty's small firm value chain (Figure 4.16) may not be perfect, but it serves a key purpose. It reminds marketers that frameworks, models and tools are not precious

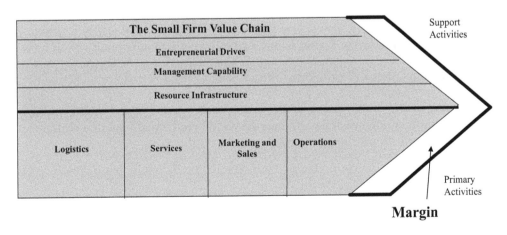

Figure 4.16 The Small Firm Value Chain

things that are beyond reproach. They can and should be adapted to suit the company. Frameworks (see the SMBF in Figure 3.39) should be designed to incorporate different approaches. A large company may well have a CSR policy and platform. Research suggests that many entrepreneurs have not even heard of CSR (Richardson, 2015). In the SMBF, a large company could be benchmarked by using the traditional VCA, whereas an SME could use McLarty's adaptation or an updated version.

4.8 Charities, not-for-profits and third-sector organisations

Kotler recognised long ago that there is more to marketing than Adam Smith's idea of a simple transaction. Kotler's social marketing theory extends to charities that are government funded (occasionally referred to as B2G). Even though the charities do not sell in the tradition fashion, they still provide services for which they receive funding. Today, charity managers are under increasing pressure to meet stakeholder expectations.

It is unlikely that the public purse is going to increase to any great extent. Charities increasingly find themselves competing for resources and income. Smaller charities are particularly affected, and many closed after the 2007 global credit crunch. Increasingly, charities are seeking to "co-brand" with either larger more-established charities or private sector companies. Clearly, any such exercises must be customer centric and should proceed only if the customers' perceptions are positive. The compatibility between the charity and the corporate brand will influence consumer decision-making. Green charities would have to avoid being tainted by any greenwashing associated with the partner brand. The public is often more forgiving of charities than private sector brands, though.

Charities often struggle to attract appropriate partners. This is improving, however, because more companies are on sustainable indices and undertake independent sustainability auditing. Benefits of co-branding include greater awareness through increased exposure, an enhance image or reputation and greater financial security. The larger partner may be a source of volunteers. Indeed, some companies (e.g. First Direct) enshrine volunteering in their HR procedures. These volunteers may bring new skills (say website design) that will have a long-lasting impact on the smaller charity's brand.

> *Example*   The Marine Stewardship Council (see www.msc.org/uk/) is an international non-profit organisation that recognises and rewards efforts to protect oceans and safeguard seafood supplies. In short, they certify sustainable fisheries. They were founded in 1996 when Unilever collaborated with WWF to create the new brand. The MSC celebrated 20 years in 2016, and having certified an increasing number of key fisheries, they have a widely recognised logo that consumers use to inform their decision-making.

Consumers' awareness and preference for ethical products are increasing. The Fairtrade mark has become a well-known logo attached to over 4500 fair-trade products, from coffee and tea to flowers and gold (Fairtrade Foundation, 2019). The growth of ethical consumerism has driven the growth of the fair-trade market. Fair trade is now on the agenda globally for leading retailers (and other stakeholders) and is being recognised by supranational organisations, including the United Nations and EC. The Fairtrade mark was introduced in the United Kingdom in 1994, and within a decade, the UK fair-trade market was worth more than £140 million; by 2012 it was worth £1.57 billion, and by 2019 most UK adults could identify the Fairtrade mark (ibid).

Charities exist to create a better society. The vast majority of people consider charities to be trustworthy, which may not be the case with politicians (of various hues) or political organisations. Most people use charities in some way, and the sector makes a substantial contribution to the UK economy, with over 200,000 registered charities generating a turnover of over £32 billion while employing almost 600,000 paid staff.

This confirms the need for charities to monitor the microenvironment and macroenvironment. Many charities became overly dependent on external funding, which often diminished their long-term marketing planning. In these days of changing funding, financial security is often no longer guaranteed.

Today businesses are more like charities with CSR and sustainability platforms, whereas charities are more like businesses with professionally run marketing campaigns. It is no longer a case of raising enough funds for a charity to achieve its objectives; stories exist of larger charities having multimillion-pound reserves and yet still heavily promoting themselves and driving fund-raising campaigns. Their argument is that it is too risky to drop out of the public's view.

Also, the life cycles of funding, processes and services are constantly reducing, and charities face increasing pressures. However, a lack of resources and (often) heavy senior management workloads have stifled strategic marketing development.

Marketing, and particularly research, is generally a weakness for charities, and many acknowledge the need for change. They need to market themselves in a coordinated way rather than rely on their usual ad hoc approach. That said, charities have always been willing to adopt a flexible approach to marketing and income generation, with staff often having the freedom to develop activities in effective and efficient ways. That said, most charities are also small businesses or SMEs with the challenges therein.

Top ten findings

1　Within relationship marketing, the theory relating to acquisition, retention or attrition of customers is well established; however, it is questionable whether effective implementation takes place.
2　Loyalty and satisfaction are not the same. Different loyalty ladders exist and present different challenges.
3　Internal marketing is an old concept, which is poorly practised by most companies. The theory has low awareness among academics. It will enable the adoption of sustainability, as it ensures that internal customers see the benefits of sustainable brands.
4　Sustainable entrepreneurship will be a key driver of sustainable development as the entrepreneurs involved seek to disrupt the old market structures.
5　Sustainable communities can influence other consumers. They can be advocates or provide potent opposition. Sustainable brands have traits akin to human characteristics. Aaker, de Chernatony and Kapferer are key authors.
6　All marketers are global marketers, and they are increasingly expected to green their supply network. Sustainability should inform market-entry methods. Hollensen is a leading author on global marketing.
7　Digital marketing provides tools that can reduce ecological footprints and improve communications with stakeholders – for example, 540-degree feedback can be

implemented by using Twitter. Many of the future macro trends concerning marketers relate to digital techniques and tools.

8 Big Data apply to very large data sets, with large volumes of data, which change
and develop rapidly. Marketers need to be careful with data, bearing GDPR legislation in mind.

9 SMEs and micro-enterprises represent 99% of all enterprises. They are major
contributor to the economy but also generate pollution. They need support in
adopting sustainable practices.

10 In a world of reduced public (government) spending, charities increasingly act like
businesses, and businesses act like charities. Third-sector organisations are growing in number and importance.

Six activities

1 What techniques would you use to support IM in an organisation of your choice?
What would the barriers be? How would you overcome them?

2 Visit http://interactive.brandrepublic.com/forward50/ and conduct further reading and research into their 50 trends driving the future of marketing.

3 A wealth of information related to global trade is available free from the UNC-
TAD site. Their World Investment Report is available from the website www.
unctad.org/diae or the organisation's investment policy hub (www. investmentpo-
licyhub.unctad.org).

4 A number of sources on FDI trends and determinants are available:

- Transparency International – see Corruption-perceptions index;
- World Bank Data and Statistics – statistics by country;
- US Bureau of Labour Statistics has data on labour costs;
- IMF Publications – World Economic Outlook;
- OECD Main Economic Indicators;
- US Trade Representative (USTR.gov National Trade Estimate Reports – pick a country);
- OECD economic surveys on developed and larger developing countries;
- CIA World Factbook (general background).

5 Some key ideas for useful data in the digital environment.

- Set up Google Alerts – for keywords, names, companies, industries – control
the volume of alerts, the sources, language and regions and get related information on posts or articles that are then emailed directly;
- Google Analytics Academy (https://analytics.google.com/analytics/academy/)
provides free online analytics courses;
- Visit free offsite tools to look for conversations and posts about brands and
organisations:

  o Social Mention (see http://socialmention.com);
  o TweetReach (see https://tweetreach.com);
  o HowSociable http://howsociable.com;

6 The Charities Commission provides extensive information on the sector. Visit
their website at www.gov.uk/government/organisations/charity-commission.

References

Aaker, J. (1997). Dimensions of brand personality. *Journal of Marketing Research*, 34(3), pp. 347–357. http://dx.doi.org/10.2307/3151897.

Aaker, D. (1991). *Managing brand equity*. New York: The Free Press.

Aksoy, L. (2013). How do you measure what you can't define? The current state of loyalty measurement and management. *Journal of Service Management*, 24(4), pp. 356–381.

Baker, M. (2009). Aided Recall and Marketing Mnemonics Guest Lecture presented By Professor Michael Baker to Leeds Business School November 2009.

Bernoff, J. and Li, C. (2011). *Groundswell, expanded and revised edition: Winning in a world transformed by social technologies*. Boston: Harvard Business School Press.

Berry, L. (1983). Relationship marketing. In: L. Berry, G.L. Shostack and G.D. Upah, eds., *Emerging perspectives on services marketing*. Chicago: American Marketing Association.

Carlson, B.D. and Donavan, T. (2013). Human brands in sport: Athlete brand personality and identification. *Journal of Sport Management*, 27(3), pp. 193–206. doi: 10.1123/jsm.27.3.193.

Cohen, B., Smith, B. and Mitchell, R. (2006). Toward a sustainable conceptualization of dependent variables in entrepreneurship research. *Business Strategy and the Environment*, 17(2), pp. 107–119. https://doi.org/10.1002/bse.505.

de Chernatony, L., Mcdonald, M. and Wallace, E. (2011). *Creating powerful brands*. 4th ed. London: Elsevier.

Dick, A.S. and Basu, K. (1994). Consumer loyalty: Towards an integrated conceptual approach. *Journal of the Academy of Marketing Science*, 22(2), pp. 99–113.

Ethical Consumer (2018). Ethical consumer markets report. Available at: www.ethicalconsumer.org/research-hub/uk-ethical-consumer-markets-report. [Accessed 9 Feb. 2019].

Fairtrade (2019). Fairtrade foundation website. Available at: www.fairtrade.org.uk [Accessed 15 Feb. 2019].

Fang, S.-R., Chang, E., Ou, C.-C. and Chou, C.-H. (2013). Internal market orientation, market capabilities and learning orientation. *European Journal of Marketing*, 48(1/2), pp. 170–192.

Freeman (2008). Ending the so-called "Friedman-freeman" debate article printed in Agle, B.R., Donaldson, T., Freeman, R.E., Jensen, M.C., Agle, B.R., Mitchell, R.K. (2008). Introduction: Recent research and new questions from Academy of Management 2007 Symposium.

FT (2012). Business in China and the importance of guanxi. Opinion MBA blog. *Financial Times* online article by Diana Mak. Available at: www.ft.com/content/9f009b85-0eee-343c-82bc-7e1c56665eea. [Accessed 10 Jan. 2019].

Fisher, R., Maritz, A. and Lobo, A. (2014). Evaluating entrepreneurs' perception of success-development of a measurement scale. *International Journal of Entrepreneurial Behaviour & Research*, 20(5), pp. 478–492.

Fussler, C. (1996). *Driving eco-innovation, a breakthrough discipline for innovation and sustainability*. London: Pitman.

Gardner, B.B. and Levy, S.J. (1955). The product and the brand. *Harvard Business Review*, March-April, pp. 33–39. http://dx.doi.org/10.4135/9781452231372.n13.

Geuens, M., Weijters, B. and De Wulf, K. (2009). A new measure of brand personality. *International Journal of Research in Marketing*, 26(2), pp. 97–107. http://dx.doi.org/10.1016/j.ijresmar.2008.12.002.

Gilmore, A., Carson, D. and Grant, K. (2001). Article SME marketing in practice. *Marketing Intelligence & Planning*, 19(1), pp. 6–11.

Haberberg, A., Gander, J., Rieple, A., Martin-Castilla, J-I. and Helm, C. (2010). Institutionalizing idealism: the adoption of CSR practices. *Journal of Global Responsibility*, 1(2), pp. 366–381.

Harridge-March, S. and Quinton, S. (2009). Virtual snakes and ladders: Social networks and the relationship loyalty marketing ladder. *The Marketing Review*, 9(2), pp. 171–181.

Harris, L.C. and Goode, M.M.H. (2004). The four levels of loyalty and the pivotal role of trust: A study of online service dynamics. *Journal of Retailing*, 80, pp. 139–158.

Hockerts, K. and Wüstenhagen, R. (2010). Greening Goliaths versus emerging Davids – theorizing about the role of incumbents and new entrants in sustainable entrepreneurship. *Journal of Business Venturing*, 25(5), pp. 481–492.

Hollensen, S. (2007). *Global marketing*. 4th ed. Instructor's Manual. Harlow: Pearson Education.

ICC (2019). The incoterms rules (2010). Article available at: https://iccwbo.org/publication/incoterms-rules-2010/[Accessed 6 Feb. 2019].

Jackson, T. (2005). Motivating sustainable consumption- a review of evidence on consumer behaviour and behavioural change; a report to the Sustainable Development Research Network January 2005. Funded by the Economic and Social Research Council's Sustainable Technologies Programme (STP).

Jobber, D. (2007). *Principles & practice of marketing*. 5th ed. Maidenhead: McGraw-Hill.

Kapferer, J.N. (2008). *The new strategic brand management*. 4th ed. London: Kogan-Page.

Kerr, I.R. (2006). *Leadership strategies for sustainable SME operation*. Business Strategy and the Environment, 15, pp. 30–39.

Kotler, P., Wong, V., Saunders, J. and Armstrong, G. (2009). *Principles of marketing*. 5th European ed. Harlow: Prentice Hall.

Margolis, J.D. and Walsh, J.P. (2003). Misery loves companies: Rethinking social initiatives by business. *Administrative Science Quarterly*, 48, pp. 268–305.

McLarty, R. (1998). Case study: Evidence of a strategic marketing paradigm in a growing SME. *Journal of Marketing Practice. Applied Marketing Science*, 4(4), pp. 105–117.

Moore, S.B. and Manring, S.L. (2009). Strategy development in small and medium sized enterprises for sustainability and increased value creation. *Journal of Cleaner Production*, 17(2), pp. 276–282.

Munoz, P. and Dimov, D. (2015). *The call of the whole in understanding the development of sustainable ventures*. Journal of Business Venturing, 30(4), pp. 632–654.

NWU (2006). *Internal marketing best practice study*. North Western University.

Pacheco, D.F., Dean, T.J. and Payne, D.S. (2010). *Escaping the green prison: Entrepreneurship and the creation of opportunities for sustainable development*. Journal of Business Venturing, 25(5), pp. 464–480.

Parrish, B. (2010). Sustainability-driven entrepreneurship: Principles of organization design. *Journal of Business Venturing*, 25(5), pp. 510–523.

Peck, H, Payne, A., Christopher, M. and Clark, M. (1999). *Relationship marketing: Strategy and implementation*. London: Taylor and Francis.

Piercy, N. (2009). *Market-led strategic change*. 4th ed. Oxford: Butterworth-Heinemann.

Rababah, K., Mohammed, H. and Ibrahim, H. (2011). A unified definition of CRM towards the successful adoption and implementation. *Academic Research International*, 1(1), pp. 220–228.

Rafiq, M. and Ahmed, P. (2000). Advances in internal marketing concept: definition, synthesis and extension. *Journal of Services Marketing*, 14(6), pp. 449–462.

Richardson, N.A. (2015). The adoption of sustainable marketing practices within the UK music festivals sector. PhD thesis. Available at: http://etheses.whiterose.ac.uk/13578/1/The%20adoption%20of%20sustainable%20marketing%20practices%20within%20the%20UK%20music%20festivals%20sector.pdf.

Richardson, N., James, J. and Kelley, N. (2015). *Customer-centric marketing: Supporting sustainability in the digital age*. London: Kogan Page.

Russell-Bennett, R., McColl-Kennedy, J.R. and Coote, L.V. (2007). Involvement, satisfaction, and brand loyalty in a small business services setting. *Journal of Business Research*, 60(12), 1253–1260.

Sachs, J. and Warner, A. (1995). Natural resource abundance and economic growth. National Bureau for Economic Research Working Paper 5398, Cambridge, Massachusetts.

Schaltegger, S. and Wagner, M. (2011). Sustainable entrepreneurship and sustainability innovation: categories and interactions. *Business Strategy and the Environment*, 20(4), pp. 222–237.

Shepherd, D.A. and Patzelt, H. (2011). The new field of sustainable entrepreneurship: Studying entrepreneurial action linking "what is to be sustained" with "what is to be developed". *Entrepreneurship: Theory and Practice*, 35(1), pp. 137–163.

Spedale, S. and Watson, T.J. (2014). The emergence of entrepreneurial action: At the crossroads between institutional logics and individual life-orientation. *International Small Business Journal*, 32(7), pp. 759–776.

Stead, R., Curwen, P. and Lawler, K. (2003). *Industrial Economics-Theory, Applications and Policy*. McGraw Hill: London.

Thomson, K., de Chernatony, L, Arganbright, L. and Khan, S. (2010). The buy-in benchmark: How staff understanding and commitment impact brand and business performance. *Journal of Marketing Management*, 15(8), pp. 819–835. https://doi.org/10.1362/026725799784772684.

Tilley, F. and Young, W. (2009). Sustainability entrepreneurs – could they be the true wealth generators of the future? *Greener Management International*, (55), pp. 70–92, Greenleaf Publishing.

UNCTAD (2008). Creative economy report 2008- the challenge of assessing the creative economy: Towards informed policy-making. Available at: unctad.org/fr/Docs/ditc20082cer_en.pdf [Accessed 3 Jan. 2013].

UNCTAD (2018). World Investment Report- Investment and new industrial policies. (United Nations publication, Sales No. E.18.II.D.4).

Verhoef, R. (2003). Understanding the effect of customer relationship management on customer share development. *Journal of Marketing*, 63 (Oct.), pp. 30–45.

Vestrum, I. and Rasmussen, E. (2013). How community ventures mobilise resources: Developing resource dependence and embeddedness. *International Journal of Entrepreneurial Behavior & Research*, 19(3), pp. 283–232.

Walker, H. and Preuss, L. (2008). Fostering sustainability through sourcing from small businesses: Public sector perspectives. *Journal of Cleaner Production*, 16(15), pp. 1600–1609. ISSN 0959–6526. http://dx.doi.org/10.1016/j.jclepro.2008.04.014.

World Bank (Article V) (2018). World bank country and lending groups. Available at: https://datahelpdesk.worldbank.org/knowledgebase/articles/906519 [Accessed 30 Dec. 2018].

Young, W. and Tilley, F. (2006). Can businesses move beyond efficiency? The shift toward effectiveness and equity in the corporate sustainability debate. *Business Strategy Environment*, 15(6), pp. 402–415. doi: 10.1002/sd.394.

Young, W., Hwang, K., McDonald, S. and Oates, C. (2010). Sustainable consumption: Green consumer behaviour when purchasing products. *Sustainable Development*, 18, pp. 20–31.

Yu-Ting, H. and Rundle-Thiele, S. (2015). A holistic management tool for measuring internal marketing activities. *Journal of Services Marketing*, pp. 571–584.

Yu-Ting, H. and Rundle-Thiele, S. (2014). The moderating effect of cultural congruence on the internal marketing practice and employee satisfaction relationship: An empirical examination of Australian & Taiwanese born tourism employees. *Tourism Management*, (42), pp. 196–206.

Zuckerberg, M. (2014). Blog posting. Available at: www.facebook.com/zuck/posts/101013 19050523971 [Accessed 4 Jan. 2019].

Index

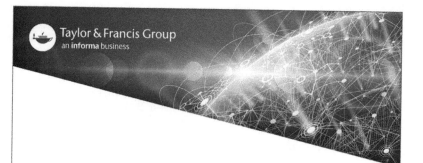